D1719895

Performance Measurement in Shared Services

MÜNSTERANER SCHRIFTEN ZUR INTERNATIONALEN UNTERNEHMENSRECHNUNG

Herausgegeben von Peter Kajüter

Band 20

Zu Qualitätssicherung und Peer Review der vorliegenden Publikation

Die Qualität der in dieser Reihe erscheinenden Arbeiten wird vor der Publikation durch den Herausgeber der Reihe geprüft.

Notes on the quality assurance and peer review of this publication

Prior to publication, the quality of the work published in this series is reviewed by the editor of the series.

Friedrich Kalden

Performance Measurement in Shared Services

Empirical Evidence from
European Multinational Companies

PETER LANG

Bibliographic Information published by the Deutsche Nationalbibliothek
The Deutsche Nationalbibliothek lists this publication in the Deutsche Nationalbibliografie; detailed bibliographic data is available in the internet at http://dnb.d-nb.de.

Library of Congress Cataloging-in-Publication Data
A CIP catalog record for this book has been applied for at the Library of Congress.

Zugl.: Münster (Westfalen), Univ., Diss., 2020

D 6
ISSN 1868-7687
ISBN 978-3-631-85045-9 (Print)
E-ISBN 978-3-631-86218-6 (E-PDF)
E-ISBN 978-3-631-86219-3 (EPUB)
E-ISBN 978-3-631-86220-9 (MOBI)
DOI 10.3726/b18738

© Peter Lang GmbH
Internationaler Verlag der Wissenschaften
Berlin 2021
All rights reserved.

Peter Lang – Berlin · Bern · Bruxelles · New York ·
Oxford · Warszawa · Wien

This publication has been peer reviewed.

www.peterlang.com

Performance Measurement
in Shared Services
Empirical Evidence from European Multinational Companies

Inauguraldissertation
zur Erlangung des akademischen Grades eines Doktors
der Wirtschaftswissenschaften
durch die Wirtschaftswissenschaftliche Fakultät der
Westfälischen Wilhelms-Universität Münster

vorgelegt von

Dipl.-Vw. Friedrich Kalden

aus Eschwege

Münster 2020

Name des Dekans: **Prof. Dr. Theresia Theurl**

Erstgutacher: Prof. Dr. Peter Kajüter

Zweitgutachter: Prof. Dr. Gerhard Schewe

Tag der Disputation: 06. Juli 2020

Preface

In recent years, Shared Service Organizations (SSOs) are of growing relevance in research and corporate practice, although managers and existing literature voice concerns about potential negative impacts of SSOs for multinational corporations. A major reason for the ongoing controversy about the effectiveness of SSOs is closely related to the shortcoming of measuring their performance.

Despite the relevance of performance measurement as a basis for a profound decision-making, performance measurement system (PMS) design in SSOs marks a blind spot in prior research. Moreover, evidence on determinants of PMS design in SSOs and its effectiveness remains scarce.

Therefore, Friedrich Kalden investigates the design, the determinants and the effectiveness of PMS in SSOs. The empirical analysis rests on field surveys with SSO managers and management accountants of 74 multinational corporations from Germany, Switzerland and Austria with an established SSO. Besides surveying experts, Friedrich Kalden held interviews with SSO managers, management accountants and process owners to unveil different viewpoints on PMS design in SSOs. Combining different research methods allows for the triangulation of empirical findings which promises a more complete picture of PMS in SSOs.

To grasp a basic understanding, the study explores PMS designs in SSOs by using three design components, namely measures, processes and actors. The results show, for example, that performance measures related to process quality prevail in SSOs and that PMS modifications are a rather neglected part in the performance measurement process. In a second step, Friedrich Kalden investigates which contingency factors are associated with PMS design in SSOs. This offers insights which determinants affect PMS design in SSOs and indicates how performance measurement actors foster PMS design by acting as promotors. Third, Friedrich Kalden's study analyzes whether PMS design relates to its effectiveness in order to derive practical recommendations. For example, the study explains to what extent PMS designs in SSOs provide support for SSO managers to achieve their objectives and reveals why more KPIs are not always more effective.

The study is the first to analyze PMS design in SSOs and its effectiveness by drawing on a PMS design score. Consequently, Friedrich Kalden increases the comparability of different PMS designs in SSOs and provides evidence on associations between PMS design and its effectiveness. The study broadens prior research by uncovering so far unexplored contingency factors in the case study analyses and by empirically testing them based on a sound theoretical foundation. The case study analyses exploit insights from the expert interviews which may be beneficial to this study's practical relevance. Therefore, the empirical analyses yield implications for managers and management accountants that use and design PMS in SSOs as well as for other practitioners working in a shared service environment.

Given the importance of PMS in SSOs in practice and the contribution of the results to the existing body of literature, I hope that Friedrich Kalden's work will receive much attention from academics and practitioners.

Münster, January 2021 Prof. Dr. Peter Kajüter

Acknowledgement

I conducted this study during my time as a PhD-student and research assistant at the Chair of International Accounting at the University of Münster. The Münster School of Business and Economics accepted the thesis as a dissertation in July 2020.

In the following lines I would like to thank everyone who supported me during this research project. First, I sincerely thank my academic teacher and supervisor Prof. Dr. Peter Kajüter who provided me with great support during my time at his chair. His high standards, critical thinking and valuable guidance at different stages of the research project have substantially contributed to this study. Likewise, I would like to express my thankfulness to Prof. Dr. Schewe and Prof. Dr. Müller, who reviewed my thesis as a second and third referee.

I am also very grateful for the support of my employer, B. Braun Melsungen AG, which made the cooperation with the Chair of International Accounting for this research project possible. In particular, I would like to thank Dr. Annette Beller, Dieter Gemmer, Sven Ritschel and Dr. Martin Lüdicke, who helped me to initiate the cooperation program with the university, thus strengthening the collaboration between academia and practice.

I want to pay tribute to my colleagues, fellow PhD students and dear friends at the Chair of International Accounting who always gave me advice when urgently needed and – equally important – plenty of precious memories. A special thanks goes to my former roommates Maximilian Saucke and Gregor Hagemann whose methodical rigor is fortunately much more pronounced than their football expertise. I will miss epic football matches in "the cage" and WiWi-Cups with Stefan Hannen and Matthias Nienaber who scored better there than in double blind reviews. I will not miss it, but I am just as grateful to Martin Nienhaus and Florian Klassmann for their suggestions on statistical data evaluation. Obviously, all remaining errors are mine. I would also like to especially thank Alexander Schulz and Stephanie Eckerth for their in-depth introduction to the exciting Münster nightlife. In times of Covid I gladly remember hilarious parties and lousy cocktails we had together with the team. I owe thanks to Henrik Schirmacher and Martin Vogelpohl for learning how to play mind games at the football table and for getting a free of charge nutrition guide on our daily way to the canteen. I am also very thankful to Kai Schaumann and Max Meinhövel for teaching me about carnival traditions and how to deal with university administration, which is a science unto itself. I further want to thank Tobias Langehaneberg and Marcel

Baki for consistently bringing me back down to earth in a world full of ambitious academics. I want to express my gratitude to Daniela Peters for her sage advice in survey research and to Moritz Schröder who is the most professor-like non-professor I know. Last but not least many thanks to my newer colleagues Christoph Mauritz and Niklas Kerkhoff with whom I could spend not enough time and whose only fault is that they had to take over my teaching duties.

I further would like to thank the student assistants Alexandra Quitmann, Katharina Högemann and Leonie Wimmer for their extraordinary commitment to support my research project during the data collection phase. Furthermore, I dedicate special thanks to my friend Martin Köhler for proofreading the particularly tricky dissertation chapters.

This research project would not have been possible without the support of my family. My education is based on the selfless support of my parents Dürten and Wolf-Arthur Kalden who, among other things, taught me that wisdom and academic degrees may be bound together but should not be confused. Most importantly, I want to thank my wife Nina for all she has done for me to make this "self-realization project" (her words) a reality. If one of the parents is chasing his own dream in Münster, this also means that the other parent in Kassel bears the main burden of caring for the child and coping with the daily routine of a long-distance relationship. There are no words to express my thankfulness that you gave me this opportunity (my words). Just this much: there should be more appreciation for the efforts of single parents in this world.

Apart from the many acknowledgements, I would also like to express a long overdue apology. For the missed moments together with you in your early childhood and for the many boring weekend afternoons in front of the laptop at home instead of being with you at the playground, I apologize to you from the bottom of my heart. It will be of little consolation, but this is dedicated to you, Luise.

Kassel, July 2020 Friedrich Kalden

Content overview

Table of contents

List of figures

List of tables

List of abbreviations

ABC	Activity based costing
Adj.	Adjusted
BPO	Business Process Outsourcing
BSC	Balanced Scorecard
Cf.	Confer
CM	Contribution margin
CoE	Center of Expertise
Coeff.	Coefficient
COMP	PMS design score
CoS	Center of Scale
C.p.	Ceteris paribus
E.g.	Exempli gratia
Ed.	Edition
Eds.	Editors
ERP	Enterprise resource planning
Et al.	Et alii
Etc.	Et cetera
EU	European Union
f.	And the following one
ff.	And the following
FY	Fiscal Year
GDP	Gross Domestic Product
GOA	Goal attainment score
HQ	Headquarters
HR	Human Resources
http	Hypertext Transfer Protocol
I.a.	Inter alia
ICS	Internal Control System
I.e.	Id est
IMF	International Monetary Fund

IT	Information Technology
KPI	Key Performance Indicator
MA	Management Accounting
MAS	Management Accounting System
Max.	Maximum
MCS	Management Control System
Min.	Minimum
MIS	Management Information System
MM	Mixed methods
MMR	Mixed methods research
MMRD	Mixed methods research design
MNC	Multinational Corporation
NIE	New Institutional Economics
NIS	New Institutional Sociology
No.	Number
O2C	Order-to-cash
OCR	Optical Character Recognition
p.	Page
P2P	Purchase-to-pay
PAT	Principal Agent Theory
PDF	Portable Document Format
PKR	Prozesskostenrechnung
PMI	Post-Merger Integration
PMS	Performance Measurement System
pp.	Pages
Q	Quarter
QDA	Qualitative Data Analysis
RQ	Research Question
SAT	Satisfaction score
SOP	Standard Operating Procedure
SSC	Shared Service Center
SSO	Shared Service Organization
Std. Dev.	Standard Deviation

Suppl.	Supplementary
U.S.	United States
USA	United States of America
Var	Variance
VIF	Variance Inflation Factor
vs.	Versus
www	World Wide Web

List of symbols

*	Significance Level
&	And
F	F-value of the F-Test
H	Hypothesis
N	Number of Observations
P	Proposition
Σ	Sum
<	Smaller than
>	Larger than
%	Per cent

1 Introduction

1.1 Motivation and research questions

In the course of globalization, multinational corporations (MNCs)[1] have been facing increasing international competition due to lowered trade barriers (*Mayer/Ottaviano* (2008), pp. 144–147), technological advancement (*Guerrieri/Meliciani* (2005), p. 491), the assimilation of consumer preferences and thus, expanding market boundaries (*Mathews/Zander* (2007), pp. 487–488). To remain a viable force in this competitive and uncertain environment, companies identify the efficient management of support processes as an important competitive advantage. Thus, developing an organization that supports globally operating business units with internal services has become a critical task for MNCs. **Shared Service Organizations (SSOs)** exclusively consolidate and perform support processes of MNC's corporate functions in a separate organizational unit. SSOs operate like a business unit under market conditions (*Bergeron* (2002), p. 3; *Janssen et al.* (2010), pp. 16–17).

By implementing SSOs, MNCs intend to reduce costs, increase the quality of internal services, standardize and automate support processes, enhance knowledge through the concentration of expertise at few locations and mitigate financial risks (*Bangemann* (2005), pp. 8–11). Prior research indicates that the implementation of SSOs leads to **cost savings** (*Aksin/Masini* (2008); *Selden/Wooters* (2011); *Sterzenbach* (2010)).[2] Further evidence suggests a higher customer orientation leading to an **improved service quality** (*Farndale et al.* (2009); *Redman et al.* (2007); *Röder* (2012); *Weschke* (2008)). Moreover, several studies

---

1   Literature does not define the term MNC consistently (*Fischer* (2006), pp. 17–21). However, MNCs differ from domestic corporations because they operate in countries other than the home market and face disparate socio-cultural contexts. According to *Baliga/Jaeger* (1984) and *Holtbrügge/Welge* (2010), the term MNC refers to a group of affiliated companies operating geographically dispersed in at least two or more countries. MNCs actively manage a portfolio of at least two foreign subsidiaries which perform core business processes on a permanent basis (Ghoshal/Bartlett (1990), p. 603). For an overview of MNC definitions see *Kutschker/Schmid* (2011). For a general discussion about typical MNC characteristics see *Tacke* (1984).

2   *Dollery/Akimov* (2007), *Fischer/Sterzenbach* (2007), *Keuper/Röder* (2009) and *Moll* (2012) provide further empirical evidence on cost savings of MNCs induced by SSO implementations.

imply an **enhanced availability of resources** for internal customers by concentrating knowledge as well as an **improved compliance** with internal guidelines and legal requirements (*Herbert/Seal* (2012); *Paagman et al.* (2015b)).

Although the implementation of SSOs seems compelling, some researchers and practitioners voice doubts that companies benefit from this concept or even suspect a **negative impact** on MNC's efficiency and effectiveness. *Cooke* finds that the loss of face-to-face contact and a lack of employee representation in a SSC model deteriorates the quality of the rendered services (*Cooke* (2006), pp. 217–220). Moreover, the consequential negative image of the SSO staff induces mistrust and shadow systems in business units, resulting in a waste of resources. *Janssen and Joha* state that cost reduction and service improvement is not always realized because the manifold motives associated with the implementation of a SSO may result in conflicting goals and thus jeopardize the expected outcome (*Janssen/Joha* (2006), p. 112).

In light of potential benefits and potential harm associated with SSOs, the **controversy** among researchers and practitioners about SSO's performance continues. By contrast, SSOs delight wide acclaim in the corporate landscape (*Aksin/Masini* (2008); *Kagelmann* (2001); *Ramphal* (2011); *Selden/Wooters* (2011); *Sterzenbach* (2010)). A survey conducted by *KPMG* among the 1,000 largest firms in German-speaking countries shows that already 74% out of the 102 responding companies established at least one Shared Service Center (SSC) (*Möller/Reimann* (2013), p. 12). Thus, the **relevance** of the SSO model in practice conflicts with the uncertainty about its performance. A major reason for this discrepancy is that measuring the performance of a SSO seems challenging as a longitudinal case study by *Herbert and Seal* stresses:

> "*Although the headline motivation was cost reduction, the net financial benefit of adopting the SSO model was actually quite difficult to measure. (…), it was extremely difficult to see how many of potential savings claimed by SSO managers could be (…) measured in practice, (…).*"

> (*Herbert/Seal* (2012), p. 91)

The findings of *Herbert and Seal* emphasize the crucial need for **performance measurement systems (PMS)** in SSOs. *Neely et al.* define PMS *"as the set of metrics used to quantify both the efficiency and effectiveness of actions"* (*Neely et al.* (1995), pp. 81–82). PMS represent an important Management Control System (MCS) used in SSOs in order to facilitate decision-making and behavioral control (*Fischer et al.* (2017), pp. 126–128). PMS aim at improving strategy implementation by the effective control of MNC's processes (*Gates* (1999); *Atkinson* (1998); *Dossi/Patelli* (2010); *Ittner et al.* (2003); *Kaplan/Norton* (1996); *Otley*

(1999)), create goal congruence through an enhanced communication platform (*Forza/Salvador* (2000); *Kerssens-van Drongelen/Fisscher* (2003); *Neely et al.* (1995); *Otley* (1999)), monitor progress (*Atkinson* (1998); *Atkinson et al.* (1997); *Neely et al.* (1995)), increase employee motivation (*Otley* (1999)), knowledge sharing (*Atkinson* (1998); *Bititci et al.* (1997); *Forza/Salvador* (2000); *Kerssens-van Drongelen/Fisscher* (2003); *Lebas* (1995)) as well as additional learning effects (*Atkinson* (1998); *Lebas* (1995)). Although there is already a fair amount of performance measurement related literature, PMS remain topical for researchers and practitioners due to continuously transforming business organizations (*Folan/Browne* (2005), p. 664). The urgent need of keeping pace with changes in markets, new technologies and an ongoing competition leads to reorganizations in MNCs and the necessity to adapt their PMS design (*Eccles* (1990), p. 134). Multicultural collaboration, knowledge work, the automation and digitalization of performance measurement processes as well as analyzing large data volumes and providing real-time performance reports are upcoming challenges that drive the change in performance measurement practices of MNCs (*Bititci et al.* (2012), pp. 313–319). While the environment is constantly changing, the pursuit for greater efficiency and effectiveness through the use of PMS remains unchanged.

Empirical studies indicate that using PMS has positive effects on companies' performance. Several studies suggest a positive influence on **organizational performance** by using PMS (*Davis/Albright* (2004); *Gleich* (2002); *Jorissen et al.* (1997); *Lingle/Schiemann* (1996); *Marr* (2005); *Raake* (2008); *Said et al.* (2003)). Moreover, empirical research finds positive effects on stock market performance if firms use PMS more extensively (*Gates* (1999); *Ittner et al.* (2003); *Said et al.* (2003)). Findings of other studies positively associate the use of a comprehensive PMS with **managers' satisfaction** (*Eicker et al.* (2005); *Ittner et al.* (2003); *Raake* (2008); *Sandt* (2004)). Further research supports the notion that PMS positively affect managerial performance in terms of **goal attainment** (*Hall* (2008); *Webb* (2004)).

Shared service related literature in general and literature with regard to PMS in SSOs in particular is essentially characterized by **anecdotal evidence** (*Shah* (1998); *Ulrich* (1995); *van Denburgh/Cagna* (2000)). Although some research addresses MCS in SSOs (*Farndale et al.* (2009); *Herbert/Seal* (2012); *Pérez* (2009); *Sterzenbach* (2010)), most studies do not focus on PMS in SSOs, but on other subjects in the field of management accounting. Therefore, these studies do not provide in-depth analyses of PMS in SSOs. Hence, the study of *Chang et al.* (2013) seems noteworthy because it focuses on PMS in SSOs, albeit it is limited to the Balanced Scorecard (BSC) developed by *Kaplan and Norton*. The low consideration of PMS in SSO literature marks a **blind spot** in management accounting research (*Keuper/Glahn* (2006), p. 85). In essence, empirical research on SSOs remains scarce:

> "*Nevertheless, researchers hitherto have not investigated [SSOs] sufficiently; [SSOs] have only been of minor importance to researchers.*"
>
> *(Janssen et al. (2010), p. 211)*

Furthermore, the literature on PMS in SSOs defines the term *Shared Service Organization* inconsistently. Due to a varying understanding in related literature, it is necessary to differentiate between the terms *SSO* and *Shared Service Center (SSC)*. Whereas the term *SSO* refers to the entire organizational structure (*Hirsch* (2016), p. 129), the term *SSC* merely defines an organizational unit that offers support processes within the SSO (*Kagelmann* (2001), p. 50). Therefore, a SSO may imply more than one SSC, whereas a SSC always belongs to a single SSO.

Although there is empirical evidence on the design and effects of PMS for many organizational forms, it may differ greatly in SSOs due to several reasons. With a view to cover different regions or different support processes, MNCs commonly establish more than one SSC that collaborate with each other (*Sterzenbach* (2010), p. 341). Moreover, SSOs frequently use outsourcing[3] of sub-processes as another possibility to reduce costs, so that SSOs need to collaborate with external service providers (*Quinn et al.* (2000), p. 15). The fact that SSOs are collaborative organizations[4] and thus entail multiple principal agent relationships, enhances the **complexity** of its PMS including a variety of operational, cultural, technical and organizational conflicts resulting from information asymmetries among the involved actors (*Busi/Bititci* (2006); *Chen et al.* (2007); *Folan/Browne* (2005)).

Apart from the geographical dispersion of SSCs, SSOs provide services to demanding customers of different regions and business segments which impose additional challenges for PMS in SSOs. Furthermore, a modern PMS in SSOs is barely feasible without relying on IT-systems that are capable of evaluating large data volumes. On the one hand, technological advancement represents a blessing to facilitating performance measurement practices. On the other hand, various IT-systems induce a heterogeneous IT-landscape causing technical barriers a PMS has to overcome. Employment in SSOs primarily requires

---

3   According to Sako (2006) outsourcing occurs when a company, which used to run a business process in-house, decides to buy the same process from an external provider.

4   According to *Huxham* (1996) collaborative organizations are corporate alliances working together towards a common aim by exchanging information, altering activities, sharing resources and enhancing each other's capability for mutual benefit and a common purpose by sharing risks, responsibilities and rewards.

profound knowledge instead of manual work. Most of the tasks for employees in SSCs demand specialized or technical knowledge even if it is a matter of *so-called* transaction-based support processes, e.g. the purchase-to-pay-process. However, the performance of knowledge-based work is difficult to measure and thus represents another challenge for PMS in SSOs (*Carter* (1998), p. 203). Since SSCs provide services, PMS might vary significantly compared to PMS in product-dominated areas (*Becker/Rech* (2013); *Bohnert* (2010); *Gleich et al.* (2010)).

Even though PMS of collaborative organizations in a multinational environment have been addressed in isolation in prior research, the composition of these elements in a new organizational model, the SSO, *is* something new for performance measurement research. Hence, collaborative organizations, such as SSOs, enhance the complexity of its PMS design:

> "(...), the community is aware of these challenges as discreet areas of research, but pays little attention to the complexity and additional challenges associated with an integrated holistic view of these areas of research."
>
> *(Bititci et al. (2012), p. 318)*

To date, neither a basic understanding of the current design of PMS in SSOs of MNCs nor its effectiveness has been empirically explored. Therefore, *Aksin and Masini* summarize a substantial **research gap** with regard to PMS in SSOs:

> "To our knowledge, there is no academic study to date that examines the link between strategy, implementation and resulting performance in SSOs. Claims are mostly based on conceptual arguments, perhaps supported by anecdotal evidence that associates certain variables and certain performance measures."
>
> *(Aksin/Masini (2008), p. 240)*

The relevance of SSOs in theory and practice as well as the ongoing controversy about benefits and additional challenges induced by this rather new organizational model forms the basis for the **three main research questions** of this study. First, this study explores prevailing PMS in SSOs to grasp a basic understanding of varying PMS designs in SSOs:

RQ 1   How are PMS in SSOs designed?

Second, the analysis investigates which contingency factors are associated with PMS design in SSOs. This offers valuable insights for the status quo and explains which determinants affect PMS design in SSOs:

RQ 2   What determines the design of PMS in SSOs?

Third, to date it remains disguised whether PMS design in SSOs is associated with its effectiveness since prior research is mostly based on anecdotal evidence. However, it seems necessary to analyze whether PMS design relates to its effectiveness in order to derive practical recommendations. For example, it remains vague to what extent PMS designs in SSOs provide support to achieve SSO's objectives in corporate practice. Therefore, the third research question is as follows:

RQ 3   What determines the effectiveness of PMS in SSOs?

The nature of the three research questions requires different research methods. Notably, this study refrains from analyzing the three research questions separately. By contrast, a **mixed method research design** (MMRD) promises a more exhaustive view on the phenomenon under research by integrating qualitative and quantitative findings. This study employs a sequential exploratory design by starting with the case studies followed by surveys. The applied sequential exploratory design allows for the refinement of the survey design. Moreover, the case study findings are exploited to refine the basic hypotheses derived from the theoretical framework. Hence, the sequential design ensures that the developed hypotheses are empirically testable by using the survey method.

Since PMS in SSOs represents a rather nascent research stream which is mainly characterized by conceptual contributions and anecdotal evidence, the first research question describes an **exploratory and descriptive research objective**. Therefore, a qualitative research approach seems best suited to explore current PMS designs. Prior performance measurement research indicates that in-depth case study analyses yield fruitful insights by conducting expert interviews (*Bourne et al.* (2003); *Franco/Bourne* (2003); *Garengo/Bititci* (2007); *Neely et al.* (2000)). Expert interviews offer access to specific knowledge about the current state of PMS in SSOs and thus give reasons for varying designs, emerging challenges and future developments. A wider range of answers compared to a questionnaire and a higher tolerance with regard to the response style provide a deeper view on PMS in SSOs. Particularly, the performance measurement process and the involved actors seem to be better explorable by using a qualitative research approach. In order to generalize empirical findings from the single case, this study also applies a quantitative research approach. MCS research commonly uses surveys to gain descriptive information about a wider population (*Easterby-Smith et al.* (2012); *Ferreira/Merchant* (1992); *Ittner/ Larcker* (2001)). Moreover, the second and the third research question pursue an **explanatory research objective** so that this study surveys a comparatively larger sample of German, Austrian, and Suisse SSOs.

Figure 1.1 summarizes the main research objectives of the study:

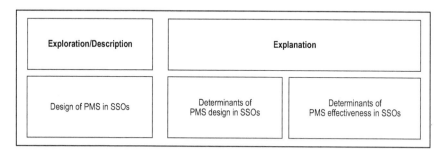

Figure 1.1: Research objectives of the study

This study **contributes** to the existing body of literature by shedding light on the rather unexplored PMS design in SSOs. It adds to the existing performance measurement literature by a thorough description of the three essential components of PMS design, namely performance measures, performance measurement processes and performance measurement actors. Particularly, the actors involved in the performance measurement process reduce a gap in prior research. This study also contributes to the nascent research stream of SSO literature by revealing the SSO's PMS design beyond prior research. Furthermore, this study is the first to analyze PMS design in SSOs and its effectiveness by drawing on a PMS design score. Therefore, this study increases the comparability of different PMS designs in SSOs and provides evidence on associations between PMS design and its effectiveness. This study adds to the existing literature by analyzing PMS effectiveness, which is far from being exhaustively explored. Since prior SSO research calls for empirical evidence on MCS determinants in SSOs, this study broadens prior research by uncovering so far unexplored contingency factors in the case study analyses and empirically testing them based on a sound theoretical foundation. Finally, this study employs a MMRD and is thus able to triangulate empirical findings from different viewpoints providing a more complete picture of PMS in SSOs. The case study analyses exploit insights from the expert interviews which may be beneficial to this study's practical relevance. Therefore, the empirical analyses yield implications for SSO managers as primary users and for SSO management accountants as primary designers of the PMS in SSOs as well as for other practitioners working in a shared service environment.

Prior to the scientific positioning, the following section presents this study's outline.

1.2 Outline of the study

The study is subdivided into eight chapters. The **first chapter** serves as an introduction to point out the motivation for this study and to emphasize the relevance of PMS in SSOs. Moreover, it presents the research questions and research objectives. Furthermore, the first chapter briefly explains the scientific positioning of this work to derive a suitable research strategy.

The **second chapter** forms the conceptual foundation of this study in two major parts. First, chapter two discusses existing definitions of the term SSO and provides a definition for this study. Furthermore, this chapter describes the main objectives of SSOs. To grasp a deeper understanding of SSOs, this chapter illustrates major design characteristics of SSOs. The second part mirrors the structure of the first part, yielding a definition for PMS and describing its main objectives. Furthermore, the second chapter derives a decent conceptualization of PMS design.

The **third chapter** provides a literature review of SSO and PMS related literature. The review exclusively focuses on empirical research which is subdivided in qualitative and quantitative contributions. Based on the findings and limitations of previous studies, chapter three identifies a research gap and illustrates this study's contribution to the existing body of literature.

The **fourth chapter** builds the theoretical foundation for this study. It outlines this study's contingency framework and elaborates on the three main theories used to derive basic hypotheses consistent to the initially introduced second and third research questions. This study builds on new institutional sociology, principal agent theory and on the promotor model to derive its hypotheses.

The **fifth chapter** presents this study's research design. It introduces qualitative case study research as well as quantitative survey research and unveils this study's MMRD. This chapter defines the term mixed methods and outlines the major objectives pursued with the selected research design. It concludes with a brief summary of essential quality criteria for this study's research design.

The **sixth chapter** contains the empirical results of the qualitative analysis. After introducing the sample selection and case company description, chapter six provides descriptive evidence on a within case analysis. Moreover, this chapter derives implications on PMS design in SSOs by exploiting the results of a

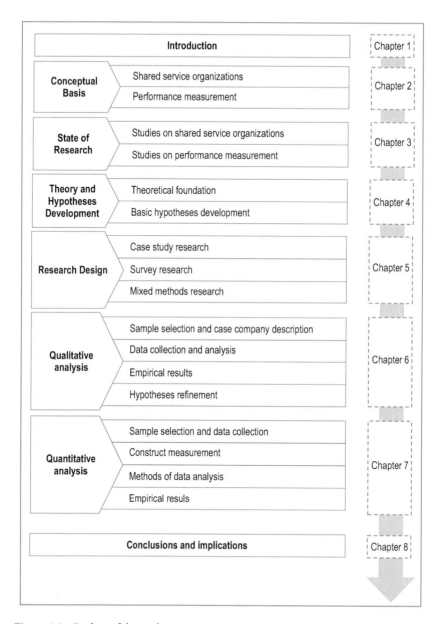

Figure 1.2: Outline of the study

cross-case analysis. Furthermore, the sixth chapter encompasses the refinement of the basic hypotheses which paves the way for the hypotheses testing.

The **seventh chapter** comprises the quantitative analysis and presents the empirical findings of the surveys. After introducing the sample selection and the data collection methods, this chapter illustrates the operationalization of the constructs under research and outlines the PMS design score. Apart from a brief description of the statistical data analysis methods, it provides descriptive evidence on PMS designs in SSOs. The seventh chapter concludes with multiple regression analyses that investigate possible associations between PMS design and its determinants and between PMS design and its effectiveness.

The **eighth chapter** concludes the main results, discusses this study's implications and describes its limitations. Furthermore, it illustrates possible avenues for future research.

1.3 Scientific positioning

This section illustrates the research project's scientific positioning for two reasons. First, it explores why the underlying research strategy has been chosen. Second, this section classifies the selected methodology among the prevailing epistemological approaches in current business economic research.

The 'Philosophy of Social Science' (*Brühl* (2016), p. 21) as a meta-science, evolved from epistemology and considers the question of how to develop cognition by scientific means (*Kornmeier* (2007), p. 7). Knowledge advancement requires true statements (*Baumann* (2008), p. 63). Hence, scientists, as potential truth seekers, should justify why a statement is true. Without any justification, other researchers are not able to verify the extent to which the scientist approaches truth. In social sciences, statements are foremost justifiable through the concepts of validity and reliability (*Brühl* (2016), pp. 40–41). Thus, the factual justification of own statements distinguishes knowledge from intuition and belief (*Kornmeier* (2007), p. 4). Moreover, knowledge differs from science. Not each single piece of information may be referred to as science. Science begins with the systematic structuring of knowledge with the purpose to accomplish scientific objectives (*Raffée* (1974), p. 13).

Popper points out that the search for truth through knowledge advancement is only one major scientific objective (*Popper/Keuth* (2009), p. 355), although it is considered by few scientists as the only worthwhile, known as pure science (*Fülbier* (2004), p. 18; *Raffée* (1974), p. 15). Other scientists emphasize the importance of criticizing the status quo and the unfolding of utopias within academic controversies as major scientific objectives (*Raffée* (1974), pp. 16–17). If knowledge advancement would be recognized as the only worthwhile objective, science lags permanently behind practice. As opposed to pure sciences, the meta-objective of applied sciences is simply to improve people's lives by using gained knowledge to derive practical recommendations (*Wild* (1993), p. 3892; *Kosiol* (1964), p. 744). Enclosed to a socio-economic environment, applied sciences target to enhance operational efficiency (*Frank* (2003), p. 283) and to solve resource scarcity at firm level (*Fülbier* (2004), p. 267).

Based on *Chmielewicz'* illustrations of a fundamental research approach (*Chmielewicz* (1994), pp. 9–11), *Brühl* defines four steps that need to be accomplished beforehand (*Brühl* (2016), pp. 23–25) in order to gain scientific knowledge. The understanding has to be mentioned as a first step, because it connects language and symbols with actions to a particular meaning. Describing phenomena in the field of business administration as a second step requires a consistent terminology. A third prerequisite is the explanation of described phenomena that reveal previously unknown causal relationships. As a fourth step, the explanation of prior causes and effects serves as an outlook to assess future developments. Only if these four stated prerequisites have been performed, researchers are capable of expanding the current body of knowledge. Therefore, this study follows the introduced four-step model. First, this study seeks to gain a sound understanding of the phenomenon under research by deriving a precise conceptualization of SSOs and PMS design. Second, this study provides comprehensive descriptive evidence on the current status of PMS design of SSOs in corporate practice. Third, this study explains current PMS designs by revealing its associations with contingency factors. Moreover, the explicative evidence unveils associations between PMS design and its effectiveness. Fourth, this study uses its findings to derive practical recommendations for future PMS designs in SSOs.

Grochla specifies this research approach by conceiving three main research strategies to gain knowledge and to derive practical recommendations (*Grochla* (1978), p. 71), namely:

- the conceptual;
- the analytical and
- the empirical strategy.

The **conceptual research strategy** aims to reveal complex associations through a predominantly intellectual simulation of reality with a view to derive practical recommendations. As a consequence, this strategy does not strive for an empirical verification. The conceptual strategy contains a speculative element instead, which is mainly reflected in the fact that variables of research models are rarely operationalized, whereby many associations remain unspecified (*Grochla* (1978), pp. 72–78).

In contrast to the conceptual strategy, the **analytical research strategy** refers directly to a particular problem. Thus, analytical research is less concerned about a comprehensive understanding of reality, but rather about applying mathematical-logical research methods to solve specific problems. However, the strong orientation of this strategy towards available mathematical algorithms and the subsequent simplification of reality may develop solutions for which a practical setting yet does not exist. Moreover, analytical research implies the risk that designed research models do not meet practical requirements, because necessary data are unavailable. Finally, those models may disregard important aspects of reality. The value of this strategy lies in yielding problem-solving blueprints that are exploitable for suitable cases (*Grochla* (1978), pp. 85–93).

The **empirical research strategy** aspires a systematic gain of experience by assessing reflections on reality and, thus, either confirm their validity or precisely not. By using qualitative and quantitative research methods, empirical research attempts to examine how accurately selected variables and measurement instruments are able to describe a particular domain of reality. Therefore, empirical researchers intend to explore, describe and explain the considered variables of the phenomenon under research. Key challenges linked to this strategy are twofold. First, an adequate operationalization is crucial to thoroughly depict the stated problem. Second, a flawed population selection causes distortions (*Grochla* (1978), pp. 78–85). With a view to the pursued research objectives, namely exploring and describing the phenomenon of PMS in SSOs in current practice, explaining PMS design by investigating its determinants and analyzing its effectiveness, this study uses an empirical research strategy to systematically assess reflections on the phenomenon under research. To address the challenges linked to an empirical research strategy, this study applies a mixed methods research design (MMRD).

The question of a meaningful combination of qualitative and quantitative research methods in a MMRD is complicated because the underlying methodologies are linked to epistemological and ontological assumptions. The combination of research methods raises the question whether qualitative and quantitative research processes are even combinable (*Hall* (2012), p. 5). Methodologies are based on epistemological theories, which are derived from ontological assumptions. Hence, this research project cannot be based solely on a single methodological viewpoint, since it also pursues an explorative research objective requiring a qualitative and a quantitative research approach. Such as many scientific disciplines, social sciences cultivated their own ontological viewpoints. Therefore, it represents only a small portion of the existing epistemology. The epistemological approaches of constructivism and critical rationalism prevail in contemporary business economic research (*Fülbier* (2004), p. 22). Both concepts

evolved from the same historical precursors, particularly the classical rationalism, the realism, the empiricism as well as the (neo-) positivism and constitute a combination of different elements extracted from the initial approaches.
Due to the fact that modern epistemological approaches already represent a
combination of varying ontological viewpoints, it seems thus feasible to combine elements of constructivism and critical rationalism.

The **critical rationalism** harks back to *Popper* and assumes that human rationality is fallible (i.e. fallibilism). According to him, gained knowledge is always
temporary and never irrevocable (*Lingnau* (1995), p. 124). Considering that
knowledge may be found to be erroneous, *Popper* rejects principles derived by
induction and prefers deduction instead (*Albert* (2000), pp. 14–15). Human
beings are capable of learning from their mistakes and approximate truth incre-
mentally. This implies that hypotheses can be tested empirically through measurable observations and are falsifiable, if they are neither limited in time nor in
space (*Keuth* (2013), pp. 16–17). Thereby, the ontological roots of critical rationalism in realism are visible, since empirical testability presumes an objective
reality, existing independently from an observer's perception (*Cappallo* (2006),
pp. 23–25). Hypotheses are either derived from conceptual models or previous
empirical research (*Fülbier* (2004), pp. 22–23). The higher the falsification risk
for a hypothesis, the more promising is its cognitive value (*Ulrich/Hill* (1976),
p. 346). As long as they are not falsified, a hypothesis is considered to be temporarily valid (*Fülbier* (2004), p. 22; *Kornmeier* (2007), p. 41).

Apart from the dominating critical rationalism, the **constructivism** is of
remarkable importance for contemporary business economic research (*Fülbier*
(2004), p. 23). As opposed to the critical rationalism, the constructivism
promotes the notion of a non-existent objective reality, since it remains a construct of human perception (*Frank* (2007), p. 2012). Indeed, the constructivism
recognizes the fallibility of human reasoning to a limited extent, which constitutes
a similarity to the critical rationalism (*Raffée/Abel* (1979), p. 6). To cope with
the selected MMRD, the underlying research approach of critical rationalism
is supplemented with a particular form of constructivism, namely **the social
constructivism**. Social constructivism emanates from *Berger and Luckmann*
and seems rather compatible with the notions of critical rationalism (*Lukka*
(1990), pp. 254–255). Similar to other constructivist approaches, the social constructivism assumes that reality is socially constructed (*Cappallo* (2006), p. 23).
Whereas positive approaches frequently neglect that manager's choices, e.g. how
to design a PMS, are influenced by societal webs of relations, social constructivism stresses an interplay between managers and social reality (*Neu* (1992),
p. 234). Although SSO managers design PMS as a consequence of their perceived

social reality, their designed PMS influences the same social reality, thus creating a continuous interplay by determining each other (*Neimark/Tinker* (1986), p. 380). It implies that socially constructed objects, such as MCS and particularly PMS, are accepted as facts and therefore of apparent objective existence (*Lukka* (1990), p. 245). Hence, the social constructivism does not fully contradict the rationalistic premise of an existing objective reality.

This study follows the critical rationalism as an underlying research approach to derive and test hypotheses with regard to possible contingency factors on PMS design. Moreover, this study analyzes possible associations between PMS design and its effectiveness. By contrast, social constructivism allows for a qualitative research approach to explore the design of PMS in SSOs. To pursue the explorative research objective, this study also investigates the interplay between the research objects and their perceived social reality. Hence, both research approaches are reflected in this study as they complement each other.

2 Conceptual basis

2.1 Shared service organizations

This section evaluates the existing and varying definitions of the term *Shared Service Organization* in order to constitute a definition for this study. Moreover, key objectives of SSOs are detailed. A major part of this section addresses the design characteristics of SSOs to better understand the organizational environment in which PMS are implemented. Furthermore, this section seeks a clear terminological distinction to alternative organizational models.

2.1.1 Definition of shared service organizations

Although the terms **shared services, shared service center and shared service organization** find an increasing use in research and practice, a general understanding in relevant literature is missing (*Brühl et al.* (2017), p. 4; *Raudla/Tammel* (2015), p. 160; *Sterzenbach* (2010), p. 3–4).[5] The lacking conceptual clarity has two different sources. First, distinct disciplines in business economic research (e.g. international management, accounting, public sector research etc.) conduct research about SSOs independently. Second, corporate practice reveals that SSOs often entail different operational functions. Moreover, SSOs are encountered in diverse industries. A widely differing corporate landscape may result in firms, which subsume diverging characteristics and objectives under the term SSO (*Sterzenbach* (2010), p. 35). Hence, this section highlights distinctions and similarities of various definitions and seeks to yield this study's definition consistent to previous literature.

Current literature unveils four different approaches to define the term SSO (*Aksin/Masini* (2008), p. 239; *Bergeron* (2002), p. 3; *Deimel/Quante* (2003), p. 302; *Pérez* (2009), p. 26; *Kagelmann* (2001), pp. 49–50; *Moll* (2012), p. 20):

- the semantic;
- the organizational;
- the effect-oriented and
- the strategy-oriented approach.

---

5   *Ulbrich* (2008), p. 34, points out that "many authors simply wrote about using shared services in orga-nizations and, for example, how to benefit from this idea, rather than actually explaining or defining what the shared services idea is really all about."

A **semantic approach** defines the individual components (1) shared, (2) service and (3) organization (or center) in order to subsequently compose the essential aspects of these components in a definition for the entire term. The component *shared* illustrates a mutual resource use from service recipients' point of view (*Deimel/Quante* (2003), p. 302). For this purpose, service recipients transfer previously owned support processes to the SSO in favor of a more efficient resource use (*Wißkirchen/Mertens* (1999), p. 85). The component *service* characterizes the services provided by the SSO. Since the adoption of SSOs involves to exclusively perform support processes, SSOs do not consider them as an tiresome task, which may pertain to a decentralized service provision. By contrast, providing support services comprises the core task of SSOs, which often entails a strong customer orientation in service delivery (*Pérez* (2009), p. 26). The component *organization* or *center* underpins the design as a separate organizational unit (*Wißkirchen* (2002), p. 34). The notion of a separate organizational unit frequently involves economic and/or legal independence (*Klingebiel/Andreas* (2006), p. 778). A well-known definition in German-speaking literature emanates from *Kagelmann,* whose definition concisely combines the three introduced components:

> "[SSOs] are organizational units that provide internal services through the mutual resource use within a corporation."
>
> *(Kagelmann (2001), pp. S.49–50)*

The essential benefit of the semantic approach is the broad interpretation of the SSO concept so that *Kagelmann's* definition remains valid as a common ground for diverging definitions with an individual emphasis (*Kagelmann* (2001), p. 50). Nonetheless, generalization implies the lack of discriminatory power. *Perez* criticizes that *Kagelmann's* definition distinguishes SSCs insufficiently from centralization within corporate functions (*Pérez* (2009), p. 25). *Moll* argues in a similar vein by challenging the discriminatory power of *Kagelmann's* definition with regard to business process outsourcing (BPO) (*Moll* (2012), p. 20).

Organizational approaches offer a more nuanced perspective towards the distinction of SSOs compared to related organizational models, such as centralization and BPO. With reference to the organizational structure, the introduced differentiation between the terms SSO and SSC is of crucial importance. *Janssen/ Joha* provide a definition, demonstrating an organizational perspective:[6]

---

6   The definitions of *Miller* (1999), p. 46, *Schwarz/Schiele* (2004), p. 40, and *Wißkirchen* (2002), p. 34, are considered as further examples for an emphasis on the organizational perspective.

"Nowadays, more and more organizations adopt service-orientation by using service centers and turning themselves into shared service organizations (SSOs)…[The] SSO … can be viewed as a set of capabilities that can be reconfigured to meet changing objectives. These capabilities are often organized in the form of shared service centers (SSCs), which can be defined as a semi-autonomous entity that provides well-defined services to other organizational entities based on predefined service level agreements."

(*Janssen/Joha (2008), pp. 35–36*)

By defining the operational process organization of SSCs, several contributions distinguish between **centers of scale (CoS)** and **centers of expertise (CoE)** (*Eichenberg/Bursy* (2016), p. 19; *Engstermann* (2015), p. 444; *Fritze et al.* (2013), p. 635).While transaction-based processes performed in CoS are characterized by high transaction volumes, expertise-based processes performed in CoE reveal a high degree of specialization (*Kagelmann* (2001), p. 89). In order to obtain a more specific distinction, several authors characterize CoS-based processes as more standardizable and with less decision-making potential compared to CoE-based processes (*Hirsch* (2016), pp. 130–131). Even though the organizational subdivision in CoS and CoE may initially appear to be a useful distinction, it seems debatable to what extent *scale* and *expertise* demonstrate a meaningful contrast. In general, it may be reasonable to distinguish processes with high economies of scale from those with low economies of scale. However, it is more challenging to differentiate between processes requiring a profound expertise from those that require hardly any expertise. Furthermore, it is difficult to categorize end-to-end support processes holistically, since exemplary CoS processes, such as the purchase-to-pay process, perform particular activities in a small number but with a demanding level of expertise. Contrarily, particular activities do not require profound expertise in exemplary CoE processes, such as settling a lawsuit, where many pages have to be scanned, too. From a psychological perspective the question arises, whether such a categorization causes demotivating effects on CoS employees.

Although the organizational science-based definition by *Janssen/Joha* specifies the organizational structure of SSOs and *Kagelmann's* definition details the individual components of the term SSO, both do not address which objectives this organizational model pursues. By contrast, **effect-oriented approaches** vary with respect to the suggested SSO objectives. Several effect-oriented approaches give priority to an improved effectiveness, e.g. through an enhanced service quality or an improved value generation (*Grant et al.* (2007), p. 522; *Schulman et al.* (1999), p. 9; *Triplett/Scheumann* (2000), p. 40). Other approaches focus on enhanced efficiency, generally illustrated by cost reduction (*Forst* (1999), p. 58;

Goh et al. (2007), p. 252; *Wang/Wang* (2007), p. 281). A popular definition combining the two main objectives of SSO emanates from *Bergeron:*

> "Shared services is a collaborative strategy in which a subset of existing business functions are concentrated into a new, semiautonomous business unit that has a management structure designed to promote efficiency, value generation, cost savings, and improved service for the internal customers of the parent corporation, like a business competing in the open market."

> *(Bergeron (2002), p. 3)*

Bergeron's definition sounds appealing because it not only points out the multilayered SSO objectives, but also suggests how to pursue these objectives while referring to a *"collaborative strategy"* and comparing SSOs to *"a business competing in the open market"*. However, naming certain objectives in a definition involves the danger of incompleteness. It is therefore questionable, whether this definition contains all essential SSO objectives (*Moll* (2012), p. 22). Furthermore, *Bergeron* identifies *"efficiency"* and *"cost savings"* as two separate objectives so that it remains vague how the notion of *"efficiency"* should be interpreted.

Several contributions seize *Bergeron's* notion of a *"strategy"*, by which SSOs accomplish their objectives (*Davis* (2005), p. 2; *van Denburgh/Cagna* (2000), p. 45; *Goh et al.* (2007), p. 252). Exponents of **strategy-oriented approaches** define shared services itself as a strategy to create value for the MNC. SSOs generate value through economic independence and responsibility, managed as a company within a company (*van Denburgh/Cagna* (2000), p. 48). In addition, service fees for internal customers should reflect cost reductions achieved by the SSOs, which may improve their competitiveness (*Schulman et al.* (1999), p. 35). Some publications of this approach specify strategies, whereby the SSOs should generate value by emphasizing process standardization, process streamlining and/or process consolidation (*Schimank* (2004), p. 171; *Triplett/Scheumann* (2000), p. 40; *Voegelin/Spreiter,* p. 831). The strategy-oriented definition of *Aksin/ Masini* unites these elements:

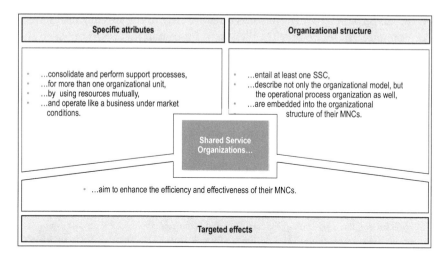

Figure 2.1: Definition of Shared Service Organizations

"Shared services is the strategy of standardizing, streamlining, and consolidating common business functions and processes in an organization, in order to improve efficiency and effectiveness with both cost reduction and overall profitability in mind."

(Aksin/Masini (2008), p. 239)

Although the definition of *Aksin/Masini* includes the SSOs' main objectives, it barely considers the organizational perspective of SSOs. Moreover, the distinction between SSO objectives and strategies remains ambiguous, since, for example, process streamlining may be regarded as a sub-objective of efficiency.

The four illustrated approaches yield a variety of SSO definitions that focus on different aspects. Despite the diverging perspectives from which SSOs are defined, certain fragments occur more frequently and are suggested by all of the four approaches. To define SSOs as precise and holistic as possible, the definition used in this study reflects the four approaches by considering recurring fragments (*Janssen et al.* (2010), pp. 213–214). Moreover, this definition not only covers recurring fragments of the aforementioned definitions but also addresses the requirements linked to this study, as shown in figure 2.1.

As a major research objective, this study analyzes the effects of PMS in SSOs. Therefore, this study examines the extent to which PMS support SSO managers to achieve their SSO objectives. Accordingly, this study's definition indicates **targeted effects** of SSO, which are expressed as aggregated as possible to avoid incompleteness. Furthermore, the study at hand analyzes possible determinants of PMS in SSO. Several determinants directly relate to the specific SSO design. For example, the design of SSO's PMS may depend on the extent to which the SSO uses service level agreements (SLAs) to manage its business relationship with internal customers. Thus, the definition used in this study entails **specific attributes** that are most commonly associated with SSOs. Again, the attributes are displayed as aggregated as possible. For the research design it is essential to distinguish between SSO and SSC so that the definition includes this **organizational component**. Nevertheless, the definition consciously does not address a possible legal and/or economic independence of SSOs since this is not necessarily valid for all of them. For the same reasons, the definition used in this study does not cover the subdivision of SSCs into CoE and/or CoS.

For clarity, the following definition is used in this study:

"SSOs consolidate and exclusively perform support processes for more than one organizational unit by mutually using resources. SSOs operate like a business under market conditions to enhance the efficiency and/or effectiveness of its MNC. SSOs entail at least one SSC and are embedded into the MNC's organizational structure."

2.1.2 Objectives of shared service organizations

With the implementation of SSOs, MNCs pursue a variety of different objectives which are set, depending on their organizational context, in diverging combinations and emphases. Due to the multitude of intentions associated with a SSO implementation, SSO related literature continuously seeks to cluster these intentions in favor of a better understanding (*Bangemann* (2005); *Deimel/Quante* (2003); *Janssen/Joha* (2006); *Paagman et al.* (2015a); *Reilly* (2000); *Kagelmann* (2001)). The objectives of SSOs play an important role in research and practice, because they help to align the individual actions of SSO managers with the MNC's strategy (*Webb* (2004), p. 929). Related literature derives **four principal objectives**:

- cost reduction;
- customer satisfaction;
- process optimization and
- compliance.

This categorization of SSO objectives in accordance with the current state of literature is subjective and implies a hierarchical order, since all SSO objectives are mutually dependent and imply goal conflicts. For example, improved lead times as a result of process optimization may have a positive impact on the perceived customer satisfaction and on the targeted cost reduction objective(s).

Cost reduction

Increasing the efficiency of the MNC's support functions by reducing costs constitutes one of the main objectives of SSOs (*Paagman et al.* (2015a), p. 5). Literature and consulting firms indicate remarkable cost reduction potentials of up to 40% that are achievable through the implementation of a SSO (*Quinn et al.* (2000); *Redman et al.* (2007); *Reilly* (2000); *Wißkirchen* (2002)). However, these figures have to be taken with a grain of salt. *Risse and Loitz* point out that one third of the MNCs fail to quantify their achieved cost reduction effects (*Risse/Loitz* (2013), p. 4). Moreover, it often remains disguised to which period the indicated cost reductions refer. Studies conducted by consulting firms may also imply a commercial proposition. Cost reduction covers an **entire set of measures**. By consolidating internal services, economies of scale emerge in two ways (*Becker et al.* (2008), p. 26): by lower costs per unit caused by, for example, an increased capacity utilization (fixed cost degression) and by reduced costs over time, for example, due to gained experience (learning curve effects). Additional cost savings may result from a decreasing number of locations providing internal services, which is commonly associated with SSO implementations (*Sterzenbach* (2010), p. 341). As opposed to a decentralized service provision, a small number of SSCs entails economies of scope by reducing accommodation and infrastructure costs, such as office rents and equipment (*Aksin/Masini* (2008), p. 249).

Another saving potential linked to the site selection consists in labor arbitrage if the SSC is located in a region with comparatively low wages (*Klingebiel* (2006), p. 499). Furthermore, the consolidation of support functions into SSCs ensures an enhanced resource efficiency since increased transaction volumes induce an increased workload per employee compared to decentralized organizational models. Hence, after implementing SSCs, MNCs are overmanned in their support functions, which results in headcount reduction (*Reilly* (2000), p. 5). If the SSO is transferred into an independent legal entity, further cost benefits may arise through the disengagement of the transferred employees from industry-specific labor agreements (*Becker et al.* (2008), p. 27).

Moreover, an increased cost awareness may yield a cost reduction effect by two levers. First, a (partly) source-based cost allocation, for instance by means of SLAs, may unfold undiscovered saving potential to the service recipients (*Janssen/Joha* (2004), p. 224). A source-based cost allocation raises the cost awareness of the service recipients with regard to their service use so that the recipients may better assess the needfulness of each required service. Second, service recipients proactively track the service provider's use of assigned resources and thus challenge an inefficient service provision by the SSO.

Customer satisfaction

Customer satisfaction is of significance in MNCs with an established SSO, particularly because services may not be provided exclusively to internal customers. According to *Sterzenbach,* more than half of the SSOs in his sample are able and willing to provide services also to external customers (*Sterzenbach* (2010), p. 354).[7] As soon as a SSO provides services to external customers, it competes against other vendors and should thus satisfy its customers to secure their loyalty (*Janssen et al.* (2010), p. 215). However, the satisfaction of internal customers is **equally challenging** since the internal customers of today commonly have been the service providers of yesterday. The consolidation of support processes in SSCs triggers the cutback of these (sub-)processes in the MNC's subsidiaries (*Truijens et al.* (2012), pp. 10–11). Nonetheless, employees who have been responsible for these (sub-)processes before, frequently remain in MNC's subsidiaries and may represent demanding SSC customers due to their professional experience. The possibility that remaining employees may perceive the process shift towards the SSO as a loss of power and reliance in their competencies additionally requires specific sensitivity in dealing with the internal customers of a SSO (*Frey et al.* (2008), p. 377).

As pointed out by *Röder,* **process and service quality** determine the perceived customer satisfaction (*Röder* (2012), pp. 243–245).[8] By implementing a SSO, MNCs usually pursue a reorganization and optimization of the integrated support processes (*Deimel/Quante* (2003), p. 303). Process quality is expressed in reduced error rates and accelerated process lead times (*Kagelmann* (2001), p. 77). A key element to achieve diminished process error rates comprises a better understanding of prior and subsequent process steps. For example, if a service requester encloses a cost center to his purchase order, the accounts payables department faces less difficulties to assign the incoming invoice to the right requester in a subsequent process step. As a result, process quality

---

7   Consulting firms operating in the field of SSOs, such as PwC, indicate comparable results (*Suska et al.* (2014), p. 37).

8   However, the causal relationship between customer satisfaction and service and process quality remains discussed controversially in literature. *Heskett's* service profit chain is a widespread theoretical concept for determining the relationship between perceived internal customer satisfaction and service quality (*Heskett et al.* (1994)). Also see *Bruhn/Stauss* (2005), p. 8, for a general discussion of the terms perceived service quality and perceived customer satisfaction. Several empirical studies indicate that internal service quality relates positively to the perceived internal customer satisfaction (*Bruhn* (2003); *Jun/Cai* (2010); *Weschke* (2008)).

increases. Reduced lead times can be achieved by avoiding duplicated efforts and parallelizing sequential process steps (*Risse/Loitz* (2013), p. 8). Automation and standardization as a particular form of process optimization are considered to be the key drivers of an improved process quality. Therefore, process standardization and automation are detailed as subordinated objectives of process optimization (*Risse/Loitz* (2013), p. 8).

There are several criteria illustrating the perceived service quality of a SSC, such as availability, responsiveness, professionalism of the SSC employees or the timeliness of their task completion (*Röder* (2012), pp. 170–171). These criteria are neither conclusive nor does its chronological order disclose a certain weighting. However, it is important to recognize that (internal) customer satisfaction, even if not stated explicitly as a primary objective by the MNC's management, is likely to be considered as a prerequisite for a smoothly running SSO. Once a SSO seems no longer able to provide the services required by the MNC's subsidiaries in an appropriate manner, other SSO objectives such as cost reduction are of less importance (*Grossman* (2010), p. 29).

Process optimization

Another objective associated with the setup and operation of a SSO consists in the optimization of administrative processes (*Kagelmann* (2001), pp. 76–77). The specific aspects subsumed under the term process optimization are supposed to contribute to other major SSO objectives. Similarly to other SSO objectives, such as compliance, process optimization is not a self-purpose. Through the reengineering of administrative processes, SSOs attempt to improve process quality, which not only contributes to an increased customer satisfaction but also to cost reduction (*Rau et al.* (2012), pp. 63–64). Furthermore, SSOs intend to **reveal cost and quality drivers** of each administrative process step. A detailed analysis of the current process results in greater transparency and facilitates the design and development of the target operating model (*Rau et al.* (2012), p. 65). Due to process optimization, SSOs may provide a consistent service availability and quality across the group.

Process standardization can be defined as the unification of processes, systems as well as roles and responsibilities by aligning them according to a defined blueprint (*Münstermann et al.* (2010), p. 31). The main reason for standardization is the identification of best practices, which should therefore be adopted across the group. A high degree of standardization increases the SSO controllability, for example, because processes are easier to benchmark among SSCs and standardized processes have few interfaces (*Lueg et al.* (2017), p. 16). In

addition, standardization allows to reduce infrastructure costs as less maintenance is required with regard to, for example, master data. An important part
is assigned to the standardization of the IT-infrastructure (*Lueg et al.* (2017),
pp. 75–76). Standardization is additionally deemed as the major precondition
to automate process steps (*Lueg et al.* (2017), p. 76). **Process automation** acts as
a lever for accelerating lead times and diminishing error rates, which may affect
the aforementioned SSO objectives positively (*Keuper/Röder* (2009), pp. 3–4).
A low degree of process standardization usually entails a low degree of process
automation (*Lueg et al.* (2017), p. 71). Process automation requires the investment in new technologies. Those investments seem worthwhile especially for
SSOs because the centralization of support processes guarantees a certain transaction volume as opposed to a decentralized service provision (*Becker et al.*
(2008), p. 27).

Compliance

Another important objective of SSOs is compliance (*Moll* (2012), p. 33). MNCs
encounter **increasing statutory requirements** for transparency and traceability of their processes by endorsing internal guidelines, standard operating
procedures (SOPs) and the extension of their internal control systems (ICS) in
order to mitigate financial risks (*Kajüter et al.* (2017), pp. 54–55). Hence, SSOs
are only able to ensure that their MNC complies with (internal) guidelines if
they meet the previously described essential conditions of process standardization (*Risse/Loitz* (2013), p. 4). Due to an increased compliance relevance, SSOs
undertake considerable efforts to meet extended documentation and information requirements. Designing strategic compliance concepts and promoting the
existing ICS are an expected outcome of process shifts to a SSO.

Other objectives

Apart from the aforementioned primary objectives, SSOs pursue other objectives. With the implementation of a SSO, MNCs also seek to enforce **organizational changes** (*Steuer/Westeppe* (2015), p. 11). Organizational changes appear
to be necessary because SSOs as a rather new organizational form require
changed roles and responsibilities of the affected employees (*Reilly* (2000), p. 8).
For instance, the implementation of a SSO often goes hand in hand with the
urgency to grasp a comprehensive, cross-departmental understanding of support processes (*Engstermann* (2015), p. 445).

Apart from the above mentioned cost advantages, **resource bundling** also
facilitates knowledge consolidation. While employees in small business units

within a decentralized organizational model often develop expertise only to a limited extent, SSOs concentrate expertise. The concentration of expertise enables knowledge sharing with little effort, reduces the knowledge outflow and develops highly specialized experts (*Krüger/Danner* (2004), p. 111). In addition, this has a positive impact on service quality (*Sterzenbach* (2010), p. 39). Moreover, business units that transfer support processes to the SSO are capable of concentrating their resources on core business processes (*Westerhoff* (2008), p. 60).

An increasing **employee satisfaction** is another objective of SSOs. The setup of market-like customer-supplier-relationships that are associated with SSOs encourages SSO employees to not consider themselves primarily as an expense factor but to contribute demonstrably to a company's value increase. The altered self-conception of SSO employees may be reflected in a higher motivation and commitment compared to central service models (*Pérez* (2009), p. 29). Moreover, employee satisfaction in SSOs improves through additional career opportunities by extended tasks and responsibilities, which are related to the consolidation of support processes (*Wißkirchen/Mertens* (1999), p. 92). Furthermore, it only seems worthwhile for MNCs to allocate a qualified and well-paid management to a SSC if it outreaches a certain number of employees (*Balling/Gössi* (2001a), p. 21).

2.1.3 Design of shared service organizations

SSOs differ in their design in a number of criteria which is important for this study, because varying design configurations may influence the design of the respective PMS. This section outlines the **five essential parameters** of SSO design (figure 2.2). First, this section elaborates on SSOs with differing functional scopes before addressing the suitability and selection of support processes for SSCs. Second, this section considers SSO's legal and economic independence. Third, the SSOs' location decisions describe another design characteristic. The fourth essential configuration parameter of SSOs consists in SLAs and charging models between a SSO and its customers. This section ends by detailing the use of IT in SSOs that also plays a role for this study's empirical analysis.

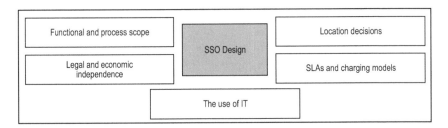

Figure 2.2: Essential design characteristics of SSOs

2.1.3.1 Functional and process scope

Functional scope

Plenty of the MNC's operational functions come into question for a relocation into a SSO. However, several empirical analyses reveal that MNCs mainly transfer support processes from the operational functions finance, (managerial) accounting, HR and IT to SSCs (*Gundavelli/Mohanty* (2004); *Kagelmann* (2001); *Sterzenbach* (2010)). A recent survey of *Deloitte* (2015) indicates comparable results, but also states that the functional scope broadens in recent years (*Pragnall et al.* (2015), p. 18). By now, more SSOs render services of operational functions, such as tax, legal, procurement, facility management or sales administration than several years ago.

Monofunctional and multifunctional SSOs are distinguishable with regard to the number of functions for which they render services. Whereas monofunctional SSOs manage support processes of a single operational function, multifunctional SSOs handle either cross-functional support processes or processes of at least two separate functions. The descriptive results of *Deloitte's* survey demonstrate an increasing number of multifunctional SSOs between 2013 and 2015. Furthermore, the study unveils a majority of MNCs that intend to expand the number of functions per SSC (*Pragnall et al.* (2015), p. 23). Nonetheless, the number of functions tells little about how many and which processes of each function are transferred to a SSC. *Sterzenbach's* analysis provides some insights, for example that managerial accounting reporting tasks are transferred to SSCs more frequently than planning tasks (*Sterzenbach* (2010), p. 349). *Sterzenbach's* results suggest that rather the transaction volume instead of the operational function is a selection criterion for SSCs. Apart from the incorporated operational functions, SSOs differ in their process scope.

Process scope

The increasing focus of MNCs on processes and the diminishing importance of functional separation promotes the formation of SSOs (*Quinn et al.* (2000), p. 102). SSOs mainly perform support processes so that the support processes of a MNC become the SSO's core processes. In favor of a precise identification of support processes for SSOs, it is necessary to concisely separate the terms core and support process.[9] Both process types combine the defining characteristics of a process, which is a set of logically linked activities that are performed to achieve a particular result (*Osterloh/Frost* (2006), p. 33). A defined incident triggers the transformation of input into an output by using resources and obeying to a certain set of rules (*Schwickert/Fischer* (1996), pp. 88–89). *Kaplan et al.* define core processes as "*...a set of interrelated activities, decisions, information, and material flows, which together determine the competitive success of the company*" (*Kaplan et al.* (1991), p. 28). The characteristics mentioned in the core process definition by *Kaplan et al.* are subsumed under the term "core competencies". Core processes provide core competencies, meeting **four specific criteria** that distinguish them from support processes (*Osterloh/Frost* (2006), p. 37):

- Company specificity: core processes are unique through the use of company-specific resources. A detachment or disposal would lead to an irreversible loss of value.
- Non-substitutability: core processes cannot be readily substituted by other processes with different problem solutions.
- Non-imitability: competitors cannot easily imitate the properties of core processes.
- Perceptible customer value: core processes create a perceptible customer value, for which the customer is willing to pay.

Processes that do not meet the above mentioned criteria are referred to as **support processes** that could be performed in SSOs.[10] Most processes performed in

---

9   *Krüger* extends the distinction between core and support processes by so-called control processes, which primarily include management processes, such as planning and decision-making (*Krüger* (1994), p. 124 ff.). *Porters* value chain model is sometimes used as a method to separate SSO processes from business processes (*Porter* (1989), pp. 234–255). However, it should be noted that the term process differs from the value chain model, e.g. by a stronger orientation towards operational functions, and should therefore not be used synonymously (*Allweyer* (2005), p. 76). See also *Olfert/Rahn* for a detailed illustration of further process differentiation possibilities (*Olfert/Rahn* (2003), pp. 28–35).

10 However, there is an ongoing controversy in literature and practice as to whether core processes cannot be successfully transferred to SSOs (*Wißkirchen/Mertens* (1999), p. 94).

SSOs do not fulfill the criterion company specificity, since they seem comparable across companies (e.g. the billing process) and most of them are suitable for outsourcing, too. The fact that many SSO processes are suitable for outsourcing may also be interpreted as an indicator for substitutability and imitability. In contrast to core processes, support processes create customer value only to a limited extent (*Osterloh/Frost* (2006), pp. 137–138).

Apart from being identified as support processes, SSO processes should meet further requirements. For SSOs, all processes come into question that have a company-wide demand and standardization potential (*Klingebiel* (2005), p. 780). If a service is requested only to a very small extent in the MNC, a decentralized service provision would appear to be more useful due to lower coordination costs. The less transaction volume, the less cost reduction potential results from a service provision in the SSO.

2.1.3.2 Location decisions

Three essential decision parameters determine the location decisions of SSOs:

- The geographic dispersion of the MNC's subsidiaries,
- the geographical distance between the MNC's headquarters (HQ) and the selected SSC site,
- the decision whether the SSC is allocated to an existing or to a new location.

MNC managers have to decide which subsidiaries should transfer their support processes or activities to the SSO. In this respect, the geographic dispersion of the MNC's subsidiaries plays a particular role (*Kagelmann* (2001), pp. 90–91).

If subsidiaries' support processes are grouped in SSCs according to their **geographic dispersion**, four major design options exist (*Krüger/Danner* (2004), p. 116): the consideration of all of the subsidiaries' processes

(1) by country,
(2) by region,
(3) globally, or
(4) a location-independent allocation of subsidiaries to SSCs.

The fact that the SSC has to consider only one national legislation and one economic area argues in favor of an allocation **by country**. Marginal cultural differences between subsidiaries of the same country facilitate a process shift. However, the critical mass of support processes should be available to pay off the SSC implementation by country (*Becker et al.* (2008), p. 33). A **regional setup** is commonly based on continents or uniform economic areas, such as the EU, in order to keep legal and cultural differences among the customers of the responsible SSC reduced to a minimum (*Kagelmann* (2001), p. 90). Furthermore, the same or at least similar time zones may be decisive for a regional allocation of subsidiaries to SSCs, for example the allocation of a South African subsidiary to a German SSC. A **global setup** is particularly suitable for MNCs, which only reach an economically sufficient transaction volume by consolidating their support processes globally. This setup is also useful for the concentration of globally distributed knowledge (*Becker et al.* (2008), p. 35).

A **location-independent allocation** of subsidiaries to SSCs is commonly done according to the subsidiaries primary business purpose and their primary business segment affiliation. Subsidiaries may vary in their primary business purpose, for instance if they are mainly responsible for selling and distributing the MNC's products and services or if they are primarily producing them. Since similar subsidiary types often have similar support processes, they may be allocated to a SSC according to their primary business purpose (*Becker et al.* (2008), p. 36). For example, in case of production companies the responsible SSC is able to perform product costing processes, while SSCs that are responsible for sales companies provide predominantly dunning and collection services. An allocation of the subsidiaries to a SSC by business segment is particularly useful if MNC's business segments are heterogeneous. SSC employees need to know the particularities of the respective business segments, because these affect the support processes (*Kagelmann* (2001), p. 91). Finally, SSCs are sometimes referred to as a *virtual SSC* by placing the geographically distributed services under a single management across locations (*Moll* (2012), p. 180). While virtual SSCs improve the enforceability of a SSO implementation because site-closure discussions are avoided, the virtual approach contradicts the SSO objectives as economies of scale are much less realizable compared to a geographic concentration (*Reilly/Williams* (2003), pp. 46–47).

These four design options do not only affect the subsidiaries' process allocation to the SSCs, but also the **number of SSCs**. Moreover, the number of SSCs depends on the support process segmentation, for example whether certain processes should be performed exclusively in a single SSC or whether each SSC performs all processes. This results in a number of different organizational combinations (*Kagelmann* (2001), pp. 96–97). For instance, a SSO may be geographically divided into several SSCs by region, whereas SSCs perform diverging support processes and serve different business segments. A possible categorization illustrates the applied classification into mono- or multidivisional SSCs and mono- or multigeographical SSCs (figure 2.3). For instance, a multidivisional and multigeographical SSC renders services to more than one business segment in more than one country.

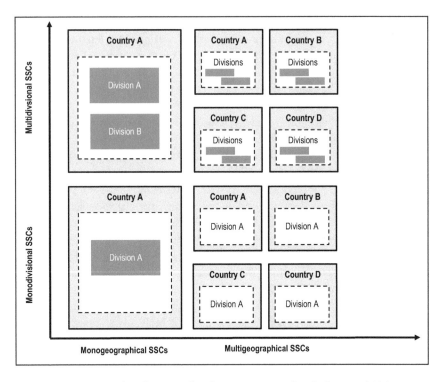

Figure 2.3: Mono- and multigeographical SSCs/mono- and multidivisional SSCs

The site selection has a significant influence on the financial advanta-geousness of SSO implementations (*Moll* (2012), p. 59). Depending on the geo-graphical distance between the MNC's HQ and the selected SSC site, **onshore, nearshore, offshore or farshore** SSC sites can be distinguished (*Gonzalez et al.* (2006), pp. 1239–1240).[11] Onshoring involves the service provision in the same

---

11 The conceptual distinction of the aforementioned translocation alternatives varies in liter-ature. *Hutzschenreuter et al.* conceive offshoring as an overriding notion and understand onshoring, nearshoring, and farshoring as offshoring forms (*Hutzschenreuter et al.* (2007), p. 24). *Klingebiel* uses the term offshoring synonymously with farshoring (*Klingebiel* (2005), p. 778). A fundamental cause of different conceptual distinctions arises from the underlying criteria used by these authors. Whereas some contributions merely base the geographical distance between HQ and SSC as a criterion, cultural proximity, a common economic area, or even the socio-economic status of a country affect the definition of terms. For an over-view of the different translocation taxonomies, see *Gonzalez et al.* (2006), pp. 1238–1240.

country in which the HQ is located. Whereas from the HQ's angle nearshoring contains the location of at least one SSC in a neighboring country, offshoring takes place in a country which is not nearby the HQ's home territory (*Jahns et al.* (2006), p. 222).

Farshoring suggests that at least one SSC of the SSO is located on another continent, which is frequently associated with lower production costs (*Farrell* (2004), p. 82).

The question of a **suitable SSC site** implies a long-term decision for the SSO so that different decision-making factors should be considered in order to yield a holistic picture (*Kajüter et al.* (2017), pp. 26–30). Key decision-making criteria with regard to the site selection are the availability and occupational qualification of the employees as well as their cultural proximity to the parent company (*Moll* (2012), p. 61). In case of a German MNC, this decision criterion argues for an onshore solution. However, the main disadvantage of onshoring is the low cost reduction potential by means of labor arbitrage (*Rothwell et al.* (2011), p. 248). Nevertheless, SSOs may use the availability and qualification of employees as a decision criterion for offshoring or farshoring solutions as well, for example by selecting a university city as SSC location. Especially in developing countries, contextual factors such as a constant power supply, an acceptable transport connection and the availability of modern information and communication technologies plays an important role for the choice of the right location (*Keuper/Glahn* (2005), p. 452). Moreover, political and legal factors may affect the SSC site selection. In addition to security aspects and a sovereign legal system, tax and labor legislation of the respective country is of particular importance for SSCs. Finally, tax relief or further subsidies can be a decisive factor for a particular location (*Schulman et al.* (1999), p. 146).

The decision whether the SSC is based at an existing or new location can be subdivided into three design alternatives (*Pfänder* (2009), p. 12). The first location alternative involves the establishment of a SSC at a location where SSC processes have not yet been performed (*Aguirre et al.* (1998), p. 8). The second location alternative suggests that support processes have already been provided at the selected site before the SSC has been established or that at least the MNC's infrastructure exists, which facilitates the SSC implementation (*Wißkirchen/Mertens* (1999), p. 98). The third location alternative implies that the corporate management is also based at the selected SSC location. By selecting a location, SSOs often face conflicting goals, precisely between initial investments and ongoing costs. For example, a SSC site selection at an already established MNC site provides an existing infrastructure and experienced employees, which leads to time savings and thus lower implementation costs.

A new SSC site is aligned to SSO-specific requirements, which may induce a more complex implementation process, but may yield higher cost reductions in the long run (*Krug* (2008), p. 27).

2.1.3.3 Legal and economic independence

Sterzenbach's results indicate that more than half of the SSOs in his sample are designed as economically and legally independent organizations (*Sterzenbach* (2010), p. 352). Both design configurations serve as a basis for behavioral control and decision-making. With regard to the **economic independence**, SSOs may be established as cost centers (input-oriented model), revenue centers (output-oriented model), profit centers or investment centers (*Anthony et al.* (2007), p. 126 ff.). Contrary to the promoted independence of SSOs, the cost center model dominates in practice (*Kagelmann* (2001), pp. 103–104). A SSO which consists of cost centers, intends to render services to the customers in an acceptable quality with the lowest possible costs. Cost center-based SSOs aim to standardize and reduce costs and cover the SSO's incurred costs by charging the rendered services to its customers (*Schimank/Strobl* (2002), p. 299). In the cost center model, cost reduction pressure is mainly created by SSO customers who do not tolerate surging service charges. The efficiency of the cost center-based SSO is evaluated by the variance between actual and planned costs (*Weber et al.* (2006), p. 34). The performance evaluation of revenue centers exclusively considers the generated revenues. However, the management of SSOs only by revenues is of theoretical relevance (*Sterzenbach* (2010), p. 352). Therefore, revenue centers are scoped out in the remainder of this study. In a profit center, the difference between center revenues and center costs results in the SSO's financial performance. Profit center models in SSOs attempt to maximize the result with simultaneous consideration of the minimum quality requirements (*Sterzenbach* (2010), p. 65). An investment center is a particular type of a profit center. Compared to profit centers, investment centers have the decision-making authority and responsibility to use a portion of their profits for investments (*Anthony et al.* (2007), p. 273 ff.). Therefore, the realized center profit should be compared to the invested capital of the SSO.

In addition to an economically independent configuration, SSOs may also be designed legally independent. The **legal independence** of the SSO offers the option to pay SSO employees regardless of existing labor agreements (*Schulman et al.* (1999), p. 146). A legally independent SSO may be perceived as an equivalent business partner by its customers (*Voegelin/Spreiter* (2003), p. 833). Furthermore, legal independence is usually associated with profit responsibility.

Legal autonomy goes hand in hand with accountability, which may result in an increased market pressure for the SSO and demands for greater transparency (*von Werder/Grundei* (2006), pp. 26–27). Moreover, legally independent SSOs might be seen as a preliminary stage for outsourcing.

2.1.3.4 Service level agreements and charging models

Another design characteristic of SSOs relates to the relationship between SSOs and its customers. In practice, SSOs usually establish SLAs as a basis for providing their services to the business units. An essential element of SLAs are charging models, which do exist in varying specifications and are outlined in this section.

Service level agreements

Campenhausen/Rudolf define SLAs as written agreements between a SSO and its customers about services to be rendered by the SSO (*Campenhausen/Rudolf* (2001), p. 90). Depending on a SSO's legal and economic independence, SLAs differ in two basic legal types: SLAs that represent a legally binding contract and SLAs without any legally binding effect, for example an intercompany agreement (*Berger* (2007), pp. 37–38). In case of a SSO that legally depends on its MNC, legally non-binding agreements are preferred since difficulties that arise from customer-supplier relationships, are solved via hierarchical coordination mechanisms instead of legal enforcement (*Kagelmann* (2001), p. 116).

With regard to the **components of SLAs**, the literature does not reveal a coherent understanding due to company-specific requirements and adaptions. However, the following contents prevail in literature and practice so that they are classified as significant for SLAs:[12]

- Involved contracting parties;
- service scope: a concise description of the services to be rendered;
- date(s) of delivery: the agreed timeline for service deliveries by the SSO;
- service quality standards: quality standards that have to be met by the SSO and which are tracked with performance measures (e.g., measuring process quality and customer satisfaction);

---

12 For a detailed overview of the following and additional criteria, see *Bergeron* (2002), pp. 207–208; *Campenhausen/Rudolf* (2001), p. 90; *Quinn et al.* (2000), p. 150; *Schimank/Strobl* (2002), pp. 295–296).

- roles and responsibilities: a detailed description of the roles and responsibilities requires a distinct activity split between the SSO and the business unit;
- charging model: the method of pricing used to settle the rendered services;
- contingencies: penalties associated with services that are provided not in the agreed quality or time;
- payment terms: the frequency and method of payment.

SLAs shape (negotiable) standards for the scope and price of the rendered services, which lead to a high degree of **transparency** regarding the cost-benefit ratio of the offered services and thus to the potential elimination of unnecessary services from a customer's perspective (*Schimank/Strobl* (2002), p. 295). In addition, SLAs provide the basis to monitor cost trends in a SSO and enable benchmarking with external service providers (*von Werder/Grundei* (2006), pp. 20–21). Hence, SLAs keep up the pressure on the SSO to increase efficiency and effectiveness. Furthermore, SLAs are useful to set objectives within the SSO (*Kagelmann* (2001), p. 117).

Charging models

SSOs charge the services they provide to customers in four different models (*Moll* (2012), pp. 75–76):

- no service charging to customers at all;
- charging according to market-oriented transfer prices;
- charging according to cost-oriented transfer prices;
- charging according to negotiation-based transfer prices.

Among others, transfer prices accomplish three important functions (*Wagenhofer* (2002), p. 2075). First, transfer prices have a coordination effect. If the SSO links transfer prices to its service delivery, the price mechanism ensures the efficient coordination of the resource use and the service provision between the SSO and its customers (*Picot et al.* (2015), p. 316). Second, transfer prices facilitate the determination of the MNC's internal profitability. The price evaluation of internal services enables MNCs to allocate the revenues and costs to the services rendered, where they actually occurred (*Coenenberg et al.* (2016), pp. 676–677). Third, transfer prices contain a motivational element since the services provided by SSO employees have a corresponding value. Thus, they are able to recognize their contribution to the MNC's success, which may increase their motivation (*Keuper/Glahn* (2005), p. 195).

No service charging from the SSO to the requesting units implies that the SSOs' costs are allocated internally to other cost centers within the company. No service charging prevents any form of a source-based cost allocation leading to deficient control mechanisms (*Bangemann* (2005), pp. 90–91).

SSOs derive **market-oriented transfer prices** by assigning prices of comparable services, which are observable on external markets (*Merchant/van der Stede* (2007), pp. 280–281). However, the application of market-oriented transfer prices requires the existence of a complete market which exists only to a limited extent. In addition, market prices are generally heterogeneous and depend on different conditions (*Wagenhofer* (2002), p. 2075).

Cost-oriented transfer prices are divided into marginal- and full cost-oriented pricing models. Therefore, the spectrum of cost-oriented transfer prices ranges from variable costs as a bottom line to full costs with additional mark-ups (*Coenenberg et al.* (2016), p. 703 ff.). Full cost-oriented pricing models include, apart from variable costs, fixed and overhead costs, too (*Coenenberg et al.* (2016), p. 549). Full cost-oriented pricing models dominate in SSO practice (*Sterzenbach* (2010), p. 370), although this concept entails weaknesses with regard to the aforementioned transfer price functions. For example, full cost-oriented transfer prices can cause an ineffective coordination of resource use and service provision, since SSO services on a full cost basis are variable costs from the customer's point of view. If SSO customers perceive service charges as comparatively high, they may generate less demand due to the full cost pricing by the SSO, although their demand seems desirable from the MNC's perspective (*Moll* (2012), p. 79). Furthermore, it seems complicated to allocate overhead costs to their source (*Coenenberg et al.* (2016), p. 703).

Negotiation-based transfer prices represent another service charging alternative. The company management does not predefine a service charge and dedicates the service pricing to the SSO and its customers, expecting that both parties negotiate for the fairest service charges (*Wagenhofer* (2002), p. 2079). The lacking practical relevance (*Sterzenbach* (2010), p. 370) emanates from the inherent conflict potential which is associated with pricing negotiations (*Coenenberg et al.* (2016), p. 720). Negotiation-based transfer prices rather reflect negotiation power and skills of both parties and less the optimal service charge (*Moll* (2012), p. 81).

Obligation to contract

The study of *Fischer and Sterzenbach* illustrates that 65% of the SSOs in their sample use contract obligations (*Fischer/Sterzenbach* (2007), pp. 40–41). Three basic contract obligation models can be distinguished. First, a complete obliga-tion to contract for the requesting business units, second, a partial obligation to contract and, third, the right of the requesting business units to select a ser-vice provider by themselves (*Hollich et al.* (2008), pp. 217–218). An obligation to contract entails the advantage of a constant service demand.

2.1.3.5 The use of IT

According to *Bangemann* "IT is the enabler for shared services" (*Bangemann* (2005), p. 65). His quote alludes to the **outstanding role of information tech-nology** during the implementation and the running operation of SSOs. The fact that SSOs often perform cross-functional support processes for various business units and countries leads to an accumulation of different IT systems within the SSO (*Krüger/Danner* (2004), pp. 114–115). This heterogeneity of the IT landscape often originates from previous autonomous efforts by divisions, regions or legal entities, which have adapted their IT systems according to their needs (*Schulman et al.* (1999), pp. 57–58). The quite rational adaptation of IT systems to local requirements causes additional complexity during the process consolidation in SSOs, which induces additional costs. Either SSO employees have to be trained for several IT systems, which may cause higher training costs and a lower service quality, or SSO employees are exclusively appointed to certain IT systems, which may result in less flexibility in per-sonnel capacity planning. Furthermore, process changes and the master data management have to be done in several IT systems, which increases compli-ance risks and error rates. Particularly, a manageable number of ERP systems as the backbone of most support processes is considered as a success factor for performing support processes efficiently within the SSO (*Bangemann* (2005), p. 65). The same applies to a smaller extent for workflow and ticketing systems as well as for self-service portals (*Furck* (2005), p. 69). The lower the degree of IT system heterogeneity, the greater the potential for process standardization and process automation, which may subsequently manifest in cost reductions (*Balling/Gössi* (2001b), p. 820).

In essence, this section illustrated that SSOs may vary in a number of design configurations. However, the discussed design characteristics do not serve as a basis to distinguish sufficiently between SSOs and other organizational forms applied by MNCs. The differentiation from related organizational models is nec-essary for the understanding of the phenomenon under research. Therefore, the following section outlines the conceptual distinction of SSOs to centralization and outsourcing.

2.1.4 Conceptual distinction to centralization and outsourcing

The implementation of SSOs does not constitute the only organizational alternative for MNCs to perform support processes. Centralization and outsourcing describe further organizational alternatives for MNCs to perform their support processes (*Becker et al.* (2008), p. 9). By implementing SSOs, companies seek to profit from the benefits of centralization and outsourcing without realizing their drawbacks (*Schulman et al.* (1999), p. 11). This section stresses that the increasing popularity of SSOs can be particularly attributed to dysfunctionalities of other organizational alternatives (*Sterzenbach* (2010), p. 96).

Centralization describes the pooling of similar tasks within an organizational unit, for example within a department, while decentralization represents the distribution of similar tasks among several organizational units (*Olfert/Rahn* (2012), pp. 128–129). SSOs and centralized departments have in common that processes or functions are separated from decentralized business units and consolidated in one area of responsibility. Both models aim at the realization of synergies and economies of scale through resource bundling (*Deimel/Quante* (2003), p. 203). In contrast to central departments, SSOs can be legally or economically independent (*Krüger/Danner* (2004), p. 114). SSOs provide their services on behalf of the operating units, while central departments are associated with a service provision regardless of customer requirements. SSOs ordinarily claim to offer competitive services in terms of service quality and pricing (*Moll* (2012), p. 24). As opposed to central departments, SSOs are sometimes allowed to supply external customers (*Wißkirchen* (2002), p. 35). The SSO's service charging rests on different transfer pricing models (*Wißkirchen/Mertens* (1999), p. 90). By contrast, central departments are managed solely cost-oriented and commonly use budgets for cost control (*Krüger/Danner* (2004), p. 114). It is noteworthy that the market-driven, service-oriented character of SSOs usually has to develop over time.

Contrary to an internal service provision by SSOs, **outsourcing** describes the transfer of support processes to an external company with the intention to optimize the MNC's service depth (*Wißkirchen* (1998), p. 139).[13] Outsourcing describes an abbreviation for the term '**Out**side **Re**source **Using**' (*Hellinger*

---

13 For the sake of completeness, reference should also be made to deviating definitions. *Hungenberg/Wulf* focus on the use of external resources: "Outsourcing can generally be understood as the resource use of external service providers to ensure operating efficiency" (*Hungenberg* (1995), p. 45). Contrarily, some definitions of outsourcing include the transfer of power within the same company (*Kagelmann* (2001), pp. 54–57).

(1999), p. 47).[14] The takeover of employees and assets by the outsourcing service provider and a long-term contract commitment represent essential characteristics of outsourcing (*Dittrich/Braun* (2004), p. 2). In essence, the organizational alternatives SSO and outsourcing denote a **make-or-buy decision**. Despite this contrasting approach to provide support services, both organizational alternatives also show similarities. By transferring their support processes to an external provider, MNCs pursue similar objectives as they do with the support process transfer to a SSO, for example cost reduction, an enhanced service quality and an increased concentration on their core business.

For both organizational alternatives the decision-making competencies over service quantity planning and performance monitoring remain in the local business units (*Wißkirchen/Mertens* (1999), p. 88). However, outsourcing has some advantages compared to a SSO. An outsourcing provider commonly acts independently and may perform formerly internal support processes more economically, because the MNC's support processes represent the core processes of the outsourcing provider (*Fischer/Sterzenbach* (2006), p. 125). In addition, outsourcing providers process higher transaction volumes because they provide the same services for several MNCs. The broader customer base of outsourcing providers compared to a SSO often leads to more know-how as the employees of outsourcing vendors apply process improvements and best practices to all customers. As opposed to large MNCs, outsourcing service providers are usually not bound to labor agreements, which enables them to calculate with lower labor costs (*Sterzenbach* (2010), p. 101). From a MNC's perspective, a significant advantage of outsourcing compared to a service provision in a SSO is the conversion of fixed costs into variable costs. Instead of preserving sufficient internal service capacities in SSOs, MNCs request the required services from the outsourcing vendor only if necessary, which may induce cost savings (*Klingebiel/Andreas* (2006), p. 982). In addition, MNCs choose the outsourcing service provider on the market, thereby increasing their flexibility (*Fritze* (2013), p. 160).

However, outsourcing is associated with **potential risks**, too. By sourcing support processes out, MNCs may lose competitiveness in the medium term. Contrary to outsourcing, SSO concepts retain the process know-how within the company, which prevents MNCs to be reliant on external parties (*Deimel/Quante* (2003), p. 302). Drawing on principal-agent theory, outsourcing service providers and MNCs may pursue diverging objectives, whereby expected cost savings are

---

14 Alternatively, the term may stem from the connection of '**Out**side' and 'Re**sourcing**' (*Dittrich/Braun* (2004), p. 1).

not realized. Compared to SSOs, outsourcing entails a higher risk that employees are not willing to accept the initiated organizational change, resulting in escalating churn rates (*Voegelin/Spreiter* (2003), p. 833). The transfer of sensitive data to a third party on a massive scale constitutes a further significant disadvantage compared to an internal reorganization through SSOs. Moreover, MNCs should consider a provider's margin and need to accept that they have little influence on the service quality provided by the outsourcing vendor (*Deimel/Quante* (2003), p. 302). Ultimately, rendering support services may require company-specific know-how that cannot be obtained from the external market (*Schimank/Strobl* (2002), p. 285). Table 2.1 summarizes the three organizational models:

Table 2.1: Distinction between centralization, shared services and outsourcing (adapted from *Kagelmann* (2001), pp. 133–134, and *Wißkirchen/Mertens* (1999), p. 90)

Distinction	Centralization	Shared Services	Outsourcing
Primary objective	Cost reduction by economies of scale and scope	Various	Variabilization of fixed costs
Coordination mechanism	Hierarchic	Mimic to market conditions	Market conditions
Legal and economic independence	Legally and economically dependent	Both	Legally and economically independent
Charging model	Cost allocation models	Transfer pricing models	Market prices
Obligation to contract	Yes	Partially	No

2.2 Performance measurement

Based on an evaluation of existing performance measurement definitions, this section provides a definition for this study. Moreover, this section discusses the objectives associated with PMS. The design of PMS in SSOs can be structured into **three essential elements**: the configuration of performance measures in a PMS, the performance measurement process and the actors that are involved in the performance measurement process. All three elements are thoroughly described in the following sections. Finally, this section integrates PMS in related conceptual frameworks, such as MCS, and seeks for a clear distinction between performance measurement and performance management.

2.2.1 Definition of performance measurement

The literature reveals plenty of performance measurement definitions, which differ greatly in their conceptual approach to this phenomenon (*Horváth/Seiter* (2009), p. 3).[15] Moreover, some studies do not define what they mean by performance measurement. This lack of conceptual clarity has three reasons. First, the dynamic development of performance measurement in corporate practice requires a continuous adjustment of generic definitions (*Klingebiel* (2001), p. 18). Second, the term performance measurement involves a high degree of complexity, because definitions refer to different performance measurement objects, such as organizational units and corporate functions or describe performance measurement as a process. Furthermore, it seems complicated to include all relevant components and objectives associated with performance measurement within a single definition (*Grüning* (2002), pp. 3–4). Third, research on performance measurement is multi-disciplinary. Research areas, such as management accounting, marketing or operations management create a variety of definitions that have little in common (*Bourne et al.* (2007), pp. 784–785). The main purpose of this section is threefold. First, this section provides a decent overview of the most relevant definitions. Second, it explains why *Neely's* (1995) performance measurement definition (*Neely et al.* (1995), pp. 80–81) represents **the most suitable definition** for this study and third, this section classifies *Neely's* definition into the existing spectrum.

Several authors choose a **semantic approach** for the definition of performance measurement by characterizing the terms *performance* and *measurement* (*Grüning* (2002); *Kretschmer* (2009); *Matheis* (2012); *Seiter* (2011)). Performance can either be defined as a potential, as a process or as an outcome (*Lebas/Euske* (2002), p. 127). Performance as a potential emphasizes the ability and willingness to provide a service and thus focuses on input variables (*Matheis* (2012), p. 16). Performance as a process considers throughput variables and elaborates on the activities that are undertaken to achieve a result (*Küng/Wettstein* (2003), p. 44). A process-oriented view allows to assign different activities to a single term, such as designing, monitoring and evaluating performance measures. Performance as an outcome variable stresses the quantitative and/or qualitative measurable result (*Matheis* (2012), p. 16). Based on the output perspective, performance can be subsumed under the terms efficiency and effectiveness (*Neely et al.* (1996), p. 424). Efficiency and effectiveness are closely linked to targets, since a target

---

15 For a detailed overview of performance measurement definitions see *Bourne et al.* (2007), pp. 789–791, *Matheis* (2012), pp. 18–19, and *Schreyer* (2007), p. 27.

serves as the reference point to define performance (*Grüning* (2002), p. 5). Therefore, performance does not only depend on the results achieved, but also on the objectives as shown in figure 2.4:

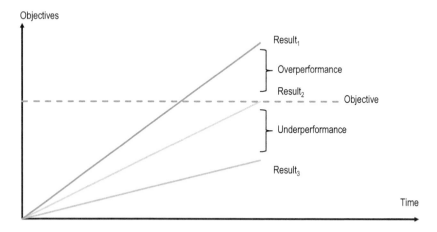

Figure 2.4: Performance as the achievement of objectives (adapted from *Kretschmer* (2009), p. 14)

Accordingly, *Gleich* (1997) addresses these two fundamental dimensions of performance, i.e. efficiency and effectiveness, in his definition:

> *"Performance measurement is defined as the composition and use of several performance measures [...] for assessing the effectiveness and efficiency [...] of different objects in the company."*
> *(Gleich (1997), p. 115)*

The viewpoint of *Gleich* (1997) details the notion of performance, albeit the term *assessing* limits the process scope of performance measurement to few activities. Other activities, such as the design, data collection and modification of performance measures are not included in this rather output-oriented view. *Campbell* describes the term measurement as an unambiguous assignment of a number to a measuring object under a certain measurement instruction (*Campbell* (1957b), p. 267). Hence, measurement determines the achieved performance of the measuring object (*Seiter* (2011), p. 102). The definition of *Zairi* (2012) equates to this **puristic-mathematical view** and offers the advantage of being almost timeless:

> *"Performance measurement has been described as the systematic assignment of numbers to entities."*
> *(Zairi (2012), p. 3)*

However, a puristic viewpoint neglects the aforementioned process and outcome perspective. In summary, it can be stated that the illustrated definitions either refer to the process or the outcome perspective. The definition of *Gleich* (1997) is closest to a combination of both views, but restricts the process perspective of performance measurement to a few activities.

Although semantic and puristic-mathematical definition approaches address important ele-ments of performance measurement, none of these approaches draws a holistic picture. Since this study analyzes different dimensions of performance measurement, this study's definition has to encompass the process and the outcome perspective of performance measurement. Therefore, the definition by *Neely et al.* (1995) serves as a basis for this study and unites the previously outlined perspectives:

- "Performance measurement can be defined as the process of quantifying the efficiency and effectiveness of action."
- "A performance measure can be defined as a metric used to quantify the efficiency and/or effectiveness of an action."
- "A performance measurement system can be defined as the set of metrics used to quantify both the efficiency and effectiveness of actions." (Neely et al. (1995), pp. 80–81)

These definitions appear to be most useful for an empirical study on PMS design in SSOs for three reasons. First, *Neely et al.* (1995) do not only provide the definition of performance measurement, but supplement it with the terms performance measure and PMS. While other contributions also define performance measurement and PMS, the distinction of the three terms in *Neely et al.* (1995) appears to be particularly precise and logically linked to each other. Since this study analyzes the design of individual performance measures, their configuration in a PMS and the performance measurement process an exact distinction of the three elements appears to be necessary. Furthermore, the empirical analysis examines the effects of PMS by addressing the perceived support for SSO managers to achieve their goals. Again, this definition seems to be suitable since it is based on the two fundamental dimensions of performance, i.e. efficiency and effectiveness. Second, *Neely et al.'s* (1995) definition unites different academic disciplines. This is especially important for research in the area of SSOs, because SSOs are explored by different academic disciplines. Third, *Neely et al.'s* (1995) understanding of performance measurement is universal so that recent developments of performance measurement in corporate practice are considered. This is crucial as the analyzed SSOs show a different degree of maturity, are located in different countries and have been implemented by MNCs of different sizes. Hence, the universality of his definition proves to be useful for an empirical study, because it subsumes the complexity of PMS design in corporate practice.

After defining the terms performance measure, performance measurement, and PMS, it is important for the empirical part of this study to understand the objectives that SSOs typically pursue with the use of PMS.

2.2.2 Performance measurement objectives

With performance measurement, SSOs pursue varying objectives. The **heterogeneity of the objectives** presented in this section provides an explanation for the large number of existing performance measurement definitions. As this study's research objective is to analyze the effectiveness of PMS in SSOs, it is necessary to address the key objectives that SSOs pursue with their PMS. Otherwise, the effectiveness of the SSOs' PMS is difficult to assess.

Undoubtedly, the primary objective of performance measurement is to measure performance (*Bourne et al.* (2007), p. 797). Since this describes a tautology, it seems understandable that many definitions do not mention it explicitly (*Atkinson* (1998); *Bititci et al.* (1997); *Forza/Salvador* (2000); *Otley* (1999)). Nevertheless, it seems noteworthy that measuring performance itself and its evaluation and communication equates to only a part of the performance measurement process. Accordingly, *McWilliams* (1996) emphasizes the knowledge gain of SSO managers during the target-setting process of particular KPIs (*Neely et al.* (2000), p. 1121). With performance measurement initiatives SSOs attempt to operationalize the previously defined corporate strategy (*Ittner et al.* (2003), p. 717). For stakeholders it is often difficult to derive clear recommendations for action from the SSO's strategy and to evaluate whether strategies have been successfully implemented (*Schreyer* (2007), p. 32). Thus, performance measurement serves as a tool for the determination of directly measurable objectives linked to the SSO's strategy. Various definitions refer to performance measurement objectives by highlighting the continuous monitoring and evaluation of effectiveness and efficiency (*Gleich* (1997), p. 115). SSOs implement PMS to continuously monitor progress but also to facilitate a comprehensive control of business processes. Controlling and monitoring business processes by means of performance measures aims to identify its drivers for success (*Lebas* (1995), p. 34). As success factors usually are prior to (financial) success, a considerable amount of contributions advocates for a balance of financial and non-financial measures in PMS (*Ittner et al.* (2003), pp. 715–716). However, the assumption that balanced PMS are more likely to achieve SSO objectives, seems to be sparsely documented (*Bourne et al.* (2007), p. 796).

SSOs intend to **achieve their operational and strategic objectives** through a transparent exposition of performance measures (*Gleich* (2002), p. 447). Conversely, performance measurement serves as an information provider for the organization enabling the SSO to develop strategies to achieve its objectives (*Kerssens-van Drongelen/Fisscher* (2003), p. 55). Therefore, PMS should support SSOs to achieve their primary objectives cost reduction, customer satisfaction, process optimization and compliance. However, a direct relation between performance measurement and the SSO's strategy is not a necessary, but a sufficient criterion, since performance measurement may only include operational objectives (*Bourne et al.* (2007), pp. 796–797). For example, it is also conceivable that a SSO's PMS aims to exclusively achieve operational objectives such as increasing the automation rate of a particular support process.

In addition, performance measurement serves as an instrument to reveal **cause-and-effect relationships** (*Lebas* (1995), p. 34). *Kaplan and Norton* argue that performance measurement supports SSOs to identify direct and indirect coherences (*Kaplan/Norton* (1996), pp. 30–31). Furthermore, a well-functioning PMS can be used to quantify the effect size between two metrics (*Schreyer* (2007), p. 33). For example, a SSO's PMS may be capable of predicting the change of a certain output-related KPI, such as cost per processed invoice, by compiling certain process-related KPIs, such as lead times and error rates. Furthermore, measuring performance enables SSO managers to set targets and allocate available resources in line with their priority. Depending on the KPI development, the SSO manager is able to conclude where to allocate available resources in his area of responsibility in order to meet the previously defined KPI targets and to recognize the impact of previously allocated resources (*Dossi/Patelli* (2010), p. 502).

Another performance measurement objective is to strengthen the **employee motivation** in SSOs (*Otley* (1999), p. 368). There are two factors that foster an increased employee motivation through the use of performance measures. First, performance measurement increases the self-responsibility of SSO employees and enables self-control of departments and teams. The notion of being directly responsible for the improvement of certain performance measures and thus contributing to the SSO's objectives is a motivating factor for many SSO employees (*Gleich* (2002), p. 448). Second, linking performance measurement to incentive systems allows a performance-based design of SSO employee remuneration, which enhances their motivation (*Atkinson* (1998), p. 555).

Performance measurement is often associated with an **improved communication** (*Forza/Salvador* (2000), p. 359). Performance measures may stimulate cross-functional communication, as the impact of one's own actions becomes visible by using a PMS (*Gleich* (1997), p. 115). Since multifunctional SSOs provide services across several corporate functions, process optimization seems particularly possible if SSO employees develop a cross-functional understanding of the MNC's support processes. Performance measures support SSO employees to understand the SSO's strategy and to discuss undesirable developments (*Kaplan/Norton* (1996), pp. 12–13). The communication of performance measures does not have to take place exclusively in formal settings, for instance in meetings. The disclosure of performance measures may also promote informal discussions between SSO employees, which contribute to an enhanced mutual understanding and knowledge sharing (*Bourne et al.* (2007), p. 797).

Furthermore, the SSOs' PMS offer the possibility to enhance the SSOs' organizational learning (*Neely et al.* (2000), p. 1120). A major effect that results from the analysis of performance measures consists in an increased **knowledge gain** for the organization since the KPI analysis enables SSO employees to permanently revise their expectations about taken actions and desired outcome (*Atkinson* (1998), p. 554).

By defining PMS objectives, SSOs lay the foundation to evaluate the effectiveness of their PMS. However, the design of a SSOs' PMS varies, depending on the SSOs' focus which PMS objectives are considered as particularly important. Therefore, the following section discusses the SSOs' alternatives for PMS design.

2.2.3 Design of PMS

The PMS design can be subdivided into **three elements** (figure 2.5):

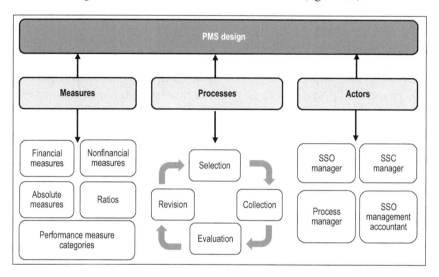

Figure 2.5: PMS design (own illustration based on *Bourne et al.* (2000), p. 757; *Kretschmer* (2009), p. 39, and *Neely et al.* (2000), p. 1143)

(1) applied performances measures,
(2) performance measurement processes,
(3) performance measurement actors.

2.2.3.1 Performance measures

Although anecdotal evidence indicates that performance measures are widely used in SSOs, it remains disguised how SSOs design their PMS. So far it remains unclear for which purposes performance measures are used. For example, it seems vague whether non-financial performance measures in SSOs are more often used as absolute measures because of the described advantages. Moreover, there is little information which dimensions of performance measures are covered in SSOs and if the used performance measures are in line with the SSO's strategy. However, understanding how SSOs design their PMS is essential to analyze which PMS designs prove to be successful to effectively control a SSO in practice.

The literature frequently uses the terms *metric, indicator* and *ratio* interchangeably for the term *measure* that is applied in this study (*Bourne et al.* (2000); *Gladen* (2002); *Ittner/Larcker* (2003); *Klingebiel* (2013)). However, several authors carefully distinguish between the aforementioned terms. *Neely et al.* (1995) point out that the term metric in a narrow sense may refer to the mere formula, how a performance measure is calculated (*Neely et al.* (1995), p. 110). In this respect, a metric only refers to the standard of measurement, while a measure systematically assigns numerical values to observations and thus quantifies (*Gladen* (2014), p. 9). Hence, performance measures capture **quantifiable information** of complex coherences in a concentrated form and inform about a SSO's development (*Küpper et al.* (2013), p. 471). SSOs have plenty of raw data available so that data are intentionally consolidated by the use of performance measures in order to yield a comprehensive but manageable overview (*Reichmann et al.* (2017), p. 19). Performance measures gauge directly observable values and instantly display their alteration (*Pütz* (2007), p. 16). Performance measures can be subdivided into **absolute and relative measures**. Absolute performance measures entail totals, differences, or mean values (*Matheis* (2012), p. 30).[16] However, absolute performance measures that are not confronted with comparative values

---

[16] Relevant literature largely agrees on the notion that performance measures capture complex coherences in an aggregated, quantifiable form. Differences emerge with regard to the structure of performance measures. For example, several anglophone contributions define performance measures only as ratios, while the German literature includes absolute measures, too. For this and the following refer to *Fischer et al.* (2012), p. 341, and *Horváth et al.* (2015), p. 286.

provide little informative power. For example, the number of automatically posted invoices provides little information about the process quality of a SSO if it is not put in relation to the total number of posted invoices. The average costs incurred by the SSOs also give SSO managers little indication which cost elements are particularly high.

By contrast, ratios put two figures into a meaningful relationship by the formation of quotients. Ratios include quotas, reference numbers and index numbers (*Gladen* (2014), p. 15). The examples of absolute and relative performance measures indicate that PMS in SSOs may contain varying performance measures. Since the performance measures in SSOs provide heterogeneous information, not only the mere number of performance measures but also the composition of the used performance measures is important.

Furthermore, performance measures can be separated into **financial and non-financial** performance measures (*Fischer et al.* (2012), p. 341). A consistent definition of non-financial performance measures does not exist in the literature. Several contributions characterize non-financial performance measures by distinguishing them from financial performance measures. For example, *Horngren et al.* (2009) define non-financial performance measures as measures which are not expressible in monetary units (*Horngren et al.* (2009), p. 266). *Ittner and Larcker* (1998) describe non-financial performance measures as the opposite of *"traditional accounting-based performance measures"* (*Ittner/Larcker* (1998), p. 205). *Fisher* argues in a similar vein by describing them as performance measures that are not directly based on cost considerations (*Fisher* (1992), p. 35). Nevertheless, normative conceptualizations emerged, too. For instance, *Klingebiel* (2013) classifies non-financial performance measures in quantitative and qualitative measures (*Klingebiel* (2013), p. 21). Quantitative non-financial performance measures are based on directly observable facts, such as the lead time of an invoice. By contrast, qualitative non-financial performance measures, bear upon indirectly observable facts, such as the employee satisfaction in the SSO (*Klingebiel* (2013), p. 22). Finally, various contributions attribute to non-financial performance measures the role of an early warning system (*Chow/van der Steede* (2006); *Fisher* (1992); *Hofmann* (2001); *Ittner/Larcker* (2003)). According to *Gladen* (2002), non-financial performance measures provide information about the future development, while financial performance measures are past-oriented since the process leading to a (financial) result has already been performed (*Gladen* (2002), p. 6).[17] Thus, non-financial performance measures

---

17 The literature addresses this role by frequently equating non-financial and financial performance measures with the terms *leading and lagging measures*. However, this

monitor their financial counterparts (*Balkcom et al.* (1997), p. 23). In addition, non-financial performance measures attempt to overcome further limitations of financial performance measures. Financial measures are criticized for being too aggregated and past-oriented in order to show managers the reasons for undesirable developments so that they are able to react in time (*Chow/van der Steede* (2006), p. 2). By contrast, using non-financial performance measures enables SSO managers to identify the activities which actually contribute to the SSO's success (*Fisher* (1992), p. 31).

Performance indicators can be distinguished from performance measures as they describe issues that can only be approximated (*Küpper et al.* (2013), p. 477). Thus, they represent not directly measurable proxies (*Matheis* (2012), p. 30). Performance indicators are an explanatory factor for an arduously foreseeable and quantifiable cause-effect relationship (*Küpper et al.* (2013), p. 477). However, since the cause-effect relationships covered by performance indicators are not directly measureable, they are less useful than performance measures (*Pütz* (2007), pp. 16–17). In general, performance indicators exhibit a strong future reference (*Matheis* (2012), p. 30). Compared to performance measures, performance indicators require a more cautious interpretation (*Klingebiel* (2013), p. 21).

In addition to the distinction between performance measures and indicators, a distinction to KPIs seems noteworthy. **KPIs** represent the proportion of performance indicators which are of decisive importance for the present and future success of an organization (*Hoffmann* (2000), p. 103). Hence, KPIs differ from performance indicators in their relevance for the SSO's success.

Performance measures are categorized in various **dimensions**. Frequently the used categorizations classify performance measures according to the functional areas in which they are implemented (*Matheis* (2012), p. 30). Another classification scheme constitutes their content-related design. In their BSC, *Kaplan and Norton* (1996) present a much-noticed content-related categorization of performance measures by drawing on four perspectives: the financial, customer, process as well as the learning and growth perspective (*Kaplan/Norton* (1996), pp. 8–10). However, many other content-related categorizations are used in practice.

---

study follows the argumentation line of *Nagar and Rajan*, who reveal in their empirical study on quality performance measures that non-financial (e.g. error rates) and financial performance measures (e.g. complaint costs) are significantly associated with future financial success. Hence, financial performance measures do not lag by default. For a detailed argumentation see *Nagar/Rajan* (2001), p. 512.

Having clarified how performance measures can be distinguished in terms of their design, the next section outlines the performance measurement process.

2.2.3.2 Performance measurement process

The classifications of performance measures presented in the previous section do not explain how performance measures are selected, designed, the necessary data collected, evaluated, communicated and revised. PMS frameworks suggest which measure types should be used, but hardly give an indication of how performance measurement should be done in daily business practice (*Bourne et al.* (2000), p. 756). Indeed, **the performance measurement process seems as crucial to SSOs** as the performance measure itself:

> „I'm not sure which is more proprietary in a scorecard – the data it contains, or the management process that went into creating it. “
> (McWilliams (1996), p. 16)

This quotation by *McWilliams* expresses widespread interest in the performance measurement process, which is **marginally reflected** in the literature compared to contributions that address its result – i.e. the performance measure (*Neely et al.* (2000), p. 1130). While several contributions address the selection and design process of performance measures, there are few contributions that focus on data collection, evaluation, and revision of performance measures (*Bourne et al.* (2000), p. 755). *Keegan et al.* developed a three-step model, which includes the integration of new performance measures into an existing PMS, but primarily concentrate on the measure design process, thus ignoring essential performance measurement process steps (*Keegan et al.* (1989), p. 45). After the publication of the BSC, *Kaplan and Norton* (1995) were exposed to criticism due to the presumption that the BSC was difficult to apply in corporate practice (*Neely et al.* (2000), p. 1127). They respond to criticism by disclosing an eight-step process that enables managers *"to put the Balanced Scorecard to work"* (*Kaplan/Norton* (2000), pp. 71–72). Their performance measurement process details the selection and implementation of performance measures, but does not focus on the data collection and revision of performance measures.

By contrast, the performance measurement process of *Neely et al. (2000)* structures performance measurement in six steps including the data collection, analysis and interpretation of performance measures (*Neely et al.* (2000), pp. 1132–1134). However, their model does not illustrate the modification of existing performance measures. *Bourne et al.* (2000) emphasize in their three-phase model the process steps of reviewing and updating existing performance measures (*Bourne et al.* (2000), p. 757). Hence, their model represents a compatible supplementation to the suggested performance measurement process of *Neely et al.* (2000). The process models of *Kaplan and Norton, Neely et al.* and *Bourne et al* supplement each other and thus serve as a conceptual basis for this study's performance measurement process in order to derive a holistic picture. It comprises the **four main process steps**: performance measure selection, data collection, evaluation, and revision. The main process steps shown in figure 2.7 are divided into a total of eleven sub-process steps. It seems noteworthy that the outlined process steps may overlap in practice (*Bourne et al.* (2000), p. 758).

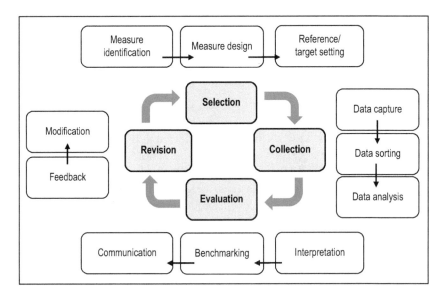

Figure 2.6: The performance measurement process (own illustration based on *Bourne et al.* (2000), p. 757, *Kaplan and Norton* (2000), pp. 71–72, and *Neely et al.* (2000), p. 1132–1134)

Selection of performance measures

The selection process of performance measures is split into three sub-processes:

(1) identification of suitable performance measures;
(2) design of performance measures;
(3) target setting for the designed performance measures.

The decision-making process leading to the selection of performance measures for the PMS is certainly valuable for a SSO because it forces the responsible decision-makers to reveal their performance priorities. Therefore, any differences in the strategic orientation of the SSO have to be ruled out during the selection process (*Neely et al.* (2000), p. 1121). Thus, the identification of the SSO's key objectives is a decisive prerequisite to design performance measures. The vast majority of performance measurement concepts agrees on the condition that selected performance measures should be derived from corporate strategy (*Azzone et al.* (1991); *Dixon* (1990); *Goold* (1991); *Kaplan/Norton* (1992); *Lynch/ Cross* (1995); *Mintzberg* (1982); *Wisner/Fawcett* (1991)). Applied to a SSO, the process step of **identifying suitable performance measures** entails five actions to be taken.[18] First, SSO managers need to identify the SSO's key objectives. Second, every SSO manager should point out his information requirements, which he needs to contribute to the SSO's key objectives. As a result, all relevant performance measurement areas within the SSO are defined. Third, a cost-benefit analysis should be done for each information requirement to detect the most promising performance measurement areas. Fourth, based on the identified performance measurement areas, SSO managers need to translate the key objectives of their areas into measures. This rather creative process step takes place in various ways, for example by holding brainstorming sessions or relying on external expertise (*Schreyer* (2007), pp. 127–129). Fifth, responsible performance measurement facilitators should perform a comprehensiveness check to ensure that all relevant performance measurement areas are covered, all possible performance measures serve a specific purpose and can be integrated into an existing PMS.

The **design of performance measures** refers to the structure of each performance measure. After the SSO management agreed on the performance measurement areas in which it wants to implement a performance measure, the SSO management decides how this measure has to be calculated. It is of particular importance to document the calculation scheme in detail to prevent calculation errors and to facilitate the communication of the selected performance measures (*Doumeingts et al.* (1995), p. 359). As illustrated, there are numerous possibilities regarding the structure of performance measures. However, some authors provide recommendations on how performance measures should be designed. *Maskell* points out that the calculation scheme should be as simple as possible so that all SSO employees easily understand the calculation scheme (*Maskell* (1991), p. 19). Furthermore, it is advisable to implement measures which allow

---

18 The following five steps are adapted from the process frameworks of *Kaplan/Norton* (2000); *Neely et al.* (2000); *Wisner/Fawcett* (1991).

for a comparison with other organizational units, such as the comparison of performance measures among different support processes, SSCs or SSOs of different MNCs (*Neely et al.* (2000), p. 1131). In order to meet the criterion of comparability, SSO managers should prefer objectively verifiable key figures (*Globerson* (1985), p. 640). Several authors recommend adopting non-financial indicators to avoid the discussed limitations of financial performance measures (*Kaplan/ Norton* (1996); *Keegan et al.* (1989); *Maskell* (1991); *Neely et al.* (2000)). As a bottom line, literature advocates for a balanced mix of different performance measure designs because different measure designs satisfy different information needs. Thus, only a balanced mix of performance measure designs provides a comprehensive picture enabling SSO managers to control their organization.

Performance measurement without a predefined **target** seems barely useful, since a target serves as a reference point to define performance (*Seiter* (2011), p. 115). In addition, a performance standard should be defined in advance in favor of a decent interpretation of the measurement result (*Grüning* (2002), p. 17). The same applies to the measurement interval which predefines the evaluation period of the measurement. Hence, the three elements performance dimension, standard and interval shape the core of the target setting process (*Cyert/March* (1963), p. 156). Usually, the target setting process involves several performance measurement actors (*Peemöller* (2002), p. 2170). Frequently, performance measurement actors negotiate not only the target for a single performance measure but rather a comprehensive target system, which entails multiple performance measures (*Seiter* (2011), p. 116). In particular, SSO managers should pay attention that the negotiated performance measure targets do not conflict with each other (*Peemöller* (2002), p. 2170). Linking performance standards with components of the SSO employees' compensation creates incentive systems (*Gladen* (2014), p. 196). These should meet the requirements of transparency, fairness and profitability (*Becker* (1995), p. 19). In essence, a transparent target setting process enables SSOs to identify and avoid target conflicts at an early stage.

Data collection

The performance measure data collection process is structured into the three process steps:

(1) data capture,
(2) data sorting,
(3) data analysis.

Data capture describes the gathering of raw data (*Bourne et al.* (2007), p. 798). Data capture also includes the selection of management information systems (MIS) out of which data are retrieved. Furthermore, the data capture process consists of data collection procedures that control which and how much data are collected. A data set becomes an information only if it has been selected and categorized according to specific criteria (*Matheis* (2012), p. 30). **Data sorting** refers to the data merging from different MIS (*Bititci et al.* (2002), p. 1277). Data can either be combined manually in a target MIS, or computer programs automatically combine data at predefined dates in a target MIS (*Bourne et al.* (2000), p. 761). It seems noteworthy that data does not always have to originate from MIS, but may be retrieved through interviews and surveys, too (*Bourne et al.* (2000), p. 758). **Data analysis** implies the detection and correction of errors, for example by duplicates that arise from data merging (*Bititci et al.* (2002), p. 1280). Moreover, data are analyzed and processed according to different criteria, such as temporal change, scale or origin. In the course of digitalization, data sorting and data analysis take a prominent role in the performance measurement process (*Kaspar/Ossadnik* (2014), p. 31). Data collection process steps offer the greatest potential for automation initiatives. In addition, SSOs are meanwhile capable of sorting and analyzing large data volumes without compromising the benefits of big data by unjustifiably high cost (*McAfee et al.* (2012), pp. 62–63). Thus, the cost of measurement determine the selected data (*Bititci et al.* (2002); *Eccles* (1990); *Lingle/Schiemann* (1996)). An increasing number of service providers specializes in analyzing existing data according to as many different dimensions as possible in order to provide new interpretation stimuli. SSOs may differ in the performance measure data collection process not only in the choice of their MIS, but also in how much effort they put into capturing, sorting and analyzing data. In addition, SSOs may vary significantly depending on the SSOs' endeavors to automate the performance measure data collection process.

Evaluation of performance measures

The evaluation process can be subdivided into three sub-processes:

(1) interpretation,
(2) benchmarking,
(3) communication.

During the **interpretation** phase of the performance evaluation, the measured values are compared against its target values which have been developed in the selection phase. Thus, the interpretation of performance measures represents an assessment to which extent the stated objectives have been achieved (*Seiter* (2011), p. 115). Organizations interpret their performance measures by using miscellaneous analytical methods. In addition to variance analyses, SSOs also use time series comparisons to assess the development of their performance measures (*Gladen* (2014), pp. 104–105). **Benchmarking** illustrates a particular form of performance measure interpretation. Performance measurement literature distinguishes between internal and external benchmarking, whereby external benchmarking is structured into functional, generic and competitive benchmarking (*Mertins/Anderes* (2009), pp. 51–52; *Weber/Schäffer* (2016), pp. 368 ff.).

The **communication of the performance measure** and its interpretation take place in a variety of ways. A commonly applied communication form are KPI reports,[19] which include the evaluation of the most important performance measures (*Krause* (2007), pp. 49–50). Performance measure results are typically shown in numbers and tables, but are also visualized in charts and diagrams (*Bourne et al.* (2000), p. 763). Elaborately designed applications, such as dashboards, gain importance. Performance measurement applications enable managers to retrieve real-time data in different visualizations and analytical models (*Hilgers* (2008), pp. 60–61). Meetings, in which performance measures are discussed, represent another communication form (*Bourne et al.* (2000), p. 761). Frequently, SSO managers not only discuss KPI reports in meetings, but also develop recommendations for actions to be taken (*Krause* (2007), p. 50). In addition to further formal communication forms, such as the use of bulletin boards, informal communication processes are also conceivable which occur spontaneously and are not subject to any pre-defined procedures (*Lingle/ Schiemann* (1996), p. 61). Other communication parameters, such as communication intervals and addressees are of significant importance for a successful communication process (*Lautenbach* (2014), p. 898). For example, it seems reasonable for SSOs to report the performance measure "employee satisfaction" only once a year, while the number of incoming invoices is reported on a daily basis. Moreover, it seems reasonable that the evaluation of employee satisfaction is made accessible exclusively to the management, whereas SSOs publish operational performance measures to the respective process managers.

---

19 The term *KPI reports* is used because this expression is primarily applied in practice. As explained in section 2.2.5.1, at this point *KPI reports* is used synonymously for *key performance measure reports*.

Revision of performance measures

The revision of performance measures is separated into:

(1) Feedback,
(2) modification.

The literature and practice neglected the revision of PMS for a long time (*Bourne et al.* (2000), p. 755). Nonetheless, a periodic review, to what extent performance measures of the SSO's PMS should be modified, appears to be necessary for two reasons (*Kennerley/Neely* (2002a), p. 1225). First, SSOs react to an altering environment by adapting their strategies over time. An altering environment also requires a **modification of performance measures**, since they are derived from corporate strategy (*Bititci et al.* (2000), p. 696). Furthermore, it may be necessary to add new performance measures and eliminate present ones because performance measurement areas have changed (*Neely et al.* (2000), p. 1134). Second, previously selected performance measures may not measure for what they were initially implemented and require an adjustment (*Grüning* (2002), p. 211).

As a prerequisite for adding, eliminating or modifying performance measures, performance measurement facilitators require a **feedback** by the PMS users (*Bourne et al.* (2007), p. 798). A frequently mentioned feedback relates to the adjustment of performance measure targets because either they have been completed or changed environmental conditions require a target revaluation (*Bourne et al.* (2000), p. 766). A commonly provided feedback by SSO management accountants who foster the PMS reveals that the benefits of selected performance measures do not justify the effort of data collection (*Bititci et al.* (2002), p. 1275). Typical feedback by SSO managers consists in the lack of performance measure suitability for decision-making or behavior control. This is expressed by the fact that certain performance measurement areas may no longer be crucial or performance measures do not track the agreed objectives (*Grüning* (2002), p. 211).

After the essential steps of the performance measurement process have been detailed, the following section outlines the performance measurement actors as the third component of PMS design. While the introduction of the performance measurement process elaborates on how SSOs measure performance, the following section explains which actors manage PMS in SSOs.

2.2.3.3 *Performance measurement actors*

This section describes the performance measurement actors as the third component of this study's conceptualization of PMS design in order to lay the foundation for the subsequent empirical analyses. The literature designates multiple groups of performance measurement actors[20] who are responsible for designing and maintaining the PMS (*Gleich* (2011), p. 317). The **SSO management accountant** in Anglo-American (*Evans et al.* (1996); *Grady* (1991); *Sharman* (1995)) and the "Controller" in German-speaking regions bear responsibility for PMS design (*Gladen* (2014); *Gleich* (2011); *Horváth et al.* (2015); *Klingebiel* (2013); *Sandt* (2004)). In the performance measurement process, a SSO management accountant coordinates not only the provision of information (e.g. data collection for selected performance measures) and the information use (e.g. reporting), but also the system design (e.g. the number of measures) and the system coupling (e.g. building links between the SSO's PMS and other existing PMS of the MNC). Thereby, a SSO management accountant synchronizes the information needs of potential addressees with the information offered by the existing PMS (*Horváth et al.* (2015), p. 125).

In the search for a suitable architect to implement their BSC, *Kaplan and Norton* distinguish **two types of SSO management accountants** (*Kaplan/Norton* (1996), pp. 310–311). First, the change agent acts as a true owner of the performance measurement process by identifying and documenting measurable objectives through his analytical abilities and using his profound knowledge for the enhancement of the PMS. Change agents have also proven their communication strength and thus are capable of solving conflicts and facilitating team building (*Kaplan/Norton* (1996), pp. 299–300). The second type of SSO management accountants attaches great importance to objectivity, auditability and integrity of financial performance measures and considers softer, non-financial performance measures as a dilution of performance standards. From the perspective of *Kaplan and Norton* only the change agent seems suitable for a holistic performance measurement by using the BSC (*Kaplan/Norton* (1996), p. 311).

In addition to the SSO management accountant, other actors take part in the performance measurement process. Particularly, **process owners** provide the PMS with valuable information, define measuring points in their processes and analyze the development of performance measures (*Matheis* (2012), p. 180). Furthermore, **SSO managers** are important for the performance measurement process (*Krause* (2007), pp. 187–188). They not only

---

20 The term "*actor*" represents only one of several denominations for groups of persons involved in the performance measurement process. *Neely* uses the term "facilitator" synonymously (*Neely et al.* (2000)), while *Kaplan and Norton* refer to an "*architect*" (*Kaplan/Norton* (1996), p. 299). In addition, the term "*promotor*" characterized by *Hausschildt* is applied, too (e.g. *Hilgers* (2008); *Schreyer* (2007)).

represent the main target group of PMS reports, but are often involved in the PMS development as SSO managers specify the objectives of their organizational units (*Gleich* (2011), p. 318). The extent to which an organization is able to establish a PMS depends very much on its standing and thus how much attention SSO managers are willing to grant to the PMS (*Bourne et al.* (2002), p. 1297). If SSO managers do not exemplify performance measurement, their employees will hardly do it. Frequently, a top management person acts as a principal or sponsor of the PMS (*Folan/Browne* (2005), p. 664). Therefore, this top manager constitutes the highest authority for all decisions with regard to performance measurement. He ensures that the development and use of the PMS finds the necessary support within the organization (*Schreyer* (2007), p. 173). **SSO employees** are also considered as performance measurement stakeholders and assist in the development and modification of a PMS. Moreover, SSO employees act as the users of performance measurement reports (*Grüning* (2002), pp. 201–202). In addition, **IT managers** take a further role in performance measurement as they provide and maintain the information systems from which the data for the PMS are obtained (*Matheis* (2012), p. 180). Finally, several contributions mention **consultants** as external actors, which are called into action especially during the implementation phase of the PMS (*Gleich* (2011), p. 317).

This section outlined that very different groups of actors are involved in the design of the PMS in a SSO. By differentiating between several groups of actors within the SSO, it can be analyzed which SSO actors particularly promote the design of PMS in SSOs.

2.2.3.4 Summary

As illustrated in the prior sections, PMS design in SSOs may vary significantly with regard to the applied performance measures, processes and involved actors. While the PMS of some SSOs may contain a large number of performance measures, other SSOs manage their performance with only a few. SSOs may also differ in the type and number of performance measurement activities and the number of actors involved. To facilitate the comparability of PMS designs of the SSOs under research, this study analyzes PMS design characterized by the interaction and numerousness of performance measures, performance measurement activities, and performance measurement actors. All of three introduced components contribute to a more or less complex PMS design, depending on their characteristics. Hence, this study examines **PMS design in terms of its complexity**. The PMS design score, which is of particular importance for the explicative analyses, rests on the introduced conceptualization of PMS design in terms of its complexity.

Notably, the term complexity can be positively and negatively connoted. In the continuum between simplicity and complexity, it is often positively connoted as a degree of differentiation or specialization (*Chenhall* (2003), p. 136). Negatively connoted, the term complexity is associated with information overload, additional costs and a lack of productivity (*O'Reilly* (1980); *Swenson* (1998)). This study does not seek to evaluate PMS design in terms of complexity as a positive or negative concept since neither empirical nor conceptual contributions in MCS research unequivocally indicate whether a more complex PMS yields greater benefits or just more costs. By contrast, the explicative analyses intend to reveal whether there is an association between PMS design and its effectiveness. Notably, this study does not focus on PMS efficiency.

Having outlined the different facets of PMS design, the following sections seek for a distinction of the term PMS compared to related terminology.

2.2.4 Conceptual distinction to MCS and performance management

2.2.4.1 Management control systems in SSOs

The introduction of MCS serves two purposes. First, it seems necessary to demonstrate that PMS are only one MCS which is available to SSO managers as current SSO literature rather ignores the full range of available management controls. Second, the framework allows for an integration of PMS into the MCS used in SSOs. In addition, the following sections differentiate PMS as the object under research from management accounting systems (MAS) and performance management. A clear differentiation substantiates which concepts are not covered by the term PMS design and are therefore not analyzed in the empirical part of this study.

MCS play an important role in SSOs since MCS encompass a variety of tools and practices that support SSOs to achieve their objectives. Academic literature engenders a myriad of MCS definitions which differ from each other, but occasionally overlap with other terms (*Abernethy/Chua* (1996); *Alvesson/Kärreman* (2004); *Anthony* (1965); *Chenhall* (2003); *Fisher* (1998); *Flamholtz et al.* (1985); *Green/Welsh* (1988); *Langfield-Smith* (1997); *Merchant/Stede* (2007); *Otley et al.* (1990); *Otley/Berry* (1980); *Ouchi* (1979); *Simons* (2013)). For a conceptual distinction, it seems advisable to distinguish between the two essential tasks of managerial accounting, namely **decision-making and control** (*Ewert/Wagenhofer*

(2014), p. 6). While decision-making is based on *what* information the system provides (i.e. accounting information), MCS primarily differ in *how* this information is used. If a SSO manager uses the PMS exclusively to gain information for his own decision-making, it is rather called a MAS instead of a MCS (*Lucey* (2004), p. 2). Even if the PMS is used by subordinates for their decision-making, this does not necessarily imply a MCS because the behavior of the employees is not controlled (*Malmi/Brown* (2008), p. 290). For example, if KPIs that are combined in a PMS exclusively to support SSO managers' ex ante decisions, it is called a MAS. If the SSO manager uses the PMS to set KPI targets for his subordinates, which align their behavior with the SSO's strategy to accomplish its objectives, it is called a MCS. Hence, each MAS may represent a MCS, depending on whether the SSO manager uses it solely for decision-making or for behavioral control (*Zimmerman* (2001), p. 424). Furthermore, it is important to characterize a system. While management controls refer to a collection of instruments, activities, roles, and practices, a MCS entail the composition of management controls for a particular purpose (*Chenhall* (2003), p. 129). For instance, if SSO managers compile single KPIs for the SSO's support processes, it does not necessarily constitute a PMS.

In essence, MCS can be separated from other MAS if they are not solely used for decision-making but also for behavioral control. Thus, a PMS may represent an MCS, but does not necessarily have to be. In addition, an essential distinction criterion between broader and narrower MCS definition marks the question which elements can be understood as management controls. The framework of *Malmi and Brown* (2008) sticks to a broader definition of MCS:

> „…*management controls include all the devices and systems managers use to ensure that the behaviors and decisions of their employees are consistent with the organization's objectives and strategies, but exclude pure decision-support systems. Any system, such as budgeting or a strategy scorecard can be categorized as a MCS.*"

(Malmi/Brown (2008), pp. 290–291)

The framework of *Malmi and Brown* (2008) presented in figure 2.7 illustrates essential MCS in SSOs. Since SSOs commonly involve several MCS, it seems noteworthy that MCS are often implemented independently from each other which is why *Malmi and Brown* (2008) refer to MCS packages instead of one comprehensive MCS (*Malmi/Brown* (2008), p. 291). The framework defines PMS as an important part of cybernetic controls that SSO managers use on a regular basis. The framework of *Malmi and Brown* (2008) defines five typologies of management controls: cultural, administrative, reward and compensation, planning, and cybernetic controls (*Malmi/Brown* (2008), p. 291).[21] The various management controls used in SSOs do not operate isolated from each other, but rather have many interrelations.

MCS related to the SSO environment are implemented in three organizational tiers. First, MCS exist at SSC level (*Schimank/Strobl* (2002), p. 285). MCS in SSCs coordinate the internal activities of a SSC to achieve its specific objectives (*Sterzenbach* (2010), p. 147). MCS in SSCs may vary depending on the center configuration since design parameters, such as SSC location, functional scope or implemented charging models affect the acceptance and use of controls. Second, MCS exist at SSO level. MCS at SSO level intend to align the objectives of each SSC with the SSO's overall goals. Third, MCS exist at group level. MCS used by the group controlling direct the SSO to pursue the MNC's objectives (*Sterzenbach* (2010), p. 147). Notably, this study investigates PMS in SSOs and thus does not reflect PMS at group level.

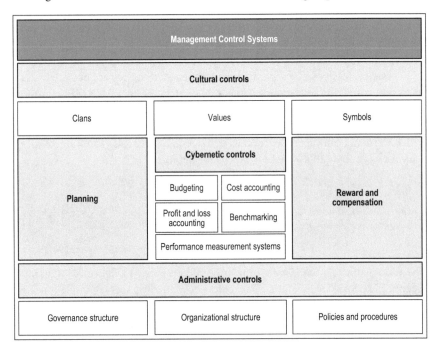

Figure 2.7: Management control systems adapted from *Malmi/Brown* (2008), p. 291.

---

21 For brevity, this section does not provide an overview of all management controls used in SSOs. Refer to *Malmi and Brown* for a summary of the five management control typologies (*Malmi/Brown* (2008), p. 291 ff.).

In essence, the applied definition of a MCS appears to be much broader than that of a PMS because it encloses other management controls, such as budgeting or cultural controls (*Chenhall* (2003), p. 129). PMS can rather be described as a specific tool out of the MCS toolbox and are classified as cybernetic controls in the *Malmi and Brown* (2008) framework. In contrast to MCS, PMS can also be used exclusively for decision-making.

2.2.4.2 Performance management in SSOs

A conceptual distinction of the terms performance measurement and performance management is challenging since the concept of performance management is not uniformly defined in the literature (*Gericke* (2002), p. 38).[22] Several contributions even use both terms synonymously (*Erdmann* (2003), p. 79). However, most contributions reach a consensus that performance measurement constitutes an important **component of performance management** (*Bourne et al.* (2003); *Cokins* (2004); *Kang et al.* (2002); *Lebas* (1995); *Leysen/van Nuffel* (2006)).

Amaratunga and Baldry (2008) define performance management as:

> "[…] the use of performance measurement information to effect positive change in organizational culture, systems and processes […]."

(Amaratunga/Baldry (2002), p. 218)

While performance measurement in SSOs focuses primarily on the mere *provision* of decision-useful information, performance management also includes the *use* of this information provided, for example in KPI reports (*Krause* (2007), p. 39). As a consequence, performance management in SSOs encompasses the two aforementioned fundamental management tasks: decision-making and behavioral control (*Hilgers* (2008), pp. 55–56). Performance management entails all activities to improve the performance of the SSO. In this respect, performance measurement and performance management follow an iterative process (*Folan/ Browne* (2005), p. 674). However, assigning individual activities, such as the analysis, communication and modification of performance measures to one of those two terms proves to be difficult (*Matheis* (2012), p. 23). For example, the communication of performance measures in a KPI report could already mark a decision of a SSO manager, because he decides which performance measures he wants to communicate to whom. At the same time, disclosing KPIs

---

22 For a detailed overview of performance management definitions see *Hilgers* (2008), pp. 50–51, and *Krause* (2007), p. 38.

seems inseparable from its communication and does not necessarily lead to a decision or behavioral control. As a result, both concepts have overlaps and vary depending on the underlying framework (*Fuchs* (2010), p. 20). Furthermore, some contributions explicitly include other MCS, such as planning, budgeting or reward and compensation systems in their performance management definition (*Ferreira/Otley* (2009); *Hilgers* (2008); *Lebas* (1995)). In this regard, several performance management frameworks also describe the interplay of different MCS, while performance measurement definitions only refer to PMS as a single MCS. *Otley* developed a widespread performance management framework in 1999, which he revised and extended ten years later (*Ferreira/Otley* (2009); *Otley* (1999)). His contribution illustrates a drawback that performance management definitions face. According to *Otley*, the term performance management entails not only cybernetic controls, such as PMS, budgeting and planning, but also informal controls, such as cultural controls or vision and strategy formation (*Ferreira/Otley* (2009), pp. 267–271). Thus, a classification of performance management into existing MCS strands seems demanding since it lacks a clear distinction to existing MCS (*Ferreira/Otley* (2009), p. 265).

In essence, it can be concluded that performance management goes beyond the scope of performance measurement as measures are not only collected, analyzed, evaluated and communicated, but actively managed. This becomes obvious with a view to the tasks of performance measurement actors. While performance measurement is typically associated with the spectrum of tasks for SSO management accountants, performance management describes an important remit for SSO managers.

Having detailed the notions of MCS, MAS and performance management, two consequences can be drawn. First, other MCS, such as cultural or administrative controls cannot be subsumed under the term PMS design and are thus not analyzed. Second, PMS design rather focuses on the provision of decision-useful information than on corrective actions that drive a SSO's performance. Thus, performance management is out of scope in the empirical part of this study.

3 State of research

This chapter reviews prior research on SSOs and on performance measurement. It provides an overview of the two research areas that are combined in this study. Thereby, it relates to the research gaps this study intends to reduce. In general, there is a great deal of empirical research on SSOs and on performance measurement. Furthermore, both research fields apply differing research approaches. Since this study's mixed methods research design (MMRD) combines qualitative and quantitative research approaches, this chapter divides prior research into **quantitative and qualitative research** (figure 3.1).

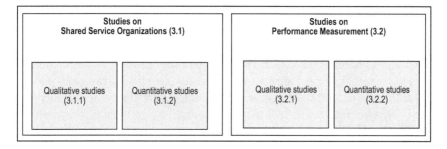

Figure 3.1: Classification of the related empirical literature

Due to the ever-increasing number of empirical studies on SSOs and on performance measurement, this literature review does not consider conceptual contributions. For the same reason the following sections omit experience reports by practitioners and anecdotal evidence. Hence, this review focuses on literature about design characteristics and empirical evidence of applied PMS in SSOs to gain insights for this study's research questions. Since there is only a small amount of empirical work related to PMS design in SSOs, this review also includes prior research that addresses this study's research questions by focusing on PMS design in terms of measures, processes and actors in other organizational models than SSOs. Moreover, this review includes prior research on determinants and effects of PMS design. By contrast, this literature review excludes research primarily concentrating on MCS. Hence, this review illustrates only a selection of prior research adapted to the research design and the research questions instead of a complete picture.

3.1 Studies on shared service organizations

3.1.1 Qualitative studies on shared service organizations

Paagman et al. (2015) draw on a sample of thirteen Dutch and New Zealand governmental organizations by conducting interviews with sixteen experts. They analyze **key motives for the adoption of SSO** by empirically validating a framework of thirteen implementation motives (*Paagman et al.* (2015a), pp. 6–8). They find that cost reduction and service quality improvements as well as process standardization are seen as the most important motives, although the interviewees were skeptical about its attainment. In addition, they state that the weighting of motives changed over time (*Paagman et al.* (2015a), p. 10). *Paagman et al.* acknowledge that their results are difficult to transfer to private firms, although their empirically validated framework draws on SSO initiatives of the private sector (*Paagman et al.* (2015a), pp. 9–10).

In a longitudinal case study of a Taiwanese trading company from 2002 to 2012, *Chang et al.* (2013) analyze the effects of a BSC introduction in a MNC's SSO. Their results indicate that the SSO employees manifest a deeper understanding of SSO's strategy after the BSC has been adopted for two years (*Chang et al.* (2013), pp. 22–23). Moreover, SSO employees grasp valuable insights into the coherences between the SSO's and the group's strategy. In a second analysis, they investigate the **effectiveness of the implemented BSC** to appropriately measure the SSO's performance and infer mixed results (*Chang et al.* (2013), pp. 21–22). SSO employees seem to be satisfied with the performance measures used in the BSC, although expressing their dissatisfaction about the lack of involvement in the performance measurement process. *Chang et al.* conclude that top-down approaches for the implementation of PMS induce negative effects (*Chang et al.* (2013), p. 23). Moreover, the communication and modification of BSC performance measures should be recurred at regular intervals.

In a longitudinal case study of a UK-based power utility corporation, *Herbert and Seal* (2012) analyze the implementation and development of a SSO. They particularly highlight the implications of this new organizational form for management accounting and come to the conclusion that the adoption of a SSO induces evolving roles and responsibilities for management accountants (*Herbert/Seal* (2012), pp. 94–95). They state that management accounting activities in SSOs are aligned regardless of individual roles, departments or functions on end-to-end processes so that management accountants increasingly become experts in process optimization (*Herbert/Seal* (2012), p. 95). In addition, management accountants in SSOs require an in-depth IT-system knowledge. Furthermore, their study reveals that benchmarking and the **use of KPIs** to quantify the achievement of the SSO's objectives get more attention with an increasing maturity of the SSO (*Herbert/Seal* (2012), p. 88). However, they only briefly describe the increasing importance of the performance measurement in their single case study so that neither the evolving performance measures nor the altering performance measurement process is addressed.

Farndale et al. (2009) conduct a case study analysis of a sample of fifteen Dutch firms to yield a better understanding of critical success factors that determine the **performance of HR SSOs**. They find that the primary objective of HR SSOs consists in an increase of service quality and a high degree of customer satisfaction (*Farndale et al.* (2009), p. 551). As main success factors they identify a profound expertise and working experience of the SSO employees as well as the implementation of an appropriate technological infrastructure and the full commitment of the MNC's top management. They also provide evidence that HR SSOs face a considerable lack of performance data as their main problem (*Farndale et al.* (2009), p. 552). They conclude that a decent PMS should be implemented as early as possible to ensure monitoring capabilities (*Farndale et al.* (2009), p. 559). *Farndale et al.* note that their results drawn from a Dutch sample are difficult to generalize (*Farndale et al.* (2009), p. 558). Furthermore, a self-selection bias seems to be an issue since they state that most participants are considered as examples of best practice.

Perez (2009) exploits a sample of twelve German firms with SSOs at an early development stage by conducting interviews and analyzing documents from 2001 to 2005. With reference to the performance measurement of early stage SSOs, *Perez* notes that most **SSOs do not use a coherent PMS**, but are limited to one-dimensional performance measurement, such as performance measures that evaluate cost saving potentials or customer satisfaction (*Pérez* (2009), p. 65). She finds that the use of SLAs requires an operative performance measurement, since otherwise a comprehensive control of the agreed service levels cannot be achieved (*Pérez* (2009), p. 65). Her inferences from the early stage SSOs about the design of performance measurement are only to a limited extent transferrable to SSOs with a higher degree of maturity. Moreover, *Perez* states that her case studies relate mainly to finance SSOs (*Pérez* (2009), p. 230).

Redman et al. (2007) conduct a case study analysis of a sample of four UK public National Health Service Organizations (NHS) that adopted HR SSOs. By conducting a total of 28 interviews, they examine **the effects of SSO implementations** in terms of employee satisfaction (*Redman et al.* (2007), pp. 1499–1502). Their results indicate mixed evidence. On the one hand, SSO employees appreciate a facilitated access to expert knowledge and a rapid learning curve (*Redman et al.* (2007), p. 1500). Results show an increased job satisfaction through a wider variety of tasks and more opportunities concerning the career development of SSO employees. On the other hand, SSO employees associate the SSO implementation with conflicting priorities and a rocky future (*Redman et al.* (2007), p. 1502). However, *Redman et al.* speculate that their results are not generalizable to mature SSOs because they emerged under the impression of a pervasive reorganization.

In summary, exploratory case study research uncovered a range of SSO design characteristics that determine the performance of this new organizational form. Moreover, qualitative research revealed the most popular objectives associated with SSO implementations. However, the gap between the postulated effects by theory and its empirical verification remains open for two reasons. First, qualitative research about the SSO effects in terms of efficiency and effectiveness is scarce. Second, firms and public sector organizations struggle to quantify the intended effects of SSO adoptions, which expresses the **urgent necessity for research on PMS in SSOs**. Particularly, research on PMS is marginally reflected in qualitative empirical research (table 3.1).

Table 3.1: Overview of qualitative studies on shared service organizations

Reference	Sample	Findings
Paagman et al. (2015)	13 Dutch and New Zealand public organizations, 2012	Cost reduction, improving service quality and process standardization are key motives for a SSO implementation.
Chang et al. (2013)	1 Taiwan firm, 2002–2012	After the implementation of a BSC, SSO employees manifest a deeper understanding of the SSO's strategy.
Herbert and Seal (2012)	1 U.K. firm, 2003–2010	SSOs represent a new organizational form that offers altered roles and responsibilities for management accountants. Management accountants face difficulties in quantifying the SSO's performance.
Farndale et al. (2009)	15 Dutch firms, 2007	Critical success factors, such as the implementation of advanced technology and top management support, determine the goal attainment of SSO managers.
Perez (2009)	12 German firms, 2001–2005	Performance measurement in early stage SSOs focuses mainly on cost-oriented performance measures.
Redman et al. (2007)	4 U.K. public organizations, 2005	SSO implementations show mixed results in terms of employee satisfaction. Results indicate dissatisfaction through conflicting priorities but positive effects on staff morale due to better career opportunities.

3.1.2 Quantitative studies on shared service organizations

By drawing on a sample of 723 internal customers of a HR SSO, *Röder* (2012) investigates **which quality criteria determine the perceived service quality** of a HR SSO. He finds that 31 quality criteria, such as the responsiveness to customer requests, professional expertise of the SSO employees and the effective use of communication channels determine the perceived service quality of an IT firm's HR SSO (*Röder* (2012), pp. 169–177). In the explanatory part of his study, *Röder* provides evidence that the SSO's service quality is positively associated with internal customer satisfaction (*Röder* (2012), pp. 243–245). However, his results are limited to a single HR SSO of an IT firm and thus not generalizable to other industries and SSOs, for example finance SSOs.

Ramphal (2011) provides **further descriptive evidence** by drawing on a sample of 64 South-African firms with established SSOs providing services of various operational functions. The results indicate that SSO implementations neither reduce costs nor increase customer satisfaction (*Ramphal* (2011), pp. 50–53). Overall, SSO customers perceive the provided service quality as dissatisfying (*Ramphal* (2011), p. 53). However, the results of his study contain little information about the background and factors that lead to the perceived poor performance of the SSOs.

In a multivariate regression analysis, *Selden and Wooters* (2011) investigate **whether organizational and environmental factors drive the adoption of HR SSOs** in 42 public sector organizations. They find that better performing governmental organizations are more likely to implement HR SSOs (*Selden/Wooters* (2011), pp. 362–363). Moreover, the feasibility of a SSO implementation is positively associated with a high degree of institutional power (*Selden/Wooters* (2011), pp. 363–364). By contrast, unionization is negatively associated with SSO adoptions (*Selden/Wooters* (2011), p. 364). However, it remains questionable to what extent the results of this particular setting can be transferred to the private sector.

In an explanatory study, *Sterzenbach* (2010) draws on the same sample as of *Fischer and Sterzenbach*, but extends their descriptive results by assessing **whether SSO design characteristics impact the SSO managers' goal attainment.** He finds that the use of SLAs is positively associated with the managers' attainment of financial objectives (*Sterzenbach* (2010), p. 398). With regard to performance measurement, the results reveal a positive association between the use of process-related performance measures and an increase in process data quality (*Sterzenbach* (2010), p. 400). In addition, the adoption of a comprehensive PMS is positively associated with the managers' attainment of financial objectives (*Sterzenbach* (2010), p. 401). However, most of his stated null hypotheses are not dismissed. Moreover, *Sterzenbach* concedes that the performance measurement part of the questionnaire is affected by a low response rate. Thus, the presented statistical inferences can be questioned.

Aksin and Masini (2008) conduct a multi-tiered cluster analysis of a relatively large sample of 139 European MNCs with an established SSO. They identified four homogenous clusters of SSO configurations and assessed whether **performance differences among the four SSO configurations** in terms of operational cost and customer satisfaction emerge (*Aksin/Masini* (2008), pp. 247–251). They find that shared service configurations consisting of relatively small SSOs that are consolidated in a few SSCs and that use SLAs extensively show the highest overall performance (*Aksin/Masini* (2008), p. 253). Furthermore, the results indicate that SSOs with a large operating scale and a pervasive geographic dispersion of their SSCs suffer from the accompanying complexity which negatively impinges on their performance (*Aksin/Masini* (2008), p. 254). With regard to their results *Aksin and Masini* issue the caveat that the applied proxies to measure the SSO's performance illustrate only few dimensions of performance (*Aksin/Masini* (2008), p. 255). They conclude that a tradeoff exists between the achievements of different SSO objectives.

Fischer and Sterzenbach (2007) analyze the design of management accounting units in SSOs and find that management accounting departments in SSOs commonly comprise less than ten employees (*Fischer/Sterzenbach* (2007), pp. 45–46). 58 SSOs of German firms completed their survey which describes a predominant use of non-financial measures (70,6%) (*Fischer/Sterzenbach* (2007), pp. 52–53). Moreover, the results illustrate that most financial performance measures relate to costs (*Fischer/Sterzenbach* (2007), p. 53). However, only a minority of 12,3% adopted a comprehensive PMS (*Fischer/Sterzenbach* (2007), pp. 54–55). Although performance measures used in SSOs are a focal point of their study, their research **does not provide any insights into the process** of selecting and evaluating performance measures. Similarly, the descriptive results do not provide information which actors are involved in the selection and analysis of the performance measures.

Kagelmann (2001) is one of the first to conduct a descriptive analysis of European SSOs by exploiting a sample of 44 MNCs with an implemented SSO. His study focuses on the design characteristics of SSOs and unveils that primarily finance processes are performed in SSOs (*Kagelmann* (2001), pp. 84–87). The majority of the SSOs in his sample uses SLAs as a control mechanism and is legally and economically independent (*Kagelmann* (2001), pp. 98–99). However, most SSOs apply cost center concepts and oblige internal customers to contract. Only a minority of the SSOs is allowed to contract with external parties (*Kagelmann* (2001), p. 119). The results show that predominantly customer satisfaction analyses, benchmarking and variance analyses are applied to measure the SSO's performance (*Kagelmann* (2001), pp. 172–173). Since the investigation of *Kagelmann* is **limited to the description of empirical findings**, the SSOs motives behind the design characteristics remain vague. Nevertheless, the majority of the SSOs in his sample indicate that the objectives associated with their adoption have been achieved in a satisfying manner.

In summary, quantitative studies on SSOs provide some evidence on performance measurement in SSOs and possible factors that affect management accounting practices in SSOs (table 3.2). However, most empirical studies focus on the used performance measures but give little information about how performance measures are selected, collected, evaluated and modified.

Table 3.2: Overview of quantitative studies on shared service organizations

Reference	Sample	Findings
Röder (2012)	723 internal SSO customers of 1 German firm, 2011	The service quality of a HR SSO is positively associated with internal customer satisfaction.
Ramphal (2011)	64 South-African firms, 2010	The implementation of SSOs neither increases customer satisfaction nor reduces costs.
Selden and Wooters (2011)	42 U.S. public organizations, 2007	Organizational factors, such as institutional power and a cultivated innovation culture foster the adoption of SSOs, whereas unionization negatively affects SSO implementations.
Sterzenbach (2010)	58 German firms, 2006	The achievement of SSO objectives depends on design characteristics of the SSO Controlling, such as the use of performance measures and SLAs.
Aksin and Masini (2008)	139 European firms, 2002	The configurational setting of SSOs has an impact on operating cost and customer satisfaction.
Fischer and Sterzenbach (2007)	58 German firms, 2006	Management accounting units in SSOs are rather small (< 10 employees). SSOs use predominantly non-financial performance measures. Only a minority has implemented a PMS.
Kagelmann (2001)	33 European firms, 1999	SSOs comprise a variety of design characteristics, such as the use of outsourcing and SLAs as well as a prevalent legal and economic independence.

By contrast, the study at hand uses a more comprehensive approach by analyzing the performance measurement process and sheds light on the most important actors that play a role for the SSOs' PMS. Apart from the empirical validation that the use of SLAs is positively associated with the SSO managers' goal attainment, research on SSOs does scarcely analyze the use of PMS in SSOs and its effects on the SSO's effectiveness and efficiency.

3.2 Studies on performance measurement

3.2.1 Qualitative studies on performance measurement

Qualitative studies on performance measurement describe the design of PMS in various organizations. **A considerable range of related empirical work** focuses on the implementation process of PMS (table 3.3). Another qualitative research stream with regard to performance measurement addresses contingency factors that determine PMS design.

Garengo and Bititci (2007) analyze **contingency factors that impact the PMS adoption** and exploit a sample of four Scottish SMEs. They extend the analysis of *Franco and Bourne* by investigating the relationships between contingency factors and performance measurement practices. They find that the composition of the management board, MIS, the firm's business model and management style influence the adoption and use of PMS (*Garengo/Bititci* (2007), pp. 814–820). The results show that PMS importance increases if firms are managed by a group of managers instead of the owners (*Garengo/Bititci* (2007), p. 815). Furthermore, they conclude that business model changes promote a more pronounced PMS design (*Garengo/Bititci* (2007), pp. 817–818). With regard to the management style, their results indicate that successful PMS implementations require an authoritative style whereas a consultative management style fits best for its daily use (*Garengo/Bititci* (2007), p. 820). However, their results are restricted to Scottish SMEs. A further drawback marks the separated analysis of the contingency factors. An analysis of interrelations between these factors might reveal further findings.

In a similar vein, *Franco and Bourne* (2003) conduct a case study analysis by exploiting a sample of eleven private and public sector firms. By conducting 24 interviews, they explore which **critical factors enable firms to effectively implement their PMS** (*Franco/Bourne* (2003), pp. 703–704). They find that nine determinants influence PMS design. Particularly, organizational culture, top management commitment as well as a coupling between compensation system and PMS have a greater impact on PMS design (*Franco/Bourne* (2003), p. 705). For instance, their results describe that a lacking support of the top management causes that PMS are less frequently modified and performance measures are less intensively evaluated (*Franco/Bourne* (2003), p. 704). This entails the risk that a PMS no longer reflects the firm's strategy. Furthermore, IT systems and further environmental factors, such as firm size and industry, impact the PMS design (*Franco/Bourne* (2003), p. 707). However, the nature of explorative case study research does not provide the ability to test the indicated relevance of their factors.

Bourne et al. (2002) expand the sample of *Neely et al. (2000)* by adding three manufacturing firms that failed to implement a PMS. By comparing the three successful PMS adoptions with their unsuccessful counterparts, their analysis yield three major differences between both groups. Their analyses support commonly suggested success factors, such as **top management commitment and MIS accessibility**, but add four blocking factors to existing empirical findings (*Bourne et al.* (2002), p. 1305). For example, they find that PMS implementations are more likely to fail if managers fear the consequences of performance measurement (*Bourne et al.* (2002), p. 1301). Moreover, an insufficient effort during the implementation phase jeopardizes potential benefits associated with a PMS in the long-run (*Bourne et al.* (2002), p. 1301). As a consequence, *Bourne et al.* suggest that management commitment should be considered as dynamic and thus changes over a project's lifetime (*Bourne et al.* (2002), p. 1308).

Bourne et al. (2000) are one of the first to **investigate performance measurement as a process**. Their sample comprises four manufacturing companies that were accompanied through all phases. They obtain data from three different sources, namely direct involvement in workshops, management meetings and semi-structured interviews (*Bourne et al.* (2000), p. 759). Results validate their conceptual framework of the performance measurement process consisting of four main phases: design phase, implementation phase, application phase and updating phase (*Bourne et al.* (2000), p. 768). They find that an initial PMS design process requires nine to thirteen months on average due to the mangers' resistance of being measured and IT infrastructure settings in order to enable the data collection of the selected performance measures (*Bourne et al.* (2000), p. 760). Due to changing contextual factors, strategy and measures evolve over time. Therefore, findings suggest a regular review of performance measures with a view to the SSO's strategy (*Bourne et al.* (2000), p. 768). Indeed, *Bourne et al.* thoroughly describe the updating phase, but take little notice of the performance measure selection as well as their data collection and analysis. Moreover, it remains open to what extent the presented phases affect the effectiveness of the PMS.

Neely et al. (2000) draw on the same sample as of *Bourne et al.* (2000) but focus on the PMS design process. Similar to *Bourne et al.* (2000), they initially developed a conceptual framework consisting of twelve phases to design a PMS (*Neely et al.* (2000), pp. 1132–1134). Subsequently, they empirically test their framework and evaluate its acceptance through a survey. Their results indicate that firms mainly focus on financial and process-related measures while ignoring performance measures related to customer satisfaction and organizational development (*Neely et al.* (2000), p. 1136). Furthermore, they find that managers tend to keep redundant measures due to the resources they invested beforehand. At the same time, managers develop new measures if necessary, which leads to a steady **increase of PMS design complexity** (*Neely et al.* (2000), p. 1136). Although *Neely et al.* modified their framework case-by-case, it seems questionable whether an assessment through a survey among workbook purchasers represents a suitable proxy to empirically validate their PMS design framework.

Table 3.3: Overview of qualitative studies on performance measurement

Reference	Sample	Findings
Garengo and Bititci (2007)	4 Scottish firms, 2006	Four factors impact PMS adoption and use, namely management style, the firm's business model, the corporate governance structure and MIS.
Franco and Bourne (2003)	11 European firms, 6 U.S. firms, 2 Australian firms and 3 U.K. public sector organizations, 2002	Nine factors determine the design of PMS, e.g. organizational culture, top management commitment, compensation links, IT support as well as business model and industry.
Bourne et al. (2002)	6 U.K. firms, 1996–1997	Successful PMS implementations are distinguished from their unsuccessful counterparts by continuous top management support and an easy data accessibility through IT systems, whereas insufficient effort and the fear of personal consequences of performance measurement blocks PMS implementations.
Bourne et al. (2000)	3 U.K. firms, 1996	The performance measurement process consists of four main phases, namely design, implementation, application and updating phase. Successful PMS continuously challenge corporate strategy.
Neely et al. (2000)	3 U.K. firms, 1993–1994	Development and empirical validation of a 12-phase model of a PMS design process.

3.2.2 Quantitative studies on performance measurement

Quantitative studies on performance measurement assess whether PMS configurations affect firm performance in a variety of ways. A couple of explanatory studies compare certain PMS configurations and their impact on financial firm performance or managerial satisfaction (table 3.4). Moreover, quantitative studies highlight differences of performance measurement practices in miscellaneous countries and yield descriptive information about the adoption of conceptual PMS frameworks in corporate practice.

Abdallah and Alnamri (2015) provide descriptive evidence on PMS design in Saudi-Arabian firms. Based on a survey sample of 72 firms they state that **financial measures are more widely used** compared to non-financial measures in current PMS designs (*Abdallah/Alnamri* (2015), pp. 601–602). *Abdallah and Alnamri* conclude that financial measures are easier to understand for MNC employees and thus more easily to implement. Their results indicate that only a minority of thirteen firms in their sample implemented a comprehensive PMS, such as the BSC (*Abdallah/Alnamri* (2015), pp. 603). However, their findings are restricted to Saudi-Arabian firms and do not necessarily apply to other settings. Moreover, their analysis remains silent on explanatory variables that drive the strong use of financial performance measures.

Dossi and Patelli (2010) survey a sample of 141 Italian firms. Their results show that on average a MNC's PMS contains sixteen performance measures of which more than 50% are financial performance measures (*Dossi/Patelli* (2010), pp. 507). Their findings indicate that MNCs primarily use financial measures although a MNC's PMS supplements financial measures with a considerable number of non-financial measures. Their regression analyses support the assumption that the **inclusion of non-financial performance measures** is positively associated with five contingency factors, namely with relative performance evaluation, an interactive PMS use, subsidiary size, headquarters nationality and subsidiary participation (*Dossi/Patelli* (2010), pp. 512–515).

Raake (2008) analyzes the PMS design and use of 79 U.S. and German based local public transport firms. Apart from descriptive cross-country analyses, her explanatory study concentrates on **PMS design factors that affect user satisfaction**. By conducting a multiple regression analysis using a subset of her sample, she finds that PMS user satisfaction is positively associated with their participation in the PMS design process and the number of performances measures (*Raake* (2008), p. 88). However, results indicate that the number of performance measures negatively affects firm performance which appears to be somewhat internally inconsistent (*Raake* (2008), pp. 90–91). This contradiction could be attributed to methodological weaknesses since, for example, a normal distribution can no longer be assumed with a sample size smaller than thirty so that her multiple regression analysis could be erroneous. Her cross-country analyses reveal that specific PMS frameworks, such as the BSC, are more prevalent in German than in U.S. firms (*Raake* (2008), p. 71).

Marr (2005) analyzes the **current state of PMS practice in U.S. firms**. He uses a sample of 780 firms which represents one of the largest samples in performance measurement research until today. Concerning PMS frameworks, he confirms the findings of *Günther and Grüning* and expands their descriptive evidence by revealing that only three BSC perspectives introduced by *Kaplan and Norton* are commonly used in corporate practice (*Marr* (2005), p. 649). Instead of using their suggested learning and growth perspective, U.S. firms tend to adapt other performance measurement areas, such as employees or innovations. His descriptive analyses illustrate that employee motivation, the communication of results and linking strategies to operational management constitute the main benefits associated with PMS design (*Marr* (2005), p. 648). He finds that spreadsheets are most commonly used to collect data and to evaluate performance measures which is contradictory to the finding that only a minority of his sample considers spreadsheets as a meaningful tool for performance measurement (*Marr* (2005), p. 650).

Based on a sample of 140 U.S. financial service firms, *Ittner and Larcker* (2003) investigate whether **PMS design affects organizational performance**. They find that firms using a broad set of performance measures earn higher stock returns compared to firms with similar strategies and value drivers that predominantly use financial measures (*Ittner et al.* (2003), pp. 727–728). Moreover, firms with a balanced set of measures experience a higher managerial satisfaction (*Ittner et al.* (2003), p. 728). However, results do not support the assumption that firm performance is positively associated with the use of existing PMS frameworks, such as the BSC (*Ittner et al.* (2003), pp. 735–736). Their results are restricted to US based financial service firms and thus may be not transferrable to other industries and countries. In addition, the survey research applied by *Ittner and Larcker* entails further drawbacks, such as response biases and endogeneity.

Said et al. (2003) conduct an archival study to analyze a similar research question. They also concentrate on the use of non-financial performance measures by exploiting a sample of 1,441 U.S. firms that use financial and non-financial measures in their compensation plans (*Said et al.* (2003), p. 200). They find that firm performance in terms of stock market returns is positively associated with the adoption of non-financial performance measures (*Said et al.* (2003), pp. 208–210). Furthermore, their results indicate that the use of non-financial measures is significantly associated with five contingency factors, such as an innovation-oriented strategy, the length of the product development cycle and industry regulation (*Said et al.* (2003), p. 211). However, *Said et al.* consider the application of non-financial performance measures only in aggregate terms and **do not differentiate between measures** relating to, for example customer satisfaction, process quality or employee satisfaction. Moreover, they exclusively rely on measures in compensation plans despite other potential applications of non-financial measures.

In a similar vein, *Günther and Grüning* (2002) investigate the **implementation, design and use of PMS** by drawing on a sample of 181 completed surveys of German firms. They state that one third of their sample does not use a PMS, whereas 17% are in the implementation phase (*Günther/Grüning* (2002), p. 6). They find that the BSC represents the most commonly used PMS (*Günther/Grüning* (2002), p. 6). With regard to the necessary modification of PMS due to changing contingency factors, their results describe that firms revise their PMS on a non-regular basis (*Günther/Grüning* (2002), p. 10). They interpret this information as a positive sign since firms seem responsive to environmental factors and predominantly do not modify their PMS according to fixed schedules. By contrast, almost half of the firms' employees consider themselves as roughly involved in the PMS implementation process which contradicts uniform recommendations uncovered by previous empirical studies (*Günther/Grüning* (2002), p. 10). Yet, the majority of the sample firms claim to be satisfied with their PMS (*Günther/Grüning* (2002), p. 11).

Gleich (2001) surveys 84 German firms with more than 1,000 employees. In addition to some descriptive information about the PMS design in current practice, he focuses on **contingency factors that impact PMS design** and conducts a cluster analysis to provide evidence whether certain PMS configurations are more successful than others. He finds that twelve contingency factors determine PMS design (*Gleich* (2001), pp. 371–382). Factors, such as competition intensity, firm size and the involvement of the management accounting department in strategic planning processes affect PMS design (*Gleich* (2001), p. 397). Moreover, PMS design complexity increases if firms are subject to continuous risk ratings (*Gleich* (2001), pp. 379–381). PMS design is operationalized through eleven characteristics, such as selected performance measures, PMS modification, performance analysis and involved PMS actors (*Gleich* (2001), pp. 203–256). The results illustrate that firms using a PMS that comprise a balanced set of financial and non-financial measures are associated with higher profitability compared to other PMS configurations (*Gleich* (2001), p. 383).

Table 3.4: Overview of quantitative studies on performance measurement

Reference	Sample	Findings
Abdallah and Alnamri (2015)	72 Saudi-Arabian firms, 2014	Financial measures are more widely used compared to non-financial measures. A minority of thirteen firms has implemented a comprehensive PMS framework.
Dossi and Patelli (2010)	141 Italian firms, 2009	Financial measures dominate in corporate practice and are supplemented with non-financial measures in the MNCs' PMS. Five determinants, such as an interactive PMS use and subsidiary size promote the inclusion of non-financial measures in the MNCs' PMS.
Raake (2008)	79 U.S. and German firms, 2006–2007	PMS user satisfaction is positively associated with the number of performance measures and their participation in the PMS design process. The omission of important performance areas negatively influences PMS user satisfaction.
Marr (2005)	780 U.S. firms, 2004	The communication of results, employee motivation and linking strategies to the operational management describe the key motives for PMS implementations. ERPs and spreadsheets are commonly used for the performance measure data collection and evaluation.
Ittner and Larcker (2003)	140 U.S. firms, 1999	Firms using a broad set of performance measures experience a higher PMS satisfaction compared to firms that predominantly use financial measures. A pronounced PMS design is associated with higher PMS satisfaction and firm's financial performance.
Said et al. (2003)	1,441 U.S. firm-year observations, 1993–1998	Firms that employ a combination of financial and non-financial performance measures have significantly higher mean levels of returns on assets and higher levels of market returns.
Günther and Grüning (2002)	181 German firms, 2000	The BSC constitutes the dominant PMS framework in practice. Compared to financial measures, non-financial measures are recognized less frequently.
Gleich (2001)	84 German firms, 1998	Competition intensity, firm size and the institutional power of management accounting determine PMS design. PMS design is operationalized through performance measure selection, PMS modification and performance analysis intensity.

3.3 Summary and research gap

In summary, the literature review on SSOs shows that only few empirical studies address MCS in general and PMS in particular. Descriptive studies on SSOs mainly focus on design characteristics, which in turn represent potential determinants of PMS design in SSOs. In essence, qualitative research on SSOs explores key objectives for SSO implementations and SSO design characteristics. However, research on SSO design characteristics and determinants that are based on German samples is largely **characterized by early adopters of SSOs** (*Keuper/ Oecking* (2008)). A minority of studies investigates which success factors impact the SSO's performance. Quantitative studies on SSOs predominantly analyze contingency factors that influence SSO implementations and determinants that affect the SSOs' success. However, contingency factors that influence the PMS design in SSOs may vary significantly from determinants that drive SSO performance. Few empirical studies unveil management accounting practices in SSO and marginally address performance measurement practices. Most of them solely refer to adopted performance measures, whereas the performance measurement process is ignored (*Sterzenbach* (2010), pp. 357–367). Apart from a low base of descriptive information on performance measurement practices in SSOs, only a few quantitative studies focus on their antecedents. Finally, SSO research neglects the effects of adopted PMS in SSOs. In particular, hypotheses obtained from exploratory case studies are seldom tested quantitatively (*Richter/ Brühl* (2016), p. 8).

Qualitative studies on performance measurement primarily explore the design of PMS in various organizations, countries and support functions. Quite a few authors compare their empirical findings with common PMS frameworks in order to determine a theory-practice gap. In addition, there is a considerable number of exploratory case studies that sheds light on the performance measurement process. However, these studies mainly concentrate on the selection and implementation of new performance measures, paying little attention to the data collection, analyses, and modification of these measures (*Bourne et al.* (2000), p. 755). Another drawback of empirical works that take a process-oriented perspective consists in the **omission of the performance measurement actors.**

The review of quantitative studies on performance measurement illustrates that most explanatory studies analyze whether specific PMS configurations are associated with firm performance and managerial satisfaction. The majority of explanative contributions assesses whether the use of non-financial performance measures affects firm performance while ignoring a variety of other PMS design characteristics. Therefore, future multivariate regression analyses should consider additional PMS design features. Quantitative studies using managerial satisfaction as a performance measure for PMS success **disregard the possible existence of different PMS user groups**. For example, a manager of a business unit may assess the effectiveness of a PMS differently than a management accountant. Research on PMS contingency factors is scarce. Thus, unknown contingency factors could be identified. Furthermore, the role of known contingency factors may change if they are applied to a new research object, such as SSOs.

Based on the outlined shortcomings of both research streams, four major research gaps are identified and addressed in this study. First, **PMS design in SSOs is rarely analyzed**, al-though it may differ greatly from performance measurement practices in other organizational forms since the SSO's specific design characteristics may impact PMS design. The strong orientation of SSOs towards end-to-end processes means that the SSOs' PMS comprises performance measures of different operational functions. In addition, the number of multifunctional SSOs increases, which may impact PMS design, too (*Pragnall et al.* (2015), p. 23). The conventional use of SLAs in SSOs entails the necessity to continually monitor the defined performance standards. An often encountered legal and economic independence of SSOs may induce legal reporting requirements that affect PMS design. Finally, the emphasis on knowledge instead of manual work (*Carter* (1998)), a strong internal customer orientation, multicultural staffing, selective sourcing and the provision of services instead of products may influence not only the PMS design compared to other organizational forms, but also the performance measurement process. Even though these determinants of PMS design are occasionally addressed independently, their empirical results remain isolated. Hence, there is a need for additional research on the combination of those drivers associated with the SSO phenomenon. Therefore, this study contributes to overcome the fragmentation of empirical findings by synthesizing PMS design determinants in SSOs.

Second, the performance measurement **process** and performance measurement **actors** yet have not been subject to extended quantitative analyses. Whereas most contributions focus on the implementation phase of PMS, this study exploits a comprehensive framework of the performance measurement process and adds an extensive descriptive analysis of all process phases to extant literature. Moreover, current research neglects the significance of performance measurement actors for the design of PMS and its effectiveness. Following the promotor model presented in the fourth chapter, this study investigates their roles and responsibilities in SSOs.

Third, research on the **antecedents of PMS in SSOs** and its success is scarce. With regard to the level of analysis, this study distinguishes three types of contingency factors. Thus, the second research questions is addressed by analyzing SSO-specific factors (e.g. functional scope and legal independence), MNC-specific factors (e.g. product diversity) and environmental factors (competition intensity and perceived environmental uncertainty). With a view to PMS success, explanatory studies that operationalize performance measurement effectiveness through satisfaction measures do not address potential differences between the perceived PMS satisfaction of its users and its creators. Hence, a dyadic research design is applied to analyze performance measurement effectiveness.

Fourth, **MMRD have not been used** in both strands of research. Compared to a purely quantitative or qualitative research approach, a MMRD promises more comprehensive results by the triangulation of data obtained by two different research methods.

4 Theory and basic hypotheses development

4.1 Theoretical foundation

This chapter details the theoretical foundation for the empirical analyses. The following section 4.11 addresses the contingency theory as a conceptual framework and meta-theory. Based on the contingency framework, this chapter introduces new institutionalism (section 4.1.2) and the promotor model as the underlying theoretical basis for the hypotheses development (section 4.1.3). Many studies disregard a sound theoretical foundation although it is of significant importance to thoroughly derive testable hypotheses. Moreover, extant SSO literature does not support a comprehensive or unifying theoretical framework and instead adapts various theoretical assumptions from other areas of research, which seems typical for a nascent research stream. Particularly, many empirical studies on the antecedents of PMS do not substantiate the selection of their determinants on the basis of a theoretical model. Hence, this study's research objective is to yield a comprehensive understanding of PMS design in SSOs and to uncover contingency factors of PMS design and its impact on the SSO's effectiveness based on a sound theoretical foundation.

4.1.1 Contingency theory

The contingency theory originates from the **system theory**[23] that is applied in various academic disciplines (*Kast/Rosenzweig* (1972), p. 460). While former

---

23 As former organizational theories increasingly face deficiencies by investigating systems' isolated components, system theory research represents a promising means of mitigation by considering social organizations (e.g. MNCs) in their entirety in order to capture their complexity (*Wolf* (2013), pp. 164–165). General systems theory and cybernetics form the two main strands of modern system theory, whereby general systems theory focuses on (relatively) open systems (*Luhmann* (1983), p. 154). These are characterized by numerous relationships with its environment and plentiful connections inherent to the system. Although the application of the general system theory to PMS research initially appears plausible, it is associated with two major drawbacks. First, the general system theory takes the view that universal relations between contextual factors and the system are not identifiable (for instance, between SSO design characteristics and the PMS) (*Wolf* (2013), p. 192). The primacy of a system-specific versus a universal contingency implies that identified relationships between PMS and its contingency factors cannot be transferred to other MNCs (single case approach) (*Brose* (1984), p. 231). Second, the general system theory remains vague in the formulation of system

organizational theorists (*Heskett et al.* (1994); *Fayol* (1970); *Taylor* (2004); *Weber* (2002)) believe that universal principles pertain in all contexts and are valid for all MNCs, contingency theory recognizes MNCs as open systems whose design and success is influenced by environmental factors (*Sorge* (1991), p. 161).[24]

Hence, the contingency approach abandons the theory of an existing optimal design alternative for all systems, as *Otley* points out:

> *"The contingency approach to management accounting is based on the premise that there is no universally appropriate accounting system which applies equally to all organizations in all circumstances."*

> *(Otley (1980), p. 413)*

Contingency research has **three main objectives**. First, contingency-based studies address which contextual factors explain the existence and particularities of different system designs and discuss how the identified contextual factors are related to the system design (*Kieser/Kubicek* (1992), p. 63). Second, contingency research suggests how contextual factors and system designs can be operationalized (*Wolf* (2013), p. 203). Third, contingency-based analyses examine the extent to which differing system designs affect their system performance, respectively how varying system configurations differ in their success (*Wolf* (2013), pp. 203–204). The aforementioned research objectives illustrate that contingency research not only explores the design or configuration of a single system, but draws inferences about system configurations that are transferable at least to a certain system type (*Wolf* (2013), p. 213). Although contingency theory emanates from system theory, the transferability of single-case solutions highlights a considerable difference between both approaches (*Jenner* (2001), p. 79). In addition, system theorists conceive the system context holistically, while the contingency approach advocates for a dissection of distinct contextual layers (*Wolf* (2013), p. 213). However, both theories underpin the great importance of interrelations between the system and its environment and thus reject a fundamentally universalistic approach (*Jenner* (2001), p. 79). Hence, contingency theory represents a **compromise** between the single case and the universalistic approach, as shown in figure 4.1:

---

objectives due to its goal plurality, yet it frequently mentions system preservation as the most important objective of organizations (*Kast/Rosenzweig* (1972), p. 456). Hence, contingency theory represents an extension of general systems theory and serves as a more suitable alternative for the theoretical framework of this empirical investigation.

24 The contributions of *Stinchcombe* (1959), *Udy* (1959) and *Woodward* (1958) are regarded as groundbreaking for the rise of contingency theory.

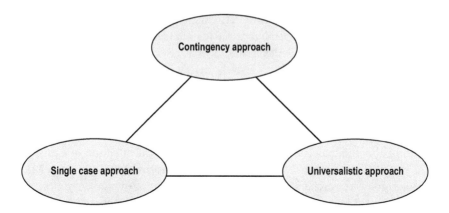

Figure 4.1: Single case, universalistic and contingency approach (adopted from *Hellriegel and Slocum* (2005), p. 6)

The popularity of the contingency approach can be attributed to its intuitive plausibility and to its suitability to **analyze the increasing complexity of organizations** whose environment is changing ever more rapidly (*Donaldson* (1999), pp. 51–52). In addition, contingency theory enables researchers to formulate hypotheses and to test them empirically (*Otley* (1980), p. 414). Thus, unresolved contradictory findings from universalistic research projects can be explained by contingency research.

Despite its widespread use, contingency theory remains **discussed controversially** (*Schoonhoven* (1981); *Tosi/Slocum* (1984)). The critique of the contingency approach can be divided into conceptual and methodological criticism. With regard to conceptual weaknesses, the contingency approach is criticized for not specifying which context variables have to be considered and how the relationships between contingency factors and systems can be modeled. Thus, contingency research entails a risk of bringing variables into relation without providing a substantial theoretical grounding (*Ulrich* (1993), p. 123). A missing conceptual strategy for the selection of potential determinants restricts the comparability of contingency-based studies. In essence, researchers doubt whether the contingency approach can be regarded as **a theory in a proper sense** (*Schmidt* (2013), p. 45).[25] Furthermore, researchers occasionally perceive the

---

25 The questionable integration of contingency theory into the existing spectrum also depends on the circumstance that the term *"theory"* is not unambiguously defined and varies due to differing ontological assumptions.

contingency approach as context-deterministic because contextual factors are generally described as independent variables, while the organizational design is operationalized as a dependent variable (*Schreyögg* (1978), p. 229). This suggests that organizational design is exclusively determined by its environment and decision-makers in organizations are incapable of influencing environmental factors. Hence, they are downscaled to mere transformers of the organizational design in a specific situation. In essence, actors are seldom involved in contingency-based research designs (*Child* (1972), pp. 8–10).

From a methodological point of view, researchers call attention to a missing link between contingency-based studies and prior research (*Wolf* (2013), p. 221). Furthermore, researchers are concerned that contingency theory scarcely provides recommendations for corporate practice due to the operationalization of complex environmental factors aggregated in a few items. On such a basis, empirical results are abstracted from reality and thus offer **barely exploitable interpretations** (*Kieser/Ebers* (2014), p. 232). Moreover, contingency-based empirical findings are often contradictory and only provide a snapshot (*Jenner* (2001), p. 82). Therefore, critics disapprove that contingency researchers scarcely conduct longitudinal studies so that situation changes and their causes are largely disregarded (*Wolf* (2013), pp. 227–228). The one-sided concentration on contingency-based cross-sectional studies leads to empirical results that are mostly based on past-oriented data. Context changes over time remain unconsidered and thus are marginally indicative for future developments. Furthermore, researchers complain that contingency research widely neglects interdependencies between contextual factors (*Jenner* (2001), p. 81). Although interaction effects between contextual factors are frequently expectable, various contingency-based studies elaborate on multicollinearity insufficiently. Many of these analyses assume a linear relationship between contingency factors and organizational design so that nonlinear relationships remain undetected (*Kieser/Ebers* (2014), p. 231). Finally, numerous contingency-based studies suffer from a small sample size which neither allows for extensive statistical analyses nor for generalizing empirical findings.

As a consequence of the aforementioned critique, this study applies contingency theory rather as a meta-theory (*Kieser* (1993), p. 75). Hence, this study stresses the consideration of contextual factors by using contingency theory as a conceptual framework for the hypothesis formulation, but embraces the necessity of additional substantial theories, namely new institutional sociology (NIS), principal agent theory and the promotor model. Figure 4.2 illustrates this study's basic model of the contingency approach. Figure 4.2 shows that performance measurements effectiveness depends on the fit between PMS design and its context.

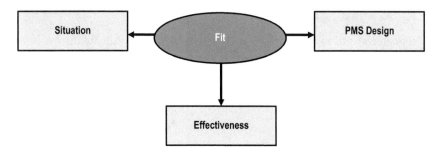

Figure 4.2: Application of the basic contingency model (adopted from *Wolf* (2011), p. 204)

The outlined critique offers **five implications** for the application of contingency theory as a conceptual framework for this study.

- First, this study counteracts the potential threat of a random contingency factor selection with a three-step model to specify potential determinants. Notably, potential determinants are derived in theory and additionally underpinned by the empirical findings of the exploratory study outlined in chapter six. This study distinguishes between (external) environmental factors, (internal) company-specific factors and (internal) SSO-specific characteristics.
- Second, the basic hypotheses detailed in section 4.2 are based on prior research and further substantial theories that are introduced in the following section. Moreover, chapter six refines the basic hypotheses by exploiting the empirical results of the qualitative study.
- Third, the research design allows for a context-open perspective by addressing performance measurement actor's room for discretion. As opposed to a context deterministic perspective, SSO managers and SSO management accountants are not only affected by their context but affect contingency factors as well, such as the PMS design. The research design reflects this basic assumption by examining a process-oriented perspective of performance measurement and the actors that are involved in the process.
- Fourth, the applied MMRD offers an enhanced interpretation of the empirical results by supplementing quantitative analyses with extensive explanations of the interviewed experts.
- Fifth, the triangulation of methods and data strengthens the obtained empirical evidence and may additionally lead to a complementation of quantitative and qualitative results. In case of contradictory results, triangulation can provide valuable insights into the causes.

4.1.2 New institutionalism

Although institutions represent the prevailing form to coordinate the behavior and coexistence of individuals in daily business practice, they illustrate only one of several alternatives since economic activities may also take place otherwise (*Coase* (1937), p. 390).

4.1.2.1 Institutionalism

Institutionalism[26] explains the emergence and structure of institutions as **surrogates for the coordination of economic activities** in deficient markets (*Picot/Fiedler* (2002), p. 242). Institutionalism seems not assignable to a single discipline of science but rather consists of numerous theoretical approaches borrowed from sociology, economics, organizational and political sciences (*Senge/Hellmann* (2006), p. 38). Hence, institutionalism subsumes heterogeneous perspectives under an umbrella term:

> "'Institutionalists vary in their relative emphasis on micro and macro features, in their weightings of cognitive and normative aspects of institutions, and in the importance they attribute to interests and relational networks in the creation and diffusion of institutions."
>
> (DiMaggio/Powell (1991), p. 1)

This study uses two essential institutionalist strands as its main theoretical foundation for hypotheses development: **new institutional economics (NIE) and new institutional sociology (NIS)**. Both institutional frameworks provide a valuable basis for the presumed influence of contingency factors on PMS and allow for general hypotheses about its effectiveness. Even though both institutional approaches are based on a strongly varying conceptualization of the term institution, they share a common epistemological ground (*Walgenbach/Meyer* (2008), pp. 152–153).[27] NIS and NIE investigate social and economic interdependencies and coordination problems of human interactions within established institutions (*Schmid/Maurer* (2003), p. 10). Thus, despite the differences in institutional understanding and the conceptualization of the involved actors' behavior, both approaches may complement each other.

---

26 The new institutionalism emerged in the seventies and is referred to as new because it expands classic institutionalism by various aspects. Classic institutionalism is greatly influenced by the works of *Selznick* (1953); *Selznick* (2011).

27 For a detailed discussion of the compatibility of NIS and NIE, see *Walgenbach* (2002), pp. 187–190.

Three institutional types

A cross-disciplinary definition of *Scott* describes institutions as *"multifaceted, durable social structures, made up of symbolic elements, social activities, and material resources"* (*Scott* (2014), p. 56). Due to its differing mechanism effects, *Scott* distinguishes three institutional types: **regulative, normative and cognitive-cultural institutions**. Regulative institutions influence the activities of institutional actors through formal and informal rules and laws that sanction or reward their behavior. Legitimacy is achieved by (legal) compliance so that institutional actors condition their law-abidance on expedience which is based on individual cost-benefit analyses (*Scott* (2014), pp. 59–62). Normative institutions are built on socially accepted and internalized values that enumerate desirable behavior and thus involve a social obligation for its actors. Institutionalized norms imply binding expectations for the actors to comply with the institutional value system which morally governs their behavior (*Scott* (2014), pp. 63–67). Cultural-cognitive institutions rest on the assumption that common beliefs and a shared logic of actions foster a constitutive pattern where institutional actors perceive their routinely performed activities as taken for granted. In contrast to normative institutions, actors in cultural-cognitive institutions are motivated intrinsically and not by moral pressure (*Scott* (2014), pp. 68–71). All of the three institutional types do not emerge in isolation, but may be interwoven within a single institution.

As *Scott's* conceptualization takes economic and social components of human interaction into consideration, it provides an eligible framework for both NIE and NIS. Apart from this broad understanding of human interaction, his institutional conceptualization is not limited to organizations, such as MNCs or SSOs, but captures established actors as well as their relationships and systems. The following section introduces NIE as the first pillar on which this study's theoretical framework rests.

4.1.2.2 New institutional economics

The term *new* institutional economics[28] originates from an extension of the antecedent neo-classical theories and explains the emergence, design and effectiveness of institutions (particularly firms) (*Held/Nutzinger* (2003), pp. 118–122). NIE does not describe a single theory but rather a collection of theoretical streams and can be subdivided into three major frameworks, namely: **property**

---

28 The term *new institutional economics* originates from *Williamson*, who originally used it only in connection with transaction cost theory, cf. *Williamson* (1983), p. 1.

rights, transaction cost, and agency theory (*Picot* (1991), p. 153).[29] The most important trigger for the development of NIE consists in the insufficiency of basic neoclassic assumptions to rationalize the emergence of institutions. In particular, institutionalists challenge the assumption that economic actors access unlimited information at all times and thus always make a rational choice in a perfect market (*Erlei et al.* (2016), pp. 46–47). In contrast to NIS, NIE focuses on the economic outcome instead of social legitimacy as the major equivalent for organizational performance (*Wolf* (2013), p. 335).

Foundation and basic assumptions

NIE relies on ten basic assumptions, of which the following four have been adopted from neoclassical theories (*Wolf* (2013), p. 336):

(1) scarcity of resources;
(2) methodological individualism;
(3) individual utility maximization; and
(4) stability of utility functions.

These four neoclassical propositions epitomize the rationally acting individual so that institutions are interpreted as arenas for efficient interactions between *homines oeconomici* (*Göbel* (2002), p. 49).[30] The following six additional basic assumptions extend the basic theoretical model of neoclassicism (*Wolf* (2013), p. 337):

(5) unequal distribution of information, knowledge, and capabilities;
(6) prevalent information structure;
(7) friction losses in economic processes;
(8) numerous interdependencies;
(9) rules regulating the possession and exchange of goods; and
(10) prevalence of institutions.

These six additional assumptions highlight that unlimited information for economic actors at all times is an illusion, whereas the **permanent existence of information asymmetries** rather approximates reality (*Williamson* (1990), pp. 50–53). An important part of the NIE represents the agency theory, which mainly addresses problems that arise in contractual relationships between a principal and an agent (*Eisenhardt* (1989a), p. 58). Since PMS represent an important

---

29 For a comprehensive analysis of all three theories, refer to *Richter/Furubotn* (2010).
30 For a detailed review of the *homo oeconomicus*, refer to *Erlei et al.* (2016), pp. 2–6.

instrument to mitigate information asymmetries between the two parties, agency theory illustrates an essential component of the hypotheses development.

Principal agent theory

Agency theory addresses design questions and emerging problems in contractual relations between a less informed party (principal) that entrusts a better informed party (agent) with an assignment (*Zeckhauser/Pratt* (1985), p. 2). The **delegation of discretionary competence** by the principal to an agent characterizes principal-agent relations. The agent is assigned to pursue the principal's objectives so that the principal's goal attainment is directly influenceable by the agent (*Meinhövel* (2004), pp. 470–471). There are a variety of principal-agent relationships observable in business practice, for example between SSO managers and SSO employees, parent company and subsidiaries, customers and suppliers or owners and managers, whereby the latter reflects the separation between ownership and control (*Ewert/Wagenhofer* (2014), pp. 357–359; *Fama/Jensen* (1983), p. 301).

Jensen and Meckling define an agency relationship as follows:

> "[…] a contract under which one or more persons (the principal(s)) engage another person (the agent) to perform some service on their behalf which involves delegating some decision making authority to the agent."
>
> (*Jensen/Meckling* (1976), p. 308)

The delegation of decision-making authority in principal-agent relationships is associated with **four premises**. First, the agent's decisions affect both the agent's and the principal's outcome (*Picot* (1991), p. 150). Second, the interests of the agent differ from those of the principal (*Schneider* (1995), pp. 48–49). For example, SSO employees may process orders with minimal effort because they know that the SSO's top management is incapable of permanently monitoring their behavior. Third, principal-agent relationships entail information asymmetries (*Shapiro* (2005), p. 264). Particularly, the principal fails to assess whether the agent's decision-making or exogenous events cause results (*Spremann* (1990), p. 572). Fourth, both sides act rationally only to a limited extent and their preference behavior stays firm over time (*Wolf* (2013), p. 364).

The information asymmetry between principal and agent shown in figure 4.3 may lead to an agent exploiting his information advantages and pursuing his own interests (*Hartmann-Wendels* (1989), pp. 716–718). This is always the case if both parties have partially conflicting objectives so that the agent has an incentive to act opportunistically (*Pfaff/Zweifel* (1998), p. 184). If there exists a state of perfect information, the principal immediately notices the agent's opportunistic behavior so that he leaves no room for discretion and thus agency problems do not emerge (*Meinhövel* (2005), pp. 67–68). The combination of existing information asymmetries and opportunistic behavior by the agent may cause **adverse selection and moral hazard**, which are referred to as major agency problems.

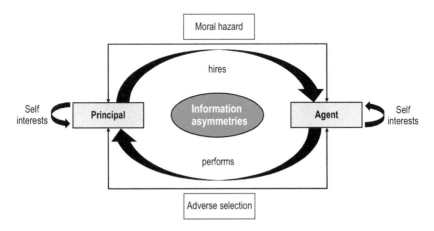

Figure 4.3: Basic principal-agent relationship (adopted from *Hagemann* (2016), p. 101)

Agency problems, agency costs and means of mitigation

Agency problems can be divided into **problems pre and post contract closing** (*Hart/ Holmstrom* (1989), p. 76). The principal is confronted with three types of agency problems: hidden characteristics, hidden action and hidden information[31] (*Küpper et al.* (2013), pp. 83–85).

Before contract conclusion, the principal is unable to assess the characteristics of the agent, for example the service quality offered by the agent. Due to the agent's **hidden characteristics**, the principal risks to select an agent offering services of poor quality (*Göbel* (2002), p. 101). Therefore, the principal is willing to pay only an average price, since he must assume an average quality (*Horsch*

---

31 The term hidden information seems somewhat misleading, because all of the three agency problems grow out of the principal's incomplete information basis, cf. *Göbel* (2002), p. 102.

(2005), p. 86). This triggers a mechanism called adverse selection,[32] whereby agents who offer an above-average service quality are forced to raid the market as they are not profitable when being paid with mean prices (*Akerlof* (1970), pp. 489–490). Adverse selection leaves the agents with an average or below-average service quality in the market, resulting in a continuously falling mean price. In the end, this mechanism provokes a market breakdown, as *Akerlof* illustrates with 'the market for lemons' (*Akerlof* (1970), pp. 495–496).

After contract conclusion, the principal is unable to monitor the agent's behavior or only at disproportionately high costs (*Göbel* (2002), p. 102). Although the principal is able to observe the outcome, he is uncertain about its formation so that the agent's performance is evaluable only to a limited extent (**hidden action**) (*Hartmann-Wendels* (1989), p. 714). Therefore, the agent has a chance to act opportunistically, for example, by deliberately slowing down (shirking) or consuming the principal's resources for private purposes (consumption on the job) (*Göbel* (2002), p. 102). Moreover, the principal encounters the difficulty of informational disadvantage with respect to the agent (**hidden information**) (*Arrow* (1984), p. 5). The agent may use his information advantage to maximize his benefits. As a result, the principal cannot assess the extent to which fringe benefits influence the agent's decision-making (*Göbel* (2002), p. 102). Hence, the agent may maximize his own benefit to the detriment of the principal. Agency problems after contract conclusion are referred to as **moral hazard** (*Richter/ Furubotn* (2010), p. 174).

Jensen and Meckling define costs that arise from agency problems as agency costs. They distinguish three cost components: **monitoring costs, bonding costs and residual loss** (*Jensen/Meckling* (1976), p. 308). The principal may monitor the agent's actions in order to minimize benefit losses through opportunistic behavior (*Göbel* (2002), p. 125). For instance, monitoring costs include incentive reimbursements and costs for the enforcement of guidelines and their compliance. Bonding costs arise if the agent reveals his actions by signaling that his behavior is in line with the principal's interest (*Jensen/Meckling* (1976), p. 308). A residual loss for the principal emerges in case of a deviation between the actual behavior of the agent and an action that maximizes the principal's benefit, while both sides invest the maximum possible in monitoring and

---

32 The term adverse selection was first established in relation to insurances as insurers are inadequately able to evaluate ex ante health risks of their policyholders. As this information asymmetry is anticipated by the policyholders, primarily high-risk individuals buy insurances leading to an unbalanced risk allocation. Cf. *Arrow* (1984), pp. 5–6.

transparency (*Meinhövel* (2005), p. 73). Agency costs represent the sum of all three components.

Since information asymmetries trigger agency costs, **potential solutions for agency problems** aim at reducing existing information asymmetries (*Göbel* (2002), p. 110). The negative consequences of information asymmetries can be reduced by creating incentives for agents to pursue the principal's objectives without exploiting the information advantage in favor of the agent. Table 4.1 supplements the previously described agency problems with potential solutions. Prior to contract conclusion, the principal may try to reveal the hidden characteristics of the available agents to minimize the risk of a wrong decision (*Alparslan* (2006), p. 29). Screening includes all activities that yield as much information as possible about the agent's characteristics (*Stiglitz* (1975), pp. 287–288). After contract conclusion the principal may monitor the agent' behavior (*Göbel* (2002), p. 112). For example, firms implement MCS to reduce information asymmetries between principal and agent. Particularly, MNCs use PMS to monitor existing agency relationships. The agent has an incentive to reduce information asymmetries as well, since he is interested in the realization of profitable agency relationships. Before contract conclusion, the agent may convincingly signal his characteristics to facilitate the principal's selection process (*Spence* (1973), p. 357). After contract conclusion, the agent may report his decision-making on a regular basis in order to transparently disclose his actions (*Breid* (1995), p. 824). In addition to the provision of voluntary information, reporting also includes the documentation of the agent's behavior (*Göbel* (2002), p. 113).

Table 4.1: Problems and potential solutions in principal-agent relationships (adopted from *Barth* (2009), p. 92; *Göbel* (2002), pp. 100 and 110)

Time of origin	Type of problem	Problem	Potential solutions	
			Principal	**Agent**
Before contract conclusion	Hidden characteristics	Adverse selection	Screening	Signaling
After contract conclusion	Hidden action	Moral hazard (e.g. shirking)	Monitoring	Reporting
	Hidden information	Moral hazard (e.g. fringe benefits)		

Performance measurement constitutes a potential means of mitigation for problems that emerge due to principal-agent relationships in SSOs. SSOs implement PMS to minimize agency problems pre and post contract conclusion.

Commonly, PMS are used after contract conclusion to monitor the agent's behavior. However, SSOs implement PMS in order to disclose its operating performance before contract conclusion, too. By disclosing performance measure reports before contract conclusion, the SSO signals its characteristics to avoid adverse selection by its customers. Hence, the existing agency relationships emerging in and around SSOs may affect PMS design in SSOs and will be specified in section 4.2.1.

4.1.2.3 New institutional sociology

Although NIE in general and the principle-agent theory in particular provide plausible explanations for the behavior of rationally acting *homines oeconomici*, they describe only a facet of human interaction, thereby mostly disregarding that human behavior comprises social and moral facets, too (*Schmid/Maurer* (2003), p. 21). In order to cover this blind spot of NIE, NIS supplements the theoretical basis of this study for the subsequent hypothesis development.

Foundation and basic assumption

The central assumption of NIS states that institutional players adapt their behavior according to the expectations of their social environment in order to gain legitimacy (*Meyer/Rowan* (1977), p. 340). Thus, NIS considers that organizations are not exclusively determined by technical and market driven rationality, but are also **striving for social legitimacy** on a larger scale (*Granlund/Lukka* (1998), pp. 156–157). Similar to NIE, NIS does not refer to a single theory, but also consists of several theoretical streams that complement each other (*Scott* (2014), p. 37). Albeit NIE and NIS share the same research interest by investigating institutions, NIS is characterized by a much broader concept of institutions (*Wolf* (2013), p. 531). In contrast to NIE, the institutional concept promoted in the NIS encompasses all actors established within an organizational field and their defined explicit and implicit rules, standards and patterns (*Mayntz/Scharpf* (1995), pp. 41–42). While NIE theories highlight the bartering of institutional actors and the resulting transaction costs, NIS addresses the questions why organizations act according to societal beliefs and how societal norms and values influence the design of institutions and their outcomes (*Steen* (2006), pp. 6–7).

Meyer and Rowan introduce the notion of existing **institutional myths** to explain an actor's behavior which is not guided by rational choice (*Meyer/Rowan* (1977), p. 341). They observed that institutional actors frequently ground their formal and informal rules on circulating narratives about unverified cause-effect relationships (*Meyer/Rowan* (1977), pp. 343–344). By seizing, imitating, and internalizing these myths, organizations foster their institutionalization within an organizational field (*Hasse/Krücken* (2015), pp. 22–23). The more myths become institutionalized within an organizational field, the more they epitomize a societal expectation, which institutional actors must comply with in order to maintain social legitimacy (*Meyer/Rowan* (1977), pp. 352–353). A societal expectation-compliant behavior of institutions improves their survival prospects and promises more stability compared to an organization striving exclusively for economic efficiency (*Meyer/Rowan* (1977), p. 340). Actors manifest institutionalized structures of societal expectation to legitimate their behavior through an existing set of rules (*Wolf* (2013), p. 542). Institutional players primarily ensure the stability of their organizations by recurrently drawing on rules and routines (*Zucker* (1983), p. 7). Rules serve as a standardized technique for actors to cope with a task. Moreover, rules serve as an instrument that allows institutional actors to estimate the likelihood of a particular behavior (*DiMaggio/Powell* (1991), p. 18). Hence, the institutional approach emphasizes the **influence of standardized procedures on institutional interaction and design** expressed in routines or SOPs (*Meyer/Rowan* (1977), p. 346).

DiMaggio and Powell build on the above assumptions by concluding that institutions embedded in the same organizational field become isomorphic over time:

> "We ask, instead, why there is such startling homogeneity of organizational forms and practices; and we seek to explain homogeneity, not variation. In the initial stages of their life cycle, organizational fields display considerable diversity in approach and form. Once a field becomes well established, however, there is an inexorable push towards homogenization."
>
> (DiMaggio/Powell (1983), p. 148)

Institutional isomorphism

Organizational fields are composed of institutions that are exposed to similar conditions and societal expectations (*Hasse/Krücken* (2015), p. 25). For example, firms operate in a similar context if they face similar competitive conditions, belong to the same industry or are subject to the same regulatory authorities. *DiMaggio and Powell* assume that firms with a similar contextual setting interact more frequently compared to firms from distinct organizational fields (*DiMaggio/Powell* (1983), p. 148). For instance, their employees meet at joint workshops, roundtables and share the same customers and suppliers. As a result, these institutions apply similar strategies and create comparable organizational structures to cope with environmental uncertainty

(*Tolbert/Zucker* (1996), p. 183). *DiMaggio and Powell* describe this process as **institutional isomorphism** and distinguish three mechanisms for its emergence: coercive, mimetic and normative isomorphism (*DiMaggio/Powell* (1983), p. 150).

Coercive isomorphism is based on peer pressure expressed by standards, regulations, laws etc. in the same organizational field (*Wolf* (2013), p. 554). For example, subsidiaries may be forced to adopt the methods, systems and procedures favored by its parent company. Mimetic isomorphism is characterized by a high degree of environmental uncertainty and describes the imitation of behavioral patterns (*Hasse/Krücken* (2015), p. 26). Firms react to uncertainties associated with organizational change by copying standardized behavior patterns from institutions in their organizational field as they are cost-effective and associated with little risk (*DiMaggio/Powell* (1983), p. 151). The transfer of organizational structures and systems from (supposedly) successful competitors illustrates a typical example in corporate practice. Normative isomorphism describes the behavioral assimilation through the influence of educational institutions and professional networks (*Hasse/Krücken* (2015), pp. 26–27). Normative isomorphism differs from coercive pressures by an inferior enforcement, while it differs from mimetic pressures by professionalization (*Wolf* (2013), p. 555). Professionalization is interpreted as the collective effort of an occupational group to define the conditions and methods of their work which constitutes necessary legitimation for their occupational autonomy (*DiMaggio/Powell* (1983), p. 152).

NIS constitutes an important theoretical basis for the analysis of PMS design in SSOs, since performance measurement in SSOs may be subject to isomorphism. NIS stresses that institutional actors, such as SSO management accountants, have an incentive to comply with organizational structures and the existing set of rules and routines in order to fulfill societal expectations (*Meyer/Rowan* (1977), p. 340). Therefore, institutional actors may become isomorphic over time to cope with the set of rules and routines prescribed by the organizational structure of its institution (*DiMaggio/Powell* (1983), p. 150). PMS design in SSOs is subject to isomorphism since the SSOs are constantly forced to adopt methods, systems, and procedures from its MNCs. Moreover, a regular exchange among SSOs at roundtables, SSO conferences or SSO-specialized management consultancies may assert pressure on SSOs to mimic the PMS designs of their peer group. Furthermore, *DiMaggio and Powell* state that institutions become isomorphic over time to cope with uncertainty (*DiMaggio/Powell* (1983), p. 150). In essence, NIS provides possible explanations for the influence of potential contextual factors on PMS design in SSOs.

4.1.3 Promotor model

The fundamental concept of the promotor[33] model emanates from the much-noticed contribution by *Witte* and addresses the research question as to which institutional actors exert influence on innovation success of organizations or systems (*Witte* (1973), pp. 4–5). Al-though the promotor model originates from innovation research, by now various business-related research domains analyze the institutional actor's involvement in organizational development by using *Witte's* model (*Gemünden* (1985); *Gemünden et al.* (2006); *Hauschildt/ Kirchmann* (1997); *Klöter* (1997); *Rost et al.* (2007); *Walter* (2013); *Walter/ Gemünden* (2013)). Instead of concentrating exclusively on the result of a development, the promotor model takes a **process perspective** to examine the contribution of individual actors during the development process (*Witte* (2013), p. 12).

The advancement of systems depends, among other factors, on the institutional actors' willingness to enforce necessary changes and their abilities to participate in the decision-making process leading to change (*Witte* (1973), p. 6). As system innovations usually involve multiple actors and activities, this complex decision-making process is characterized by the existence of personnel and technical barriers (*Rost et al.* (2007), p. 341). Therefore, *Witte* distinguishes **barriers of unwillingness and barriers of ignorance** (*Witte* (1973), pp. 6–9).

Barriers of unwillingness emphasize the persistence of the status quo. Institutional actors perceive their current conditions as known and familiar so that both the behavior of actors and the system configurations seem calculable (*Witte* (2013), p. 13). The uncertainty about future conditions which is associated with a successful enforcement of innovations fosters the desire to maintain the status quo (*Witte* (1977), p. 50). However, barriers of unwillingness describe not only the actors' passivity driven by the hope of preserving the status quo, but also their intention to actively hamper the decision-making process (*Hauschildt/ Schewe* (2000), p. 97). This may happen under the prerequisite of limited resources if a system innovation competes for resources with another innovation project (*Witte* (1973), p. 7).

Barriers of ignorance characterize the perceived uncertainty about new objectives, operating procedures, rules and alternative measures that are closely

---

33 The terms "champion" and "gatekeeper" are sometimes used synonymously for the term "promotor". However, the champion and the gatekeeper model have been developed independently from *Witte's* promotor model. For a detailed analysis of the gatekeeper model refer to *Allen* (1970). For a discussion on the champion model refer to *Chakrabarti* (1974); *Howell/Higgins* (1990); *Schon* (1963).

related to innovations (*Witte* (2013), p. 14). Innovations presuppose that institutional actors are capable of identifying novel coherences, for instance to develop new performance measures or targets. Therefore, innovations force institutional actors to elevate existing expertise (*Witte* (1977), p. 52). If their expertise is insufficiently developed to participate in system innovation, actors consequently interfere innovations in order to maintain the well-known system (*Rost et al.* (2007), pp. 341–342).

The described types of resistance may be overcome by enthusiastic individuals, who are called promotors. *Witte* defines promotors[34] as:

> *"…individuals who actively and intensively support the innovation process."*
>
> *(Witte (1973), pp. 15–16)*

According to the defined barriers, he identifies two promotor types, namely **the power promotor and the know-how promotor** (*Witte et al.* (1989), p. 151). Power promotors actively foster an innovation process through hierarchical power and the provision of resources (*Witte* (1973), p. 17). His hierarchical position allows the power promotor to impose sanctions on opponents and to shield innovation facilitators (*Rost et al.* (2007), pp. 342–343). Therefore, an authentic power potential seems sufficient without having to use it regularly (*Witte* (1973), p. 17). The power promotor primarily helps to overcome barriers of unwillingness (*Hauschildt* (2001), p. 332). Moreover, organizations need know-how promotors to overcome barriers of ignorance (*Rost et al.* (2007), p. 343). Know-how promotors support innovation processes through their specific expertise, without their hierarchical position being relevant (*Witte et al.* (1989), p. 152). Through their expertise, these individuals contribute to make the most effective use of an innovation by recognizing emerging problems and detecting possible solutions (*Witte* (1973), p. 18). Notably, expertise is not restricted to a single institutional actor, but may rather be provided by several actors from various organizational areas. The promotor model challenges the assumption that a single key person decisively drives the successful outcome of an innovation process (*Folkerts/ Hauschildt* (2002), p. 8). In contrast to the champion model, it introduces a distribution of promotor roles which highlight a necessary labor division for a successful innovation process (*Hauschildt/Schewe* (2000), p. 97).

---

34 *Witte* consciously avoids the notation promoter to prevent the misconception that his definition is restricted to the sponsorship of an individual or object (*Witte* (1973), p. 16).

Hauschildt and Chakrabarti expand *Witte's* dyadic promotor model into a troika by adding a **process promotor** (*Hauschildt/Chakrabarti* (2013), p. 67 ff.). Process promotors are required to overcome administrative barriers (e.g. non-responsibility and indifference) that become apparent with a growing organizational and innovation project complexity (*Hauschildt* (2001), p. 332). Process promotors break down administrative barriers relying on their organizational knowledge and establish a link between power and know-how promotors (*Hauschildt/Kirchmann* (2001), p. 44). Process promotors avoid isolated strategies for solving problems and are instead in close contact with both the institutional actors involved in the innovation process and with the actors affected by the innovation (*Rost et al.* (2007), p. 344). Their diplomatic skills enable them to act as interpreters who translate technical vocabulary into business language and vice versa (*Hauschildt/Chakrabarti* (2013), p. 78). Hence, process promotors coordinate the innovation process (*Hauschildt/Kirchmann* (2013), p. 93). Furthermore, *Gemünden et al.* introduce **relationship promotors** who overcome dependency barriers that are caused by an asymmetric balance of power between institutional actors. Relationship promotors are characterized by their networking competencies and thus are able to maintain powerful relationships within the organization and to external parties (*Gemünden et al.* (2007), p. 409). They break bottlenecks for the necessary knowledge transfer and build reliable relationships between previously unknown institutional actors (*Rost et al.* (2007), p. 344).

Notably, the four introduced promotor types are not necessarily distributed among four institutional actors. A single actor may embody several promotors and a single promotor type may be exercised by several actors. Figure 4.4 summarizes the promotor model and section 4.1.3 applies the described promotor model to PMS design in SSOs.

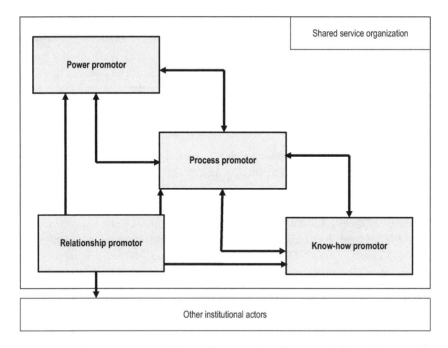

Figure 4.4: The promotor model (own illustration based on *Hauschildt/Kirchmann* (2001), p. 42)

4.1.4 Summary

The nascent SSO research stream does not provide a unifying framework for the empirical analysis of its management control practices. Thus, the following section integrates the outlined theoretical perspectives into **an overriding theoretical framework** in order to derive hypotheses that explain PMS design and its consequences on PMS effectiveness. This study draws on a contingency framework by stressing the importance of contextual factors that determine PMS design in SSOs. PMS are perceived as systems whose design and success depends on its environment so that an optimal design alternative for each contextual setting seems non-existent. Due to its lack of analytical specificity, the study at hand supplements the contingency framework with three further basic theories, which allow for the identification of potential influencing factors and their subsequent testing.

The first two theoretical pillars are based on the **new institutionalism**, thus emphasizing the institutional context in which PMS are designed. Although the two introduced institutional strands NIE and NIS show considerable differences, both are based on institutionalism and therefore compatible with each other. NIE and in particular the outlined principal-agent theory highlight the individual utility maximization based on rational decision logic as the major driver for human interaction. NIS stresses the primordial need for social legitimacy. The subsequent hypotheses development applies both theories to substantiate the selection of relevant contingency factors that surround PMS design in SSOs.

This study considers PMS as a possible means of mitigation for arising information asymmetries between a principal and an agent. The multitude and nature of existing agency relationships indicates an influence on PMS design. Hence, the following section applies **agency theory** to derive hypotheses that investigate the impact of internal contextual factors emerging from agency relationships on the SSO's PMS design. For clarity, this study subdivides internal contingency factors into SSO-specific and MNC-specific contextual factors. Moreover, agency theory allows for the formulation of hypotheses on the effects of PMS design in SSOs. With regard to the limited explanatory power of NIE, this study uses **NIS** to identify additional contextual factors. Since SSOs are exposed to the MNC's expectations, institutional isomorphism may influence performance measurement practices in SSOs. Furthermore, NIS states that isomorphism describes a promising strategy of institutions to cope with environmental uncertainty. Hence, the study at hand uses NIS to develop hypotheses that comprise a broader set of internal and external contextual factors.

The third theoretical pillar constitutes the **promotor model** which has been introduced to shed light on PMS design in SSOs from a process perspective. The promotor model is applied to investigate whether the previously detailed promotor structures are identifiable within the performance measurement process in SSOs. Since promotors appear in the context of institutions, the promotor model seems consistent with the institutional view. The three theoretical pillars are neither independent nor mutually exclusive.

4.2 Basic hypotheses development

This section develops the basic hypotheses for the subsequent empirical analyses. The basic hypotheses derived from this study's theoretical framework are refined with the empirical results of the qualitative study and tested in the subsequent quantitative study. The hypotheses postulated in the following represent alternative hypotheses and form the counterpart to null hypotheses, which negate the postulated effect (*Auer* (2016), pp. 107–108). The empirical testing aims to reject the null hypotheses and to keep the alternative hypotheses. The basic hypotheses are formulated **non-directional**, whereas the hypotheses refinement as a result of the qualitative study allows for the formulation of directed hypotheses. Each hypothesis is assigned to at least one research question. Since the first research question focuses on the status quo of the PMS design in SSOs, it provides purely descriptive evidence. Instead, the hypotheses are linked to the second and third research question. While the second research question attempts to ascertain determinants that influence PMS design in SSOs, the third research question addresses associations between PMS design and PMS effectiveness.

4.2.1 Determinants of PMS design in SSOs

The gained insights provided by **NIS allow for three important implications** for the hypotheses development of this study. First, institutionalists assume that institutional isomorphism illustrates a strategy to cope with perceived environmental uncertainty. Therefore, PMS design in SSOs may also be determined by external contextual factors within an organizational field, such as the perceived competitive environment. In essence, NIS allows for the development and testing of hypotheses that entail a broader set of potential contextual factors influencing PMS design. Thus, it is expected that:

H_{1a}: *There is an association between the external context and PMS design in SSOs.*

Second, SSOs are usually exposed to the MNC's expectations so that SSO managers have an incentive to legitimate their actions complying with the MNC's formal and informal procedures. Therefore, existing systems, methods and the organizational structure at corporate level may impact the SSO's PMS design. For instance, there is little chance that SSOs implement MIS and MCS regardless of the MNC's existing system landscape, even though an independently designed MIS or MCS would be more advantageous at SSO level. Third, NIS highlights the importance of standardized processes, routines and patterns for the emergence of institutional isomorphism. The standardization of processes and SOPs plays an important role in SSOs. Thus, the degree of process standardization and standardized behavioral patterns of SSO employees may affect PMS design. Hence, it is hypothesized that:

H_{1b}: *There is an association between the MNC context and PMS design in SSOs.*

As outlined in the previous sections, agency relationships may determine PMS design in SSOs. In general, five main principal-agent relationships are derivable from agency theory, in which SSOs use performance measurement as a method to reduce information asymmetries between the two parties (figure 4.5).

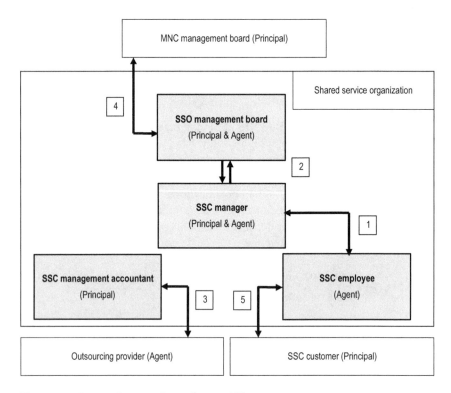

Figure 4.5: Principal-agent relationships in SSOs.

First, the relationship between SSO managers and their employees constitutes a principal-agent setting. The objectives of SSO employees may conflict with the SSO's objectives so that employees follow their own agenda, for instance by reducing their effort. Therefore, a PMS reduces the risk of moral hazard by measuring the SSO employee's performance, such as the number of processed transactions per employee. Thus, SSO managers quickly detect performance differences among SSO employees. Hence, PMS design may differ, for example, due to the number of SSO employees or due to their geographic dispersion.

A second form of a principal-agent relationship exists between the SSO management board and the management of the subordinated SSCs. Again, performance measurement is required to monitor the decision-making of the SSC's management to harmonize diverging objectives. Therefore, the number of SSCs within a SSO may have an influence on PMS design.

Third, SSOs may act as a buyer of external services, particularly if subprocesses are transferred to an outsourcing provider. Commonly, performance measures are institutionalized in SLAs between the SSO and the outsourcing provider. Therefore, the SSO's PMS is supposed to monitor the performance measures agreed with the outsourcing provider in the SLA. By using the SSO's PMS, the SSO management accounting is able to assess whether the agreed service levels are met by the outsourcing partner.

Fourth, the SSO management board acts not only from a principal's perspective, but also appears as an agent. Regardless of whether SSOs are designed legally independent, the SSO management board is expected to account for their actions to the MNC's group management board, analogous to a subsidiary's role. Therefore, SSOs use their PMS to inform the MNC's group management about recent developments. A comprehensive reporting, based on the SSO's PMS enables the SSO management board to convincingly assure the group management board that the SSO is acting in line with the MNC's expectations. Hence, the composition of the group management board and the support given by the MNC's top management, may impact PMS design in SSOs.

Fifth, the SSO acts on behalf of its (internal) customers so that reporting represents an effective means to reduce information asymmetries. Prior to contract conclusion, the SSO employees may signal the SSO's characteristics to potential customers, such as the offered service quality and price developments by using its PMS. Even in case of an obligation to contract signaling illustrates a meaningful measure to initiate a customer-supplier relationship, since a transparent disclosure of the SSO's characteristics reduces a subsidiary's resistance to transfer support processes to the SSO at an early stage. Hence, the SSO customers' requirements may influence PMS design. In essence, PMS design and its complexity is owed to the number and nature of the existing principal-agent relationships within the SSO and thus contributes to the solution of multiple agency problems.

The number of potential agency relationships in SSOs does not allow for a directional hypothesis. However, the literature reviewed in chapter three suggests that effects on the PMS design resulting from agency relationships in SSOs are detectable. Therefore, this study aims at testing the following non-directional hypothesis:

H_{1c}:   *There is an association between SSO design characteristics and PMS design in SSOs.*

The **promotor model offers explanatory perspectives** for the existence of promotors in the performance measurement process in SSOs. The necessity of financial and human resources to implement and maintain a PMS suggests the existence of a **power promotor** who is able to provide resources. The performance measurement process is associated with various actors so that hierarchical enforcement is essential for the required contribution by each party. SSOs commonly engage in a variety of support processes of different operational functions and encounter a globally dispersed customer base with heterogeneous requirements. This heterogeneity is reflected in the PMS so that the purposeful selection of performance measures and their evaluation demands a high degree of expertise. Therefore, SSOs may involve **know-how promotors** to enable a meaningful performance measurement. The prevailing complexity in SSOs suggests that **process promotors** are of significant importance to practice and enhance performance measurement. The number of potential actors involved indicates an enormous coordination effort. Moreover, a well-functioning PMS depends on the existing connections between the SSO and its environment. The SSO's relationship to the parent company's top management and to the group controlling may be important PMS design in SSOs. Relationships to various organizational units, such as the sales and the procurement organization of MNCs, external service providers as well as to SSO customers are equally crucial to assert a continuous improvement of performance measurement in SSOs. Hence, it is stated that:

H_{1d}:   *There is an association between promotors and PMS design in SSOs.*

4.2.2 Effectiveness of PMS design in SSOs

Performance measurement is considered to be effective when it achieves the objectives that have been set before its implementation. However, SSOs pursue **varying objectives** with their PMS. An effective PMS design contributes to achieve the SSO's objectives and is able to reduce information asymmetries between the participating actors. Depending on the context, institutional actors may appear as agents or principals. Due to the multitude of existing principal agent relationships, the effectiveness of the SSO's PMS depends on its capability to reduce information asymmetries among the performance measurement actors. Nevertheless, it is ambiguous whether a certain PMS design is associated with a higher degree of effectiveness, since a more complex PMS design does not necessarily has to be more effective. Hence, it is expected that:

H_2:   *There is an association between PMS design in SSOs and its effectiveness.*

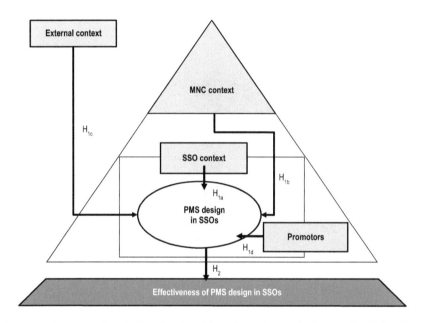

Figure 4.6: summarizes the five developed basic hypotheses which are refined after the case study analyses.

5 Research design

This chapter introduces qualitative case study research as one of the two research methodologies used in this study's research design. Moreover, this chapter provides an overview of quantitative survey research as the second methodology applied in this study. Furthermore, it integrates both research methodologies into this study's mixed methods research design (MMRD).

5.1 Qualitative case study research

Qualitative case study research denotes the **predominantly used methodology in SSO research**, which underpins its exploratory nature and the generally growing popularity of qualitative research designs (*Richter/Brühl* (2016), p. 7). The inadequacies of quantitative research and the accompanying criticism of a quantitative primacy in social sciences revealed the necessity of a methodological alternative (*Flick* (2014a), pp. 12–13). Based on symbolic interactionism and ethnomethodology, qualitative research focuses on the interpretation of social interaction in order to alleviate the divide between theory and perceptible social reality (*Mayring* (2016), p. 10). *Flick* points out:

> "Qualitative research is oriented towards analyzing concrete cases in their temporal and local particularity and starting from peoples expressions and activities in their local contexts."

(Flick (2014a), p. 21)

In order to counter the criticism that qualitative research does not meet scientific criteria, qualitative researchers agree on a number of basic principles for the analysis and interpretation of concrete cases.

Basic principles of qualitative research

Various representatives of qualitative research programs unveiled essential principles of qualitative research (e.g. *Corbin et al.* (2014); *Flick* (2014a); *Lamnek* (2005); *Mayring* (2016); *Wrona* (2005)). The following eight characteristics may be supplemented by other criteria and are thus not exhaustive. Nevertheless, they constitute **a common thread** for the multitude of varying qualitative research designs:

(1) openness;
(2) contextuality;

(3) totality;
(4) interpretative paradigm;
(5) reflexivity of the researcher and the research;
(6) appropriateness of methods and theories;
(7) circularity of the research process;
(8) intersubjective traceability.

The principle of **openness** emphasizes the interpreting character of qualitative research (*Mayring* (2016), pp. 27–28). Openness with a view to the object of the investigation, the investigation situation and the available research methods intends to counteract the information-reducing selection of standardized data collection techniques (*Lamnek* (2005), p. 21). Whereas quantitative research aims to test hypotheses, qualitative research also strives for its generation and refinement. Therefore, this study interviews SSO managers and SSO management accountants to generate and refine hypotheses that are tested in the subsequent quantitative study. Another feature of qualitative methodology stresses the **contextual dependence** of social interaction. Qualitative research attempts to grasp the entire complexity of the research object by being mindful of existing relationships between the research object and its context (*Wrona* (2005), p. 4). The basic principle of contextual dependence is in line with this study's second research question on determinants of PMS design in SSOs and corresponds to the underlying contingency framework. **Totality** points out that an isolated analysis of individual aspects without making references to the research object as a whole is a risky endeavor. The analytical separation into individual variables is indeed meaningful, but requires a reconciliation and interpretation in the overall context (*Mayring* (2016), p. 33). During the analysis of the empirical results, it is thus important that this study analyzes the case in its totality (within case analysis) and the individual components of PMS design in SSOs which are compared across the available cases (cross-case analysis). Qualitative research is based on the epistemological stance that reality is not directly observable, but has to be interpreted by the researcher (*Wrona* (2005), p. 4). Hence, the **interpretive paradigm** of qualitative research alleges to analyze phenomena in a more sophisticated way compared to quantitative research programs (*Kromrey* (2013), p. 529).

Qualitative research does not deem the interaction between the researcher and the research object as an intervening variable, but rather conceives it as an opportunity to grasp a better understanding (*Flick* (2014a), p. 16). Therefore, the researchers' and the subjects' **reflections** on their interaction become fruitful findings of qualitative research (*Mayring* (2016), p. 32). The **appropriateness of methods and theories** is another central characteristic of qualitative research. The object under investigation determines the selection and evaluation of the methodology and not vice versa (*Flick* (2014a), p. 15). Thus, it seems necessary to individually adjust the research design to the research object. Appropriateness also implies methodological rigor, for instance through a thorough documentation of the research process (*Mayring* (2016), p. 29). While quantitative research presents a linear sequence in the research process, qualitative research highlights a **circular approach** by closely meshing data collection and analysis (*Wrona* (2005), pp. 13–14). **Intersubjective traceability** refers to the aspiration of researchers to disclose the individual steps of the investigation process (*Lamnek* (2005), p. 24). Only in this way empirical evidence is comparable among researchers.

This study uses the empirical results of the qualitative study for **four purposes**. First, the empirical results of the conducted case study research serve to explore all relevant dimensions of PMS design in SSOs. The analysis of the case studies elaborates on the important aspects of performance measurement and unveils its essential contextual conditions (*Creswell et al.* (2007), p. 245). Second, qualitative results are used to refine the basic hypotheses outlined in chapter four. Third, the case study analysis provides valuable support for the operationalization of the quantitative research design (*Lamnek* (2005), pp. 306–307). For example, the qualitatively gained insights facilitate the quantitative operationalization of theoretical concepts in an appropriate manner so that inquirer and respondent have a congruent understanding. Fourth, this study uses the case study findings to illustrate, deepen and expand the quantitatively yielded empirical evidence (*Lamnek* (2005), pp. 307–308).

Case study research

Case studies approach 'real-life phenomena' in depth (*Flyvbjerg* (2006), p. 235). Case study research is based on the assumption that contextual conditions are inseparably contingent upon the investigated phenomenon and research designs should therefore encompass the phenomenon and its context (*Eisenhardt/Graebner* (2007), p. 25). Hence, *Yin* defines case studies as follows:

> "A case study is an empirical inquiry that investigates a contemporary phenomenon in depth and within its real-life context, especially when the boundaries between phenomenon and context are not clearly evident."

> (*Yin* (2013), p. 18)

Case studies are primarily suitable in nascent research streams in which the research objectives are not yet clearly identified and the data required to formulate hypotheses have not yet been obtained, such as PMS design in SSOs (*Eisenhardt* (1989b), pp. 547–548). Case study research describes not only a data collection technique, but also comprises the necessity to review existing theoretical frameworks, the design logic and the data analysis (*Lamnek* (2005), pp. 298–299). Case studies are based on several sources of knowledge so that data obtained from different sources can be triangulated (*Stake* (2011), pp. 443–444). Case study research can be subdivided into **exploratory, descriptive or explanatory case studies** (*Yin* (2011), p. 5). Exploratory case studies attempt to refine the research questions and hypotheses for a subsequent study and improve the subsequently used research method (*Scapens* (1990), p. 265). While descriptive case studies interpret the analyzed phenomenon comprehensively in its context, explanatory case studies pursue the detection of possible cause-and-effect relationships (*Yin* (2011), p. 5). All three case study research dimensions allow for several case study designs.

As shown in figure 5.1, *Yin* defines **four basic case study research designs** (*Yin* (2013), p. 46). The dotted lines between the case and its context emphasize the imperative to analyze the case in connection with its environmental conditions. Researchers apply single case designs particularly if they suspect a critical or unique case (*Scapens* (1990), p. 273).

A critical case is capable of seriously testing an existing theory in order to confirm, expand, or challenge it (*Yin* (2013), p. 47). Another rationale for single case designs is to describe typical cases that occur on a regular basis and thus may be representative for a certain group of research objects (*Scapens* (1990), p. 272). Revelatory cases are usually investigated in single case designs, since the studied phenomenon is not or only scarcely accessible to science so that even a single case promises rich empirical findings (*Yin* (2013), pp. 48–49). Moreover, qualitative research applies single case study designs in longitudinal studies to analyze changes over time (*Yin* (2013), p. 49). Whereas single-case designs entail the risk of turning out to represent something different than initially expected, multiple-case designs offer greater robustness because they allow for the literal or theoretical replication of empirical evidence (*Yin* (2013), p. 54). Both the duplication of findings by using a different case (literal replication) and contrasting results between cases due to altered treatments under control of the researcher (theoretical replication) strengthen the robustness of the empirical analysis (*Borchardt/ Göthlich* (2009), pp. 36–37).

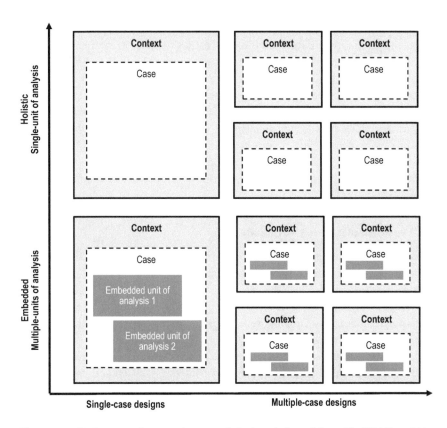

Figure 5.1: Basic types of case study research designs (adopted from *Yin* (2013), p. 46.)

The necessary number of cases depends on the existence and strength of alternative explanations challenging the yielded empirical findings (*Yin* (2013), p. 58). Apart from the fragmentation into single-case and multiple-case designs, *Yin* distinguishes holistic and embedded case study designs (*Yin* (2013), p. 50). In contrast to holistic case designs, embedded designs involve more than one unit of analysis, e.g. different actors within a single organizational unit. Holistic case designs are usually applied if logical subunits are not identifiable.

As opposed to the quantitative part, the qualitative study intends to explore the PMS design in SSOs rather than testing existing theories or hypotheses. In accordance with the four outlined objectives of the qualitative research design, this study can be assigned to the **exploratory case study research**. As such, the qualitative part of this mixed method study exploits an embedded multiple-case design since there are no indications for a unique or revelatory setting. By contrast, the exploratory nature of this qualitative study is accompanied by the necessity to validate gained insights by its replication through additional cases. Furthermore, this study analyzes PMS design in SSOs on two different levels. In order to capture diverging facets of performance measurement, this study collects and analyzes data from both SSO managers and SSO management accountants. The subsequent quantitative part also reflects these two units of analysis by applying a dyadic questionnaire design. Consistent to the contingency framework outlined in chapter four, the applied multiple-case design devotes particular attention to the context in which performance measurement takes place.

5.2 Quantitative survey research

Quantitative social science research stands in the tradition of natural sciences and primarily uses structured, standardized data collection techniques, resulting in numerically measured values that are subject to statistical analyses (*Döring/Bortz* (2016), p. 14). In contrast to the qualitative paradigm, quantitative research strategies apply sequentially structured research processes in order to **test theoretically derived hypotheses**. A sequential research approach implies that standardized instruments, such as a survey, do not change during the data collection. In addition to the survey research presented below, experimental research and psychometric tests are referred to as the most important quantitative methodologies (*Döring/ Bortz* (2016), p. 15). As opposed to verbal descriptions, which are mainly used in qualitative techniques, quantitative methods assign attributes to numerical values (*Riesenhuber* (2009), p. 7). Therefore, quantitative data are processed considerably easier compared to qualitative data so that quantitative research usually draws on large, preferably representative samples. Hence, a substantial advantage of quantitative research strategies consists in the generalizability of empirical results for the sample's basic population. Quantitative research broadly wipes out the researcher's subjectivity and considers interactions between the researcher and the object under investigation as noise. The quantitative research approach aims at the ongoing development of existing theories (*Stein* (2014), p. 136).

Survey research

Questionnaires are the most frequently used research method in quantitative research (*Döring/Bortz* (2016), p. 398). *Birnberg et al.* define survey research as a methodology that *"employs a standardized approach in order to collect information from sampling units to make inferences about the population"* (Birnberg *et al.* (1990), p. 35).[35] Survey research collects verbal and numerical self-reports from participants in written form. The distribution, completion and return of questionnaires is documented and typically analyzed statistically. Quantitative survey research implies that researchers use standardized questionnaires, which consist of mostly polar questions and cannot be modified by the participant (*Döring/Bortz* (2016), p. 405). Surveys are conducted either face-to-face, by mail, via the internet or on mobile devices (*Merchant/Otley* (2007), p. 791). The survey mode differs by the variants paper-pencil and online surveys. A particular survey mode represents the **online survey** applied in this study, by which a researcher sends out an electronic questionnaire usually via e-mail so that participants complete the questionnaire on a computer or mobile device (*Manfreda/Vehovar* (2009), p. 264). Compared to paper-pencil surveys, online surveys are administrated more cost-efficiently, since the researcher is no longer dependent on postal correspondence. Moreover, online surveys are sent out and completed in a considerably shorter period of time (*Bandilla* (2002), p. 1). Furthermore, survey research differs by means of an active or passive sampling. While an active sampling indicates that potential participants are actively selected by personal invitation, passive sampling presumes a wide spread of the questionnaire so that a sample is formed in a self-selection process (*Döring/Bortz* (2016), p. 400). Finally, survey research projects differ in the choice of their target group. Self-reports from affected parties and expert opinions are obtainable through surveys (*Döring/Bortz* (2016), p. 400). This study follows an active sampling strategy due to the fact that only a selected target group of experts is able to give information about PMS design in SSOs.

Questionnaires are primarily used in social sciences to assess trends in corporate practice, to test theories by using a large sample of firms or individuals, and to supplement data collected from case studies (*van der Stede et al.* (2005), p. 656). Compared to other methodologies, such as case studies, survey research offers a wide range of **advantages**. Questionnaires are more efficient compared to case studies, since many observations can be collected by a large number of participants in a relatively short period of time at comparatively low costs (*Riesenhuber* (2009), p. 7). Moreover, respondents perceive the completion of a questionnaire as more discret and anonymous than an interview situation (*Fowler* (2013), p. 71). Survey research allows the researcher to yield data from

---

35 Notably, the literature review of *de Leeuw and Dillman* reveals many definitions of the term *survey* which differ in their components, criteria and emphasis. For a detailed review on survey definitions, see *Leeuw et al.* (2009b), pp. 2–4.

the field without entering it. An essential motive of survey research consists in the possibility to quantitatively estimate the distribution of a population's characteristics, even though the researcher obtains the required information from only a small part of the population (*Rea/Parker* (2005), p. 4). Hence, the generalization of the sample's empirical results illustrates the main objective of survey research (*van der Stede et al.* (2005), p. 666).

Despite the aforementioned advantages, survey research also entails **disadvantages and risks**, particularly with regard to the desired generalizability of empirical results. As opposed to interviews, survey research implies a loss of control over the respondent's behavior, for instance that a non-targeted respondent completes the questionnaire. Compared to interviews, survey research entails the risk of a non-response bias (*van der Stede et al.* (2005), pp. 669–670). Since the researcher has a decisive influence on the wording and response format, expectancy effects may occur (*Birnberg et al.* (1990), p. 44). In addition, further measurement errors may appear that are directly related to the respondent's or researcher's abilities to design respectively complete the questionnaire. The advantage of survey research to collect data anonymously and discretly conflicts with the objective to generate objective information, because survey research mostly relies on unverified self-reports (*van der Stede et al.* (2005), p. 675). Self-reports entail subjective biases, such as recall, incentive and halo effects (*Birnberg et al.* (1990), p. 49). Due to the fact that surveys represent a generic instrument, it abstracts from the respondent's context. Therefore, a questionnaire contains only few peculiarities of the respondent's natural environment (*Birnberg et al.* (1990), pp. 50–51). In principle, survey research should be mindful of providing the opportunity to participate in the research project to all members of the target population (*Dillman/Bowker* (2001), p. 57).

By contrast to the qualitative case studies, the quantitative survey aims to yield descriptive empirical evidence on the current state of PMS design in SSOs in a much broader sense by drawing on a larger sample. Using a larger sample allows for resilient inferences about the sample's basic population (*Riesenhuber* (2009), p. 7). Furthermore, the survey research design enables to test hypotheses that are derived from the conceptual framework and refined by the qualitative case studies so that explanatory empirical results supplement the gained descriptive findings of the quantitative study.

This survey research applies a **dyadic multi-actor design**, by sending out two questionnaires to different target groups (*Pasteels* (2015), pp. 2–3). The first questionnaire is addressed to the SSO managers and contains questions on SSO design characteristics and further contextual factors that may impact PMS design in SSOs. The second questionnaire is addressed to the SSO management accountants and contains questions on the design of the PMS, the performance measurement process and the involved actors. Both questionnaires contain questions on the perceived effectiveness of the PMS. This study applies a dyadic multi-actor design for two reasons. In line with the promotor model adopted in the theoretical framework of this study, the quantitative survey research design analyzes the most important performance measurement actors in SSOs since they play a significant role in the performance measurement process and influence the design of PMS. As the applied MMRD intends to combine and triangulate the quantitative and qualitative results, it seems useful to choose the same sampling unit as in the case studies by surveying SSO managers and SSO management accountants (*Pasteels* (2015), p. 3). Second, endogeneity illustrates an ubiquitous problem in survey research which can be reduced by using a dyadic multi-actor design (*Kajüter/Nienhaus* (2016), p. 517). A common source of endogeneity represents the common method bias that seems preventable by tapping various information sources (*van der Stede et al.* (2005), p. 666). Hence, the effectiveness of the PMS design in SSOs is investigated independently from its design.

In addition to the aforementioned criteria of survey design, online surveys should consider further criteria to reduce the **four major sources of error in sample surveys**, namely non-response error, non-coverage error, sampling error and measurement error (*Leeuw et al.* (2009b), p. 4). In order to ensure the highest possible response rate and to alleviate non-coverage error, the questionnaires are offered in a paper pencil version and online to the participants (*Leeuw et al.* (2009a), p. 302). The potential participants are actively selected via an online search in professional networks. Prior online research ensures that the identified participants are part of the target population and have the necessary information available to complete the questionnaire (*van der Stede et al.* (2005), p. 666). The two essential criteria to assess the survey participants' eligibility are their stated job description and more than one year of professional experience. As far as practicable, the participants are approached by telephone beforehand to exclude non-targeted respondents and to achieve a higher response rate (*Dillman* (1991), p. 230). In addition to the preliminarily provided oral explanations via telephone, a personalized mail with the links to the questionnaires including additional notes is sent out so that technical or content-related barriers are reduced to a minimum. Furthermore, the participants are given sufficient time for answering the questionnaires and several follow-up reminders are sent out (*Dillman* (1991), p. 239).

Moreover, a total of five additional measures are taken to **increase the response rate** and to **reduce measurement error**. First, both questionnaires are available in German and English. Whereas the English version copes with the international SSO environment, the German version of the questionnaires suits the scope of the study to analyze PMS design in SSOs of the German-speaking world. SSCs that are located in Germany employ many non-German-speaking employees. By contrast, a majority of German-speaking participants has to be expected who complete questionnaires more easily in their mother tongue. In order to preserve conceptual, functional and measure equivalence in the English version, both questionnaires are back-translated to ensure translation accuracy (*Brislin* (1970), pp. 214–215). Second, each participant is assured of a comprehensive management summary with the most important empirical results as an incentive to complete the questionnaire (*Dillman* (1991), p. 231). Third, particular attention is paid to the use of question-writing principles, response alternatives and their consistency (*Porst* (2009), pp. 95–114). Fourth, the online questionnaire layout is designed by using the university's official corporate design and an appealing introduction (*Dillman* (1991), p. 239). The questions are ordered according to *Dillman's* general recommendations on questionnaire design (*Dillman* (1991), pp. 233–234). Fifth, it is ensured that a questionnaire can be completed in less than twenty minutes.

The web surveys developed for this study are based on the methodological principles for the design of online surveys by *Dillman and Bowker* and can be subdivided into **technical and formatting-related means of error mitigation** (*Dillman/Bowker* (2001), pp. 65–68). Technical measures include, for example, the use of protected, personalized links and an automated screen optimization (*Dillman/Bowker* (2001), p. 66). Formatting-related measures comprise the integration of a status bar to indicate the progress of the respondent and the abandonment of drop-down menus (*Dillman/Bowker* (2001), p. 59). All of the hereby addressed questionnaire design criteria were subject to extensive pre-testing that involved three experts from consultancy firms, three practitioners from SSOs of European MNCs and academics who were familiar with the survey research methodology. Having outlined case study and survey research, the following section combines both research approaches in the MMRD.

5.3 Mixed methods research design

This section serves four purposes. First, it defines the term mixed methods to establish a common understanding of this study's research design. Second, this section outlines the main objectives pursued with a MMRD. Third, it details the sequential exploratory research design as a particular MMRD which is applied in this study. Fourth, this section describes the essential quality criteria that this study's MMRD has to fulfill.

5.3.1 Definition of mixed methods

The increasing and interdisciplinary spread of mixed method (MM) approaches in the international arena leads to an expansion of existing research methodologies (*Kuckartz* (2014), p. 10). Until the 1980s, qualitative and quantitative research have taken root as two methodological views, which partly have been regarded as incompatible **paradigms**. Since then, the emerging combination of qualitative and quantitative elements within a mixed methods research (MMR) framework constitutes a third (pragmatic) approach (*Morgan* (2007), p. 65). The international prevalence of MMR approaches inevitably follows a greater variety of conceptual interpretations of this "third research paradigm"[36] (*Denscombe* (2008), p. 271). Although "mixed methods" represents the most common term for this research approach, it is also used under a number of other terms, for example *"triangulation"*, *"multiple methodology"* and *"mixed research"* (*Johnson et al.* (2007), p. 118).[37] The term *"methods"* is often interpreted broadly so that MM is not only concerned with data collection and data analysis methods, but also involves basic epistemological assumptions in a wider sense of a methodology (*Greene* (2006), pp. 93–95). Even though varying definitions from different perspectives illustrate the result of an international and interdisciplinary MM research community, *Johnson et al.* identify five major definition criteria (*Johnson et al.* (2007), pp. 118–123).[38] These are used in current literature in regular recurrence and constitute the MM **definition** used in this study (*Kuckartz* (2014), p. 32):

---

36 In addition to the term "third research paradigm" coined by *Johnson/Onwuegbuzie* (2004), p. 14, MMR is also referred to as a "third methodological revolution" (*Teddlie/ Tashakkori* (2010), p. 697) or as a "third research community" (*Teddlie/Tashakkori* (2009), p. 3).

37 *Campbell and Fiske* introduced the concept of triangulation already in 1959 (*Campbell/ Fiske* (1959)). Although triangulation is sometimes equated with MM, they differ greatly. For a general overview of the term "triangulation", refer to *Flick* (2014c). For the term "multiple methodology" refer to *Smith* (2006). For the term "mixed research" refer to *Onwuegbuzie/Johnson* (2006).

38 The following five definition criteria are based on nineteen different MM definitions (*Johnson et al.* (2007), pp. 118–123).

(1) MM combine quantitative and qualitative research approaches.
(2) The combination of quantitative and qualitative methods in an MM research project does not have to be used in all but at least in one phase of the research process.
(3) MMR ranges from a mere combined data collection to a methodologically melted worldview and language.
(4) The choice of a MMRD can be based on the research question and on the researcher's normative standards.
(5) MM pursue one or more research objectives that are not (or not to the same extent) achievable with a mono-methodic research strategy.

This MM definition can be delineated from mono-methodological and multi-methodological research approaches (*Azorín/Cameron* (2010), p. 96). While mono-methodological research uses either a quantitative *or* qualitative research methodology, multi-methodological research employs more than one research method (*Teddlie/Tashakkori* (2006), p. 14). In a multi-methodological research design, several quantitative *or* qualitative research methods are applicable so that a multi-methodological research design might not be congruent with a MMRD (*Bergman* (2011), p. 272).

5.3.2 Objectives of a mixed methods research

As stated in the definition above, MMR promises a more complete picture of the research object compared to mono-methodic research approaches (*Kuckartz* (2014), p. 53). MMR is largely characterized by the three major research object-ives: **triangulation, (further) development and extension** (*Greene et al.* (1989), p. 259).[39] As shown in figure 5.2, triangulation can be broken down into the three subordinate objectives convergence, complementarity, and divergence (*Erzberger/Kelle* (2010), p. 466).

---

39 *Greene et al.* interpret triangulation by limiting the term to convergence. Thus, complementarity and initiation represent separate objectives in their presentation. For a review of other potential MMR purposes, see *Collins et al.* (2006), pp. 74–75.

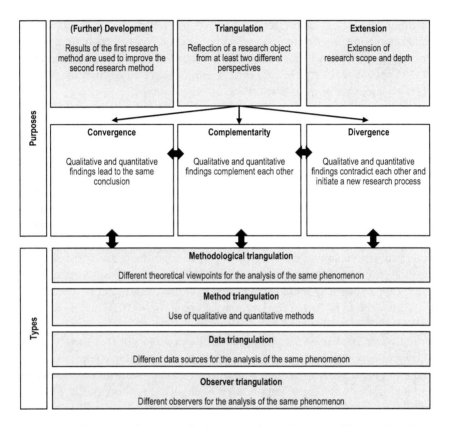

Figure 5.2: Objectives of mixed methods research (own illustration following *Denzin* (1978); *Greene et al.* (1989) and *Tashakkori/Teddlie* (2003))

The most commonly used interpretation of triangulation consists in the convergence of research results obtained from different research methods (*Fielding* (2012), p. 127). *Denzin* separates between internal (qualitative *or* quantitative) and external method triangulation (qualitative *and* quantitative), whereby only the latter has a commonality with MMR (*Denzin* (1978), p. 301). The use of different research methods that describe converging empirical findings may underpin the validity of the research construct by reducing common method bias (*Denzin* (1978), p. 304). A second purpose of triangulation is expressed by complementarity and aims at enriching and refining empirical results since MM combine the strengths of both methods and reduce their weaknesses (*van Griensven et al.* (2014), p. 368). Thus, MM achieves a more mature interpretation of empirical findings (*Erzberger/Kelle* (2010), pp. 469–470). The third purpose of triangulation is effected if quantitative and qualitative methods describe contradictory findings when analyzing the same phenomenon (*Greene et al.* (1989), pp. 259–260). As a consequence, contradictory findings may initiate new research questions or hypotheses (*Flick* (2014b), p. 228).

Furthermore, *Denzin* distinguishes **four triangulation types**: methodological triangulation, method triangulation, data triangulation, observer triangulation and derivable combinations of these types (*Denzin* (1978), pp. 297–298). All triangulation types reflect on the same phenomenon from different perspectives (*Flick* (2014b), p. 225). Triangulation intends to reveal the influence of different theories, methods, data sources and researchers on the research object (*Thurmond* (2001), pp. 254–255). Apart from triangulation, the (further) development of methods illustrates a research objective of MMRDs (*Greene et al.* (1989), pp. 257–258). Sequential MMRDs offer the advantage to refine empirical results by exploiting the insights gained through the use of a first research method (*Kuckartz* (2014), p. 58). For example, the empirical results of the qualitative case studies may lead to an adjustment of this study's sample selection for the survey research. Therefore, the empirical results of MMRDs may be superior to research designs that employ a single method.

Moreover, the use of MM may lead to the extension of the research scope (*Caracelli/Greene* (1993), p. 196). In contrast to triangulation complementarity, extension is primarily associated with the extension of the whole research project and not with the mere amplification of empirical results (*Kuckartz* (2014), p. 59).

5.3.3 Development of the mixed methods research design

As MMR pursues different research objectives and addresses varying research questions, a wide range of MMRDs exist (*Collis/Hussey* (2013), p. 292). Therefore, *Creswell's* typology **classifies MMRDs** on the basis of the dimensions timing, weighting, mix and theoretical perspective as illustrated in figure 5.3.

The first dimension approaches the chronological order of the methods used in the research design, which can be implemented concurrently or sequentially (*Creswell* (2013), p. 207).[40] A concurrent design is useful if the largest possible amount of data has to be collected in a given time, while a sequential design is

---

40 For the sake of clarity, *Creswell's* dimensions for MMRDs are explained by using the term methods. Since MM goes beyond a mere method combination, the combination of different methodologies and epistemological assumptions is implicitly included.

more time-consuming but offers the opportunity to refine the second research method (*Teddlie/Tashakkori* (2006), pp. 20–21). The weighting indicates how the researcher prioritizes the two methodologies within his research design. A "pure" MMRD weights qualitative and quantitative methods to the same extent (*Johnson et al.* (2007), pp. 124–125). The dimension "mix" elaborates on the use of qualitative and quantitative elements during different phases of the research process (*Creswell* (2013), p. 207). Notably, research methodologies can be already mixed in the conceptualization and planning phase (*Johnson et al.* (2007), p. 122). Furthermore, MMRDs can be categorized according to the application of a theoretical framework on which the research design rests (*Mertens* (2015), p. 808).

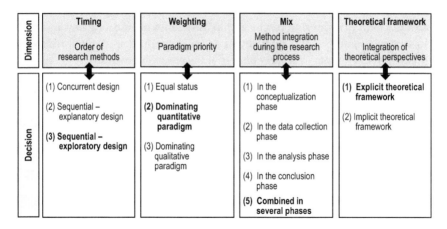

Figure 5.3: Dimensions of mixed methods research designs (own illustration following *Creswell et al.* (2003), pp. 167–177)

This study uses a **sequential exploratory design** beginning with qualitative case studies and followed by a quantitative survey research design. Although a paradigm priority is difficult to assess, this study follows a **dominating quantitative paradigm** for two reasons. First, the qualitative results are mainly used to complement the quantitative results and not vice versa. Consequently, the survey results take a more important role in this study's empirical part. Second, the survey study consumed considerably more time during the research process. In accordance with the research gap unveiled in chapter three, the qualitative part intends to shed light on the comparatively unexplored phenomenon of PMS design in SSOs. Moreover, the applied sequential exploratory design also allows for the development and refinement of the questionnaire design. Only through the profound interviews with SSO managers and SSO management accountants within the case study context all relevant dimensions of PMS design are captured. At the same time, constructs derived from literature are dropped since case study findings indicate that they are of minor relevance in corporate practice. As outlined in chapter four, this study relies on an **explicit theoretical framework**. Therefore, the case study results are exploited to refine the basic hypotheses developed from the theoretical framework. The sequential design ensures that developed hypotheses are empirically testable through the questionnaires. The quantitative part intends to generalize the case study results. Moreover, the survey analyses also investigate whether the quantity distribution of performance measurement characteristics indicated by the case studies pertains for a larger sample. Furthermore, the used sequential exploratory research design aims to extent the empirical results of the case studies by revealing new insights. As shown in figure 5.4, this study draws on the **combination of qualitative and quantitative elements in several phases** of the research process.

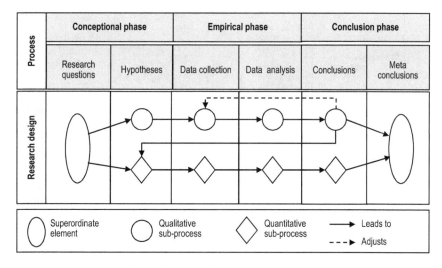

Figure 5.4: This study's mixed methods research design (own illustration following *Collins et al.* (2006), p. 71 and *Schulz* (2018), p. 74)

5.3.4 Quality criteria in mixed method research

The definition of criteria for the quality of empirical findings constitutes a focal point in quantitative and qualitative empirical research (*Himme* (2009), p. 499).

Since MM combines quantitative and qualitative research approaches, quality criteria of both research approaches are relevant. In addition, the **quality of the method integration** per se has to be considered (*Ihantola/Kihn* (2011), pp. 44–45). Due to the ambiguous interpretation of quality criteria in both research paradigms, *Tashakkori and Teddlie* introduce the concept of "inference quality" for method-integrative approaches, which is composed of design quality and interpretive rigor (*Tashakkori/Teddlie* (2008), p. 113). *Onwuegbuzie and Johnson* supplement their framework by adding the concept of legitimation to address threats to validity due to the combination of methods (*Onwuegbuzie/Johnson* (2006), p. 57). *Dellinger and Leech* combine the two above-mentioned models with traditional quality factors in qualitative and quantitative research, as illustrated in figure 5.5.

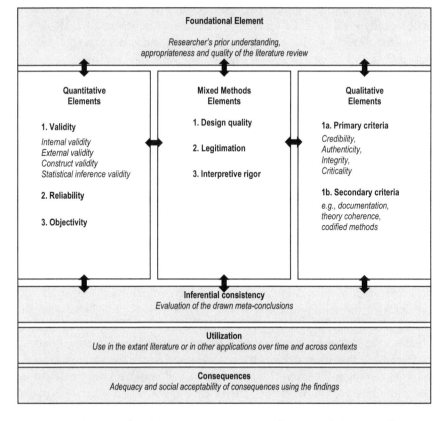

Figure 5.5: Elements of quality criteria in MMR (own illustration following *Dellinger and Leech* (2007), p. 322)

Quality criteria for quantitative research

Quantitative research primarily refers to the criteria of classical test theory: **validity, reliability and objectivity** (*Campbell* (1957a), pp. 297–298). **Validity** determines the accuracy of a measuring instrument and thus tests whether the instrument measures what it is supposed to measure (*Stier* (2013), p. 51). Validity in quantitative research can be separated into internal and external validity, construct validity and inference-related validity (*Döring/Bortz* (2016), p. 93). Internal validity exists if the change of a dependent variable can be attributed unambiguously to the modification of an independent variable (*Döring/Bortz* (2016), p. 99). External validity describes the extent to which the results of a study are generalizable (*Döring/Bortz* (2016), p. 102). Construct validity is given when the measured relationships of the operationalized constructs correspond to the underlying theory (*Döring/Bortz* (2016), p. 98). Statistical inference validity prevails if the descriptive and inferential statistical analyses are conducted correctly so that a researcher is able to demonstrate that connections between variables are statistically significant. Moreover, statistical inference premises that a theoretically and practically significant effect size exists in the population (*Döring/Bortz* (2016), p. 106). **Reliability** is a measure for the trustworthiness of the measurement instrument and thus indicates whether it consistently generates similar measurement results without a remarkable measurement error (*Hair et al.* (2010), pp. 45–46). **Objectivity** is defined as the evaluation of a measurement result independently from the observer. Objectivity implies that the researcher has little (interpretative) influence on the empirical findings, for example by his external appearance or his values and beliefs (*Döring/Bortz* (2016), p. 184).

This study uses a series of statistical tests, such as omnibus tests, to verify the validity of the survey research results. In addition, the data of the quantitative sample must meet several conditions, such as the central limit theorem or variance homogeneity. The procedures for assessing validity are presented in a separate section in chapter seven. Since this is a cross-sectional study, the reliability of the survey instrument can only be verified to a limited extent, although both surveys were subject to extensive pre-tests. Compared to the case studies, questionnaires are much less susceptible to influence by the observer. Nevertheless, this study's research design cannot assure complete objectivity. In order to reduce the interpretative influence to a minimum, the questions in the questionnaires and the e-mail letters are composed in a neutral language. Moreover, only completed questionnaires flow in the empirical analyses to exclude manual changes of raw data by the observer.

Quality criteria for qualitative research

Qualitative research relies on varying, controversially discussed conceptions of quality criteria so that an established framework of quality factors is non-existent (*Onwuegbuzie/Leech* (2007), p. 233). *Whittemore et al.* consider the lack of unifying validity framework to be a great difficulty for qualitative researchers and propose the use of the **four primary quality criteria** credibility, authenticity, criticality and integrity (*Whittemore et al.* (2001), p. 534). This study draws on these primary criteria as they are essential for all qualitative inquiry, albeit they have to be supplemented by secondary criteria for their application to a specific research project. Credibility refers to the required assurance that the interpretations of the data's meaning are trustworthy. Authenticity is linked to credibility and comprises an accurate portrayal of the meanings and experiences perceived by the research participants (*Whittemore et al.* (2001), p. 530). A critical appraisal of the employed research design and of the obtained empirical findings seems a necessary third criterion to guard against constructional and interpretive flaws. Furthermore, integrity in each phase of the research process involves self-awareness for the subjectivity of a researcher's interpretation (*Whittemore et al.* (2001), p. 531).

To satisfy the outlined primary criteria, this study employs **secondary quality criteria** according to *Steinke's* prominent suggestions for a classification of quality criteria in qualitative research (*Steinke* (1999), pp. 205–248). A complete documentation of the research process represents a mandatory criterion for an intersubjective traceability (*Flick* (2014b), p. 491). Therefore, data collection and analysis methods, such as interview guidelines, transcription rules and conducted analyses are disclosed in the subsequent chapters. The application of codified methods improves transparency on how the researcher analyzes data. Thus, this study applies a structuring-thematic coding by using the qualitative data analysis (QDA) software MAXQDA (*Mayring* (2015), pp. 50–59). The criterion of indication considers not only the appropriateness of the methods of data collection and analysis but also methodological decisions during the research process. Indication includes the question to what extent method selection and sampling strategy are appropriate with regard to the research objectives (*Steinke* (1999), pp. 216–221). PMS design in SSOs represents a nascent research stream, which advocates for the exploratory case study research design used in this study. The sampling strategy is described in chapter six.

Empirical data are compulsory in connection with the development and the testing of theories. In contrast to quantitative research strategies, empirical embeddedness is crucial not only for the hypotheses testing, but for hypotheses development, too (*Steinke* (1999), p. 221). Therefore, this study intends to develop and refine hypotheses on PMS design in SSOs by exploiting the empirical findings of the conducted case studies. Another quality criterion is to point out the limitations of the empirical results instead of generalizing them speculatively so that their authenticity and credibility suffers (*Thole* (2003), p. 62). Limitations also indicate the extent to which the findings are transferable. This study's limitations are thoroughly outlined in chapter eight after the presentation of the empirical results. The quality criterion of theory coherence implies that hypotheses developed from the case study analyses should be closely connected to the outlined theoretical framework (*Steinke* (1999), p. 241).

Quality criteria for mixed methods research

Dellinger and Leech define the three quality criteria **design quality**, **legitimation** and **interpretive rigor** for MMR. The **design quality** of a MMRD results from the following components: suitability of the MMRD to answer the research question, consistency within the quantitative and qualitative design components as well as analytical and design adequacy (*Tashakkori/Teddlie* (2008), p. 113). Design adequacy refers to the quality and rigor of the applied research procedures and methods, whereas analytical adequacy addresses the appropriateness of data analysis (*Tashakkori/Teddlie* (2008), p. 114). Since the three research questions of this study are based on an explorative, descriptive and explanative research objective, an MMRD seems to be particularly suitable for answering this study's research questions. Moreover, the questionnaires of the quantitative study are based on the interview guideline of the qualitative study and thus illustrate a consistent structure and sequence of questions. All research questions are addressed in both the case studies and the questionnaires so that the components PMS design in SSOs, determinants of PMS design and effectiveness of PMS design are treated consistently in both studies. The design adequacy of the questionnaires and the pool of questions is validated in multiple ways. For example, the questionnaires and the pool of questions are subject to extensive pre-tests in order to eliminate linguistic inaccuracies, incomprehensible technical terms, layout flaws etc. To ensure the appropriateness of the data analysis, the case study analyses follows the acknowledged concept of structuring-thematic coding. Furthermore, using QDA-software ascertains traceability on how the data is analyzed. The analysis of quantitative data follows established statistical methods, such as multiple regression analyses. To assess the quality of the data analysis, this study uses several statistical quality criteria, e.g. the adjusted R^2 and the variance inflation factor.

MMRDs ought to deliver credible, transferable and confirmable conclusions to gain legitimacy among scholars (*Onwuegbuzie/Johnson* (2006), p. 52). *Johnson and Onwuegbuzie* identify nine major types of **legitimation** for MMRDs whereof three criteria are of particular importance for this study's MMRD: sample integration, weakness minimization and commensurability (*Onwuegbuzie/ Johnson* (2006), p. 57). Sample integration refers to the extent to which meta-inferences can be drawn, although the qualitative and quantitative samples differ from each other (*Onwuegbuzie/Johnson* (2006), pp. 56–57). To secure the integration of the qualitative and quantitative sample in the discussion of the empirical results, this study employed a nested sampling scheme so that the qualitative sample represents a sub-set of the quantitative sample. Weakness minimization addresses the question how well the researcher is able to compensate the weaknesses of an employed method by the strengths of another method. Since this study uses a sequential MMRD, weaknesses of the case study analysis are addressed in the quantitative part, such as a lacking anonymity during the interviews and a limited generalizability of the case study results (*Onwuegbuzie/ Johnson* (2006), p. 58). Moreover, commensurability indicates the extent to which a MMRD reflects a mixed worldview that purposefully combines both paradigms. Therefore, the scientific positioning outlined the basic epistemological assumptions on which this study rests and described its compatibility with the selected research strategy.

Interpretive rigor consists of the three criteria consistency, distinctiveness and integrative efficacy (*Tashakkori/Teddlie* (2008), p. 113). Consistency involves the compatibility of the empirical findings with existing theories as well as the coherence between the drawn inferences and the empirical data. Therefore, this study relates to the developed theoretical framework during the discussion and interpretation of the empirical findings. Distinctiveness describes the plausibility of the drawn conclusions from the results compared to other possible conclusions. Integrative efficacy addresses the quality of the drawn meta-conclusions that are made from qualitative and quantitative results (*Tashakkori/ Teddlie* (2008), pp. 115–116). A systematic consolidation of qualitative and quantitative findings at the end of this study's empirical analysis allows for an evaluation of integrative efficacy.

Additional criteria

Furthermore, *Dellinger and Leech* supplement **four additional quality criteria** as overriding elements that are applicable to this MMRD. A **foundational element** addresses the researcher's prior understanding and the appropriateness and quality of the literature review (*Dellinger/Leech* (2007), p. 323). An appropriate and critical selection and compilation of prior research in chapter three increases the quality of this MMRD. The literature review is composed analytically and the findings are used consistently for the theoretical and methodical orientation of the MMRD. **Inferential consistency** assesses the extent to which the meta-conclusions drawn from the qualitative and quantitative results are consistent with the research objectives and the research design (*Dellinger/Leech* (2007), p. 325). The conclusions at the end of this study demonstrate to what extent the research questions are answered and whether the research objectives have been achieved. In addition, the limitations emphasize the confined integrability of qualitative and quantitative results. By adding utilization and the consequences as further quality criteria, *Dellinger and Leech* distinguish between the interpretation and application of empirical results. **Utilization** relates to the relevance of the results for existing and future research and its application in practice, while **consequences** primarily aim at the social acceptance of these implications (*Dellinger/Leech* (2007), p. 325). The latter two quality criteria are not verifiable in this study, as the relevance and acceptance of the empirical findings will become apparent in the long run.

Having clarified the quality criteria of quantitative, qualitative and MM research and how those specific quality criteria are addressed in the course of this study, the following chapter presents the empirical analysis of the case studies.

6 Qualitative analysis

The qualitative analysis is subdivided into four main parts. Section 6.1 presents the sample selection for the case study analyses and provides descriptions of the case companies. Section 6.2 presents the data collection process and the interview characteristics. Moreover, this section outlines the data analysis procedures applied for the qualitative analysis. Section 6.3 analyzes PMS design in SSOs, the determinants of PMS design and its effectiveness in two ways. First, the empirical results are presented as firm level cases to grasp the case in its totality. Second, section 6.3 draws on a cross-case analysis to investigate the components of PMS design in SSOs across the available cases. This allows for a comparative analysis of the cases and yields commonalities and differences in PMS design. Section 6.4 discusses implications of the qualitative results and refines the developed basic hypotheses which are tested in the quantitative part of this study.

6.1 Sample selection and case company description

6.1.1 Case company selection

This study's case selection rationale is based on the first research question and on the rationale of mixing qualitative and quantitative approaches. The selected cases ought to yield a holistic picture of PMS design in SSOs of MNCs in German-speaking countries.

Sampling designs entail two major elements: the **sampling scheme** and the **sampling size** (*Collins et al.* (2007), p. 271). The sampling scheme describes the selection rationale, whereas the sample size expresses the number of selected cases. Notably, the MMRD presumes that the selected sampling strategy takes the quantitative and the qualitative sample into consideration to be capable of combining their results (*Collins et al.* (2007), p. 270). While the sample size in explorative case study research depends on the theoretical saturation (*Glaser/Strauss* (1967), p. 61), the sampling scheme varies according to whether the researcher intends to cover the field as wide as possible or to analyze a phenomenon as deep as possible (*Flick* (2014a), p. 123). A random case selection is not a preferable sampling scheme since multiple-case designs are limited in their sampling size and thus barely yield statistically representative results (*Wrona* (2005), p. 24). Hence, two sampling schemes come into consideration: the theoretical and the statistical sampling design (*Flick* (2014a), p. 115). Whereas the theoretical sampling represents a gradual approach where case selection decisions are made in the process of data collection and which is particularly suitable if little prior knowledge is available, a **statistical sampling scheme** a priori defines the sample according to certain criteria (*Flick* (2014a), pp. 115–118). This study builds on prior knowledge and thus uses a statistical sampling scheme based on two primary criteria and four secondary criteria. A statistical sampling presupposes a known population size and the ability to estimate the distribution of relevant criteria within the population (*Flick* (2014a), p. 138). The population size of the qualitative study is known beforehand since the number of MNCs with an established SSO in German-speaking countries is limited. Due to the fact that the participants of the qualitative study are recruited at roundtables, the essential SSO characteristics and the main features of the PMS of the participating firms are also available.

The following two primary **selection criteria** intend to foster a high degree of variation among the cases so that each case yields particularities of PMS design in SSOs. The first primary case selection criterion is the **SSO's size**. PMS design in SSOs may vary depending on their size since this criterion implies various other case characteristics, such as the availability of resources as well as the process and organizational complexity which has to be reflected in the PMS. In contrast to large SSOs, smaller SSOs may not be able to operate with large controlling departments so that performance measurement tasks may be distributed among several actors. The second primary criterion is the **industry**. It is conceivable that PMS design in SSOs differs according to the industry because, for example, the support processes implemented in SSOs vary among service and manufacturing companies. Furthermore, the competition intensity may differ across industries so that the design of PMS in SSOs may vary.

In addition to these two core criteria, this study is constrained by four **secondary conditions** for the sample selection which are either due to this study's research design or applied for practical reasons. First, the case companies apply to the definition of a MNC. Thus, the firms should operate with at least two foreign subsidiaries, which permanently demand the SSO's services. Companies that are only active nationally or do not undertake any substantial foreign direct investments are less suitable for this study since important contingency factors that may impact performance measurement practices in SSOs, such as the perceived environmental uncertainty, the geographical dispersion of the SSCs or the multigeographical service provision are not adequately observable. Second, the MNCs obviously have to maintain a SSO and a PMS. Third, it is important that at least one SSC of the case company's SSO is located in a German-speaking country as geographical proximity to the interviewees facilitates face-to-face interviews. The planned interview duration of at least one hour per interview partner indicates that the interviews should be conducted in the mother tongue of the participants. Interviews in the mother tongue promise more detailed answers and thus provide more ample results. Fourth, the access to the field represents another constraint, since SSOs remain a sensitive topic for MNCs. In order to secure comparability among the qualitative and quantitative sample, the case companies should ensure interviews with a SSO manager and a SSO management accountant as both embody essential promotors of the performance measurement process. Furthermore, this study exploits a sequential nested sampling design so that the qualitative sample represents a subset of the larger quantitative sample to yield interpretive consistency (*Collins et al.* (2007), p. 276). The sampling scheme yielded a **sample size** of seven firms which are presented in the following section.

6.1.2 Case company description

This section presents a brief description of the case companies to give a general overview of the MNC's setting in which performance measurement takes place. The names of the case firms represent pseudonyms in order to comply with the confidentiality ensured to the participating firms. Each pseudonym characterizes the firm's industry. The firm's fundamental characteristics are anonymized so that firms cannot be identified while ensuring an assessment of the essential sample characteristics. This study anonymizes the interviewees in such a way that pseudonyms mirror their current job title, but are harmonized to the extent that job titles remain comparable across all cases.

Case #1 – MedTechCo

MedTechCo is a medical and pharmaceutical device company headquartered in Germany. The company manufactures disposable hospital supplies as well as products and services related to surgery and dialysis. MedTechCo generates more than € 5 billion in annual sales and employs more than 50,000 employees. The company encompasses more than 200 subsidiaries which are dispersed across more than 80 countries. Apart from the company's domestic market, MedTechCo has a strong market presence in Asia and the US. The family-owned company is privately held. MedTechCo implemented its SSO in 2015. The company's SSO has four SSCs on two continents which employ more than 100 employees.

Case #2 – CommCo

CommCo is a German telecommunications company. The network provider renders communication services for fixed lines, mobile phones and offers digital television as well as internet access. CommCo is one of the largest communication service providers throughout Europe with more than € 60 billion in annual sales and operating with more than 60,000 employees. The company incorporates more than 250 subsidiaries which are located in more than 50 countries. Apart from the company's home market, CommCo undertakes major investments in the US and Eastern Europe. CommCo is a publicly traded company. The case company established its SSO in 2014. CommCo's SSO consists of five SSCs located in Europe with more than 1,000 employees.

Case #3 – ChemCo

ChemCo is one of the largest chemical producers in the world and manufactures a wide range of chemicals, plastics, agricultural products, coatings as well as oil and gas. ChemCo generates more than € 60 billion in annual sales and has more than 100,000 employees. The case company comprises more than 250 subsidiaries which operate in more than 80 countries. Apart from the case company's domestic market, particularly the US and the Asian market contribute to the company's growth. ChemCo is listed on a German stock exchange. The company installed its SSO in 2002. The company's SSO contains four SSCs on three continents which employ more than 2,500 employees.

Case #4 – PharCo

PharCo is a German-based pharmaceutical company and produces pharmacy medicines, laboratory chemicals, test kits and liquid crystals. PharCo is one of the largest pharmaceutical companies in the world generating more than € 15 billion in annual sales with more than 50,000 employees. Apart from the home market, the case company shows a strong market presence in the US and in Central Europe. PharCo has more than 200 subsidiaries which operate in more than 60 countries. The company is publicly quoted on a German stock exchange. PharCo implemented its SSO in 2012. The company's SSO has four SSCs on three continents and operates with more than 250 employees.

Case #5 – AgriCo

AgriCo is an American company that manufactures agricultural, construction, and forestry machinery. Apart from the US market, AgriCo established major manufacturing sites in Western Europe, Asia and South America. The case company is a world leader for tractors by generating more than € 25 billion in annual sales and employing more than 50,000 employees. The company incorporates more than 60 subsidiaries which are dispersed across more than ten countries. AgriCo is listed on a US stock exchange. The company established its SSO in 2007. AgriCo's SSO maintains ten SSCs on two continents with more than 250 employees.

Case #6 – HealthCo

HealthCo is a pharmaceutical and life sciences company headquartered in Germany. HealthCo produces human and veterinary pharmaceuticals, consumer health medication and agricultural chemicals. The case company is one of the largest pharmaceutical and chemical companies worldwide with more than € 40 billion in annual sales with more than 100,000 employees. HealthCo encompasses more than 300 subsidiaries and operates in more than 70 countries. Apart from the home market, HealthCo undertakes major investments in Western Europe, the US and Asia. HealthCo is a publicly traded company. The company implemented its SSO in 2002. HealthCo has two SSCs on two continents which employ more than 1,000 employees.

Case #7 – EngineerCo

EngineerCo is a German-based mechanical engineering company. The case company predominantly manufactures printing presses and has a considerable worldwide market share in this business segment. EngineerCo generates more than € 2 billion in annual sales and has more than 10,000 employees. The company comprises more than 70 subsidiaries which operate in more than 30 countries. Apart from the domestic market, EngineerCo established major manufacturing sites in Central Europe, in the US and in China. The company is publicly quoted on a German stock exchange. EngineerCo installed its SSO in 2007. The case company's SSO has four SSCs on three continents which employ more than 50 people.

The case descriptions reveal that the cases differ in their **fundamental characteristics** which promises a compelling cross-case analysis. Whereas MedTechCo represents the only privately held firm within the sample, HealthCo has the most complex legal structure by operating with more than 250 entities. With regard to the MNC size, EngineerCo exemplifies the smallest case company in terms of annual sales and employees, while ChemCo belongs to the largest MNCs according to those two size proxies. Notably, MedTechCo pertains to the group of firms which is engaged in the most countries, although it ranks among the case companies with the smallest annual sales. ChemCo has the largest SSO by means of SSO employees, whereas EngineerCo and AgriCo belong to the group of MNCs with the smallest SSOs. Apart from ChemCo, HealthCo is the company with the most mature SSO. By contrast, HealthCo established less than four SSCs which is the lowest number among all case companies. Table 6.1 summarizes the fundamental characteristics of the seven case companies.

Table 6.1: Fundamental characteristics of the case companies

Case company	Case #1 – MedTech Co	Case #2 – Comm Co	Case #3 – Chem Co	Case #4 – Phar Co	Case #5 – Agri Co	Case #6 – Health Co	Case #7 – Engineer Co
MNC annual sales[a]	< 10	> 50	> 50	10–50	10–50	10–50	< 10
MNC employees[b]	50–100	50–100	> 100	50–100	50–100	> 100	< 50
MNC Subsidiaries	200–250	> 250	> 250	200–250	< 200	> 250	< 200
MNC countries	> 80	50–80	> 80	50–80	< 50	50–80	< 50
Ownership	private	public	public	public	public	public	public
SSO employees	< 500	500–2,000	> 2,000	< 500	< 500	500–2,000	< 500
SSO maturity[c]	< 5	< 5	> 15	5–15	5–15	> 15	5–15
Number of SSCs	4–6	4–6	4–6	4–6	> 6	< 4	4–6

[a] Annual sales of the FY 2015 are stated in € billion, [b] Number of employees is stated in thousands, [c] SSO maturity is stated in years

6.2 Data collection and analysis

6.2.1 Data collection

In contrast to quantitative data collection techniques, qualitative research projects analyze non-standardized data. Non-standardized data are usually available in written form and describe social phenomena in such a way that they grasp the conditions, meaning and structures that are inherent in the phenomenon (*Kleining* (1995), p. 13).

Apart from the observation, the oral interview describes the most commonly used method in qualitative research (*Marschan-Piekkari/Welch* (2004), p. 13). Since this qualitative study aims at developing hypotheses to be tested in the subsequent quantitative study and to improve the survey instrument, expert interviews appear to be the most suitable interview type. Expert interviews provide an in-depth look at the phenomenon and allow for the collection of sensitive data (*Scholl* (2015), p. 38). Based on the degree of standardization, expert interviews are distinguished in fully standardized, semi-structured and non-standardized interviews (*Gläser/Laudel* (2010), p. 41). This study conducts **semi-structured interviews** that use a pool of questions but do not direct the interviewee's answers (*Gläser/Laudel* (2010), pp. 41–42). The interviews are based on a guideline that contains questions to be answered obligatory by each participant and thus provide orientation (*Lamnek* (2005), p. 658). Semi-structured interviews enable the interviewer to freely choose the order of the questions, their precise formulation and the number of asked questions (*Bogner et al.* (2014), p. 28). In addition to the transcribed and documented interviews, the collected data includes **additional material**, such as publicly available information (e.g., annual reports, press articles, company websites). Moreover, several experts offered internal documentation, such as management presentations, organizational charts and reporting files. Hence, this study uses multiple data sources to triangulate the case study findings which enables a deeper understanding of the topic (*Scapens* (1990), p. 275).

The data collection phase for the seven case studies started in April and ended in December 2016. The interview process can be subdivided into four major stages (figure 6.1) which are presented throughout the following sections:

Figure 6.1: The interview process (adapted from *Poplat* (2013), p. 104)

Interviewee identification

Three different **SSC roundtables** served as a platform to engage potential SSO managers for an interview. The SSC roundtables appeared particularly appropriate for a first contact because they are events that are voluntarily attended by the SSO managers. Hence, the participating companies signal a specific interest in SSO related topics. Therefore, a participation in the research project by these managers was more likely. The SSO managers were identified as the gatekeepers for this research project as they are able to make informed statements about their SSO and to establish a contact to the SSO controlling department. The SSO managers were proactively approached to ensure a case selection in accordance with the sampling rationale. Whenever a SSO manager signaled his willingness to participate in the research project, prior telephone calls were arranged in order to explain the general outline of the project.

Furthermore, this study applied a **snowball sampling strategy**, since it is an effective strategy to acquire further participants (*Meuser/Nagel* (2008), p. 464). During the prior telephone calls, further information about the organization of the PMS design in the SSO of the case company was gained so that this information was used to identify further potential interviewees. Either during the prior telephone calls or during the face-to-face interviews, the SSO managers were asked to identify further performance measurement actors who were subsequently approached in the follow-up process. All interviewees were German so that the interviews were conducted in their mother tongue. Moreover, it was discussed during the prior telephone calls whether the SSO managers have the necessary information about the SSO and about its PMS and how much professional experience they had gained with the subject (*Gläser/Laudel* (2010), pp. 117–118). Depending on the performance measurement actor in the interview, further questions from the pre-developed pool of questions were asked in addition to the obligatory questions (*Gläser/Laudel* (2010), pp. 178–182). The additional questions were not provided to the interviewees to enable an open discussion and thus to avoid framing effects (*Scholl* (2015), pp. 68–69).

Interview preparation

Prior to the interviews, the interviewees were provided with a research exposé and a tailored **pool of interview questions** (*Gläser/Laudel* (2010), p. 42; *Mayer* (2013), p. 38; *Meuser/Nagel* (2008), pp. 472–473; *Scholl* (2015), p. 68).[41] Furthermore, the participants were asked for the permission to record the conversation and to transcribe it afterwards. All interviewees agreed with the procedure, which strengthens the reliability of the results (*Witzel/Reiter* (2012), p. 4).

---

41 See appendix A for this study's pool of interview questions.

Furthermore, it was principally offered to sign a non-disclosure agreement in order to foster the interviewee's trust in the confidentiality of the data collection process. The pool of questions for each interviewee contained a set of questions from the pre-developed pool of questions based on the conceptualization in chapter two.

Apart from an introductory definition of terms, the interview guideline comprises **four main parts:**

  I The context of performance measurement,
  II SSO objectives,
  III Design of the performance measurement system,
  IV Performance measurement effectiveness.

The first section of the guideline includes questions on the environment in which performance measurement takes place. This section is subdivided into two parts. Part A entails questions on the MNC's organizational structure and specific contextual factors that may impact the SSO's performance measurement. Part B sheds light on the MNC's SSO and gathers information about the general organizational setup of the SSO. It also comprises questions about the SSO controlling and further possible contingency factors. The second section investigates the objectives that are pursued by implementing a SSO. The third section represents the largest part in the interview guideline and requests information on how the SSO designs its performance measurement. This section incorporates the three dimensions of performance measurement as conceptualized in chapter two (measures, processes, actors). The fourth section of the interview guideline collects data about possible effects of the PMS. Apart from questions about the most important performance measurement objectives, this part reviews the current satisfaction with the PMS and its acceptance among SSO employees. The last part of the guideline also incorporates questions that address to what extent the stated objectives have been achieved.

The interview guideline exclusively comprises open-ended questions since close-ended questions direct the interviewees with pre-conceptions of the interviewer. Prior to the first interview, the relevance and the comprehensibility of the pool of questions were subject to several **pre-tests** with two practitioners working in a SSO and two research assistants who are familiar with case study research based on interviews (*Lüdders* (2016), pp. 99–103; *Mayer* (2013), p. 45).

Interview execution

All interviews were conducted **face-to-face**, since related literature advocates for this approach and argues in favor of richer data compared to interviews via telephone (*Gläser/Laudel* (2010), p. 153; *Scholl* (2015), p. 29). Face-to-face interviews have at least three advantages. First, the interviewer is capable of gathering not only verbal but also non-verbal information, for example gestures, body language, mimic or visual cues (*Scapens* (1990), p. 274). Second, face-to-face interviews enhance a more personal relationship between interviewer and interviewee, which is beneficial to the quality of answers (*Scholl* (2015), pp. 37–38). A more intimate conversation atmosphere also encourages informal remarks and thus contributes to a deeper understanding. Third, some experts prepared presentations and presented their PMS reporting during the interviews, which facilitated the interviewer's understanding and stimulated further inquiry (*Gläser/Laudel* (2010), p. 154). Furthermore, interviews that lasted longer than one hour were interrupted by breaks to avoid a lapse of concentration of the conversation partners.

At the beginning of each interview an easy opening question was asked about the occupational career of interviewees to create a pleasant atmosphere. Moreover, the final question of each interview asked for other aspects that were not discussed during the interview. During the interviews, attention was paid that the questions varied in their degree of difficulty and in their specificity to ensure a **pleasant course of conversation** (*Mayer* (2013), p. 37).

Interview post-processing

Student research assistants transcribed the recorded interviews in accordance with a transcription guideline. All **interview transcripts** are based on the same standardized template which comprises the documented statements of the interviewees, the pre- and post-script as well as additional administrative information. The pre-script incorporates general information on the interview, such as the interview code, date and time of the interview, the interviewee's job title and the interview length. The post-script entails additional information, such as company-specific abbreviations. Notably, the interview transcripts have to be verbatim reports to ensure methodological rigor (*Meuser/Nagel* (2008), p. 476; *Scholl* (2015), p. 72). All interview transcripts are prepared in the interview language. The transcription guideline contains the following seven transcription rules based on suggestions by *Kuckartz* (2016):

- The transcript anonymizes all personal information, for example by assigning an alphanumeric code [P1] to each interviewee,
- confidential company information is encoded by using [XYZ],
- grammatically wrong sentences as well as dialects and slang are adapted to standard German,

- filler words, such as 'hmm' are left out,
- amendments to the spoken word are highlighted in square brackets,
- non-verbal communication are typed in italic and brackets,
- input of the interviewer is typed in bold and prefixed with his initials.

After the transcription, each transcript was reviewed carefully to avoid misunderstandings and enhance transcription quality (*Gläser/Laudel* (2010), p. 194). This study uses **in-text quotations** which have been translated from the German original quote. As suggested by *Thurmond*, the translations have been reviewed by research assistants (*Thurmond* (2001), p. 255).

6.2.2 Interview characteristics

The qualitative study is based on a total of **twelve interviews** with experts. The interview length adds up to a total of 874 minutes, resulting in 196 transcribed pages (table 6.2). Five SSO managers, five SSO management accountants, and two process managers participated in the interviews, reflecting the views of three key groups of performance measurement actors. The interview duration ranged from about 50 minutes to almost two hours.

The extent to which the interviewees are able to provide deep insights into the performance measurement of their SSO can be estimated by the two indicators professional background and experience of the interviewees.

First, the **professional background** and the job title imply the extent to which the interviewee is involved in the performance measurement process and in how far he is able to provide information about the SSO design and its particularities. The five participating SSO managers are responsible for either the entire SSO (managing director) or a SSC (head of SSC/senior vice president). The five SSO management accountants are either department managers (director), team managers (e.g. head of performance controlling) or senior managers without personnel responsibility. Three management accountants work in the SSO controlling department, while two management accountants work for the SSO governance department. The two process managers are senior managers responsible for the P2P and the O2C process. The professional background of the interviewees indicates that all participants have deep insights in the PMS design of their SSOs. Particularly the SSO managers are able to provide detailed information on their SSO's characteristics and the effectiveness of the SSO's PMS.

Table 6.2: Interview characteristics of the case companies

Case company	Number of interviews	Interview length (in min.)	Number of transcribed pages
Case #1 – MedTechCo	2	138	31
Case #2 – CommCo	2	98	24
Case #3 – ChemCo	1	113	18
Case #4 – PharCo	1	115	28
Case #5 – AgriCo	1	90	24
Case #6 – HealthCo	3	162	35
Case #7 – EngineerCo	2	158	36
Total	**12**	**874**	**196**

Second, the **professional experience** of the interviewees indicates their expert knowledge. While the SSO managers and process managers have an average professional experience of more than ten years (of which more than five years are SSO-specific professional experience), the SSO management accountants have on average six years professional experience (three in a SSO). The professional experience of the interviewees implies a high level of expertise about the performance measurement practices in their SSOs.

6.2.3 Data analysis

Due to their specificity, qualitative data analysis methods are difficult to classify. *Gläser and Laudel* distinguish **four qualitative data analysis methods** (*Gläser/Laudel* (2010), pp. 44–48):

- free interpretations,
- sequential analysis methods,
- qualitative content analysis methods and
- coding methods.

Since the free interpretation does not require the disclosure of the analysis method and thus does not represent an intersubjectively traceable method, it is not considered for this study. Sequential analysis methods, such as objective hermeneutics according to *Oevermann*, analyze the thematic and temporal links between the statements. Objective hermeneutics generates conceivable interpretations of a text passage and examines them until all inadequate interpretations can be excluded. Due to the effort required to analyze all possible interpretations of each text passage, this procedure is also omitted for this study.

The qualitative content analysis evaluates transcripts by systematically extracting information on a rule-based procedure (*Flick* (2014b), p. 416). Thus, the content analysis differs from the other approaches mainly in two aspects. First, the qualitative content analysis does not remain attached to the source text, but extracts information and processes that information separately from the text. Second, qualitative content analysis develops its category system ex ante. Particularly, the qualitative content analysis according to *Mayring* prevails in German-speaking countries (*Mayring* (2015)). This study refrains from its application because the ex ante setting of evaluation categories limits the explorative potential of the interviews. A grounded theory approach, for example according to *Glaser and Strauss* or *Charmaz* represents a special form of a coding method. The grounded theory is not a pure analysis method as it combines data collection and analysis in a cyclical process (*Charmaz/Belgrave* (2010); *Corbin et al.* (2014); *Glaser/ Strauss* (1967)). This inductive approach aims at grounding (mid-range) theories (*Strübing* (2014), p. 68). However, as this study has already made some theoretical assumptions, this approach seems less suitable for this study's qualitative data analysis.

This study applies the **structuring-thematic coding** for the analysis of the qualitative data. Structuring-thematic coding represents another coding method and describes an interplay between induction and deduction in the data analysis process.

Although the structuring-thematic coding uses superordinated categories derived from theoretical considerations (basic hypotheses), it also uses an

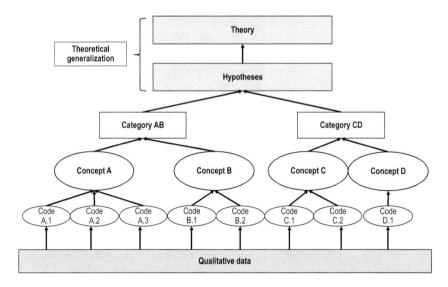

Figure 6.2: Structuring-thematic coding (adopted from *Denscombe* (2007), p. 394)

inductive coding paradigm, which allows for the formation of new subordinated categories (*Kuckartz* (2010), p. 86). Therefore, the data analysis process may result in a refined theoretical generalization.

The structuring-thematic coding can be subdivided into the **four steps** coding, thematic sorting, sociological conceptualization and theoretical generalization (figure 6.2) (*Denscombe* (2014), p. 394; *Mayer* (2013), pp. 51–55; *Mayring* (2015), pp. 11–12; *Meuser/Nagel* (2009), pp. 476–477). **Coding** describes the process of assigning concepts to text passages in the transcript (*Gläser/Laudel* (2010), pp. 209–210). In the context of qualitative content analysis, a concept is associated with the interpretation of the code which abstracts from the verbatim record and assigns a meaning to the text (*Mayring* (2015), p. 51). The **thematic sorting** into concepts is driven by the structure of the interview guideline that predefined the ordering of the initial concepts (*Mayer* (2013), p. 53; *Scholl* (2015), p. 72). If concepts prove to be inappropriate or have to be subdivided, they are modified or new concepts are generated during the coding process (*Meuser/Nagel* (2009), p. 476). **Sociological conceptualization** refers to the search for patterns that can be subsumed under a category name (*Mayer* (2013), p. 54; *Scholl* (2015), p. 72). A category describes the umbrella term for different concepts that are linked to each other (*Gläser/Laudel* (2010), p. 205; *Mayer* (2013), p. 49). This third step enables an identification of similarities and differences among the case companies which facilitates the cross-case analysis (*Gläser/Laudel* (2010), pp. 246–249). For all three steps the qualitative data analysis (QDA) software MAXQDA has been used (*Gläser/Laudel* (2010), p. 201). QDA-software creates transparency and intersubjective traceability due to a comprehensible documentation of the whole data analysis process (*Sinkovics et al.* (2008), p. 709). The fourth step arranges the content according to the categories and thus abstracts from the single case view in favor of a **theoretical generalization**. Theoretical generalization results in new or refined hypotheses (*Gläser/Laudel* (2010), pp. 267–275). Having outlined the data collection process and the used method for qualitative data analysis, the following section presents the empirical findings of the case studies.

6.3 Empirical results

The empirical results of the qualitative case study analysis are subdivided in two major parts. Section 6.3.1 presents the within-case analysis and thoroughly describes the PMS design in SSOs for each case. Section 6.3.2 outlines the cross-case analysis which compares the PMS design in SSOs and its contingency factors across all cases in order to derive implications for the hypotheses refinement in section 6.4.

6.3.1 Within-case analysis

6.3.1.1 MedTechCo case

The SSO of MedTechCo emerged from two main motives. First, several analyses and an external benchmarking revealed that the group's finance and controlling function does not perform its processes and tasks efficiently. Second, managers of the finance and controlling organization held several roles, which led to **ambiguous areas of accountability** and thus to conflicting goals:

> *"I had corporate functions, I offered services for subsidiaries on a smaller scale and was responsible for the reporting of the parent company. As a result, our subsidiaries never knew who they were talking to. Were they talking to the local controller of the parent company, who is looking at the transfer prices of his company or were they talking to the corporate controller, who just wants to change the corporate process? Hence, the next step was a clear distinction between local tasks, services and corporate areas of responsibility. Although a hodgepogde works somehow, it always leads to the processes not being handled very well because an employee does not have the know-how for ten different finance processes."*

> *Head of SSO (MedTechCo), Interview #1, p. 2*

MedTechCo's SSO has been established in 2015 and encompasses only finance and controlling processes. The SSO initially focused on the P2P process as it assumed the greatest **savings potential** here:

> *"We started the shared service project three years ago and we are operating worldwide. We went live with the first support process – the P2P process – [...] and already transferred 85% of the group's transaction volume in Europe into our SSO. The difficulty with the further roll-out to the other continents is that we are operating on four ERP systems."*

> *Head of SSO (MedTechCo), Interview #1, p. 1*

As a major advantage, the SSO manager of MedTechCo describes the harmonization of the MNC's IT systems prior to the establishment of its SSO. Furthermore, MedTechCo considers a homogeneous IT landscape as a prerequisite for process standardization. However, four ERP systems still cause a partially decentralized process handling so that different teams work on the same processes but on four different systems. Nevertheless, MedTechCo globally maintains the master data and a global chart of accounts across all four systems, which prevents a strong differentiation of its four ERPs. A high degree of process standardization entails the advantage for MedTechCo's SSO that its employees do not have to be trained for varying systems and processes. A typically higher fluctuation of employees in SSOs compared to the group necessitates highly **standardized processes**:

> *"At that time, we decided to set up a global master data system [...]. This was an important contribution to the SSO and is still the basis why we are comparatively fast in the roll-out of our finance processes today. We have already triggered process standardization quite early. The other important issue is that it is easier to train SSO employees in one instead of two processes. In SSOs, fluctuation rates are commonly higher as employees want to advance in their careers [...]."*

> *Head of SSO (MedTechCo), Interview #1, p. 4*

In addition to cost reductions and process standardization, MedTechCo focuses on improving **process quality** and compliance with regulatory requirements and internal guidelines by implementing their SSO:

> *"We did not exclusively use the shared service concept to reduce the costs of our finance organization. This aspect automatically comes into play when I think about improving process quality. Particularly, because in the past there were enormous quality differences among certain regions. [...] Moreover, compliance issues also play an important role."*

> *Head of SSO (MedTechCo), Interview #1, p. 6*

MedTechCo's SSO primarily uses its PMS to determine the SSO's objective achievement. In terms of measures, MedTechCo's PMS mainly consists of

non-financial performance measures with reference to process quality and process automation. Therefore, MedTechCo's PMS foremost focuses on the SSO objective of improving process quality. However, MedTechCo's PMS almost exclusively contains performance measures for the P2P process and less for other support processes of the SSO. Moreover, the PMS barely contains measures with regard to further SSO objectives, such as reducing costs or ensuring compliance:

> *"With regard to performance measures related to our processes, I have to confess that our PMS is not sufficiently advanced yet. At first, we initially have to think about which sub-processes we want to monitor at all. On which measures do I have influence in the SSC and on which I do not? At the moment, I'm still looking for a suitable model [...]."*

> *Head of SSO (MedTechCo), Interview #1, p. 13*

The low degree of PMS maturity and the uncertainty about which SSO objectives should be reflected to what extent in the PMS have an impact on the performance measurement process. MedTechCo copes with the uncertainty of which measures correspond to the SSO's strategy by seeking **inspiration from outside**. However, MedTechCo does not adopt new measures, but adapts suggestions according to their own needs:

> *"I also adopt ideas from magazines or congresses to use it in our brainstorming sessions and then adapt what is important to us."*

> *Head of SSO (MedTechCo), Interview #1, p. 14*

Nonetheless, the **performance measure selection process** in MedTechCo's SSO does not always seem to be transparent to all performance measurement actors. This also affects the target setting for certain performance measures. If the selection process and the performance measure target setting process take place in isolation from each other and with different groups of performance measurement actors, it entails the risk that performance measures do not measure what they should. Thus, performance measure targets may have a demotivating effect:

> *"The fact that we want to include the order reference as a KPI in our PMS has just been handed down to me as I started here. [...] I do not know how the target for the performance measure 'processed invoices per FTE' was set. But I do know that it is a fundamental measure in our reporting. [...] Apart from that, I'm thinking on my own what would be, for example, a good target for an error rate."*

> *SSO Management accountant (MedTechCo), Interview #2, p. 3*

Overall, MedTechCo's management accountant describes the data collection process for providing the monthly KPI reporting as complex. Particularly, the performance measure data collection process is time-consuming due to the large data volumes that have to be processed. As a consequence, MedTechCo is about to procure an analysis tool that is capable of evaluating and visualizing large data volumes. MedTechCo mainly performs **variance analyses** to assess the SSO's current performance level. By contrast, MedTechCo's SSO barely uses an internal benchmarking because it fears negative effects for behavioral control:

> "We have already received the request if we could benchmark our three European SSCs and establish a regular reporting. However, we never did that because it could demotivate our SSC teams. [...] If the Polish SSC and the Spanish SSC notice that the German SSC always adulates itself by bragging with 18,000 invoices per FTE and the two other SSCs are at 9,000, it has a demotivating effect. Particularly, because this difference may be due to the fact that they process other invoices which are more complicated. [...] Moreover, the quantity distribution is an issue. At least in the early days of the SSC in Poland, the SSO management transferred invoices to Poland that are rather simple to process, because they wanted to train the new employees first. If you look at the SSC benchmarking you might say: 'Why are they still so slow in this SSC? What are they doing all day? You already process the easiest invoices.' Such already existing rivalries should not be fostered by my KPI reporting, because that does not yield any benefits."

SSO Management accountant (MedTechCo), Interview #2, p. 6–7

MedTechCo's SSO controlling department adjusts the KPI reporting cycle according to the user groups. Essentially, the SSO reports performance measures with reference to the support processes on a daily basis to the operating units in the SSCs. Aggregated performance measures are reported on a monthly basis to the SSO management. The rather reactive approach to performance measure selection and target setting, the lack of transparency in the performance measurement process, the tedious data collection and an insufficient involvement of key performance measurement actors are the main reasons for a **dissatisfied SSO management** with respect to its PMS:

> "At the moment I am rather dissatisfied with our PMS. The effort to collect the required data is too high. The contents are quite good, but there is also a lot of information missing, such as flow times [...]. We also need to talk more regularly with our SSC customers to better use the information from our PMS. A lot of information is already there, but it's still incomplete and needs to be generated faster and in a more automated way because its collection is very costly at the moment."

Head of SSO (MedTechCo), Interview #1, p. 11

Nevertheless, the SSO management and the SSO controlling department have initiated a policy shift towards a stronger **integration of SSO employees** into the performance measurement process. By now, SSO employees are encouraged to discuss the meaningfulness of new or altered performance measures and may suggest possible alternatives. The process managers are also required to integrate the performance measurement into the communication with their teams and to use KPI analyses as a basis for lean management initiatives:

> *"[...] since we discuss performance measures, our employees are capable of understanding how they are calculated. The acceptance by the SSO employees is an indication for me whether a specific measure works. If the SSO employees accept a measure, I can also make it available to a manager."*
>
> *Head of SSO (MedTechCo), Interview #1, p. 11*

6.3.1.2 CommCo case

CommCo emerged in the mid-nineties as a private firm from the state-owned German Federal Post Office. The historical background as a state-owned company still impacts CommCo's current SSO in three aspects. First, CommCo had a very **fragmented organizational structure** as its subsidiaries mainly evolved from formerly state-owned post offices in German cities. Since the implementation of a SSO involves the consolidation of support processes, CommCo faces a specific challenge with regard to its number of locations:

> *"There was a post office in almost every major city that had its own HR and accounting department. For many years attempts have been made to consolidate the sites in several steps. [...] The problem exists, because CommCo has this historical background."*
>
> *Managing Director SSO (CommCo), Interview #3, p. 2–3*

Second, CommCo focuses more on the domestic market compared to other MNCs of this size. The internationalization of CommCo just started with its privatization so that a large part of CommCo's business still takes place in Germany. As a consequence, the SSO is guided by the needs of German SSO customers, who are particularly interested in **service quality**:

> *"If you look at CommCo's annual report, you may recognize that a very large part of its business is still running in Germany. Of the 400,000 employees, around 200,000 are employed in Germany. This already shows the importance of the domestic market. [...] In essence, I think that's how CommCo is perceived nationwide: if one thing has to be right, then it's the service quality [...]."*
>
> *Managing Director SSO (CommCo), Interview #3, p. 3*

Third, a significant proportion of SSO employees are **civil servants**. The administration of civil servants and public employees is more complex compared to SSOs, which have only regular employees as there are specific employment laws for civil servants. Nonetheless, employing civil servants in CommCo's SSO also facilitates the intended site consolidation, since they are easier to relocate than regular employees:

> *"In our HR departments, we face the situation that still one third of our SSO employees are civil servants. With regard to the civil servants administration you have to consider laws. You cannot simply delegate their administration into a subsidiary [...]. This means that [...] we will have to work with many legal entities in the long run. There are several issues that make CommCo more complicated than other companies that evolved in the private sector. [...] Therefore, the transformation process itself is problematic but during the actual implementation the peculiarities of employing civil servants even helps you."*

> *Managing Director SSO (CommCo), Interview #3, p. 2–3*

Since 2016, CommCo's SSO includes not only finance and accounting processes, but also support processes from the operational functions controlling, HR and procurement resulting in **multifunctional SSCs**. This enables CommCo to perform end-to-end support processes in their SSCs. Therefore, CommCo's SSO uses the PMS across functions so that, for example, it measures flow times for the entire process and not just for the subprocesses of each operational function. Due to the low maturity level of the multifunctional SSO, silo mentality still poses a problem so that the operational functions do not yet collaborate in the desired intensity. A close cooperation along the process chain promises to detect causal relationships between the subprocesses:

> *"At the moment you can still see: this is a buyer and this is an accountant. But they should become P2P managers. In order to promote this convergence, I am looking for KPIs that show me to what extent we have the end-to-end process in mind. But I know that I am struggling with it."*

> *Managing Director SSO (CommCo), Interview #3, p. 6*

CommCo's SSO uses a PMS that is based on the **BSC**. All three SSCs use their own BSC:

> *"For our three SSCs, we have [...] built a BSC with the well-known perspectives, namely the financial, the employee, the customer and the process perspective."*

> *SSO Management accountant (CommCo), Interview #4, p. 1*

The measures within the four perspectives are closely linked to the SLAs of the respective SSCs and its customers and vary due to the diversity of SLAs. The SSO management accountant emphasizes that SLAs are an important control mechanism of CommCo's SSO and that the **SLA design** is closely linked to the PMS. Each support process performed by the SSO (the service line) also uses its own BSC, albeit it primarily contains process-related performance measures.

The top KPIs of the BSCs at the service line level are merged into one BSC for the entire SSC. The most important KPIs of the SSC BSCs are grouped into a superordinated management scorecard for the entire SSO. Notably, the management scorecard and the BSCs of the SSCs encompass predominantly performance measures with reference to process quality and process automation.

New performance measures for the PMS of CommCo's SSO are primarily generated due to two triggers. First, there is an impetus from the SSO's management to investigate a particular performance measurement area. Second, during the everday operations problems emerge which need to be solved by the process owners. In order to ascertain whether a process change has successfully contributed to problem solving, the process managers monitor their actions by using performance measures. For the **performance measure selection**, it is of particular importance for the process managers that they can influence the KPI development based on their actions:

> *"The selection process for our performance measures is simple. We exchange ideas on possible measures with the service line. We suggest alternatives for potential measures, and the service line chooses an alternative because it is ultimately held responsible for that measure. [...] By which measures the service line would like to be benchmarked? In general, they always take the performance measure that they are most likely to influence."*

> SSO Management accountant (CommCo), Interview #4, p. 4

According to CommCo's SSO controlling department, the target setting approach for performance measures is considered as poorly developed. Currently, there is no standardized approach to set performance measure targets so that very different target setting procedures occur. In addition to coordination efforts between the service lines and the SSO controlling to compromise on targets, the SSO controlling department prefers the use of an external benchmarking. An external benchmarking entails the advantage that possible targets are set independently from individual interest so that the use of arbitrary objectives induced by principal-agent relationships can be mitigated. Nevertheless, an **external benchmarking** entails the necessity to select a peer group that is precisely fitting to CommCo in order to enable a meaningful comparability:

> *"I want to have a decent benchmark for each performance measure wherever possible. There are many benchmarking opportunities, such as the SSC roundtable or Hackett. [...] But we use special systems at CommCo that are not available elsewhere. Thus, we simply had to set goals internally. They are set arbitrarily. They are set according to a gut feeling, experience, expert knowledge, management requirements, whatever."*

> SSO Management accountant (CommCo), Interview #4, p. 6

Due to the fact that CommCo uses twelve different ERPs, collecting data for performance measures is challenging. Moreover, CommCo's SSO controlling relies on data from departments that do not belong to the SSO to calculate its performance measures. Furthermore, the SSO agreed upon activity splits between the SSO and CommCo's subsidiaries. Hence, performance measures that aim at an end-to-end process are based on a relationship of dependency between the SSO and its customers. The PMS has not been modified until recently. After a reorganization, the SSO controlling department started to make **major modifications** in its PMS for two reasons. First, because the SSO omitted to continuously modify its PMS so far. Second, because the environmental conditions of the PMS have changed so that the SSO's strategies to achieve its objectives have changed:

> "I have been here for three months now. We are at the stage where we are able to eliminate about half of the KPIs in our PMS. [...] Some systems that were monitored with our performance measures were not even existent anymore. [...] At the same time, new topics have developed in recent years. For example, robotics is currently running big. We are about to install chatbots in our service hotlines. These are topics that did not exist three years ago and now you have to define KPIs. How efficient are our new applications that we are launching?"
>
> *SSO Management accountant (CommCo), Interview #4, p. 3*

In essence, the SSO management accountant and the SSO manager are satisfied with the modifications they made with respect to their PMS, but both see room for improvement. While the SSO controlling needs to better understand the business model of its service lines in order to play an advisory role in the performance measurement process, the process managers do not yet conceive the SSO's PMS as a chance to improve their daily work but rather consider the PMS as a threat that sanctions their individual performance:

> "It is very important that a PMS does not represent a solely theoretical concept. [...] I believe the key point is that the easier a performance measure is to understand and the more transparent a PMS is designed, the safer it is that you can work successfully with your KPIs. With regard to the KPI target setting, I'm convinced that only a negative deviation creates action. Hence, a negative deviation per se is not bad. However, you have to be careful that the SSO employees are not afraid of personal sanctions so that in case of a negative KPI deviation their annual bonus is immediately reduced to zero. This creates a corporate culture that is just bad. My managers in the service lines still look at our PMS too much as an instrument to patronize them. They still do not perceive our PMS as a common steering tool by which we try to steer the SSO in a better direction."
>
> *Managing Director SSO (CommCo), Interview #3, p. 9–10*

6.3.1.3 ChemCo case

ChemCo operates with a mature SSO, which has been implemented as a greenfield approach fifteen years ago. Unlike many other SSCs, the German SSC of ChemCo is not located next to the corporate headquarters, but has been established in a larger German city. This location decision has three major implications for ChemCo's SSO. First, the SSO employees have not been transferred from the corporate functions into the SSO. Thus, the majority of SSO employees does not have any corporate experience. As a consequence, SSO employees have been hired according to the SSO's job requirements. For example, ChemCo's SSO has put emphasis on language competencies when selecting new employees for the accounting and controlling functions. Second, ChemCo's SSO is not bound to corporate labor agreements allowing the SSO to establish new compensation models. Third, the site selection has been determined by a sufficient availability of employees with the required competencies. Therefore, labor arbitrage has not been the most important criterion when selecting the SSC location. The SSO's site selection seems in line with its **objectives**, which do not exclusively encompass cost reduction:

> "With the implementation of shared services, our top management had the vision: 'I get the same thing much cheaper – maybe 30% cheaper, but it's the same thing'. [...] And it's true, establishing a SSO yields labor arbitrage. You can yield it again if you relocate your SSC to a country with even more favorable wages while going through the whole process again. However, saving labor costs and getting the same cheaper is admittedly attractive, but not enough. By implementing a SSO, the management implicitly wants a better governance, a higher quality and it wants more flexibility in corporate transactions, too."

> *Managing Director SSO (ChemCo), Interview #5, p. 1–2*

With regard to the **SSO's structural complexity**, the managing director of ChemCo's SSO highlights that SSOs are not a panacea, because they also entail disadvantages. Particularly, he challenges the prompt emergence of multifunctional SSOs since multifunctional SSCs create interfaces that did not exist before. Interfaces may lead to turf battles between corporate functions, local organizational units and the SSO. Moreover, multifunctional SSOs may induce more conflicting goals concerning the governance of support processes:

> "What I have achieved through multifunctional SSOs is the following: I have taken some of the responsibilities away from the corporate and from the local functions. [...] In other words, I created headquarters that governs the corporate functions, such as accounting and HR, and I have SSCs in my SSO that are responsible for the process governance, such as P2P or hire-to-retire. As a consequence, the governance of the corporate functions inflates unnecessarily in order to monitor the SSCs. Moreover, an inflated governance induces a

sharper separation between corporate functions and SSCs. [...] Hence, the collaboration between functions in end-to-end processes does not necessarily improve just because we're introducing shared services.

Managing Director SSO (ChemCo), Interview #5, p. 2–3

By contrast, SSOs are comparatively well able to standardize and optimize support processes:

"What will be better is the following: assume that ChemCo has 100 subsidiaries and would like to change something in their support processes. For example, ChemCo would like to define a standardized process. Without a SSO, ChemCo had to talk to 100 subsidiaries to explain the process changes, make the changes and monitor if these changes persist. By using a SSO, I now have a single person in charge, who is in a position to coordinate and assess all these process changes. What are the differences between the 100 subsidiaries? What do we consider as a good standard? Successively rolling out a standardized process to 100 subsidiaries works comparatively well with the shared service model. At least better than a somehow self-coordinated mechanism among 100 subsidiaries. My experience with shared services is that an increased coordination efficiency is actually a more significant leverage to reduce costs than labor arbitrage."

Managing Director SSO (ChemCo), Interview #5, p. 3

The critical attitude towards universally applicable concepts is also reflected in the performance measurement of ChemCo's SSO. For its PMS development, ChemCo's SSO did not follow an established model or relied on external support from consulting firms. Instead, ChemCo's SSO is convinced that a PMS has to be tailored according to its own environment and that a PMS model cannot be used for all SSOs in the same way. Based on the notion that ChemCo's SSO emphasizes its **unique contingency factors**, the SSO manager shares the belief that only ChemCo's own abilities and actions allow for a meaningful PMS. In accordance with ChemCo's internal locus of control, the SSO's managing director highlights that performance measurement effectiveness is built on the SSO's competences and not by external forces, such as lean management or six sigma initiatives:

"We did not rely on external support and asked ourselves instead, where we are and where to go. [...] Whatever performance measurement model you select, the starting point is always your own circumstances and what can be achieved in your own environment. [...] Growing by your own challenges is a continuous competence development. But can you measure that? Yes, for example, by measuring that I receive fewer complaint calls."

Managing Director SSO (ChemCo), Interview #5, p. 6

The strong **internal locus of control** is expressed by the fact that ChemCo's SSO barely adopts performance measures that are frequently used by other SSOs. The managing director of ChemCo's SSO exclusively uses a personnel deployment ratio to manage the entire SSO. Therefore, he considers the relationship between FTEs that have been initially transferred to the SSO and currently deployed FTEs. Moreover, ChemCo's SSO management board analyzes the development of average personnel costs per operating unit. The SSO management board deliberately limits itself to a single performance measure to avoid micromanagement:

> "A BSC is not really what we need. [...] 90% of our costs are labor costs. To control a SSC, you can moderately discuss about the rent of our office building. IT costs play a certain role, but these are usually managed by other units and we're just the users. [...] In order to manage such a SSC we only need a single performance measure, namely: 'How much staff do I use?' [...] The deployment ratio sets further objectives, which then lead to other KPIs that are looked at intensively if we identified room for improvement."

> *Managing Director SSO (ChemCo), Interview #5, p. 8*

Although ChemCo's SSO uses many known performance measures, they do not collect, for example, process measures on a regular basis. ChemCo's SSO refrains from institutionalizing its performance measurement for three reasons. First, many performance measures are not an objective themselves, but can only temporarily support the achievement of a SSO objective. Second, many performance measures address activities in subprocesses so that their interpretation seems difficult for all KPI reporting addressees. However, ChemCo's SSO agrees to introduce measures on request from the SSO's customers, if these measures enable correctives for the SSO and its customers. Third, an **institutionalized performance measurement** involves considerable costs:

> "A backlog is only interesting to me if a subsidiary calls and complaints: 'this does not work, we're heading for the year-end closing and it looks bad. You lost control.' Then I'm going to ask my teams. Could you measure the backlog? Could you show me how you want to get it under control? Why are you quiet when they are nervous? We are using performance measures, such as the backlog. [...] However, the backlog itself is not an objective. We do not strive for zero backlog. [...] To control a SSC, you do not need many KPIs. Maybe if you need to evaluate a launched improvement action. But two years later you may not need them anymore. That makes performance measurement difficult. Defining measures, compromising on a common definition, perhaps even automating performance measures – all this takes a considerable amount of time, costs a lot of money and nerves. For performance measurement purposes, you can set up entire organizational units that operate with lean-six-sigma and all these tools."

> *Managing Director SSO (ChemCo), Interview #5, p. 7–8*

Moreover, organizational units that are primarily responsible for performance measurement partly contradict ChemCo's philosophy of an internal locus of control. From the SSO management's point of view, performance measurement units do not represent a vote of confidence for the process managers and partly relieve them from bearing responsibility. Furthermore, the expert highlights that most activities in ChemCo's SSO are knowledge-based and thus it is challenging to develop performance measures that map the employee's competences. Although the SSO uses pulse checks and churn rates to measure the satisfaction of its employees, these measures only provide insufficient information about the expertise available in the SSO. Although performance measurement analysis tools provide improved transparency about the current performance, they do not improve performance. Thus, ChemCo's SSO assumes that the implementation of analysis tools in favor of a transparent performance measurement is at the expense of performance management.

In essence, ChemCo's SSO is aware of its rather unique approach and is quite satisfied with its performance measurement and what has been achieved so far. The expert stresses that ChemCo's performance measurement aspires to be comprehensible for all relevant performance measurement actors and **improves communication**. Particularly, ChemCo's SSO pays attention to the direct applicability of the findings from performance measurement activities:

> "A PMS must be clear, it must create transparency at the relevant spots, it must be accepted and understood by employees and by managers. It should also be of a manageable complexity. [...] Modification at recurring intervals, traceability, and feasibility are decisive factors for the effectiveness of a PMS."
>
> *Managing Director SSO (ChemCo), Interview #5, p. 17*

6.3.1.4 PharCo case

PharCo has a fairly experienced SSO that exists for almost ten years. In addition to a SSC in Germany, PharCo also uses two low-wage locations in Asia, primarily to perform P2P and O2C processes. Moreover, PharCo established a SSC in Eastern Europe. When setting up its SSO, PharCo selected a mixed approach. While one SSC in Southeast Asia has been set up as a new legal entity, PharCo located the remaining SSCs at an already existing site. The second SSC in Asia has been added to PharCo's SSO when the MNC has made a larger acquisition so that the SSO had to integrate the SSC of the acquired company. In general, PharCo's SSO has been strongly occupied in integrating new subsidiaries, which have been added due to PharCo's expansion strategy in recent years. Based on the experience of the post-merger integration of new subsidiaries, PharCo's SSO has decided to terminate the implementation of activity splits between local subsidiaries and SSCs, but to **transfer the entire finance organization** of a subsidiary into the SSO. Only a CFO remains as a counterpart for the managing director of the local subsidiary and a so-called accounting business partner who is responsible to coordinate activities between the subsidiary and the SSO:

> *"In total, approximately 200 employees with over thirty nationalities are now working for the SSO providing the full range of finance and accounting services. They perform not only the transactional accounting processes, such as accounts payable and accounts receivable but also other activities, such as general ledger, tax, management accounting tasks, etc. We started some time ago to refrain from the activity split between the local subsidiaries and our SSCs so that we meanwhile pursue a full service approach. Therefore, we gradually transfer the entire financial function of the subsidiaries into the SSO."*

> *Head of SSO Process Excellence (PharCo), Interview #6, p. 2*

PharCo launched a one-ERP project to harmonize its IT landscape. A **homogeneous IT landscape** is also advantageous for PharCo's SSO as a manageable number of ERP systems enhances the standardization of support processes. However, in the course of several acquisition projects, PharCo had to integrate new ERP systems in a relatively short period of time so that a harmonization of the IT landscape no longer seemed enforceable. Moreover, PharCo's operating divisions enforced to design their IT landscape mostly independently of each other according to their business requirements as their requirements are too far apart to compromise on a global ERP system. As a result, PharCo's SSO has adapted its strategy and by now defines standard processes as far as possible across systems. This also has an influence on the SSO's PMS, since, for example, performance measures have to be automatable, evaluable and comparable across systems:

> *"We always had many ERP systems in our SSO. In 2007, we initially decided that we only provide services to subsidiaries working on a globally defined ERP template. However, our doctrine changed with our first major acquisition. In fact, our first major integration project started with Oracle. As a result, a variety of ERP systems emerged over time with which we now have to work."*

> *Head of SSO Process Excellence (PharCo), Interview #6, p. 9*

Although PharCo's SSO exists for almost ten years, the SSO's performance measurement is still in the early stages, mainly because of the acquisition wave in recent years. Quite unusually, the SSO's PMS comprises a **large set of KPIs**:

> *"Our PMS now has a total of 280 KPIs for some time now. 'KPIs' in quotation marks, because these are not really KPIs. We have a data pool of 280 performance measures that we collect automatically and manually. [...] We usually schedule a monthly meeting to discuss our performance measures. In these meetings, we discuss a total of three KPIs per service line. Particularly, we analyze the KPI development of the last three months. Apart*

from the SSO management, also process managers participate in these meetings if their expertise is required."

Head of SSO Process Excellence (PharCo), Interview #6, p. 14

The low priority of performance measurement activities in PharCo's SSO is also expressed by the fact that performance measurement is not yet part of the SSO controlling department. Even though recent performance measurement activities, such as the monthly KPI reporting discussions were coordinated by the SSO controlling department, the main part of performance measurement has been under the responsibility of the process managers. The low importance of performance measures in the operational management of PharCo's SSO becomes apparent as for most KPIs targets are not yet set. Moreover, the SSO rarely derives specific actions to counteract negative KPI developments after analyzing its KPIs. Due to this unsatisfactory situation with regard to the SSO's performance measurement, PharCo's SSO has initiated a reorganization project. In addition to an internal performance measurement reorganization initiative, the SSO also has decided to consult **external expertise**:

> *"For the reorganization of our performance measurement, we have asked for external support. [...] However, even before we received external support we got started with an internal reorganization project so that both projects overlapped. [...] Thus, we were already going in the direction that we want to implement a pyramid structure for our PMS. That means, whenever you see an effect on a superordinate KPI level, it should be explainable with the subordinate KPI levels. This pyramid structure ensures a certain consistency."*

Head of SSO Process Excellence (PharCo), Interview #6, p. 18

Apart from the notion that the prospective PMS encompasses performance measures that are consistently linked to each other, the reorganization project primarily intends to establish a KPI driven culture in the SSO. The pyramid structure of the new PMS is important to enable a KPI driven culture, because performance measurement has to be used by all hierarchical levels of the SSO as a tool for performance improvement. Thus, performance measurement **involves all relevant actors**, such as the SSO employees, the process managers and the SSO customers. Moreover, the SSO's new PMS incorporates a closer integration of performance measures that are used to control the SSO and performance measures that are used in SLAs to drive customer-supplier relationships:

> *"Another change that we want to make in our PMS is that we subdivide our KPI set into internal and external KPIs. The external performance measures are particularly relevant to our SLAs that we agreed on with our customers. Moreover, external KPIs primarily describe a strategic level, which we usually discuss with the SSO management. The internal KPIs are more important on a tactical or operational level. This fragmentation should*

answer the question: who discusses which issues in which frequency and with which actors? [...] Another aspect of the PMS reorganization is the extension of the performance measurement scope towards end-to-end processes. We need performance measures by which we can analyze to what extent prior activities of other organizational units have a negative impact on our indicators. But at the moment we are lacking of instruments that enable us to act [...]."

Head of SSO Process Excellence (PharCo), Interview #6, p. 17

Furthermore, the extension of the performance measurement area towards the reflection of the entire end-to-end process describes another requirement for the optimized PMS. An end-to-end process scope seems the best way for the SSO manager to visualize causal relationships between performance measures. The gained **transparency** allows to link specific actions for improvement to the KPI analysis. Overall, PharCo's SSO manager emphasizes that the prospective PMS should provide greater flexibility than the previous KPI pool of 280 measures. Accordingly, he suggests to no longer track measures just in case, but rather define new performance measures if necessary and eliminate them after a successful improvement:

"Our PMS should be transparent so that it enables us to locate problematic issues in our support process. [...] Moreover, we do not need a static PMS, but a PMS that allows for a flexible response to a specific situation. We need a flexible PMS so that you can replace an indicator, for which you have achieved a target by a new one. [...] You should be able to immediately replace a KPI as soon as the indicator has improved as a result of the taken actions. Hence, our future PMS should offer this flexibility."

Head of SSO Process Excellence (PharCo), Interview #6, p. 25–26

6.3.1.5 AgriCo case

AgriCo is a MNC from the Midwestern United States: the so-called bible belt. As the largest manufacturer of agricultural machinery in the US, the group generates more than 50% of the annual sales in its domestic market. Although AgriCo has a fairly mature SSO that exists for almost ten years, its SSO initiatives have so far focused on economies of scope instead of a cost reduction through economies of scale or a pooling of experts. The consolidation of corporate functions at a few locations plays a far greater role in AgriCo's SSO concept than a more effective and efficient rendering of support processes through a cross-functional end-to-end analysis. The implementation of the SSC in Germany has been **initiated by expats** from the USA:

"AgriCo is a globally dispersed corporation and there have always been SSC initiatives by the US headquarters. However, these initiatives were often designed solely to concentrate

employees in two or three cities. There has never been a process-oriented approach for our SSCs, which puts emphasis on end-to-end processes. Our SSCs consist of former corporate functions that have been migrated to a SSC. The shared service approach came to Germany about ten years ago with the American finance directors of AgriCo, who came to Germany as expats for two to three years."

Head of SSC Germany (AgriCo), Interview #7, p. 1

AgriCo established a SSC in the US, Brazil, India, and China. In addition to the SSC in Germany, AgriCo also has SSCs in France, Spain, Poland, and Finland. All SSCs have been established at existing production or distribution sites. As the SSCs have emerged from regional initiatives in the sense of a mere concentration of corporate functions, AgriCo has united the regional approaches to a global finance SSO. Apart from the general ledger accounting, the accounts payable and the accounts receivable departments, the SSCs also include asset accounting, payroll accounting and the travel expense processing. However, the SSCs do not perform all of the mentioned processes but differ from each other in their process scope. AgriCo's strategy with regard to the European SSCs remains vacillating according to the Head of the German SSC. The SSO manager perceives the development of the European SSCs and the American SSC at varying speeds and attributes the more advanced development of the US-based SSC to diverging **support from AgriCo's top management**:

"Five years ago, we decided to turn the regional shared service initiatives into a global SSO. In other words, I am now reporting to the USA. Everything is globally dictated by our SSC in the US. They define the performance measures we should use. Whether or not the globally predefined measures correspond to our regional SSC is a completely different question. [...] So let's conclude: the American SSC is considerably more developed compared to AgriCo's German SSC. However, the American SSC has also received greater support from our top management over the past years. That is to say, they rapped over the subsidiaries' knuckles much more than here in Europe so that the US subsidiaries have been challenged to transfer their support processes to the American SSC."

Head of SSC Germany (AgriCo), Interview #7, p. 7

After integrating the regional shared service initiatives into a global SSO, AgriCo has changed its focus from a mere site consolidation to a standardization of locally varying support processes and a gradual automation of sub-processes. The lack of process standardization in most support processes until today also has a negative impact on the performance measurement of AgriCo's SSO, as the process performance measures are barely comparable. Due to the lacking comparability of the process KPIs, the PMS of the SSO primarily incorporates aggregated performance measures for the SSO management reporting. However, these aggregated measures are of **minor decision usefulness** for the Head of the SSC in Germany to control his organization. Therefore, the SSCs usually operate with additional performance measures in addition to the KPIs that have to be reported mandatorily to the SSO's PMS in the US:

> *"As you presumed, I have to create my own [performance measures] together with my management team and with my supervisor. [...] Because somehow I have to control my SSC, and the predefined performance measures from the US are not sufficient for this purpose. For example, the head of the SSC in Poland has also developed her own performance measures."*
>
> Head of SSC Germany (AgriCo), Interview #7, p. 12

This is aggravated by the fact that the SSC and the SSO management barely communicate with each other with respect to performance measurement issues. Thus, it remains unknown to the SSC in Germany whether the performance measures reported to the USA are even used. By pre-defining the set of measures, the SSO management misses the opportunity to learn which performance measures developed by the SSCs have proved to be successful for the SSC's control. For example, the Head of the SSC in Poland has developed performance measures that also matter to the SSC in Germany as these employee-related measures aim at the competence development of SSO employees. Overall, the globally driven performance measurement process across the SSCs is confined to report a **pre-defined KPI set** to the SSO's management:

> *"In plain language: you cannot do anything at all with these performance measures. They are too aggregated for my purposes. Above all, I need measures in the accounts payable department, because we have quite standardized processes there. [...] With these performance measures I would like to analyze the efficiency of our SSC. The lead times for individual process steps are important to me, for example the required time to verify an invoice, the time required to release an invoice, the time required to complete a payment run, the time required to communicate with our suppliers, etc."*
>
> Head of SSC Germany (AgriCo), Interview #7, p. 14

The performance measurement process for the performance measures of AgriCo's German SSCs is determined by an outward view. The selection of new performance measures and their **target setting** process focuses on the exchange with SSOs from other companies and academic research. Through an external benchmarking and a constant communication with SSOs that are perceived as pioneers in the field of performance measurement, AgriCo's SSC wants to ensure to not miss significant developments in this field and generate ideas for its PMS modification:

> *"First, we set targets for performance measures based on their development over the past years. A second possibility is benchmarking with other companies. We meet with other SSCs in the close proximity and exchange ideas. [...] A third possibility consists in specialized literature. There are enough SSC articles and shared service conferences where companies and academic research present their latest developments."*

> *Head of SSC Germany (AgriCo), Interview #7, p. 17–18*

In essence, the SSC manager is not really satisfied with the PMS. He assumes that the performance measures are widely accepted by the SSC employees as the individual performance measures are not used to monitor the performance of the employees. By contrast, those measures indicate developments of the SSC performance so that the SSC management is able to discuss latest developments with the SSC employees. The expert emphasizes that the measures are not used as a sanctioning mechanism. The SSC manager regrets the lack of cooperation with regard to performance measurement topics between the SSC Germany and the SSO management. Furthermore, the SSC manager is **not satisfied with his PMS** because performance measures are based on inadequately standardized processes. Therefore, the performance measure analysis across processes or SSCs seems superficial. The expert would prefer a PMS development towards a model established in theory, such as the BSC, since it would limit the number to a few but meaningful performance measures. Moreover, the SSC manager advocates for an institutionalized performance measurement that supports the SSC management:

> *"I'm not satisfied at all with my PMS. Or let's say: I'm satisfied, because I am able to control my SSC to some extent. But I don't have any support. I'm doing everything by myself. I'm creating and analyzing performance measures all by myself and [...] I'd like to have more standardized processes connected with well-defined performance measures."*

> *Head of SSC Germany (AgriCo), Interview #7, p. 21*

6.3.1.6 HealthCo case

HealthCo's SSO exists for nearly twenty years and exclusively performs accounting, controlling, and finance processes. HealthCo considered to extend the SSO model to other functions in the recent past but so far without reaching a decision. The high degree of the SSO's maturity also leads to a high geographical dispersion of its SSCs and to dispersed subprocesses. Overall, HealthCo distinguishes three types of SSCs in their SSO. **Back-offices** mainly perform subprocesses that have high transaction volumes and require little communication with customers, suppliers and with HealthCo's organizational units. **Front-offices** also handle subprocesses with high transaction volumes, but often get in touch with SSO stakeholders so that language skills are of particular importance for front-offices. Third, there are so-called **global offices**, which process low transaction volumes and usually have a high specificity. Furthermore, HealthCo's SSO includes a department called 'design and build', which governs the support processes and thus specifies how processes should be performed and optimized in the back- and front-offices. Moreover, the local subsidiaries installed an accounting business partner who represents the interests of the SSO customers and serves as an interface between the SSO and the SSO customer. In addition, the corporate accounting, controlling and finance is subsumed under the term functional leadership, which governs the finance function of the group and encompasses departments, such as the group accounting.

This organizational structure allows for a distinct control of the SSO and the SSO's essential objectives. The separation into back, front and global offices enables a further labor division within the support processes yielding further cost reductions. The 'design and build' function ensures a high degree of process standardization and thus also contributes to a high degree of compliance with legal and internal requirements. However, such an organizational structure also creates **additional interfaces**, which lead to inefficiencies through an increased coordination and communication demand. The risk of inefficiencies increases if process governance and process execution are not only organizationally but also geographically separated due to the intended labor arbitrage:

> *"It is important to us that our SSO governance stays in touch with the daily challenges of the local units. It is important that we are not just working in our ivory tower and making decisions over the heads of the local units or the SSCs. [...] We want to do more for the operational business in the future than we did in the past. Because this is where the action is and not in our administrative processes. [...] The organizational structure of our SSO has economic advantages and it also has advantages in terms of quality, transparency and standardization. But you also create a lot of interfaces. [...] From my point of view, you cannot always relocate a subprocess somewhere, because it is less costly. You have to be aware that you create an interface with each process shift."*
>
> Head of SSO Performance Controlling (HealthCo), Interview #9, p. 16

The organizational structure of the SSO also affects HealthCo's performance measurement. The geographical distance between the SSO units and the number of interfaces requires a high degree of control. Moreover, the external conditions in which HealthCo's SSO operates may influence the performance measurement. If **regulatory requirements** of countries change, process improvements may be possible that were not possible before. This allows for altering measuring points of KPIs and a different performance measure development. Digitalized administrative processes in local tax authorities ensure a higher level of auto-mation of SSO processes and thus for improved process performance measures:

> *"For example, if you look at the processing of electronic invoices. I know exactly that there are 'terrific' countries where you can say good-bye to an electronic invoice exchange, because they have these legal requirements that an invoice must have an authorized sig-nature and an official company stamp. Otherwise, the invoice is not legally compliant. But we always monitor the extent to which legal requirements evolve. For instance, there are now tendencies in Russia, Latin America, and Turkey, where exactly this change of mind is taking place in the local tax authorities. Because they also recognize that the electronic processing of invoices yields benefits for them."*

Head of SSO Governance (HealthCo), Interview #8, p. 18–19

For the Head of HealthCo's SSO governance, process standardization constitutes the prerequisite to automate support processes. All process changes requested by SSO customers have to be approved by the SSO governance so that deviations from the standard processes remain exceptional. The importance of process standardization in HealthCo's SSO is closely related to the SSO objective of min-imizing the risk that the processes execution violates legal requirements since standardized processes are easier to monitor compared to customized processes with multiple exceptions.

With regard to **performance measurement targets**, standardized processes enable a greater comparability. External benchmarking plays an important part in the SSO's target setting process for performance measures. External benchmarks as reference values for performance measures provide a comparatively independ-ent view of what is achievable. Nonetheless, external benchmarks are associated with the risk that different underlying conditions are not explicitly taken into account when setting targets for performance measures. Therefore, HealthCo's SSO governance adjusts target values from an external benchmarking:

> *"With regard to the performance measure targets, I am guided by external benchmarks. Knowing that Hackett gives me international numbers, I analyze how far Hackett's pro-posed KPIs can be adopted to our SSO. A good deal of our business takes place in Asia so that we face very different conditions from our peer group suggested by Hackett. I try to adjust Hackett's suggestions according to our conditions and then set a target value. I do not set a value before making sure that the SSCs are able to provide the support to push the KPIs to the next level together with our customers."*

Head of SSO Governance (HealthCo), Interview #8, p. 22

An important objective for the performance controlling of HealthCo's SSO is the automation of the data collection for the calculation of performance meas-ures. For this reason, the department has made extensive modifications of the

SSO's PMS in the recent past. The Head of the SSO Performance Controlling emphasizes that changed environmental conditions consistently lead to **changes in the PMS**:

> *"In the beginning of 2015, we enforced a 'big bang' PMS modification. Thereby, we elimi-nated 18 of our 60 performance measures, which were designed before my time in the per-formance controlling department. This was the result of discussions and analyses. [...] We change our organization regularly and therefore have to adapt our KPI landscape to this new organizational structure."*
>
> Head of SSO Performance Controlling (HealthCo), Interview #9, p. 30

However, PMS modifications in HealthCo's SSO are intended not only to auto-mate data collection and improve comparability, but primarily to improve the SSO's performance. Only if performance measures enable performance improvements, the effort spent on performance measurement is justified. In es-sence, the experts are satisfied with their PMS and perceive a high acceptance of the PMS among the SSO employees. However, they see two risks that could undermine the **PMS acceptance**. First, performance measures have to remain understandable. Second, KPIs lull the process managers into a false sense of security, because a good KPI development does not indicate a need for action:

> *"From my point of view, the acceptance of the PMS is quite good. Of course you have to differentiate. I think I'm not exaggerating when I say that the SSCs are working very inten-sively with this data. [...] However, we have already experienced a dwindling acceptance in meetings between accounting platforms and the management when they have to google the presented KPIs to be able to follow the discussion. In general, the feedback I get is that we created some transparency that was not there before. That's positive. My negative remark is that some managers are too gullible with regard to KPIs. They believe that if they improved all of their KPIs, there is no more action required."*
>
> Head of SSO Governance (HealthCo), Interview #8, p. 33

6.3.1.7 EngineerCo case

The SSO of EngineerCo has been implemented ten years ago in the course of the firm's **restructuring phase** after an industry crisis. Thus, EngineerCo intended to reduce its administrative costs by establishing the SSO:

> *"Over the past years, the top priority for EngineerCo has always been on cost savings. Because we had to restructure and downsize ourselves. [...] Further objectives, such as quality improvements and risk minimization, which are rather non-monetary objectives, have not been pursued in the meantime. It means that we first had to prove that we can do the same less costly. Not better, but less costly. We have to be clear [...]: we come from a situation over the past few years in which we have moreover reacted than acted. We*

have had declining sales volumes for years so that the SSO's focus has been exclusively on capacity and FTEs."

Head of SSO Governance (EngineerCo), Interview #11, p. 12

EngineerCo's SSO has three SSCs: one SSC next to its headquarters in Germany, a second in Malaysia and a third in the US. A peculiarity of EngineerCo's SSO is that the SSC in Malaysia is subordinated not only technically but also disciplinary to the SSC in Germany. All three SSCs have been established next to existing EngineerCo sites, as neither the critical mass nor the required initial investment has been available for a new legal entity during the restructuring phase. Therefore, the SSCs legally belong to the respective subsidiary where they are located. EngineerCo's SSO is a pure finance SSO and provides services in the area of accounts payables and accounts receivables, general ledger accounting, inventory and fixed asset management, cost accounting, period end closing and travel expense accounting. During the restructuring phase, EngineerCo also had to dismiss employees working for the finance, accounting and controlling functions. In accordance with the severance scheme, the layoffs affected foremost employees with a low job tenure and without a family so that rather older employees remained in the SSO. By now, EngineerCo has overcome the restructuring phase and the MNC generates a profitable sales growth. However, EngineerCo's SSO faces the problem that several SSO employees are about to retire and new employees have to be recruited. Thus, mastering the demographic change is a key challenge for the SSO in the coming years.

In addition to the challenging age structure, EngineerCo's SSO provides services for a **heterogeneous customer portfolio**. First of all, SSO customers differ in their size. In smaller subsidiaries, it is quite common for employees to fulfill tasks from multiple areas of responsibility as the subsidiary's transaction volumes are low and thus a comparable degree of specialization as in the SSO is not possible. The lower degree of expertise implies a higher communication effort for the SSO's performance measurement. Second, the organizational complexity of the SSO customers also influences the SSO's performance measurement. Customer preferences vary depending on the organizational design of the subsidiary. For example, the dunning process performed by the SSO is of higher importance for EngineerCo's sales companies than for its production companies, while the latter emphasize the meaning of the SSO's product costing services. Hence, the SSO's KPI reporting has to be based on customer preferences:

"First of all that is a question of size. There are many employees in our subsidiaries who unite multiple tasks in one person. The accounts receivable accountant also performs tasks belonging to accounts payables, the controller also performs general ledger activities, the

service technician also places orders for the procurement department etc. Many employees work for several areas of responsibility as it seems efficient to them. From a group perspective, this is not always efficient. [...] Second, it is a question of the subsidiaries' organizational complexity. [...] I believe that you notice huge differences between a small sales company in Indonesia and a large production company in Germany. I believe that you notice know-how differences."

Process manager (EngineerCo), Interview #12, p. 7

EngineerCo's SSO uses a PMS, which is based on the BSC. The SSO's BSC is composed of six subordinated BSCs which measure the performance of the six major support processes in the SSO. The BSC mainly contains financial and process performance measures. The number of measures varies by process, whereby most performance measures are used in the P2P process. EngineerCo's SSO manager points out that the varying number of performance measures depending on the support process is owed to the fact that he struggles to develop performance measures for the other support processes. The performance measure targets are primarily **based on the recommendations and expertise of the process managers**. On the one hand, this approach seems plausible as process managers are most suited to assess which performance improvements are possible in their processes. On the other hand, the principal-agent relationship between the SSO and the process manager entails the risk of moral hazard, such that the process managers only set goals that are achievable without spending much effort. However, if performance measure goals are too easy to achieve, this barely induces a need for action:

"These performance measure objectives are our own commitments. [...] We need a reference point which we consider as the standard performance level. [...] For example, we have set a target value which in my opinion reflects an acceptable backlog level. [...] A backlog below the reference point is good and if the backlog exceeds the reference point, then we would have to analyze whether we have to adjust the target value or whether we have to investigate the causes. For us, this is a kind of tachometer."

Process manager (EngineerCo), Interview #12, p. 17

In addition to the lack of inventiveness to create additional measures, the automation of the data collection process also plays a role for the KPI selection. EngineerCo's SSO pursues this pragmatic approach for two reasons. First, the SSO is afraid of the effort accompanied by a manual data collection. The SSO manager suspects that a huge manual effort does not completely pay off in the form of an improved controllability and transparency through manually collected performance measures. Second, manual performance measure data collection is prone to error so that decisions made on an obscure database can be costly. Nevertheless, this pragmatic approach involves the risk that the PMS is not based on EngineerCo's SSO strategy, but on the **feasibility of the data collection process**:

> *"Apart from the manual effort, which I am not willing to approve with regard to the performance measure data collection – because the employees are actually supposed to process invoices and not to collect KPI data – manual data collection is error-prone. Therefore, we have analyzed which data we get out of the system automatically. And it turned out that the P2P process is more predestinated to collect KPI data than in other areas, such as fixed assets or cost accounting."*

> *Head of SSO Governance (EngineerCo), Interview #11, p. 31*

An important recipient of the SSO's KPI reporting are the SSO customers. Since the SSO customers formerly administered the support processes by themselves, they represent a particularly critical clientele. As a result, EngineerCo's SSO feels in the need to report the SSO's progress in terms of process quality and cost reduction as transparent as possible to the SSO customers. The KPI reporting of EngineerCo's SSO is tailored according to the expectations of the customers and thus has a positive effect on the **customer satisfaction**:

> *"This may sound a bit clumsy, but at least some parts of our KPI reporting are comparable to an accountability report. If we transfer the support processes from the legal entities to the SSO, the customer expects that we will perform accounts receivables processes or whatever at least as good as the entity did before. But usually they expect us to be better and to provide our services to a lower service fee. In this respect, it is an accountability report, because a shared service approach is not necessarily perceived uncritically right from the start. Thus, the KPI reporting serves the SSO to prove that we achieved a lot for our customers."*

> *Process manager (EngineerCo), Interview #12, p. 24*

Overall, EngineerCo's SSO managers are only partially satisfied with their PMS. The Head of SSO governance criticizes the unstructured approach during the implementation of the PMS and its usability in day-to-day operations. The BSC has emerged mainly bottom-up by consolidating performance measures of the main support processes into a BSC and has not been derived from the SSO's strategy. The rather unstructured bottom-up approach entails the disadvantage that performance measures have not been coordinated across the SSO's performance measurement areas, which induces conflicting goals. Furthermore, the SSO managers note that the PMS development has been mainly driven by the objective to reduce costs due to the restructuring phase in the recent past:

> *"We analyze how much costs the SSO has saved. However, we do that on a very abstract level. We know how many FTEs the P2P process had before we implemented the SSO. We also know how many employees in the P2P process work after we implemented the SSO and*

what an employee costs. Based on this, we perform a delta calculation. Hopefully, we have the right number. [...] But at the moment, I am not really capable of making a meaningful statement about the benefits that the SSO yields. [...] What are the SSO benefits with regard to risk management or quality improvements?"

Head of SSO Governance (EngineerCo), Interview #11, p. 32

Therefore, the BSC of EngineerCo's SSO does not allow for meaningful statements about the current **SSO performance** in terms of risk management and service quality so that the PMS does not entirely support the SSO managers in achieving all relevant SSO objectives. In addition, the SSO managers realize that the SSO employees' interest in performance measurement has declined significantly. Thus, it is questionable to what extent all relevant performance measurement actors accept the PMS.

6.3.2 Cross-case analysis

The following sections analyze the PMS design in SSOs, its contingency factors and its effectiveness across all cases. While the within case analysis puts emphasis on dissecting the PMS design in the particular context of the respective SSO, the cross case analysis yields differences and similarities of the PMS design between the SSOs of the cases under research. The cross-case analysis is divided into three sections. The first section investigates the context in which PMS design takes place. The second part elaborates on PMS design in SSOs. In accordance with the conceptualization of PMS design in SSOs, this section is sub-divided into the three PMS components (measures, processes and actors). The third section analyzes the effectiveness of PMS design. Notably, the cross case analysis follows the structuring-thematic coding for qualitative data analysis outlined in section 6.2.3. Therefore, the codes extracted from the interviews (e.g. "guideline", "customized software") are ordered thematically into concepts (e.g. "formal standardization", "factual standardization"). These concepts, which vary from case to case, are grouped into categories (e.g. "degree of process standardization"). The hypothesis refinement builds on the cross-case analysis and condenses the categories to theoretical constructs.

6.3.2.1 Context of PMS design in SSOs

6.3.2.1.1 External context

In line with the basic hypotheses development, the following sections are subdivided into an external context, a MNC-specific context and a SSO-specific context. In order to systematize the contingency factors of PMS design in SSOs, the following sections use sub-headings for the categories developed during the qualitative data analysis according to the structuring-thematic coding technique.

Perceived environmental uncertainty and competition intensity

Overall, the interviews indicated that most SSO managers perceive the environment of their MNCs as neither particularly predictable nor do they experience a great uncertainty. However, the interviews suggest that the smaller case companies perceive their environment as more uncertain as compared to the larger ones. While CommCo and ChemCo are a little concerned about a changing external environment, PharCo, AgriCo and MedTechCo less fear that external conditions will affect the SSO.

MedTechCo's SSO manager stresses that **customer behavior** has an impact on the SSO's KPIs:

> *"The behavior of customers clearly has an impact on my output in the SSO. Will my invoice volume rise or fall? [...] In other words, I must always keep an eye on our customers in order to estimate the expected order intake..."*

Head of SSO (MedTechCo), Interview #1, p. 7

The SSO manager of HealthCo emphasizes that the **political and legal environment** has an impact on the SSO's support processes. Altered legal requirements often induce process changes or are even responsible if a process is performed in a SSC or remains with the local subsidiary:

> *"If I am not legally allowed to scan, digitize and edit an invoice in a SSC which is located abroad, then I have to refrain from it. Unfortunately, the invoice processing within the country is a legal requirement in many countries. Hence, we do not deal with the subsidiaries for the time being, unless there are developments in these countries so that an electronic invoice exchange is possible. Then we are going in with our SSO squad and say: '... we are taking over from now on'."*

Head of SSO Governance (HealthCo), Interview #8, p. 18

Based on the experience of EngineerCo's restructuring phase during the past years, the EngineerCo expert perceives the general conditions for his company as rather volatile and uncertain. Moreover, he points out that the restructuring phase affects the SSO's PMS:

> *"It has to be said that the targets for our KPIs date back to a time before the restructuring phase of EngineerCo when we still had 28,000 employees. At that time, we had a completely different transaction volume of 1,000,000 invoices. Today, we only process 600,000 invoices. Needless to say, the restructuring phase also influences our performance measures."*

Head of SSO Governance (EngineerCo), Interview #11, p. 25

In general, the interviewed SSO managers observe a **competitive environment** for their MNCs. All experts perceive particularly the price competition of their MNC's as very intense. The experts shared the opinion that their MNCs better survive in a tough price competition if the SSO is able to provide services at competitive costs since the support processes administered by the SSO entail a large part of the MNC's administrative costs. Moreover, the SSO managers of HealthCo and MedTechCo highlight the competition intensity for new products on global markets. A competitive environment also affects the resources assigned to the SSO as described by ChemCo's expert:

> "As I said, my management team receives very demanding objectives and they have to ask themselves how they can positively influence the use of their resources. This is what we are heading for: build competences, understand your processes, and automate them to deliver services in a competitive environment that is certainly not the most favorable at the moment."

> *Managing Director SSO (ChemCo), Interview #5, p. 8*

Table 6.3 summarizes the external context of PMS design in SSOs:

Table 6.3: External context of PMS design in SSOs

External context	MedTech-Co	Comm-Co	Chem-Co	Phar-Co	Agri-Co	Health-Co	Engineer-Co
Perceived uncertainty	Medium	Low	Medium	Medium	Medium	Low	High
Competition intensity	High	High	High	High	High	High	High

6.3.2.1.2 MNC context

Product differentiation and organizational structure

With the exception of EngineerCo, all SSO managers of the case companies indicate that their firms' products and services differ to a large extent. A high degree of **product differentiation** also poses a challenge for the SSO's service provision because the MNC's subsidiaries (i.e. the SSO customers) confront the SSO with varying preconditions and requirements. The process manager of EngineerCo states that the complexity resulting from the MNC's varying development, manufacturing and sales processes has to be reflected in the PMS:

> "For us, the greatest difficulty consists in making progress with the small subsidiaries in a predominantly international environment. We have little difficulty with the large production companies here in Germany. [...] In other countries, we encounter difficulties with

the small units because they are much more oriented to sales processes. Therefore, it is not
always possible to adopt the standard processes of the SSO in a precisely fitting manner and
to map their processes all properly in our PMS."

Process manager (EngineerCo), Interview #12, p. 6

Two organizational structures prevail in the case companies. While CommCo, PharCo and EngineerCo are structured according to business segments, ChemCo, MedTechCo, AgriCo and HealthCo have a matrix organization in place. The SSO manager of ChemCo emphasizes that a matrix organization implies more counterparts as compared to an **organizational structure** by segment or region. According to an expert of MedTechCo, the SSO has to coordinate its activities in the P2P process with the central procurement department and the local business units. A matrix organization entails equally ranking accountability and reporting relationships between functions and business units, thus resulting in cross-jurisdictions. HealthCo's SSO manager voices concerns with regard to the emergence of interfaces in matrix organizations:

"Looking at the organizational aspect as a whole, I would conclude that a matrix organi-
zation creates many interfaces. [...] Our matrix basically entails three to four dimensions.
While in the past the buyer was sitting right next to the accountant and both were able to
talk to each other, today there is a continent between them. [...] This is something which is
not negligible when considering the shared service approach."

Head of SSO Performance Controlling (HealthCo), Interview #8, p. 16

The addressed interfaces in matrix organizations also increase the coordination effort in the performance measurement process. For instance, a higher number of potential reporting addressees are involved and measuring points have to be defined across the existing interfaces. Moreover, the number of hierarchical levels contributes to the MNC's organizational complexity. The SSO management accountant of CommCo points out that the more hierarchical levels exist in the MNC, the more sophisticated are the reporting requirements in the performance measurement process. Commonly, KPI reports vary according to the hierarchical level in their information content, which also leads to a higher processing effort.

IT infrastructure and top management support

All experts stress that **ERP systems** play an outstanding role in the MNCs' IT system landscape, since they map almost all business and support processes of the company. The experts of PharCo, AgriCo, HealthCo and EngineerCo state that their companies implemented several ERP systems suggesting a rather heterogeneous system landscape. However, all four case companies aim at harmonizing their ERP systems. During the interviews, the SSO managers of MedTechCo and HealthCo describe the harmonization of the ERP landscape as the most important premise for the effectiveness of shared service initiatives, since only a harmonized IT landscape enables process standardization:

> "In 1997, we began to harmonize our SAP systems. This is basically the prerequisite for the formation of a SSC. The final step before establishing a SSC is to ensure a certain degree of process standardization. This sequence should be adhered to, meaning that non-standardized processes should not be transferred to a SSC, because by doing this you only relocate activities from A to B without exploiting the economies of scale."

Head of SSO Governance (HealthCo), Interview #8, p. 13

The SSO manager of EngineerCo indicates that ERP systems play an important role for the performance measure data collection process. The more ERP systems the MNC uses, the more data sources have to be tapped to collect the required data for calculating the performance measures. This often results in an increased data consolidation effort and in more plausibility checks:

> "We do not have an integrated system to collect the data for the corresponding performance measures. At the moment, we experience difficulties to extract the data for the performance measures that we are using today. Although we have a software that merges, edits and publishes the required data, [...] there is a lot of manual work needed to extract the data. [...] All the data that we use for the KPIs are derived from the SAP systems."

Head of SSO Governance (EngineerCo), Interview #11, p. 5

Apart from the ERP systems, the case companies use a myriad of other IT systems, which also contribute to the homogeneity (or heterogeneity) of the IT landscape. Therefore, the SSO manager of ChemCo emphasizes that IT-systems should be customized locally only to a very limited extent in order to avoid that formerly standardized processes drift apart. One expert of HealthCo underpins the importance of a centralized procurement of new software for all subsidiaries, which prevents the business units from using different IT systems for the same process:

> "A good example is how we used to handle travel and entertainment expenses. At that time we found 70 different travel expense solutions worldwide in our group. Every single solution was perhaps not so bad from a local perspective, but not from the group's point of view. Because every single IT system had to be implemented, running costs occurred, it had to be maintained and technical know-how had to be provided. This means that from the group's point of view this made no sense at all."

Head of SSO Governance (HealthCo), Interview #8, p. 15

All experts highlight the relevance of the **MNC's top management support** to achieve the SSO's objectives. The expert of ChemCo constitutes that the establishment of ChemCo's SSO led to conflicting goals, since particularly the subsidiaries have to transfer competencies to the SSO. The power shift from the subsidiaries to the SSO is only achievable with the MNC's top management support. According to AgriCo's SSO manager, a major reason for an insufficient top management support stems from an ambiguous allocation of responsibilities for the SSO's support processes:

> *"In my opinion, every firm needs a COO alongside a CFO. A guy who really cares about the administrative processes in a firm. Every firm should have that. But AgriCo does not. We have the board members who are concerned with their areas of expertise, such as finance or HR. Apart from that there are board members responsible for the product divisions, who are also responsible for production, development and sales. However, it is a fundamental error in organizations that these people are doing HR, finance and bits and pieces."*

> Head of SSC Germany (AgriCo), Interview #7, p. 23

Group controlling

All case companies indicate that their MNCs have a **group controlling department**. Moreover, all group controlling departments bear the responsibility for the group's PMS. However, the SSO managers of MedTechCo, ChemCo, AgriCo, HealthCo and PharCo suggest only a weak cooperation between the SSO and the group controlling. Thus, the interconnections between the group's PMS and the SSO's PMS remain poorly developed:

> *"In the end, we are only using the same platform with our PMS as the group controlling does with their PMS, although there are certainly other PMS in our business divisions. We are already using a central platform, in which we import the performance measure data. But we have no direct connection to the group's PMS so that you cannot speak of a shared dashboard [...]."*

> Head of SSO Process Excellence (PharCo), Interview #6, p. 21

Nonetheless, the experts of EngineerCo and CommCo stress that they have discussions on a regular basis about the SSO's KPIs with their colleagues from the group controlling department. Furthermore, CommCo's SSO management accountant mentions institutionalized meetings which promote a closer cooperation with the group controlling:

> *"To put it in concrete terms, we are directly connected with the colleagues from the group controlling. The service line controllers are located on the same floor as the group*

controllers. And of course the three heads of the service line controlling are sitting in the same executive meetings as the heads of the group controlling teams."

SSO Management accountant (CommCo), Interview #4, p. 11

Table 6.4 summarizes the MNC context of PMS design in SSOs:

Table 6.4: MNC context of PMS design in SSOs

MNC context	MedTech-Co	Comm-Co	Chem-Co	Phar-Co	Agri-Co	Health-Co	Engineer-Co
Product differentiation	Diversi-fied	Diversi-fied	Diversi-fied	Diversi-fied	Diversi-fied	Diversi-fied	Speciali-zed
Organizatio-nal structure	Matrix	Segments	Matrix	Segments	Matrix	Matrix	Segments
IT-system landscape	Homo-genous	Homo-genous	Homo-genous	Heteroge-nous	Hetero-genous	Hetero-genous	Hetero-genous
MNC top management	Suppor-tive	Suppor-tive	Suppor-tive	Cautious	Cautious	Cautious	Cautious
Relationship to group controlling	Little coopera-tion	Close coopera-tion	Little coopera-tion	Little coopera-tion	Little coopera-tion	Little coopera-tion	Close coopera-tion

6.3.2.1.3 SSO context

Geographic dispersion and legal as well as economic independence

The **geographic dispersion** of the SSCs illustrates two case study findings. First, all SSOs of the case companies implemented a SSC onshore in their country of origin. With the exception of ChemCo all other case companies located one of their SSCs next to the headquarters' site. One of the main reasons for HealthCo to establish a SSC affiliated to the headquarters is that the domestic market is of significant importance for HealthCo. Moreover, the education of the employees and achieving a critical transaction volume for the establishment of a SSC are arguments in favor of an onshore SSC:

"The SSC in Germany is affiliated to EngineerCo's parent company. The SSC in Malaysia is affiliated to the local subsidiary. Thus, we use the existing organizational structure in the respective country where we established a SSC. With the size our SSO currently has, a greenfield approach makes no sense."

Head of SSO Governance (EngineerCo), Interview #11, p. 2

Second, all case companies established another SSC in Europe, whereby most of them are located in Eastern Europe. Moreover, all case companies implemented at least one SSC outside Europe in a low-wage country. The expert of PharCo substantiates the popular opinion among practitioners that the most important factor for the establishment of a farshore SSC is labor arbitrage:

> "We have a SSC site here in Germany, we have a location in the USA and are currently establishing two new sites. We are implementing a SSC in Poland, and we are setting up a site in the Philippines. [...] With our two new SSC locations, we intend to perform the same tasks at lower costs."
>
> *Head of SSO Process Excellence (PharCo), Interview #6, p. 4*

The case study findings indicate mixed results with regard to the **legal and economic independence** of SSOs. Whereas the experts of ChemCo, CommCo and HealthCo state that their SSOs are designed as a legally and economically independent entities, the other case companies are neither legally nor economically independent. The interviews with EngineerCo's experts reveal that achieving a minimum size is a prerequisite for the legal independence of the SSO. Furthermore, EngineerCo's SSO manager assumes a higher complexity with the SSO's legal and economic independence, for example through a separate annual financial statement. By contrast, CommCo's SSO manager finds significant advantages in a legally independent SSO due to the possibility of establishing a remuneration system which is independent from the parent company. Moreover, the SSO manager of MedTechCo associates a higher transparency and accountability for the SSO's business activities and a higher identification of the employees with their entity:

> "The project team at that time suggested that the SSO should be set up as an independent legal entity. I still believe that this is the best concept, because it is clearly defined and visible, which employees work for the SSO. The operating result is transparent for the entity and a shared identity is created. You are an independent organization, everyone fights for the achievement of this entity's objectives and you can easily measure the economic performance in the P&L. In our current set up, the SSCs are integrated into the legal entities of the respective countries. In Germany, it is the parent company. You may also have the possibility to make the economic results visible via our cost accounting, but you are always part of a huge parent company with its special rules."
>
> *Head of SSO (MedTechCo), Interview #1, p. 2*

Center concepts and SSO configuration

Apart from HealthCo, all other case companies ensure the economic accountability of their SSOs by using **cost centers**. According to MedTechCo's SSO manager, the main reason for controlling the SSO by using cost centers is that the

SSO does not aim at making profits. MedTechCo's SSO manager seeks to cover all occurred costs and to keep the service charges for the SSO customers at a constant level. One expert of EngineerCo describes the simple monitoring of the SSO's cost development by using a cost center concept:

> "We have a look at our cost centers every month. For that reason, all department heads meet with the SSC head once a month and we go through all the topics. [...] When things get out of hand, we agree on appropriate measures."
>
> *Head of SSO Governance (EngineerCo), Interview #11, p. 30*

Solely MedTechCo and AgricCo operate with monofunctional SSCs which perform finance and accounting processes. By contrast, the SSOs of the other case companies evolved into **multifunctional SSOs** which bundle several functions, such as finance, IT, and HR at one location:

> "We established the multifunctional SSO of CommCo since the first of January. The new multifunctional organization emerged from the former SSC for finance and accounting. The processes from the procurement area, the internal reporting factory and HR [...], joined the former finance and accounting SSC."
>
> *Managing Director SSO (CommCo), Interview #3, p. 1*

HealthCo's SSO manager argues that multifunctional SSOs yield more economies of scale and scope. However, with regard to the performance measurement, a PMS for multifunctional SSOs seems to be more challenging since the process landscape becomes more heterogeneous and the SSO controlling has to consider the particularities of the different corporate functions, for example during the performance measure analysis.

The interviews reveal that all SSOs of the case companies provide their services for several geographic regions and most of them for multiple divisions. MedTechCo's SSO manager describes that a monodivisional and monogeographical service provision was the precursor of MedTechCo's **multigeographical SSO** since in an initial step the subsidiaries within a single country were bundled at one location. AgriCo's SSO operates monodivisionally and multigeographically which was not the result of a strategic initiative, but emerged from the historical development of the MNC:

> "The services provided in and the background of the SSCs is absolutely different. [...] For example, in Finland we acquired a company called TimberCo fifteen years ago, which produces forestry machines. TimberCo has several smaller sales companies in Norway, Sweden, England, and Ireland. In the meantime, the acquired subsidiary in Finland provides the support services for the sales companies, quasi as a SSC. However, AgriCo has not established a SSC in Finland, but TimberCo has simply been labeled as such."
>
> *Head of SSC Germany (AgriCo), Interview #7, p. 4*

Obligation to contract and use of SLAs

With the exception of EngineerCo, all SSOs of the case companies state that their subsidiaries are completely or at least partially subject to a **contract obligation**. The SSO managers of the case companies elaborate on two major advantages of an obligation to contract for internal customers. First, the SSO manager of MedTechCo emphasizes that the mandatory purchase of SSO services ensures to achieve a critical mass in a relatively short period of time and planning certainty for the subsequent periods. Especially planning certainty facilitates the implementation of standardization and automation projects, since these usually require an initial investment and only pay off with sufficient transaction volumes. Second, CommCo's SSO manager finds that the compulsory service provision for subsidiaries requires less coordination effort because the SSO does not have to enter into regular negotiations with its internal customers:

> "I do not believe that the relationship between the internal customers and the SSO can really be controlled by a pricing mechanism. Ultimately, the internal customers are obliged to contract anyway. But I do know that there are colleagues from other companies who experience it differently. In any case, we have opted for an obligation to contract so that we discuss the planned transaction volumes with customers only once a year. No further discussion necessary."
>
> *Managing Director SSO (CommCo), Interview #3, p. 7*

Apart from AgriCo, all SSOs of the case companies use **SLAs** to design their relationships with internal customers. One expert of HealthCo points out that SLAs have implications for the SSO's performance measurement because a SLA design often entails process quality and customer satisfaction measures. In order to monitor to what extent the agreed service levels are kept, the SSO needs a PMS design that corresponds to the SLA design:

> "We report KPIs that measure the cycle times and performance of the SSC. These are so-called SLA KPIs, which measure an agreed service level between us and the local units. [...]. For example, in the P2P process, the agreed objective in the SLA is that an invoice should not stay in a SSC for more than two days. As you can see, in 2015 invoices spent an average of four days [in the SSC]."
>
> *Head of SSO Performance Controlling (HealthCo), Interview #8, p. 24*

As opposed to the other case companies, AgriCo refrains from using SLAs because the design of SLAs involves a considerable effort. CommCo's SSO manager highlights that the SLA monitoring and reporting encompasses a substantial resource consumption in the SSO controlling department:

"However, you should also know that we decided to design SLAs as simple as possible. I know that there are also firms that design SLAs in a more sophisticated way. That is quite cool, but with the size we have, I would be forced to build a team of thirty or forty employees, who are exclusively concerned with this SLA topic."

Managing Director SSO (CommCo), Interview #3, p. 7

SSO controlling and SSO customers

Except of AgriCo, PharCo and EngineerCo, all SSOs of the case studies have their own controlling department. ChemCo and HealthCo implemented a controlling department in each of their SSCs, whereas MedTechCo and CommCo have a controlling department for the entire SSO. EngineerCo's SSO manager explains that their SSO is not allowed to establish a **SSO controlling department** due to the MNC's persistent resource scarcity. As outlined before, cost reduction remains the most important objective for EngineerCo's SSO manager. Labor costs are by far the largest cost driver in SSOs so that ChemCo's SSO manager considers the extent to which he invests in SSO management accountants very carefully. In the end, ChemCo's SSO has to regain the labor costs of a SSO management accountant by means of an improved control and decision support:

"We do not need another performance controlling department. These departments often try to analyze things from numbers and try to make recommendations. [...] A performance controlling with transparency tools for process optimization does not replace the sense of responsibility. The decision-making needs to be done in addition to the controlling. Thus, the question remains: how much do you invest in such departments and how much do you invest in a good management? Or are you doing both? This is not easy to explain to your staff. If you overload your organization with such controlling instruments, this is not a big vote of confidence in your managers."

Managing Director SSO (ChemCo), Interview #5, p. 15

With regard to the **controlling tasks** in SSOs, the case study findings illustrate that SSO management accountants mainly perform genuine controlling tasks. One expert of EngineerCo mentions cost accounting as an important task for the SSO controlling. Moreover, budgeting, planning and reporting are essential duties for SSO management accountants. The SSO management accountants of MedTechCo, HealthCo and CommCo describe KPI calculations and analyses as an essential component of their daily work. However, the interviews with the experts of MedTechCo and CommCo reveal that SSO management accountants also partly take over tasks which are not related to genuine controlling tasks. By contrast, EngineerCo's process manager states that he performs genuine controlling tasks, because a SSO management accountant simply does not exist. Blurred boundaries for the responsibility of controlling tasks may lead to an insufficient task fulfilment provoking that the responsible employees conceive their performance measurement process as dissatisfying, as described by MedTechCo's SSO management accountant:

> "Apart from the SSC controlling, I am still responsible for many other processes and participate in various projects [...] In addition, I am also responsible for our communication strategy with the suppliers. I am thinking about communication concepts and, if possible, design the relevant websites. I try to establish communication channels for our suppliers to make our workflows more accessible to them. At the same time, I am responsible for other projects, for example, the audit preparation of the purchase-to-pay process. [...] With my current resources, I am able to report the most important performance measures, but we still have significant room for improvement."

> *SSO Management accountant (MedTechCo), Interview #2, p. 2*

In essence, most of the SSO managers perceive their **SSO customers** as demanding with regard to the SSO's service provision. MedTechCo's SSO manager states that the SSO customers are very sensitive to service fee changes. Particularly, if SSO customers believe that they have no influence on the service fee development, their acceptance decreases. ChemCo's SSO manager points out that a number of ChemCo's SSO customers is concerned about the SSO's service quality, as many of the local subsidiaries have recently provided these services by themselves. ChemCo's SSO manager also mentions that the responsiveness of the SSO is of great importance to the SSO customers. Although CommCo's SSO manager underpins that the SSO has demanding customers, the interview reveals that CommCo's SSO measures only to a limited extent whether the SSO meets their customers' requirements:

> "If you take our customer service in Germany as an example: the customer service performance measures are very much designed to measure responsiveness. In the SSO, we are already collecting performance measures about how satisfied the employees in the local units are with our call handling, which issues we are able to solve after the first contact and how many incidents have to be passed to the second or third support level. [...] However, our SSO can still learn a lot from the customer service. They are at a very advanced stage and we have to get there as well."

> *Managing Director SSO (CommCo), Interview #3, p. 8*

Process standardization

Process standardization is one of the most important SSO objectives. The results unveil that all SSO managers of the case companies consider standardization as a prerequisite for other SSO objectives, particularly for process automation:

"A comment on standardization: at EngineerCo, we observe that if we standardize a process, we also have the possibility to automate it. And with these two steps, we have the opportunity to tackle the three other objectives: cost savings, quality improvement, and risk minimization. In essence, we have a great interest in standardization and try to push it to the next level."

Head of SSO Governance (EngineerCo), Interview #11, p. 12

Overall, the results stress that SSO managers perceive their processes as rather standardized. However, CommCo's SSO manager notices a considerable difference between the degree of **formal standardization** that is visible by, for example, the existence of established guidelines, a comprehensive process documentation as well as templates and the **factual degree of standardization** that is observable in the daily work practices:

"As it is often the case in such large, complex firms shaped by its particular history: the roll-out of a standard software or a guideline does not automatically ensure the desired process standardization, because everyone tries to butt in their own customizing. And every single customizing that does not correspond to the standard process makes it more difficult for the SSC. Because it is as simple as it sounds: the more standardized the process, the more savings in the SSO."

Managing Director SSO (CommCo), Interview #3, p. 3

By contrast, AgriCo's SSO manager argues for necessary deviations from the standard processes in the interest of the MNC since the standard process is not applicable for some SSO customers. He concludes that SSOs still have to take local particularities into account.

In a similar vein, one expert of HealthCo recommends a differentiated assessment of process standardization in SSOs due to country-specific requirements. Particularly, local information systems cause constant deviations from the standard process:

"I would say that process standardization is the prerequisite for a truly efficient and effective SSO. However, we must consider country-specific requirements. Those are not created in our company, but will be brought to us from the outside, particularly from legal and tax requirements. [...] These are basic requirements so that we have to adapt our process according to the respective national regulations."

Head of SSO Governance (HealthCo), Interview #8, p. 10

In essence, the case study results indicate that there are considerable deviations between the formally documented standard processes and their daily execution in SSOs. This could have a negative impact on other SSO objectives. As outlined by EngineerCo's SSO manager, the gap between formal and factual standardization might be even bigger since the standardization degree for the SSOs' support processes is difficult to measure.

Power and know-how promotors

The fact that the case study interviews are conducted with SSO and SSC managers, SSO management accountants and process owners suggests that the PMS design in SSOs involves several actors. MedTechCo and PharCo's SSO managers state that different actors have to contribute to the PMS design in order to be a successful management tool. CommCo's SSO manager supports this point of view and adds that the effectiveness of performance measurement initiatives in SSOs depends on the presence of actors who are willing to invest resources into the PMS:

> *"For me it is essential that the PMS is promoted from all sides. From the employees who designed the PMS, but also from other actors who regularly use the PMS, such as the operative business and the management. A PMS has to be used jointly, otherwise it is useless."*

Managing Director SSO (CommCo), Interview #3, p. 10

In order to support the PMS as **power promotors**, performance measurement actors need to have resources at their disposal. In addition, power promotors can decide which performance measurement initiatives they are willing to grant their limited resources to. This holds especially true for higher hierarchical levels. Particularly, the SSO managers of ChemCo, CommCo and MedTechCo see themselves in a position to decide on scarce resources:

> *"[...] how much am I willing to invest to become even better? [...] Are there new areas of activity that must be looked at and developed? This also plays a role, because the really important resources are always scarce."*

Managing Director SSO (ChemCo), Interview #5, p. 3

However, AgriCo's and EngineerCo's SSO managers constitute that they are not in a position to support the PMS with sufficient financial and human resources. Apart from themselves, both SSO managers have no idea who else would support the further development of the PMS. The non-existence of a power promotor dissatisfies them to the degree that they feel left alone with all the performance measurement activities in their SSO.

SSOs are commonly responsible for a variety of processes from different operational functions. This results in a broadly diversified customer base, which originates from different countries and business areas and thus imposes heterogeneous requirements for the SSO. A PMS which intends to map the described complexity in order to allow for a meaningful decision-making and control requires a high degree of expertise. All experts of the case companies share the opinion that the process owners contribute with their process-specific expertise to the development and improvement of a meaningful PMS:

> *"The performance management team manages the PMS, but the suggestions [for new performance measures] come from our process experts, for example from the GPO of our purchase-to-pay process who works together with his [...] departments in the SSC."*

> *Head of SSO Performance Controlling (HealthCo), Interview #9, p. 2*

Apart from suggestions for new performance measures, process managers provide information on a realistic target setting for certain performance measures. EngineerCo's SSO manager indicates that the process managers support him during the evaluation of the performance measure development. HealthCo's SSO management accountant describes that process managers inform the SSO controlling whether performance measures need to be adjusted. In essence, the process managers of the case companies support the PMS with their know-how and can thus be considered as **know-how promotors** for the PMS design in SSOs.

Process and relationship promotors

The complexity of SSOs leads to a considerable coordination effort with regard to the performance measurement process. **Process promotors** help to overcome administrative barriers through their organizational knowledge. The interviews with PharCo's and EngineerCo's SSO managers suggest that predominantly the process owners take over the role of the process promotor. This is an unexpected finding for two reasons. First, process managers are usually responsible for a single process and thus a comprehensive institutional network and an intensive collaboration with other areas of the SSO is not necessarily expected for this group of performance measurement actors. Second, the coordination of the performance measurement process is a genuine remit of management accounting. Hence, it is expectable that the SSO controlling fills the role of the process promotor. For example, CommCo's and HealthCo's SSO controlling departments coordinate performance measurement activities, for example by initiating meetings and brainstorming sessions as well as implementing feedback loops for the modification of performance measures. A reason why the SSO controlling is considered as a process promotor only by CommCo and HealthCo may be due to the fact that not all SSOs implemented a management accounting unit:

> *"Thus, a SSC controlling unit does not exist yet. I am saying 'yet', because that is where we want to go. There is still no central [KPI] tracking, where all [KPIs] are collected and evaluated. That is why we have established these meetings some time ago that we are heading*

more in the direction of KPIs. [...] Today, the service lines themselves bear the responsibility
[to track their KPIs]."

Head of SSO Process Excellence (PharCo), Interview #6, p. 15

A well-functioning PMS in SSOs depends to a large extent on the cooperation of the performance measurement actors with organizational units outside the SSO. Without relationships to areas that work closely together with the SSO, for example the group controlling, it seems difficult to overcome dependency barriers caused by an asymmetric balance of power. This also includes connections to outsourcing service providers and the IT, since the power of these relationships also impacts a successful performance measurement. PharCo's SSO manager acts as a **relationship promotor** by getting in touch with other departments regarding the SSO's PMS. Thus, he is able to initiate cross-departmental collaborations:

> *"In my role as the Head of Process Excellence, I am involved in various meetings. If we see*
> *something going wrong somewhere according to our indicators [...], this is automatically a*
> *trigger for me or my team, [...] where we get in touch with these units. This means that we*
> *will continue the cooperation [with other organizational units] because we are automati-*
> *cally involved."*

Head of SSO Process Excellence (PharCo), Interview #6, p. 26

In a similar vein, the SSO managers of CommCo and MedTechCo build relationships to other departments to develop the SSO's PMS. Moreover, the interviews reveal that the role of the relationship promotor is not assigned exclusively to SSO managers, but assumed by several actors. ChemCo's SSO manager believes that SSO management accountants are in a position to further develop the PMS design using their relationships to the IT department and the group controlling. By contrast, HealthCo's SSO manager notices that the purchase-to-pay process owner communicates with the procurement department about the SSO's PMS design on a regular basis. AgriCo's and EngineerCo's SSO managers state that nobody in their organization establishes relationships with other departments in order to improve the PMS.

Table 6.5 summarizes the SSO context of PMS design:

Table 6.5: SSO context of PMS design

SSO context	MedTech-Co	Comm-Co	Chem-Co	Phar-Co	Agri-Co	Health-Co	Engineer-Co
SSC locations	Farshore	Nearshore	Farshore	Farshore	Farshore	Farshore	Farshore
Legal independence	No	Yes	Yes	No	No	Yes	No
Center concept	Cost center	Cost center	Cost center	Cost center	Cost center	Profit center	Cost center
Functional configuration	Mono-functional	Multi-functional	Multi-functional	Multi-functional	Mono-functional	Multi-functional	Multi-functional
Geographical configuration	Multi-geographical	Multi-geographical	Multi-geographical	Multi-geographical	Multi-geographical	Multi-geographical	Multi-geographical
Contract obligation	Yes	Yes	Yes	Yes	Yes	Yes	No
Use of SLAs	Extensive	Extensive	Extensive	Moderate	No	Moderate	Extensive
SSO controlling	Yes	Yes	Yes	No	No	Yes	No
SSO customers	Demanding	Demanding	Modest	Demanding	Demanding	Demanding	Modest
Standardization degree	Medium stage	Global standards	Global standards	Medium stage	Early stage	Global standards	Medium stage
Power promotor	SSO manager	SSO manager	SSO manager	SSO manager	Nobody	SSO manager	Nobody
Know-how promotor	Process manager	Process manager	Process manager	Process manager	Process manager	Process manager	Process manager
Process promotor	SSC manager	SSO Controller	SSC manager	Process manager	SSC manager	SSO Controller	Process manager
Relationship promotor	SSC manager	SSC manager	SSO Controller	SSC manager	Nobody	Process manager	Nobody

6.3.2.1.4 Summary

In essence, the case study results indicated that most SSO managers perceive the **environment** of their MNCs as neither exceptionally predictable nor as unpredictable. However, the cross-case analysis reveals that particularly the smaller case companies perceive a comparatively higher environmental uncertainty. Moreover, all experts constitute a competitive environment for their MNCs. Several experts indicate that the perceived environmental uncertainty and the competitive environment affect PMS design in SSOs.

With regard to the MNC-specific context factors, all experts observe a rather high degree of **product differentiation**. Furthermore, the case companies are either structured according to business segments or the MNCs implemented a matrix organization. The cross-case analysis illustrates that case companies with matrix organizations are exposed to multiple interfaces which impacts the performance measurement process.

All experts emphasize that the MNC's **ERP systems** are of significant importance for the SSO and thus may influence PMS design. Particularly, the performance measure data collection process depends on the MNC's IT systems. All experts share the opinion that **MNC's top management support** represents a decisive success factor to implement an effective PMS. With regard to the group controlling, the case study results suggest that all group controlling departments use a PMS on group level. However, the cross-case analysis finds little evidence on a close cooperation between the SSO and the **group controlling**.

All case companies established a SSC in their country of origin, whereby the majority of the case companies located their SSCs next to the headquarters' site. Moreover, the case study findings point out that the SSCs are **geographically dispersed** so that all SSOs implemented another SSC in Europe and at least one SSC outside Europe in a developing country. The cross-case analysis presents that about half of the MNC's SSOs operate as **legally and economically independent** organizations.

The majority of the case companies is controlled by **cost centers** so that profit centers are of minor importance. Moreover, the cross-case analysis finds that most SSOs provide services for more than one operational function which may lead to a more challenging PMS design compared to monofunctional SSOs. The case study results reveal that all SSOs provide their services for **multiple geographic regions and divisions**.

The interviews with the experts demonstrate that most of the SSOs **oblige the SSO customers to contract**. The majority of the case companies uses **SLAs** to define their customer relationships. The findings indicate that SLAs may affect the selection of performance measures for the SSO's PMS. Most SSO managers in this case study's sample describe the SSO customers as rather demanding which results in additional requirements for the KPI reporting. The cross-case analysis illustrates that particularly the smaller case companies refrain from establishing a **SSO controlling** department since it is associated with considerable costs. The interviews with the SSO management accountants reveal that they primarily perform genuine controlling tasks, such as budgeting, cost accounting and performance measurement. However, several case company experts find blurred responsibilities for controlling tasks.

All SSO managers of the case companies constitute that **process standardization** and automation are major prerequisites to achieve their SSO objectives. In essence, the interviews with the SSO managers highlight that most managers perceive the SSO's support processes as rather standardized. However, the case study findings unveil considerable deviations between the formal and the factual degree of process standardization which affects the performance measurement process.

The cross-case analysis demonstrates that various actors are involved in the performance measurement process. Most of the experts share the opinion that SSO managers act as **power promotors** by supporting performance measurement activities with financial and personnel resources. However, the case study findings indicate that the absence of power promotors for PMS design in SSOs may lead to helplessness and dissatisfaction with regard to the SSO's PMS. All experts of the case companies point out that process owners promote the SSO's PMS design by contributing with their process-specific expertise so that process owners slip into the role of **know-how promotors**.

However, the cross-case analysis yields ambiguous results regarding the role allocation of **process promotors** for the SSO's PMS design. The case study findings show that mostly SSO managers and process owners foster PMS design by coordinating performance measurement activities across the SSO's organizational units. Furthermore, the interviews demonstrate that several performance measurement actors cooperate with departments outside the SSO in order to develop the SSO's PMS design. Therefore, the cross-case analysis cannot assign a certain performance measurement actor to the outlined conceptualization of process and **relationship promotors**.

6.3.2.2 PMS design in SSOs

6.3.2.2.1 Performance measures

The interviews with the SSO management accountants suggest large differences among the SSOs with regard to the **number of performance measures**. Whereas

HealthCo's PMS contains 90 performance measures, MedTechCo's SSO management accountant has just four performance measures available in his PMS. The
larger case companies (in terms of annual sales volume), such as CommCo (50
measures) and ChemCo (30 measures) use more performance measures compared to the smaller companies, such as AgriCo, EngineerCo (10 measures each)
and PharCo (11 measures). As a major reason for the low number of performance measures, the SSO management accountants of MedTechCo, PharCo and
AgriCo argue that the PMS of their SSOs is still under development. EngineerCo's
SSO manager states that he has no other performance measures in mind which
allow him to meaningfully control the SSO. CommCo's and HealthCo's SSO
management accountants assume that the number of performance measures in
their PMS will be reduced because some measures are not used anymore. Both
SSO management accountants have recently taken up their jobs and are willing
to significantly modify the PMS of their SSOs in the near future. ChemCo's SSO
manager states that he is currently satisfied with the number of performance
measures in his PMS.

Looking at the **performance measure categories**, the importance of performance measures with reference to process quality and productivity stands out.
All experts mention that their PMS encompasses process-related performance
measures. MedTechCo's SSO manager intends to increase process quality by
using his PMS:

> *"I need a measurement system to identify errors in the processes. I need to know
> which quality level and which errors are generated by the different stages of the pro-
> cess chain."*

Head of SSO (MedTechCo), Interview #1, p. 7

Apart from performance measures with reference to process quality and process automation, cost-profit-related measures and measures with reference
to customer satisfaction play an important role in the PMS of the SSOs. The
SSO manager of CommCo highlights the prevalence of financial KPIs in
his PMS:

> *"We have designed this [PMS] in an entirely classic way. We mainly track financial KPIs."*

Managing Director SSO (CommCo), Interview #3, p. 8

By contrast, performance measures with reference to employee satisfaction and
organizational development are barely used in the SSO's PMS of the case companies. Only ChemCo and HealthCo use measures that relate to the organizational
development of the SSO, such as the language competencies of the SSO employees.
The interview with ChemCo's SSO manager suggests that process-related

performance measures are easier to design as compared to performance measures with reference to employee satisfaction and organizational development.

The SSO's PMS of AgriCo, HealthCo and EngineerCo contain more non-financial than financial measures. The predominance of **non-financial performance measures** may follow a general trend towards the use of non-financial measures since related literature emphasizes the importance of non-financial measures for a SSO's effectiveness (*Ittner/Larcker* (2003), p. 2). This finding seems also consistent with the above mentioned prevalence of process-oriented performance measures. By contrast, the SSO's PMS of CommCo and PharCo is dominated by financial performance measures. The SSO manager of EngineerCo states that financial performance measures are preferred by the corporate management in order to assess the SSO's performance. However, he disapproves the dominance of financial KPIs in EngineerCo's SSO, because other SSO objectives apart from cost efficiency are poorly incorporated in the SSO's PMS. The proportion of financial and non-financial performance measures in ChemCo's and MedTechCo' PMS is near-balance.

The proportion of **absolute measures and ratios** is difficult to assess for the SSO management accountants. The SSO management accountants of CommCo, PharCo and HealthCo operate with a rather balanced PMS regarding absolute measures and ratios. The difficulty of estimating the proportion of absolute measures and ratios may be due to the fact that ratios require absolute measures:

> "I could say: we do not use absolute measures, because we track 20,000 invoices per year and per employee. Nevertheless, absolute numbers are at the basis of these measures."
>
> *SSO Management accountant (MedTechCo), Interview #2, p. 4*

The SSO management accountants of MedTechCo and HealthCo state that the proportion of absolute measures and ratios has no particular significance for their PMS. For them, it is important that absolute measures and ratios are better or worse suited depending on the purpose of the analysis.

Apart from CommCo, no other SSO of the sample companies links its performance measures with the remuneration system. CommCo's SSO Manager believes that only by **linking performance measures to compensation systems** KPI targets are consistently pursued by organizational units. By contrast, PharCo's Head of SSO Process Excellence raises doubts on the effectiveness of financial incentive schemes and points out that by linking performance measures with compensation systems false incentives are also possible. The case company findings of CommCo and EngineerCo suggest that variable remuneration components are only applied for senior hierarchical levels. The fact that employees in lower hierarchical levels in MedTechCo's SSO do not financially benefit from the achievement of their KPI targets, may impinge on the motivation of MedTechCo's SSO employees at lower management tiers:

"I wrote an e-mail to my boss in which I asked whether we should establish target agreements. For example, the increase of the e-mail ratio could be assigned at a 100% to my area of responsibility [...] I wrote this mail nine months ago [...] No update yet."

SSO Management accountant (MedTechCo), Interview #2, p. 4

Linking performance measures to variable remuneration may reduce moral hazard in MedTechCo's SSO. If the management accountant of MedTechCo does not receive any other incentives, he has an interest to shirk and may stop calling suppliers to convince them of sending invoices via e-mail which improves the e-mail ratio. This would not be in the SSO manager's interest. Moreover, the interview with EngineerCo's SSO manager reveals that a difficult quantification of target agreements describes another reason for a restrictive coupling of performance measures and variable remuneration:

"[Demographic change] is a performance measure that is linked to the variable remuneration of the SSC heads [...] because EngineerCo has to shoulder this issue after the restructuring phase. [...] If you shrink from 20,000 to 12,000 employees, you can imagine that we had to dismiss the young co-workers with a short period of employment at EngineerCo. [...] Necessarily, we try to counteract this development through apprentices or trainees. [...] Such an objective is difficult to measure. And certainly not measurable at the flick of a switch, but only by a rule of thumb."

Head of SSO Governance (EngineerCo), Interview #11, p. 31

Table 6.6 summarizes performance measure design in SSOs:

Table 6.6: Performance measure design in SSOs

Measures	MedTech-Co	Comm-Co	Chem-Co	Phar-Co	Agri-Co	Health-Co	Engineer-Co
Number of measures	4	50	30	11	10	90	10
Dominating measure category	process quality	financial	process quality	financial	process quality	process quality	process quality
Composition of measures	rather balanced	financial measures prevail	rather balanced	financial measures prevail	non-financial measures prevail	non-financial measures prevail	non-financial measures prevail
Measures linked to variable remuneration	no	yes	no	no	no	no	no

6.3.2.2.2 Performance measurement process

As outlined in the conceptual basis, the performance measurement process can be divided into four sub-processes (measure and target selection, data collection, measure evaluation and measure modification). Therefore, the results of the cross-case analysis are arranged according to the four sub-processes of performance measurement.

Performance measure selection

The cross-case analysis suggests that the SSOs approach the **performance measure selection** very differently. Whereas ChemCo gains ideas for new performance measures from journals and scientific articles, MedTechCo and AgriCo develop their performance measures according to the trial-and-error principle. AgriCo's SSO manager states that he brings the idea for a new performance measure quickly to an implementation and subsequently adapts the measure continuously until he feels able to effectively control the running operations with the new measure. HealthCo and EngineerCo select performance measures based on an external benchmarking. HealthCo uses the results of a recently conducted *Hackett* benchmarking. EngineerCo's SSO manager joins discussion forums, such as SSC roundtables to generate ideas for new KPIs. CommCo develops new performance measures by using brainstorming sessions. Essential triggers for the SSOs to initiate a brainstorming session are issues in current operations and escalations by the management:

> "An escalation by the management is certainly a trigger. The management is blamed and urgently needs facts and figures. […]. Second option: We see a challenge in our day-to-day operations. Thereupon we get together with the service lines once a month and discuss if we are able to solve the problem with the current KPI set or if they need supplementing KPIs."
>
> *SSO Management accountant (CommCo), Interview #4, p. 4*

Moreover, the interview with EngineerCo's SSO manager suggests that he conditions the performance measure development on the data availability in the IT system:

> "To put it straight: performance measures have to be available automatically. It is useless if I have a measure by which I can possibly control, but at the same time an employee has to manually create a list. […] Instead, the [performance measures] have to be available in the IT system."
>
> *Head of SSO Governance (EngineerCo), Interview #11, p. 21*

This sample's SSOs define **performance measure targets** by using four strategies. First, MedTechCo, CommCo and EngineerCo base their targets on previous year's figures. Second, ChemCo defines performance measure targets by an internal benchmarking between their SSCs in Europe, Asia and South America. Third, AgriCo's SSO manager describes that expectations of the MNC's management define performance measure targets. This seems plausible insofar as the MNC's management is usually involved in the SSO's strategy development. However, it is questionable whether performance measures based on perceived management expectations are always best suited to control and monitor the SSO. EngineerCo's experts point out that performance measures which exclusively aim to meet the corporate management's expectations are rather used as an accountability report than as a critical self-evaluation of the SSO. Fourth, PharCo, EngineerCo and HealthCo use the experience of the SSO process managers to select performance measure targets. However, target setting based on the experience of process managers may place SSO managers in a dilemma. On the one hand, HealthCo's Head of Performance Controlling stresses that process managers are the only ones who can set and assess achievable goals for their processes in absence of external benchmarking possibilities. On the other hand, the statement of EngineerCo's process manager illustrates that it is *his* process to be monitored so that moral hazard occurs if process managers set targets for themselves:

> "But the target value [for the backlog] is simply based on the experience of the business we already know for years. One of our predeterminations. [...] We defined this. I do not know from the outside what is good or bad. This is a value that we have agreed on and set as the benchmark. Nobody said that three [days] are fair enough, four [days] are bad and two [days] are outstanding. [...] I can think about whether I am going to castigate myself [with two days] or if a benchmark of four days is a little bit too relaxed."
>
> *Process manager (EngineerCo), Interview #12, p. 19*

Performance measure data collection

This sample's SSOs mainly use ERP systems and spreadsheets to **collect the required data** for their performance measures. CommCo's SSO management accountant describes that data from the ERP systems are subtracted at first and subsequently edited in spreadsheets. The interviews reveal that MedTechCo, HealthCo and CommCo use software solutions based on ERP systems with the possibility to analyze big data. According to MedTechCo's SSO management accountant these software solutions gain popularity in SSOs for two reasons. First, they solve the bottleneck caused by the limited data collection capacity of spreadsheets so that these IT solutions are able to exploit large data volumes.

Second, they are able to visualize data streams and have extended analysis possibilities compared to spreadsheets:

"And because we have this Excel solution until now [...], we do not have the possibility to map these twenty extra lines per invoice into Excel. [...] The new analysis tool allows us to track every single document from a huge stream of data and to limit this data stream to the essential channels. This allows for a visualization of data: what is the most common way an invoice takes during its processing? [...] But also: how often does someone click before the invoice is finally processed?"

SSO Management accountant (MedTechCo), Interview #2, p. 6

All experts indicate that data collection for performance measures is a resource-intensive subprocess. EngineerCo's SSO manager emphasizes that data needs not only to be collected from back-end systems but also aggregated, validated, and edited. Thus, all SSO management accountants of the case companies seek to reduce the data collection effort for performance measures. CommCo's SSO management accountant reports that in the past the SSO needed to collect data from back-end systems and subsequently edit retrieved data for further processing. In order to reduce the data collection effort CommCo's SSO outsourced data collection activities to the MNC's IT department:

"I define a report how I would like to analyze the figures. [I] define this with the IT colleagues responsible for the SAP systems and they ensure the data retrieval from the back-ends, prepare the data and make it available to me monthly, weekly or daily, depending on the scheduled reporting cycle. The bottom line is that we have a central data source that we use. In other words: we no longer tackle back-end systems by ourselves, but we use our IT instead."

SSO Management accountant (CommCo), Interview #4, p. 5

With the exception of CommCo and AgriCo, all other case companies struggle to automate performance measure data collection, although the SSO managers of PharCo and MedTechCo suspect automation potential in this subprocess. PharCo's Head of Process Excellence points out that performance measures in these categories are accessible from databases only to a limited extent:

"We are computing [the performance measures] automatically for the most part, but there are also qualitative issues, which are entered manually. We are working on such issues like customer satisfaction. In that case, we use a combination of a [satisfaction] rating scale, where you can easily select a rating, as well as notes that can be entered. However, we think [the CFOs] would not be happy if they are asked to complete a questionnaire every month. That is why we committed ourselves to once a year."

Head of SSO Process Excellence (PharCo), Interview #6, p. 20

Evaluation

The case studies reveal three different possibilities to **analyze performance measures** in SSOs. The SSO management accountants of MedTechCo and ChemCo predominantly use variance analyses to evaluate performance measures whereas CommCo's, PharCo's and AgriCo's SSO management accountants mainly perform time-series comparisons. HealthCo's and EngineerCo's accountants additionally analyze the SSO's performance with an internal and an external benchmarking. However, EngineerCo's SSO manager believes that SSO management accountants rarely evaluate the measures by themselves, but in cooperation with the process managers:

> *"I send out the [performance measure] analyses to the respective process managers. Because I do not know why the PO-ratio in Switzerland at once increased by 5%. This has to be interpreted by the person in charge who takes care of the country. He adds his comments to the report."*

> *Head of SSO Governance (EngineerCo), Interview #11, p. 23*

HealthCo's SSO participates in an external *Hackett* benchmarking, which benchmarks a considerable number of performance measures among MNCs with SSOs, such as the administrative costs per transaction among SSOs. Since an external benchmarking is associated with considerable costs, EngineerCo's SSO performs an internal benchmarking instead by comparing the same performance measures between EngineerCo's SSCs. The interview with EngineerCo's SSO manager suggests that the comparison of performance measures across SSCs provides insights about different modes of operation in the SSCs and thus initiates process improvements. However, HealthCo's process manager states that internal benchmarking is less intensively applied in HealthCo's SSO due to the limited comparability of the SSCs. The SSCs of HealthCo provide different services and are responsible for different countries with different requirements:

> *"The problem is comparability. If we stick to the invoice issue: the processing of invoices will take more time in China. The fact that processing an ordinary invoice in Shanghai is more expensive than in Manila is not a novelty to me. I cannot conclude from this that I need to transfer the Chinese invoices to Manila and afterwards it will be less expensive. If [we benchmark], we would have to take a country-specific view, because countries vary in their complexity. Because you have to look at the legal and fiscal complexity of the processes in each country."*

> *SSO Process manager (HealthCo), Interview #10, pp. 28–29*

The interviews with the SSO management accountants suggest that SSOs predominantly use tables, charts, and diagrams to **publish analyzed performance**

measures. CommCo's, MedTechCo's and EngineerCo's SSO management accountants create reports in *Excel* and publish the resulting tables and diagrams either as a PDF or as a *PowerPoint* presentation:

> *"We have a transaction that stores this data from the ERP overnight into a file, which we edit by using an Excel-macro. [...] This results in a management summary, which is a PDF with the performance measures for the last two and a half months and comprises five to seven pages [...]. This file is made available to every country manager.*

> *SSO Management accountant (MedTechCo), Interview #2, p. 5*

The SSO managers of HealthCo and CommCo state that their SSO controlling departments already develop dashboards, in which the user obtains a visualization of the most important performance measures in an aggregated and neatly arranged form. The interview with PharCo's Head of Process Excellence emphasizes PharCo's ambition to allow the dashboard users modifying those reports and to retrieve real-time data:

> *"We want to build an appropriate management dashboard. Depending on which preferences someone has, he will be able to create his own report. In processes, such as P2P and O2C, we want to create something similar to the manufacturing industry. [...] Each team has its monitor with the main indicators. You can see intraday trends and you are able to identify problems. In the future system, we will have the possibility to look at real-time data."*

> *Head of SSO Process Excellence (PharCo), Interview #6, p. 17*

The analysis of the **reporting frequency** reveals that CommCo's, PharCo's, AgriCo's and HealthCo's management accountants report their performance measures primarily on a monthly basis. By contrast, ChemCo and EngineerCo installed a quarterly reporting whereas MedTechCo's SSO management accountant provides a daily performance measure reporting. However, MedTechCo's management accountant indicates that the reporting frequency varies depending on the hierarchical level of the report recipients. In MedTechCo's SSO lower hierarchical levels receive reports at shorter time intervals compared to their management:

> *"Two management reports: one of them goes on a monthly basis to the SSC head. [...] The other one is called the daily report. However, hardly anyone in our management team uses it. It is rather used by the employees [...]."*

> *SSO Management accountant (MedTechCo), Interview #2, p. 8*

According to EngineerCo's SSO manager, the frequency of performance measure reports is affected by the length of the customer relationship. EngineerCo's SSO customers that already receive SSO services over a longer period of time also have longer reporting intervals compared to rather new SSO customers:

> *"We found that [...] there is meanwhile so little to discuss, because our performance is convincing. [...] If the customers are satisfied [...] and the prices are fair, we will provide reports in a longer interval instead of a quarterly reporting. We would certainly not do this with a subsidiary that we have just boarded [...] rather we would provide [our reporting] more often to them."*

> Head of SSO Governance (EngineerCo), Interview #11, p. 24

Moreover, the interview with MedTechCo's SSO management accountant highlights that he does not take it as an offence if SSO employees or customers scrutinize performance measures, but rather considers discussions about performance measures as a positive sign that their analyses support the ongoing development of the SSO:

> *"Our PMS and its reporting have frequently been called into question by our employees. But I consider this as something positive in case you are able to explain the KPIs to your employees [...] and only that the question comes up is already something good. [...] For example, if we have a technical problem and the daily report does not update itself, they ask for it at the latest after two or three days. By this, I recognize that our performance measures are being discussed."*

> SSO Management accountant (MedTechCo), Interview #2, p. 13

Hence, informal communication among SSO employees about performance measures might be another indicator to what extent the PMS is embedded in the organization apart from a formal KPI reporting to the SSO's management. A PMS which is seldom discussed, struggles to motivate SSO employees or to yield learning effects.

Revision

The cross-case analysis yields varying findings with respect to the **performance measure modification frequency**. Whereas in AgriCo's and EngineerCo's PMS no performance measures have been added, eliminated or changed within the last twelve months, the SSO managers of ChemCo and MedTechCo claim to have modified their PMS several times over the last twelve months. The fact that two case companies did not make any changes to the SSO's PMS raises the question whether changing environmental conditions should have an impact on the SSO's PMS. For MedTechCo's and ChemCo's SSO managers it is unequivocal that process changes and changing legal requirements cause modifications of performance measures in the SSO's PMS. Thus, the PMS of MedTechCo's and ChemCo's SSO is in a continuous transformation:

> *"The fact that a PMS is evanescent seems out of question to me. [...] There are certainly performance measures, which have to be adjusted constantly, because processes change and whenever a process changes, I must also react with my PMS. I handle that quite flexible. If I notice that it is necessary to adapt something in certain [performance measurement] areas, I do it ad hoc [...]."*
> Head of SSO (MedTechCo), Interview #1, p. 14

However, MedTechCo's SSO manager admits that the continuity of the PMS is of significance in order to understand and compare trends over a longer period of time and to convey steadiness to report recipients:

> *"Consistency has the advantage of making certain developments more transparent over several years. [...] This continuity is also important for the recipients of the performance measure reports. If I bother them every month with a new structure, they instantly tell me off because they just do not understand it anymore. This is the worst thing that can happen to you. As soon as someone no longer understands your measures, they will not ask about it anymore [...]. This has to be avoided."*
>
> Head of SSO (MedTechCo), Interview #1, p. 14

The interviews with the SSO management accountants of CommCo, HealthCo and PharCo suggest that their SSOs made substantial changes in their set of performance measures within the past twelve months. This rather implies a '*big bang*' modification approach than a continuous PMS adjustment. In the case of CommCo and HealthCo, substantial PMS modifications are also associated with a personnel change in the SSO controlling department as both management accountants recently started their jobs.

Table 6.7 summarizes performance measurement process design in SSOs:

Table 6.7: Performance measurement process design in SSOs

Processes	MedTech-Co	Comm-Co	Chem-Co	Phar-Co	Agri-Co	Health-Co	Engineer-Co
Measure selection through…	trial & error	brainstorming	papers & articles	brainstorming	trial & error	benchmarking	benchmarking
Target setting through…	previous year's figures	previous year's figures	internal benchmarking	process manager's experience	management expectations	process manager's experience	previous year's figures
Data collection	partially automated	largely automated	partially automated	partially automated	largely automated	partially automated	poorly automated
KPI analysis focus	time series comparison	target vs. actual	time series comparison	target vs. actual	target vs. actual	external benchmarking	internal benchmarking
Main reporting frequency	daily	monthly	quarterly	monthly	monthly	monthly	quarterly
Modification within the last 12 month	few but steadily	big bang	few but steadily	big bang	no modification	few but steadily	no modification

6.3.2.2.3 Performance measurement actors

As outlined in the conceptual basis, PMS design involves a range of performance measurement actors. The interviews in the case studies suggest three groups of actors that play an important role for PMS design in SSOs: the SSO and SSC managers, the SSO management accountants and the process managers.

All interviewed **SSO and SSC managers** state that they are involved in performance measurement activities. Since the PMS of the SSO is still under development, the three SSO managers of MedTechCo, PharCo and AgriCo are strongly involved in the implementation of the PMS for their SSOs. Their main tasks are the selection and implementation of a suitable tool to map the new PMS and the selection of the most important performance measures. In addition, the SSO managers of MedTechCo, CommCo and ChemCo explain that they are responsible to set targets for the selected performance measures:

> *"One aspect of the PMS is that as a SSC manager I always have to know: what is my current status with regard to my goal attainment? The other task for me is to define: how do we measure goal achievement in our [performance measurement] system? Which KPIs are important to manage my SSC?"*

> *Head of SSO (MedTechCo), Interview #1, p. 7*

However, the analysis illustrates that AgriCo's SSC management team additionally evaluates performance measures and performs an internal benchmarking between the German and the Polish SSC. This appears to be due to the fact that AgriCo's SSO has not yet established a SSO controlling department:

> *"There is no special performance controller that takes care of [the PMS]. I have to create performance measures with my management team or with my supervisor."*

> *Head of SSC Germany (AgriCo), Interview #7, p. 12*

All SSO managers of the case studies indicate a broad agreement about the necessity of a controlling department within the SSO. However, the cross-case analysis reveals that AgriCo, EngineerCo and PharCo do not have a SSO controlling department and subsequently no **SSO management accountants**. Thus, it remains a controversial issue which organizational unit of the SSO is best suited to coordinate performance measurement activities. CommCo's SSO manager points out that an institutionalization of performance measurement in a SSO controlling department promises a distinct area of responsibility for SSO management accountants. If performance measurement activities are performed by the SSO management accountants, the SSO's PMS benefits through the knowledge gain and specialization of the SSO management accountant. Moreover, the

SSO management accountant is *the* person in charge for coordinating the performance measurement process:

> "We have structured the controlling for [our SSO] as follows: We have management accountants that deal with our eight service lines and additionally we have an area which is called 'Transformation and Performance Controlling'. This includes the performance measurement and also the [...] reporting for the entire SSO. The tracking of business cases and its compilation for further roll-outs, scope extensions and so on are bundled in this unit together with the performance controlling. What we are doing in performance controlling is strongly based on KPIs."

Managing Director SSO (CommCo), Interview #3, p. 4

The cross-case analysis finds that the **process managers** are involved in the performance measurement process in all SSOs of the case companies. With regard to the SSO's PMS, process managers fulfill three major tasks. First, the EngineerCo process manager states that he is involved in the evaluation of the performance measures. Without process managers, it is difficult for EngineerCo's SSO manager to analyze process KPIs so that he is reliant on the process manager's expertise. Second, HealthCo's process manager describes the definition of KPI requirements for the PMS as one of his tasks in order to effectively control the support processes. Third, the interview with HealthCo's process manager emphasizes that the process manager is involved in the creation of new performance measures in order to set meaningful measuring points to assess the SSO's performance:

> "As a GPO I am part of the Process Ownership and Governance Organization in our SSC. My task is to orchestrate the requirements of the different process owners with respect to our PMS. And beyond that I help to define the KPIs of today. In addition, I pay some attention whether a performance measure is meaningful at all and whether it is measurable. Thus, I actually play quite a role in the design of the PMS."

SSO Process Manager (HealthCo), Interview #10, p. 3

Table 6.8 summarizes performance measurement actors in SSOs:

Table 6.8: Performance measurement actors in SSOs

Actors	MedTech-Co	Comm-Co	Chem-Co	Phar-Co	Agri-Co	Health-Co	Engineer-Co
SSO/SSC manager involvement	set targets	set targets	set targets and define measures	set targets and define measures	poorly involved	poorly involved	set targets
SSO management accountant involvement	data collection and reporting	analysis and reporting	data collection and reporting	non-existent	non-existent	analysis and reporting	non-existent
Process manager involvement	analyze measures	analyze measures	analyze measures	analyze measures	set targets & analyze measures	set targets & analyze measures	analyze measures

6.3.2.3 Performance measurement effectiveness

The cross-case analysis demonstrates that the SSO managers of the case companies assess the effectiveness of their PMS differently. The SSO manager of CommCo emphasizes that CommCo's PMS can be described as effective since it supports him to **meet the objectives** of cost reduction as well as process quality and enables the SSO to ensure compliance with internal policies. By contrast, EngineerCo's SSO manager struggles to identify suitable performance measures which enables EngineerCo's SSO to achieve its objectives. The lack of applicable measures impedes the effectiveness of EngineerCo's PMS:

> "In the other performance measurement areas [...] we have hardly found any performance measures that help us to manage our SSO's effectiveness. The only [effectiveness] we are measuring is: what is the benefit for EngineerCo generated by the SSO? However, we only measure this on a very abstract, financial level. But in terms of quality or risk minimization, I am not able to analyze anything. I cannot grasp a deeper understanding of the SSO's benefits apart from reduced costs. And that is problematic, because our SSO has not only the objective to reduce costs, but also to optimize processes and to avoid risks. This is what makes my life very difficult at the moment."

Head of SSO Governance (EngineerCo), Interview #11, p. 32

Therefore, EngineerCo's SSO manager is rather unsatisfied with the current status of the SSO's PMS. The SSO manager of HealthCo outlines that the **degree of PMS satisfaction** depends on whether the performance measurement actors are able to directly influence the KPI development. Furthermore, he states that an effective PMS is characterized by the fact that performance measures are defined and evaluated transparently for all performance measurement actors:

"I guess we can be satisfied with the PMS. [...] I think the performance controlling team is doing a good job of analyzing the SSO's performance as transparently as possible ..."

Head of SSO Performance Controlling (HealthCo), Interview #9, p. 34

PharCo's SSO manager mainly uses the SSO's PMS to identify room for process improvements. Consistently, this objective has the highest priority and is thus being pursued with high intensity. Apart from the identification of potential for process optimization, the SSO management accountant of MedTechCo stresses that the communication of results and the understanding of causal connections constitute major objectives pursued with the implementation of MedTechCo's PMS:

"A decent PMS allows me to communicate performance measure data with rigor and subsequently discuss it with the person in charge so that we are able to perform a comprehensive, detailed analysis of complex problems that currently bother us."

SSO Management accountant (MedTechCo), Interview #2, p. 12

However, the interviews with the SSO managers of MedTechCo, AgriCo and EngineerCo also yield two major reasons for a **diminished PMS effectiveness**. First, the EngineerCo's employees seem to use the PMS to account for their individual performance rather than recognizing it as a MCS to analyze and improve the SSO's performance:

"The SSO employees consider [the PMS] probably rather as a scourge than as a helpful tool. Because who would propose a measure that measures himself? I would not do that at all and neither would you."

Process manager (EngineerCo), Interview #12, p. 34

Thus, the SSO employees' acceptance of the PMS as a tool for improvement seems to have an influence on PMS effectiveness. Second, the SSO managers of AgriCo and MedTechCo fear that the limited allocation of financial and personnel resources to the PMS impairs the effectiveness of the SSO's PMS:

"We are far from where we want to go. [...] But I am already quite satisfied as it runs. However, I also know very well that our PMS should look differently someday. Currently, I am rather dissatisfied with the limited resources I am able to invest in our PMS."

SSO Management accountant (MedTechCo), Interview #2, p. 12

Moreover, the cross-case analysis finds that the design and maintenance of the PMS in the SSOs of MedTechCo, AgriCo and EngineerCo is done as a part-time job which underpins the notion of scarce resources for PMS design.

Table 6.9 summarizes PMS effectiveness in SSOs:

Table 6.9: PMS effectiveness in SSOs

PMS effective-ness	MedTech-Co	Comm-Co	Chem-Co	Phar-Co	Agri-Co	Health-Co	Engineer-Co
PMS objectives	communicate results	communicate results	create transparency	create transparency	reveal cause and effect relationships	create transparency	improve processes
Satisfaction	rather unsatisfied	rather unsatisfied	satisfied	rather unsatisfied	unsatisfied	rather satisfied	rather unsatisfied

6.3.2.4 Summary

Overall, all experts relate to the underlying conceptual framework of PMS design. The cross-case analysis finds large differences among the case companies' SSOs with regard to the **number of performance measures** in their PMS. The majority of this sample's SSOs focuses on measures with reference to process quality. Moreover, non-financial performance measures either already dominate in the PMS of the case companies or gain importance. With one exception, the case companies do not link the SSO's performance measures to remuneration systems.

With respect to the performance measurement process the analysis showed that the case companies use different approaches to **select measures** for their PMS. Brainstorming sessions and the trial-and-error principle are most commonly applied by this sample's SSOs. **Performance measure targets** in the case companies' SSOs are usually based on previous year's figures or on the process manager's experience, whereas the latter one may induce moral hazard. Most SSOs of the case companies undertake considerable efforts to automate the **data collection process** for the calculation of performance measures. However, the cross-case analysis suggests that all SSOs struggle to automate this resource-intensive sub-process due to large data volumes and a heterogeneous

IT-landscape. The experts illustrate that performance measures are mainly analyzed by using three methods: time series comparisons, variance analyses, which compare the actual figures with the KPI targets and benchmarking. Furthermore, the findings indicate that performance measures in SSOs are predominantly reported on a monthly basis, although a quarterly and even a daily reporting frequency exists in three case companies. The cross-case analysis reveals that the **modification of the PMS** seems to be a rather neglected part of the performance measurement process. Two case companies in this sample do not modify their PMS at all. The large time intervals between performance measure modifications in combination with substantial changes in the SSO's PMS in two case companies implies *big bang* modifications instead of a continuous improvement.

The interviews with the experts reveal three major groups of performance measurement actors. First, **SSO and SSC managers** select and define performance measures which they intend to implement in their PMS. Moreover, they are usually responsible to set KPI targets. However, the cross-case analysis finds that SSO and SSC managers are reliant upon the support of process managers when setting KPI targets. Second, **SSO management accountants** are responsible for collecting performance measure data and analyzing KPIs. In addition, SSO management accountants usually play an important role when setting up a KPI reporting for the SSO. However, the cross-case analysis finds that three case companies do not have a SSO management accountant because establishing a SSC controlling department is associated with considerable costs. Third, the experience and knowledge of **process managers** is often used in SSOs to analyze performance measures. Moreover, SSOs depend on the expertise of process managers in order to define meaningful indicators and targets for performance measures.

With regard to the **PMS effectiveness**, the cross-case analysis indicates mixed results. Three SSO managers describe their PMS as effective since the PMS supports them in achieving the SSO's objectives. However, the results stress that not all PMS of the SSOs in this sample contribute to the achievement of SSO objectives. Furthermore, the interviews describe that an effective PMS creates process transparency so that SSO managers are able to unveil room for improvement. However, the case companies still struggle to reach full process transparency. Finally, the SSO managers emphasize that an effective PMS makes cause and effect relationships visible and facilitates the communication of the SSO's current performance.

The insights gained from the within-case and the cross-case analysis not only provide an empirical in-depth look into the current state of PMS design in SSOs in MNCs, but can also be used to supplement the quantitative study. Therefore, section 6.4 uses the results of the qualitative study to refine the basic hypotheses for the quantitative study.

6.4 Hypotheses refinement

The hypothesis refinement is sub-divided into five sections. The following section considers the external context of SSOs that may influence PMS design in SSOs. The second part of the hypothesis refinement refers to MNC-specific contingency factors on the PMS design, while the third section contains SSO-specific factors. The selection of potential contingency factors is built on the basic hypotheses presented in chapter four and the case study findings. The external and MNC-specific context factors are derived from the NIS and supplemented with the case study findings. The SSO-specific contingency factors refer to the NIS, the agency theory and the promotor model. Therefore, the third section on SSO-specific factors is structured according to the three underlying theories. Consistently, the case study findings are also included in this part. The fourth section refines the hypothesis with regard to the influence of PMS design in SSOs on its effectiveness. The fifth section summarizes the hypotheses refinement.

6.4.1 External context

Several contingency-based contributions in MCS research consider **perceived environmental uncertainty** as an important determinant of the external environment for MCS in MNCs (*Chapman* (1997); *Ezzamel* (1990); *Merchant* (1990)). MNCs experience environmental uncertainty due to two major reasons. First, environmental turbulence induced by an unpredictable behavior of the market participants or by rapidly developing technologies may trigger uncertainty in a MNC (*Chenhall* (2003), p. 137). Second, rapidly changing political and legal conditions can lead to uncertainty. Particularly, the HealthCo case reveals that quickly changing legal and economic conditions drive an increased need for information. Several authors suggest that a high degree of perceived environmental uncertainty is associated with more complex MCS (*Chapman* (1998); *Chenhall/Morris* (1986); *Gordon/Narayanan* (1984)). MNCs facing environmental uncertainty attempt to cope with it by gathering more information. The need for more information is expressed by more complex MCS, such as a PMS. In accordance with NIS, *Granlund and Lukka* state that additional uncertainty may also be induced by peer pressure in an organizational field (*Granlund/Lukka* (1998), p. 167). Therefore, this study assumes that perceived environmental uncertainty is linked to PMS design complexity. Hence, it is expected that:

H_{1a_1}:   *The perceived environmental uncertainty is positively associated with PMS design complexity in SSOs.*

Another important external contingency factor is the perceived environmental hostility (*Chenhall* (2003), p. 137). The perceived **competition intensity** represents a particular form of environmental hostility. Competition intensity is not limited to competition for market shares and customers, but also for resources and personnel necessary for manufacturing products and services. Prior research indicates that a high degree of competition intensity perceived by MNCs results in a higher reliance on cybernetic controls (*Imoisili* (1986); *Khandwalla* (1972); *Otley* (1978)). As outlined in *Malmi and Brown's* MCS framework, PMS appertain to the group of cybernetic controls (*Malmi/Brown* (2008), p. 291). The EngineerCo case highlights that MNCs facing a difficult competitive environment tend to have confidence in formal MCS, as MCS usually provide quantifiable, reliable information. Moreover, the EngineerCo case unveils a strong emphasis on financial measures during its restructuring phase, which supports the notion of an association between a high degree of competition intensity and a strong reliance on formal controls. It also becomes apparent that MNCs try to cope with competitive pressures by designing more complex MCS. Based on the case study findings and prior contingency-based MCS research, it seems likely that a highly competitive environment affects the SSO's PMS design. Hence, it is assumed that:

H_{1a_2}:   *The competition intensity is positively associated with PMS design in SSOs.*

6.4.2 MNC context

The work of *Khandwalla* illustrates that more diversified products and services lead to more complex MCS (*Khandwalla* (1972), p. 283). Further studies that investigate the impact of **product diversity** on other MAS, such as cost accounting systems, confirm these findings (*Drury/Tayles* (2005); *Schoute* (2011); *Schröder* (2014)). Product diversity also affects the administrative support processes of a MNC, as different business segments lead to diverging sales, manufacturing and distribution processes. SSOs, which take care of administrative processes, commonly provide services to different business divisions of the MNCs and to subsidiaries that focus on, for example production or sales processes. The process heterogeneity in the SSOs induced by product diversity may be reflected in the design of the SSO's PMS, because the PMS has to cover all relevant performance measurement areas. The EngineerCo case describes that product and service diversity among the MNC's subsidiaries also affects the performance measurement process. Increasing heterogeneity in sales, manufacturing and distribution processes caused by product diversity necessitates an extension of the PMS, since diverse processes cannot be controlled with the same performance measures. Moreover, product diversity impedes the comparability measures during the performance measure evaluation resulting in a higher coordination and communication effort in the performance measurement process. In accordance with previous research, the case study findings imply that an increasing product diversity of the MNC fosters the SSO's PMS design. Hence, it is hypothesized that:

H_{1b_1}: *The MNC's product diversity is positively associated with PMS design in SSOs.*

The MNC's organizational structure plays an important role for MCS design (*Chenhall* (2003), p. 146). The **MNC's organizational complexity** can be described in many different ways. This study is based on the conceptualization of organizational complexity by *Blau and McKinley* who emphasize the influence of hierarchical, functional and occupational complexity on organizational outcome (*Blau/McKinley* (1979), pp. 694–695). Therefore, it is conceivable that a complex hierarchical structure of the MNC also has an influence on the performance measurement of the SSO, since, for example, an increasing number of hierarchical levels is associated with an increasing number of recipients of KPI reports. Moreover, a stronger functional differentiation of the MNC may have an influence on MCS in SSOs. The AgriCo case highlights that only a cross-functionally used performance measurement offers meaningful insights. The stronger the MNC's functional differentiation, the more coordination effort may be required for the SSO's PMS design. Hence, it is expected that:

H_{1b_2}: *The MNC's organizational complexity is positively associated with PMS design in SSOs.*

Contingency-based literature emphasizes the impact of information technology on MAS (*Al-Omiri/Drury* (2007); *Brandau et al.* (2013); *Granlund/Malmi* (2002)). In modern times, the application of MCS without the simultaneous use of IT systems seems barely feasible (*Chenhall* (2003), p. 144). Thus, all seven case studies emphasize the influence of the **MNC's IT infrastructure** on the SSO's PMS design. Particularly, the CommCo case illustrates that the heterogeneity of IT systems affects the performance measurement process. For example, a large number of different ERP systems complicates the data collection process for performance measures. Moreover, not only the performance measure data collection may be contingent on the MNC's IT infrastructure, but also the performance measure evaluation since support processes with high transaction volumes require the analysis of large data volumes in order to yield meaningful process performance measures. Providing a KPI reporting in multiple IT systems that have different user groups also results in a more challenging PMS design for the SSOs. Hence, it is hypothesized that:

H_{1b_3}: *The MNC's IT infrastructure heterogeneity is positively associated with PMS design in SSOs.*

MCS are considered as tools that primarily managers use interactively for decision making and behavioral control (*Malmi/Brown* (2008), pp. 290–291). *Simons* highlights the relevance of top managers when it comes to the implementation of MCS (*Simons* (1991), p. 49). Applied to PMS design in SSOs, the support of the MNC's top managers is key for a successful implementation and development of PMS. In addition, NIS stresses that SSOs are subject to institutional isomorphism. Therefore, SSO managers and employees may anticipate and mimic the behavior of the MNC's top management in order to cope with their expectations. Hence, if the SSO managers and employees perceive that the MNC's top managers support the SSO's PMS, for example by regularly requesting KPI reports, the SSO employees mimic their dedication to the SSO's PMS and get more involved in PMS design. The ChemCo and the CommCo case describe the importance of the **MNC's top management support** for the SSO's PMS design. Both case studies find that the SSO's PMS provides information to top managers about how their SSO strategy is being implemented. If the SSO's PMS is constantly questioned by the MNC's top managers, it can no longer be used as a basis for decision-making and behavioral control. Thus, the MNC's top management support is particularly important for PMS design in SSOs. Hence, it is postulated that:

H_{1b_4}: *The MNC's top management support is positively associated with PMS design in SSOs.*

Drawing on NIS, *DiMaggio and Powell* state that institutions become isomorphic over time to cope with uncertainty (*DiMaggio/Powell* (1983), p. 150). With regard to its PMS, mimetic isomorphism seems to be a reasonable strategy for SSOs as it is economic for the SSO to mimic the MNC's PMS (*Hasse/Krücken* (2015), p. 26). Moreover, imitating the performance measurement of the MNC's group controlling reduces the risk for the SSO management to be called into question by the group management or group controlling, as critique of the SSO's PMS would recoil on the PMS of the MNC's group controlling. In this respect, an **intense collaboration between the SSO and the group controlling** seems advantageous for the SSO's management. Furthermore, a close cooperation in performance measurement activities is also useful for the group controlling since it reduces information asymmetries between the SSO and the group. The PharCo case demonstrates that a close collaboration between the SSO and the group controlling enhances plausibility checks during the performance measure data collection. Given that the PMS of the group controlling is usually more mature and thus more advanced, an intense collaboration between the group and the SSO implies the adoption of more elaborated performance measurement practices and thus may impact PMS design in SSOs. Hence, it is hypothesized that:

H_{1b_5}:   *The collaboration intensity between the SSO and the MNC's group controlling is positively associated with PMS design in SSOs.*

6.4.3 SSO context

The empirical works of *Kagelmann* and *Sterzenbach* reveal that SSOs disperse their SSCs at different locations around the world (*Kagelmann* (2001), pp. 91–92; *Sterzenbach* (2010), p. 347). The geographic dispersion has different causes, such as mirroring the strategic focus of the MNC's business units or due to the SSO's objective to generate labor arbitrage. **Geographic dispersion of SSCs** is usually associated with cultural and language heterogeneity as well as with a geographical distance between the SSO management and the SSC heads (*Kagelmann* (2001), p. 90). These challenges may affect PMS design in SSOs in two ways. First, an important objective of PMS is to improve the communication within the organizational unit, which also includes overcoming linguistic and cultural barriers. For example, it is obvious that a KPI reporting in German and English requires more (communication) effort by the SSO controlling department and thus causes a more complex performance measurement process. A meeting of all SSC heads with the SSO's management in order to analyze the KPI development also involves more difficulties due to the different cultural backgrounds of the managers. Second, geographical distance creates a higher information asymmetry between the SSO management and the SSC heads compared to a pure onshore SSO so that a more elaborated PMS design promises to be a remedy for moral hazard. Particularly, the ChemCo case illustrates that the geographical dispersion gives the SSO management food for thought about a further development of their performance measurement. Hence, it is expected that:

H_{1c_1}:   *The geographical dispersion of SSCs is positively associated with PMS design in SSOs.*

Sterzenbach's contribution has already conceptualized and tested the **SSO's legal and economic independence** as a potential determinant for MCS in SSOs (*Sterzenbach* (2010), pp. 377–378). Leaving aside the fact that he could not find a significant association, he did not explicitly refer to the PMS design in SSOs as a dependent variable. Nevertheless, it seems conceivable that legally and economically independent SSOs may determine PMS design in SSOs, since the SSO management is held accountable for the SSO's development by their MNC. Profit responsibility also implies that the SSO has to continuously track its economic development in order to remain capable of acting. Therefore, a PMS supports SSO managers to transparently monitor the SSO's economic development. By contrast, legal and economic independence is also accompanied by the fact that the SSO is no longer part of a large corporation. Regarding the SSO's performance measurement, this may simplify the data collection, analysis and communication of financial performance measures as fewer reconciliations and plausibility checks are required. The CommCo case illustrates that a clear delineation of the SSO's and the MNC's profit responsibility facilitates the performance measure evaluation. Moreover, profit responsibility independently from the MNC may foster a higher cost sensitivity in the SSO since new reporting software or analysis tools have to be paid out of the SSO's own pocket. Based on the two contradictory lines of argument, this study postulates an undirected hypothesis. Hence, it is assumed that:

H_{1c_2}:   *The SSO's degree of legal and economic independence is associated with PMS design in SSOs.*

The findings of *Sterzenbach* and *Kagelmann* suggest that SSOs primarily use cost and profit centers to organize their economic areas of accountability

(*Kagelmann* (2001), p. 104; *Sterzenbach* (2010), p. 353). Since **center concepts** represent an important SSO design configuration, their adoption may also have an impact on its performance measurement. For example, it is likely that SSOs using profit centers, which entails profit responsibility for their SSO managers, require a broader set of performance measures because they cannot confine themselves to cost measures. By contrast, SSOs that are exclusively organized as cost centers are able to avoid a broad set of performance measures related to revenues and profits so that these SSOs may use less performance measures. The case studies indicate that SSOs, which ground their areas of responsibility solely on cost centers, facilitate the performance measurement process since the analysis of financial performance measures is rather limited to cost divergence analyses based on predefined budgets or on the discussion of cost development ratios, such as administration costs per FTE. Given the prevalence of SSOs in the case studies that exclusively use cost centers, it is hypothesized that:

H_{1c_3}:   *The SSO's cost center concepts are negatively associated with PMS design in SSOs.*

The case study findings and *Sterzenbach's* empirical results unveil that SSOs often do not restrict their full range of services to just one corporate function, geographic region or business segment of the MNC, but render services of more than one corporate function across geographic regions for multiple business segments instead (*Sterzenbach* (2010), pp. 348–351). Notably, the CommCo case illustrates that multifunctional SSOs gain importance as SSOs focus on cross-functional end-to-end support processes. Moreover, a successfully operating monofunctional SSO leads to a rising interest of the MNC's top management to initiate a scope extension to further functional areas. The performance measurement of multifunctional SSOs appears to be more complex, because it has to encompass more support processes and thus faces an extension of its performance measurement areas. Moreover, the processes of multifunctional SSOs strongly differ from each other. The application procedure of HR departments for new employees cannot be monitored by using the same performance measures as for the P2P process. An extension of the SSO's service portfolio to several regions and business units also implies that the performance measurement expands, as the number of SSO customers and thus the number of performance measurement actors is growing. Furthermore, particularities of the MNC's business segments may affect PMS design, such that support processes for dialysis centers differ from administering public hospitals, as pointed out by the

MedTechCo case. Therefore, it seems plausible that a growing **structural complexity of the SSO** drives PMS design. Hence, it is supposed that:

> H_{1c_4}: *The SSO's structural complexity is positively associated with PMS design in SSOs.*

The **obligation for SSO customers to accept SSO services** represents another potential contingency factor for PMS design. *Sterzenbach* has already tested this contingency factor for MCS in SSOs, but did not find a significant association (*Sterzenbach* (2010), pp. 390–391). The descriptive results of *Sterzenbach* and *Kagelmann* suggest that the majority of the SSOs obliges their customers to contract, regardless of the costs incurred in the SSO (*Kagelmann* (2001), p. 121; *Sterzenbach* (2010), p. 354). The case study findings confirm their results and quote a lower coordination effort as a significant advantage of contract obligations for SSO customers. Contract obligations reduce negotiations about quantities and service pricings between the SSO and its internal customers to a minimum. With regard to the SSO's performance measurement, the possibility for SSO customers to be able to refuse services or to negotiate the conditions of a service provision requires a higher effort. Without an obligation to contract, SSOs have to regularly review customers' purchase quantities and take a closer look at the sales generated with their customers. Furthermore, free negotiations affect SLAs and thus, SLA performance measures need to be monitored in greater detail. By contrast, a detailed monitoring of the purchase quantities for SSOs whose customers are obliged to accept their services seems less crucial. The purchase quantities and the price development are ex ante fixed. Therefore, SSOs whose customers are required to accept the SSO's services may operate with a less complex performance measurement. Hence, it is expected that:

> H_{1c_5}: *The obligation for customers to buy SSO services is negatively associated with PMS design in SSOs.*

The empirical results of *Kagelmann* and *Sterzenbach* reveal that the majority of the SSOs apply SLAs to design their relationships with internal customers (*Kagelmann* (2001), p. 118; *Sterzenbach* (2010), p. 355). Since SLAs often include performance measures with reference to process quality and customer satisfaction, **SLA design** represents another potential determinant of PMS design. The HealthCo case demonstrates how SLAs are designed and monitored by the SSO's PMS and HealthCo's performance controlling department.

HealthCo's SSO compiles a separate SLA reporting with the most important performance measures of the SLAs, which is discussed in regular meetings with its internal customers. The more aspects the SLAs govern, the more aspects have to be monitored to realize whether both parties comply with the agreement. As exemplified in the HealthCo case, SSOs often use performance measures to monitor SLAs. Thus, it seems conceivable that SLA design will affect PMS design in SSOs. Moreover, SSOs and their customers are also characterized as principal agent relationships since information asymmetries between both sides exist and thus moral hazard may occur. The interplay between SLAs and performance measurement is able to mitigate undesirable behavior of both parties, for example by providing a regular SLA KPI reporting. Hence, it is hypothesized that:

H_{1c_6}: *The SLA design is positively associated with PMS design in SSOs.*

Sterzenbach's investigation uncovers that using performance measures in the SSO controlling department is positively associated with the attainment of specific SSO goals as perceived by the SSO managers (*Sterzenbach* (2010), pp. 400–401). This finding represents an indicator for the relevance of PMS design in SSOs. However, *Sterzenbach* also describes that performance measurement embodies just one MCS among many in SSO controlling departments (*Sterzenbach* (2010), pp. 364–366). Apart from performance measurement, cost accounting, planning, budgeting, and risk management are important elements in the daily work of the SSO management accountants. Given the limited working time SSO management accountants are able to spend on these controlling tasks, it seems obvious that the most widely used MCS of SSO management accountants become the most sophisticated ones. As a result, a strong emphasis of the SSO's controlling department on performance measurement influences PMS design in SSOs. The case study findings reinforce this assumption by the fact that most SSOs operate with a small number of SSO management accountants. Since few SSO management accountants are responsible for many controlling tasks, they are even more subject to time constraints and limited resources. Therefore, their **focus on performance measurement tasks** may have a decisive influence on PMS design. Hence, it is assumed that:

H_{1c_7}: *The focus of the SSO controlling department on performance measurement tasks is positively associated with the SSO's PMS design.*

The relationship between the SSO customers and the SSO represents another principal agent setting, where the SSO acts as an agent on behalf of the SSO customers. Since information asymmetries arise between both parties, a regular KPI reporting signals that SSOs are acting in their interest. Moral hazard may occur, because the SSO has an interest to operate as cost-efficient as possible so that this could be detrimental to the service quality. As SSO customers differ in their requirements, the SSO controlling may reflect varying **customer requirements** in their performance measurement (*Kagelmann* (2001), pp. 78–79). For example, if a low error rate is particularly important for a number of SSO customers, SSOs may provide additional process quality measures to these customers. A customized KPI reporting according to customer groups with specific needs is certainly beneficial to the SSO's customer relationships, but implies a more complex performance measurement. The more demanding the SSO customers are, the more effort is required by the SSO's performance measurement to adequately monitor all relevant needs. The interviews in the case studies confirm that regular meetings with the SSO customers to discuss the current development of customer satisfaction measures contribute to a more complex performance measurement process. Hence, it is hypothesized that:

H_{1c_8}:   *The variety of SSO customer requirements is positively associated with PMS design in SSOs.*

An important SSO objective consists in the standardization of their support processes, since standardization increases the SSO's controllability, enables the identification of best practices and constitutes the essential prerequisite for process automation (*Lueg et al.* (2017), p. 76). To enable a more nuanced perspective on process standardization, *Tempel and Walgenbach* distinguish between formal and factual standardization (*Tempel/Walgenbach* (2007), p. 14). While formal standardization refers to the existence of official guidelines, SOPs etc., factual standardization is defined by the actual execution of standardized processes in the SSO. Drawing on NIS, standardization is considered as a catalyst of isomorphism (*Tempel/ Walgenbach* (2007), pp. 13–14). Support processes, which become more similar and thus provide less maneuvering room for their execution, also require a less multi-faceted PMS since the same calculation schemes for performance measures are applicable to different support processes and the performance measure data collection is more likely to be automated. Standardized processes ensure fewer reconciliations among performance measurement actors and fewer plausibility checks. The CommCo case illustrates that not only formal but also factual standardization is of importance for PMS design in SSOs. For instance, a formally documented SOP only results in less effort, if local requirements do not induce factual deviations from the formally documented standard process. Only if the formal and the factual **degree of process standardization** increases, it seems conceivable that the design of PMS in SSOs is less elaborate. Hence, it is expected that:

H_{1c_9}: *The SSO's degree of process standardization is negatively associated with PMS design in SSOs.*

The performance measurement process involves varying groups of actors. SSO managers play an important role in the performance measurement process, as they usually define the objectives which are associated with the implementation of a PMS (*Gleich* (2011), p. 318). SSO managers also decide which human and financial resources can be assigned to the PMS design in SSOs. Therefore, SSO managers usually bear the responsibility for the further development of the PMS (*Witte* (1973), p. 17). Drawing on the promotor model, SSO managers may take the role of **power promotors** as they act as sponsors for the SSO's PMS (*Folan/Browne* (2005), p. 664). Their hierarchical position allows them to allocate resources to PMS design in SSOs and to overcome barriers of unwillingness. The CommCo case demonstrates that the presence of a power promotor in a SSO has a positive impact on the PMS design, as more resources flow into the performance measurement process and performance measurement actors become more important in their organization. If PMS power promotors are existing in the SSO, they foster the daily work with the PMS and encourage the SSO employees to familiarize with the PMS. The constant engagement in PMS activities promotes a pronounced PMS design. Hence, it is stated that:

H_{1d_1}: *The existence of power promotors is positively associated with PMS design in SSOs.*

PMS design in SSOs requires a high degree of expertise, since the SSO's PMS has to include varying support processes from different operational functions. As process owners are usually responsible for the processes performed in a SSO, they should have a profound understanding of the support processes so that they are able to define meaningful performance measures. In addition to a deep understanding of the SSO's processes, a process manager is the person in charge to assess the development of performance measures in his area of responsibility. He is able to provide explanations for KPI developments. Moreover, the data collection for the performance measure calculation requires knowledge of the information systems. The EngineerCo case indicates that process owners may act as **know-how promotors** since they contribute to the PMS design with their knowledge about the SSO's information systems. This knowledge enables them to overcome barriers of ignorance so that they assist SSO managers and SSO management accountants in the performance measurement process with their specific expertise (*Rost et al.* (2007), p. 343). In essence, the existence of know-how promotors in SSOs facilitates PMS design as know-how promotors enable a deep understanding of performance measurement activities in SSOs among all performance measurement actors. Hence, it is expected that:

H_{1d_2}: *The existence of know-how promotors is positively associated with PMS design in SSOs.*

This study's conceptualization of PMS design indicated that PMS design encompasses a considerable number of performance measures, performance measurement activities and actors. The different facets of PMS design require a high coordination effort, which is usually assumed by SSO management accountants. In addition to the coordination of the performance measurement actors and activities, SSO management accountants provide methodological competence which enables them to take care of the performance measurement process. SSO management accountants overcome administrative barriers by acting as a project manager of the SSO's PMS (*Hauschildt* (2001), p. 332). Similar to other project managers, SSO management accountants do not improve the PMS design on their own, but rather use the expertise of the know-how promotors and demand resources for the PMS development from the power promotors (*Hauschildt/Kirchmann* (2001), p. 44). In accordance with the promotor model, SSO management accountants may thus serve as **process promotors**. The CommCo and the HealthCo case reveal performance measurement actors who feel responsible for the ongoing development of the PMS, who ensure a coordinated performance measurement process and involve all affected actors. Hence, it is assumed that:

H_{1d_3}: *The existence of process promotors is positively associated with PMS design in SSOs.*

SSOs promote a holistic view of end-to-end processes instead of a strict functional separation. Mapping end-to-end processes in a PMS leads to a number of interfaces with organizational units that do not belong to the SSO (e.g. the MNC's group controlling). Furthermore, the SSO's PMS design needs to capture interfaces between the SSO and its customers as well as to external service providers. For example, the causes for the development of certain performance measures that are part of the SSO's PMS can be traced back to preceding process steps that are done by other departments. Thus, the SSO's PMS design relies on the support of other organizational units. The better the SSO's performance measurement actors succeed in establishing reliable relationships to other institutional actors, the more meaningful the PMS could be designed (*Gemünden et al.* (2007), p. 409). The PharCo case illustrates that particularly SSC managers are committed to build and deepen relationships with other organizational units, SSO customers and external service providers. Drawing on the promotor model, it is thus conceivable that SSC managers act as **relationship promotors**. Due to their exposed position, SSC managers are able to overcome dependency barriers by ensuring the knowledge transfer across the boundaries of the SSO (*Rost et al.* (2007), p. 344). The presence of relationship promotors in a SSO facilitates networking with other institutional actors (e.g. with SSO customers or other organizational units). These actors supply the SSO's PMS with information and thus contribute to the continuous improvement of the PMS design. Hence, it is hypothesized that:

H_{1d_4}: *The existence of relationship promotors is positively associated with PMS design in SSOs.*

Figure 6.3 summarizes the four outlined hypotheses on PMS design promotors in SSOs.

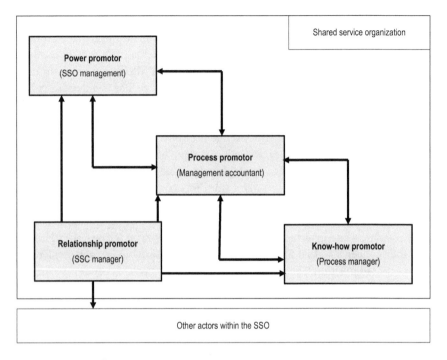

Figure 6.3: PMS design promotors in SSOs

6.4.4 Performance measurement effectiveness

In addition to analyzing potential contingency factors of PMS design, this study investigates a possible association between the SSO's PMS design and its **effectiveness**. The effectiveness of PMS has been subject to prior research (e.g. *Ittner et al.* (2003); *Said et al.* (2003)). Performance measurement supports SSO managers to implement strategies in order to achieve their objectives (*Gleich (2001), pp. 418–420; Ittner et al.* (2003), p. 717; *Sterzenbach (2010), p. 430*). Furthermore, PMS allow for a continuous monitoring of the SSO's support processes and to evaluate the SSO's performance (*Gleich* (1997), p. 115). The more information the PMS provides for SSO managers, the higher the likelihood that SSO managers are able to assess the current level of the SSO's performance. Thus, the PMS enables SSO managers to derive action plans and to better achieve their goals. The HealthCo case highlights that a PMS ensures transparency, which facilitates decision-making. The MedTechCo case reveals that a constant communication about performance measure developments strengthens the problem-solving competencies of the SSO employees and thus enables process improvements.

A nuanced perspective on performance measurement effectiveness offers the introduced principal-agent theory. The principal-agent theory illustrates that information asymmetries induce moral hazard. A SSO's PMS supports SSO managers to reduce moral hazard, such as hidden action and hidden information by SSO employees. An effective monitoring by using the SSO's PMS diminishes undesirable behavior, such as shirking. More information provided by the SSO's PMS entails the ability to align the decision-making and behavior of the SSO's employees to the SSO's strategy. Hence, the extent to which SSO managers are able to reduce moral hazard by using the SSO's PMS depends very much on its design.

By contrast, more information may lead to an information overload. For example, performance measure developments may contradict each other or are simply not convertible into action because the gathered information from the SSO's PMS exceeds human processing capacities. Therefore, information overload induced by a complex PMS design may paralyze the SSO's decision-making. The EngineerCo case emphasizes that a PMS may serve to measure individual performance, which usually does not contribute to the satisfaction of the involved performance measurement actors. Moreover, the ChemCo case illustrates that a complex performance measurement requires a considerable amount of resources that may be appointed to manage the SSO's performance instead of measuring its effectiveness.

Since the positive influence of PMS design on effectiveness prevails in literature, this study derives a directed hypothesis to analyze the impact on the SSO's performance measurement effectiveness. Hence, it is assumed that:

H_2:   *The PMS design in SSOs is positively associated with its effectiveness.*

6.4.5 Summary

Based on the empirical results of the case studies and the theoretical framework the previous sections refined the basic hypotheses developed in chapter four. The refined hypotheses will be tested in the following quantitative study. Figure 6.4 summarizes the overview of all hypotheses as well as the underlying theories and illustrates that new institutionalism serves as a theoretical foundation for the hypotheses refinement. Agency theory, NIS and the promotor model form a sound theoretical framework to analyze contingency factors on PMS design in SSOs. This study uses NIS in combination with the case study findings to derive hypotheses for the external and MNC-specific determinants. NIS is a powerful tool to explain the isomorphism of the SSO's PMS in order to cope with MNCs' methods, systems and guidelines. Furthermore, NIS offers perspectives to explain how the SSO's PMS design is affected by environmental uncertainty. Since a number of information asymmetries arise between the SSO actors, this study draws on agency theory that is supplemented with the case study results to derive hypotheses for SSO-specific context factors. Moreover, this study builds on principal-agent theory to derive a hypothesis for the assumed association between PMS design and its effectiveness. The promotor model serves as a basis to analyze the association between PMS promotors and PMS design in SSOs. Therefore, the hypotheses H_{1d_1} to H_{1d_4} investigate whether the outlined four types of promotors impact PMS design in SSOs.

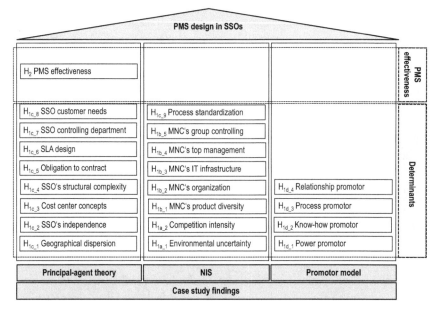

Figure 6.4: Overview of hypotheses and underlying theories (adopted from *Hagemann* (2016), p. 130)

7 Quantitative analysis

The quantitative analysis is subdivided into four main parts. Section 7.1 presents the sample selection for the survey study and provides a description of the sample characteristics. Moreover, section 7.1 describes the data collection process and the response rates. Section 7.2 outlines the construct measurement of PMS design in SSOs and PMS effectiveness. Furthermore, section 7.2 reveals the operationalization of the explanatory and control variables. Section 7.3 describes the methods of data analysis which are applied in the subsequent empirical investigation. Section 7.4 presents the results of the quantitative analysis.

7.1 Sample selection and data collection

7.1.1 Sample definition

Since this study analyzes PMS design in SSOs of MNCs located in German-speaking countries, only firms above a certain size threshold and operating at several locations are considered in this sample. Therefore, this study builds on publicly quoted firms that are located in Germany, Austria or Switzerland and generate annual sales of at least € 100 million as of 31st December 2015 from the *Compustat* database. Furthermore, firms with less than 500 employees are excluded because the presence of a SSO seems rather unlikely in such firms. These selection criteria yield a total of 478 firms (net of duplicates). Using the same selection criteria, this study draws a total of 778 privately held firms from the database *Amadeus*. Hence, the **initial sample** covers **1,256 firms** (table 7.1).

Table 7.1: Sample selection

	Germany	Switzerland	Austria	Total
Number of listed firms located in German-speaking countries with at least 500 employees and € 100 million annual sales as of 31st of Dec 2015	291	136	51	478
Number of privately held firms located in German-speaking countries with at least 500 employees and € 100 million annual sales as of 31st of Dec 2015	489	82	207	778
Initial sample	**780**	**218**	**258**	**1,256**
less firms without a SSO	-484	-109	-129	-722
less firms operating exclusively in their country of origin	-39	-17	-11	-67
less liquidated firms	-32	-11	-13	-56
less cross-listed firms	0	-8	-5	-13
less other reasons	-5	-1	-1	-7
Final sample	**220**	**72**	**99**	**391**

As information about SSOs in MNCs is not available in databases, all remaining firms are subject to an internet search. The first five pages of a search engine are skimmed to yield information about the company in connection with the words 'shared service', 'service center', 'SSC' or 'SSO'. Furthermore, professional online networks are searched for employees who indicated in their profile that they work for the SSO of their MNC. As a consequence, a total of 722 firms are subtracted from the initial sample since they do not have a SSO. A total of 67 firms are subtracted from the initial sample as they do not meet the definition of a MNC. In particular, these are law firms, airports and hospitals. 56 other firms are excluded because they have been liquidated. Moreover, 13 firms are eliminated because they are publicly quoted in more than one of the three countries and to avoid duplicates. Seven firms are removed due to other reasons, mainly because they were founded less than two years ago, making the existence of a SSO unlikely. The **final sample** consists of **391 MNCs** located in Germany, Austria or Switzerland with established SSOs (= population).

7.1.2 Sample characteristics

Figure 7.1 illustrates the **distribution by country** of all 74 MNCs that completed at least one of the two questionnaires (Questionnaire A for SSO managers, Questionnaire B for SSO management accountants). The majority of the participating MNCs is located in Germany, while almost a third of the firms is based in Austria and Switzerland. These proportions roughly correspond to the initial sample.

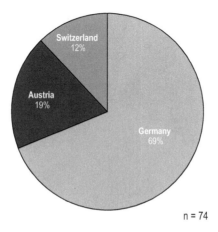

Figure 7.1: Sample distribution by country

Figure 7.2 summarizes the sample **distribution by industry**. In order to provide a meaningful industry classification of the sample firms and to ensure comparability with other studies, this study uses the Standard Industrial Classification (SIC), which is commonly used in current literature. Thus, the sample is subdivided into ten groups, which are taken from the first two levels of the SIC. For reasons of clarity and comprehensibility, the SIC terms are slightly modified. Figure 7.2 shows that all major industries in the sample are represented by at least 3%. Compared to *Sterzenbach's* study, retail and consumer firms (22%) are slightly more represented and form the largest industry group with sixteen firms (*Sterzenbach* (2010), p. 337). However, it should be noted that *Sterzenbach* classifies his sample using a total of eighteen industry groups based on self-statements of the respondents so that both classifications are comparable only to a limited extent.

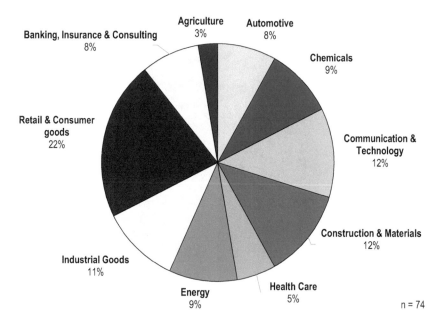

Figure 7.2: Sample distribution by industry

Table 7.2 illustrates the **size of the sample firms**. The four key figures net sales, number of employees, subsidiaries and countries with established subsidiaries serve as proxies for company size and are also drawn from the *Compustat* and *Amadeus* databases. Since the initial sample has been drawn in 2015, the presented key figures also relate to the fiscal year (FY) 2015. The analysis of this sample's net sales reveals two insights. First, a mean of € 26 billion net sales suggests that SSOs are implemented in comparatively large MNCs. Notably, one MNC is an outlier as it generates significantly more sales than the other companies of the sample with more than € 200 billion annual turnover. Since the median tends to be more robust against outliers it is displayed in the table 7.2 as well as the first and the third quartile. Second, the presented standard deviation indicates enormous size differences within the sample. A total of eight MNCs generate less than € 500 million annual turnover. The number of employees supports these two implications and reveals that the largest 25% MNCs of the sample operate with more than 84,000 employees.

Table 7.2: Fundamental characteristics of the sample firms

Key figures FY 2015	Mean	Std. dev.	Q25	Median	Q75
Net sales[a]	26,289.67	40,377.37	1,588.54	11,789	28,863
Number of employees	75,140	107,247	8,944	30,712	84,183
Number of subsidiaries	145	183	30	66	200
Number of countries with established subsidiaries	51	45	16	42	70

[a] Net sales are stated in € million.   n = 74

The number of subsidiaries and the number of countries with at least one established subsidiary are supplemented as non-financial key figures to characterize the MNCs' size. Both figures indicate that the implementation of SSOs seems particularly prevalent in globally dispersed MNCs with a considerable number of legal entities.

In addition to the sample firms' characteristics, the **respondents' characteristics** are of particular interest in survey research. The respondents' characteristics serve as an indicator for the data reliability and quality (table 7.3). For this study, the professional experience within the MNC and the professional experience within the SSO is relevant to evaluate the respondents' ability to provide proficient information. With an average of 13 years of professional experience in the MNC and almost 6 years of experience in SSOs, the participants represent a rather experienced group.

Table 7.3: Respondents' characteristics

(in years)	SSO Managers (Questionnaire A)		SSO management accountants (Questionnaire B)	
	Mean	Std. dev.	Mean	Std. dev.
Professional experience in the MNC	13.0	9.0	12.1	8.3
…thereof in the SSO	5.8	4.7	6.0	4.6

Figure 7.3 summarizes the **current position of the respondents** as a second indicator for data quality. While questionnaire A is addressed to the SSO managers and thus to the PMS users, questionnaire B is addressed to the SSO management accountants and thus to the PMS designers. The analysis of the SSO managers' current job position provides expectable results, since the majority of the participants take a leadership role within the SSO and thus use performance measurement for decision-making and behavioral control. 96% of the respondents indicate that they are responsible for staff. Consequently, the largest group of respondents describes their current job title as Head of SSC or SSO. Notably, 9% of the respondents are board members, predominantly CIOs. Although management accountants with a total of 51% still constitute the largest group of respondents for questionnaire B, 27% of the respondents are process managers who perform performance measurement activities in addition to their process responsibility. Interestingly, 9% of the respondents indicate that performance measurement in their SSOs is located in teams who are mainly responsible for optimizing processes. This finding suggests blurred lines between genuine management accounting tasks, such as decision support, and process optimization tasks. In essence, the conceptual role of the SSO management accountant in current literature (*Sterzenbach* (2010), pp. 147–150) contradicts this study's findings. With regard to the promotor model conceptualized in chapter four, the analysis in section 7.4 investigates whether management accountants exclusively occupy the role of process promotors and whether process owners exclusively represent know-how promotors.

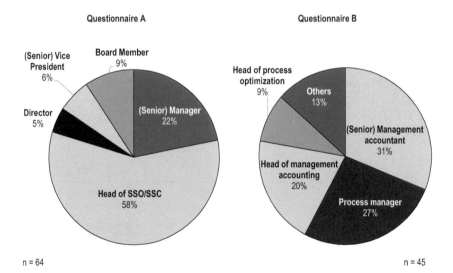

Figure 7.3: Current job title of the respondents

7.1.3 Data collection

Questionnaire characteristics

The survey data was collected with **two questionnaires in a dyadic research design**. Questionnaire A addresses SSO managers and contains four sections, while questionnaire B addresses SSO management accountants and encompasses three sections. Both questionnaires are based on the theoretical analyses outlined in chapter two, the prior research presented in the literature review and the empirical results of the case studies. Section A of questionnaire A encloses general information about the MNC and its environment, whereas section B considers the MNC's SSO design. Both sections gather potential determinants that may influence the PMS design and thus are the source for the explanatory variables in the multiple regression analyses. In addition, Section B yields descriptive findings on the status quo of the SSO design in German-speaking countries. Section C encompasses questions on the performance measurement effectiveness in the SSO and thus refers to the third research question. Effectiveness is measured in several dimensions so that the SSO managers' goal attainment, the overall satisfaction with the PMS and its general acceptance among SSO employees are addressed. Section D concludes questionnaire A by collecting personal information from the respondents. This is used for the description of the sample. The sections C and D in questionnaire A are identical to the sections B and C in questionnaire B. Information about PMS effectiveness is collected for both groups to analyze whether the perception of performance measurement effectiveness in SSOs differs between the designer and the user of the PMS. Section A in questionnaire B elaborates on PMS design in SSOs and forms the basis for answering the first research question. Section A is concerned with the distinct facets of PMS design (measures, processes and actors).

While the pool of interview questions for the qualitative study contains exclusively open questions, most of the 60 questions in the two questionnaires are close-ended in order to allow an efficient statistical analysis. Textboxes in the questionnaires are only created to enter numerical values or to allow self-framed answers, which prevents from disregarding important aspects. Close-ended answers are mainly presented as rankings and seven-point rating scales since they mitigate the risk of extreme response styles compared to five-point *Likert* scales and thus generate more reliable results. Table 7.4 summarizes this study's **questionnaire characteristics**.

Table 7.4: Characteristics of the two questionnaires

Questionnaire	Section	Topic	No. of questions	No. of pages (offline version)
Questionnaire A for SSO managers	A	Company's profile	14	7
	B	SSO's profile	13	
	C	PMS effectiveness	4	
	D	Personal profile	1	
Questionnaire B for SSO management accountants	A	PMS design	23	9
	B	PMS effectiveness	4	
	C	Personal profile	1	

Response rates

The **data collection** for the quantitative study took place between April and July 2017 and lasted for a total of four months. After the potential respondents were contacted via telephone and indicated their willingness to participate in the study, individual links to the online questionnaires were sent via e-mail. Upon request participants also received the questionnaires as a PDF. After the expired deadline (usually two weeks after the questionnaires were sent out), all participants who had not completed at least one questionnaire were contacted again by telephone. After another two weeks, a second reminder was sent via e-mail. Finally, a third and last reminder was sent out.

The response rates describe the proportion of completed questionnaires in relation to the final sample (table 7.5). In 53 firms the identified target person could not be contacted by phone or mail. In most of these cases, the corporate switchboard refused to put the research assistants through to the target person, or the researched target person had already left the company and an alternative contact person could not be found. Moreover, the number of respondents decreased by 97 firms, which were generally not willing to participate in research projects. In most cases, this approach was justified by the large number of research inquiries or by data protection concerns. For the latter, the provision of a non-disclosure agreement (NDA) was offered. In essence, **241 questionnaires** were sent out whereof 71 respondents completed questionnaire A (53 questionnaire B). In relation to the final sample, this equates to a response rate of 18.2% (for questionnaire A) and 13.6% (for questionnaire B). With reference to the sent-out questionnaires being the denominator, the **adjusted response rate I** is 29.5% (22.0% for questionnaire B). The adjusted response rate II indicates the proportion of completed questionnaires in relation to the total of 112 (84) attempted questionnaires.

Table 7.5: Response rates

	Questionnaire A	Questionnaire B
Final sample	**391**	**391**
…thereof not available	53	53
…thereof generally not participating in surveys	97	97
Sent-out questionnaires	**241**	**241**
…thereof not attempted	129	157
…thereof not completed	41	31
Completed questionnaires	71	53
Response rate	**18,2%**	**13,6%**
Adjusted response rate I	**29,5%**	**22,0%**
Adjusted response rate II	**63,4%**	**63,1%**

Due to the rather low response rate, **feedback from non-participants** via mail and telephone was collected whenever possible (figure 7.4).

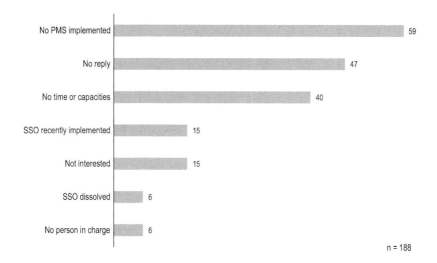

Figure 7.4: Feedback from non-participants

The number of non-participating MNCs (188) incorporates MNCs which did not complete both questionnaires (241 questionnaires – 53 completed questionnaires A and B = 188 questionnaires). Overall, potential respondents refused to participate in the study for two main reasons. First, the feedback indicates that 31% of the non-participating SSOs have not implemented a PMS and thus were unable to complete the questionnaires (figure 7.4). This finding implies that a significant proportion of SSOs control their organization without relying on a PMS. Second, 21% of non-participants indicated that they have no time or capacities to participate. Furthermore, several MNC just recently implemented their SSO so that they could not yet make reliable statements.

The rather low response rate indicates that the sample may be affected by a non-response bias. This study therefore compares early and late responses as proposed by *Armstrong and Overton* (*Armstrong/Overton* (1977), pp. 396–402). The **non-response bias test** reliably estimates the direction and magnitude of the non-response bias. The test procedure of *Armstrong and Overton* assumes that late respondents are comparable with non-respondents (*Armstrong/Overton* (1977), p. 397). This study conducts the test for the essential constructs of both questionnaires and the fundamental characteristic SSO size. For questionnaire A, the non-response bias test uses both measures for performance measurement effectiveness, namely goal attainment and satisfaction, as both measures play a central role in the subsequent analyses of the SSO manager questionnaire. In addition to the SSO size, the test for questionnaire B uses the three components of PMS design as the main construct of this questionnaire. In line with the suggested approach of *Armstrong and Overton*, the test defines the early and late respondents by means of waves (*Armstrong/Overton* (1977), p. 397). Hence, this study defines early respondents as those who answered before the first reminder, whereas late respondents are those who have responded after the last reminder. Due to the small sample size the two-sample *Wilcoxon Mann Whitney* test is used. Table 7.6 indicates **no significant difference** between both samples.

Table 7.6: Non-response bias test for questionnaire A

Measure	Early respondents (mean)	Late respondents (mean)	p-value
n	21	18	
Goal attainment	0.41	0.41	0.762
Satisfaction	0.50	0.53	0.848
LN SSO size	5.85	5.44	0.426

This finding suggests that a measurement error due to non-response bias is unlikely. The same pattern emerges for questionnaire B (table 7.7). This test also shows that the results of the early respondents do not significantly differ from those of the late respondents. Al-though both tests do not reveal any significant differences, the SSO size implies that larger SSOs have responded first and smaller SSOs tend to be the late respondents.

Table 7.7: Non-response bias test for questionnaire B

Measure	Early respondents (mean)	Late respondents (mean)	p-value
n	18	19	
Performance measures	0.40	0.38	0.650
Performance measurement process	0.43	0.42	0.364
Performance measurement actors	0.32	0.35	0.820
LN SSO size	5.86	4.85	0.150

7.2 Construct measurement

This section clarifies which indicators are used to measure the theoretical constructs and how these constructs are operationalized as items in the two questionnaires. This study aggregates formative indicator variables to scores for construct measurement. Hence, these scores form the components of PMS design and of performance measurement effectiveness. All scores are latent constructs which are not directly observable and thus in need of explanation. Therefore, the operationalization of questionnaire items not only rests on the detailed theoretical concepts, but is enhanced by the empirical results of the case study analyses in order to foster content validity. The scale development for the used items is in line with *DeVellis'* set of specific guidelines (*DeVellis* (2016), pp. 73–114).

With regard to the relationship between the theoretical construct and the indicators, it is important to distinguish between reflective and formative measurement models (*Döring/Bortz* (2016), p. 229). In reflective measurement models, the theoretical construct causes the indicators that are considered as effects. By contrast, this study applies a **formative measurement model** and thus assumes that the used indicators determine the construct to be measured (*Jarvis et al.* (2003), pp. 200–201). The used formative indicators compose a score for the PMS design and for the aggregated performance measurement effectiveness. Both scores are divided into sub-scores in order to perform further analyses. Notably, formative indicators may be very dissimilar to one another in terms of content and do not necessarily correlate with each other (*MacKenzie et al.* (2005), p. 712). However, the used proxies should always be the result of theoretical reasoning (*Diamantopoulos/Riefler* (2008), p. 1192). As opposed to reflective measurement models, formative indicators do not necessitate the same antecedents and consequences (*Jarvis et al.* (2003), p. 203).

7.2.1 Operationalization of the constructs under research

7.2.1.1 PMS design score

The operationalization of the **PMS design score** is based on the three dimensions described in section 2.2 (measures, processes and actors). Furthermore, this study's case study results are exploited to operationalize the questionnaires as comprehensible as possible for the respondents. To operationalize PMS design, this study applies a PMS design score which allows to condense multidimensional content into a single, comparable, and communicable value. The quality of the score depends essentially on whether all relevant performance measurement dimensions are reflected. Since the used indicators show different measuring units, they have to be standardized to a uniform measuring unit with a value between zero (lowest possible complexity) and one (highest possible complexity) (*Döring/Bortz* (2016), pp. 277–278). This study uses a total of twelve components that are merged into the **three subscores** performance measures (MEAS), performance measurement process (PROC), and performance measurement actors (ACT). The three subscores are averaged and subsequently aggregated into the PMS design score (COMP). All elements of the three subscores are equally weighted. The following sections outline the operationalization of the questionnaire items used in the PMS design score.

Notably, the PMS design score represents a necessary tool since the latent construct PMS design is not directly and objectively observable. Therefore, the weighting of the subscores and the assignment of the questionnaire items to the respective constructs remains a controversial issue. However, the formation of the score is guided by two basic rules. First, formative measurement models suggest to choose manifest over latent variables whenever possible. Therefore, it seems, for example, more advantageous to survey the number of modified performance measures compared to an implicit question, such as: *how much did your PMS change within the last 12 month on a scale from one to seven*? Due to the requirements and quality criteria for survey research, this study cannot collect exclusively manifest variables (e.g. the completion of a question related to a manifest variable takes more time; there is a higher risk that the respondent aborts the completion; it is not always possible to collect a manifest variable for a theoretical construct). Second, the assignment of the items to the three subscores (MEAS, PROC, ACT) is based on the conceptualization of PMS design in chapter two (measures, processes, actors). For instance, the item modification intensity may also be assigned (in a modified form) to the subscore MEAS. However, extant literature considers the modification of performance measures rather as a process step and thus this study assigns modification intensity to the performance measurement process (subscore PROC).

7.2.1.1.1 Performance measures

The **subscore MEAS** consists of three elements, which are composed of several questionnaire items. The first subscore element operationalizes the **number of performance measures** used in the SSOs' PMS. It is assumed that a higher number of performance measures enhances PMS design. The questionnaire item A.1 has been used in a similar vein by (*Raake* (2008), p. 154). In contrast to her operationalization, this study discards preset intervals for performance measure numbers but requests the current number of used performance measures from the respondents. Compared to the use of ordinal scales the determination of manifest variables seems more precise and advantageous for formative measurement models. The transformation of the variables into the design score is based on a logarithm function, since it is expected that the PMS maturity level increases rather convergingly than linearly with a growing number of performance measures (*Libby/Waterhouse* (1996), p. 141). Moreover, the explanatory notes to this question point out that performance measures have to be counted only once if they are reported to different users or hierarchical levels in the same manner.

The second element comprises the **number of performance measurement categories**. This element assigns the used performance measures to the six categories *costs, customers, process quality and productivity, process automation, employees, and organizational development*. The more performance measurement categories the SSO covers, the higher the PMS design score. Performance measurement categories are also addressed by *Raake* in a similar way (*Raake* (2008), p. 155). However, she operationalizes performance measurement categories as a binary variable so that a further differentiation into six categories grasps a deeper understanding. As described in section 2.1.3, the performance measure categories are derived from the most essential performance measurement areas in SSOs. Based on the empirical findings of the interviews, this study condenses the categories used in the questionnaire to the six most important ones in order to lower the time exposure for the respondents to an acceptable level.

The third component of the subscore MEAS refers to the percentage of the performance measures that are linked to the variable remuneration system. **Performance measures linked to the remuneration system** are expected to attract more attention compared to performance measures that are not compensation-related. Performance measures and target levels affecting the remuneration need to be precisely defined and documented in order to prevent ambiguity with respect to the bonus payments (*Tuomela* (2005), p. 314). The link between PMS and remunaeration system adds to the PMS design score. This element is also adapted from *Raake*, who instead prefers a five-point rating scale (*Raake* (2008), p. 155).

7.2.1.1.2 Performance measurement process

The **subscore PROC** comprises eight elements. The operationalization of the questionnaire item A.4 follows the performance measurement process described in section 2.2.5.2. The first element addresses the **performance measure selection** process and entails seven questionnaire items. The items refer to different approaches in the selection process so that varying approaches of the SSOs are measured on a seven-point rating scale (*1 = not at all … 7 = completely*). The more intensely the SSO employs different approaches for the selection of performance measures, the higher is its score. The operationalization is essentially based on the empirical findings of *Neely et al.*, whose case study analyses revealed varying performance measure selection processes (*Neely et al.* (2000), pp. 1127–1130).

In a similar vein, six items are used to consider the **target setting process** for performance measures in order to assess the SSOs' strategies how performance measure targets are set. PMS, whose performance measure targets originate from different sources, imply a higher process complexity, since this involves a higher effort. For example, it is less sophisticated to derive reference values for performance measures only from an internal benchmarking compared to additionally realizing an external benchmarking to gain further reference values.

The operationalization of item A.10 rests on the case study results of *Bititci et al.* (2002) and *Bourne et al.* (2002). The FTEs that are appointed to gather the necessary data for the SSOs' performance measures serve as a proxy to evaluate the complexity of the **data collection process**. It is assumed that a larger number of FTEs assigned to each of the six operationalized process steps reflects a more complex data collection. For example, an elaborate formatting and visualization of performance measures is certainly desirable from the reporting users' point of view. However, this is manifested in the effort involved during the performance measure data collection. The data aggregation from different back-end systems into the target system illustrates another source for process complexity driven by a heterogeneous MIS landscape. In order to avert the threat of biased variables due to different working hour models of the SSO employees, item A.10 prefers the measuring unit FTE over headcounts. Explanatory notes on the questionnaire item provide a calculation example for the conversion of headcounts to FTEs.

In addition to the number of FTEs used, the automation degree of the data collection process provides information on the complexity of this subprocess. As described by *Chenhall*, employed technologies play an important role for MCS and in particular for the performance measurement process (*Chenhall* (2003), p. 139). In contrast to highly specialized support processes with many exceptions, SSOs strive for standardized processes that are well-analyzable. Standardized processes foster the **automation of data collection** for the SSOs' performance measures, since measurement points can be defined without exceptions. The findings of the interviews indicate that the automation degree varies greatly between the aforementioned performance measure categories. Therefore, this score element is operationalized by using the outlined six categories. For instance, it is conceivable that process-related performance measures, such as productivity measures, have a higher degree of automation compared to employee satisfaction measures since the latter are often based on surveys. Notably, item A.10 is reverse coded because a higher degree of automation in the performance measure data collection process implies less complexity.

Another element of the PROC score encompasses the evaluation of performance measures. The **analysis frequency** consists of four items and indicates on a seven-point rating scale how often SSOs perform certain performance measure analyses. The more frequently an analysis (e.g. a variance analysis) is performed, the higher the PMS design score for this subprocess. Item A.13 is informed by the empirical work of *Dossi* and *Patelli* whose findings unveil applied methods for relative performance evaluation and by the results of *Fischer et al.* who investigate benchmarking in the context of SSOs (*Dossi/Patelli* (2010), pp. 521–522; *Fischer et al.* (2017), p. 127).

Furthermore, the **reporting frequency** of performance measures represents an indicator of the performance measurement process complexity since a KPI reporting seems more challenging in shorter intervals. Item A.12 has already been used in a similar manner by *Grüning* ((2002), p. 340). In contrast to his operationalization, the respondents are allowed to choose between eight instead of six intervals, namely: *daily, weekly, monthly, quarterly, semi-annually, annually, less regularly than annually, and irregularly.* This ordinal scale yields a greater differentiation of reporting intervals. For the same reason, this study uses a seven-point instead of a five-point rating scale. As the reporting frequency also varies depending on the performance measure category, reporting frequency is operationalized for each performance measure category and averaged afterwards.

Dossi and *Patelli* emphasize the importance of informal communication to discuss performance measures (*Dossi/Patelli* (2010), pp. 522–523). According to their findings this study seizes the notion of an **informal reporting frequency** in questionnaire item A.14. The more frequently SSO employees are willing to discuss the developments of certain performance measures, the higher the need for information. It is expected that a higher information need implies a more complex communication process and thus elevates the PROC score. This item also employs a seven-point rating scale.

The last element of the PROC score refers to the **modification of performance measures**. The review process has been empirically addressed by the investigations of *Bourne et al.* (2000), *Grüning* (2002) and *Raake* (2008). *Grüning* and *Raake* use ordinal scales to operationalize modification frequency (*Grüning* (2002), p. 341; *Raake* (2008), p. 155). However, the frequency provides little information about the extent and nature of measure modifications in SSOs. Hence, this study supplements the reporting frequency by analyzing the amount of added and eliminated performance measures. The number of modified measures is directly observable and thus included in the PROC score as a logarithm function analogous to item A.1.1 and A.10. The more measures are modified the higher the PMS design score.

7.2.1.1.3 Performance measurement actors

The third **subscore ACT** addresses the involvement of performance measurement actors as a driver of PMS design. It consists of an element containing eight questionnaire items. The inclusion of relevant actors has been subject to few contributions in extant literature (*Folan/Browne* (2005); *Gleich* (2002); *Kaplan/Norton* (1996)). With regard to survey based performance measurement research the operationalizations of actors in the surveys of *Raake* (2008) and *Grüning* (2002) act as a stimulus for this study's operationalization. As opposed to *Grüning* who merely focuses on the involvement of performance measurement actors during the PMS implementation phase, this study broadens the scope by addressing their involvement during the measure definition, modification, and reporting phase. Furthermore, the surveys of *Grüning* and *Raake* cover only two groups of actors: the employees and the top management (*Grüning* (2002), p. 337; *Raake* (2008), p. 155). However, conceptual literature suggests that more than these two groups of actors are involved in the performance measurement process in SSOs. Therefore, item A.18 comprises **eight potential performance measurement actors** in SSOs and operationalizes their involvement in three essential performance measurement subprocesses. This proxy implies that an increasing number of involved actors induces an increasing PMS design complexity.

Table 7.8 describes the calculation scheme for the transformation of the questionnaire variables into each subscore and the PMS design score. Each item refers to a question in section A of questionnaire B, which is attached in appendix C.

Table 7.8: The PMS design score

	PMS design score (COMP)	
Item	**Subscore/element**	**Calculation scheme for score-transformation**
	Performance measures (MEAS)	
A.1.1	Number of performance measures	$f(x_i) = \dfrac{\ln(x_i)}{\ln(\text{max. no. of performance measures})}$
A.1.2	Number of performance measure categories	For each of the **six** performance measure categories the respondent scores $\dfrac{1}{6}$, if covered.
A.6	Performance measures linked to the remuneration system	$f(x_i) = \dfrac{x_i}{100}$
	Performance measurement process (PROC)	
A.4	Performance measure selection	For each of the **seven** line items: $f(x_i) = \dfrac{1}{6} * (x_i - 1) * \dfrac{1}{7}$
A.7	Target setting	For each of the **six** line items: $f(x_i) = \dfrac{1}{6} * (x_i - 1) * \dfrac{1}{6}$
A.10	Data collection	$f(x_i) = \dfrac{x_i}{\text{max. no. of FTEs}}$
A.11	Automation degree[a]	For each of the **six** line items: $f(x_i) = 1 - \dfrac{1}{6} * (x_i - 1) * \dfrac{1}{6}$
A.13	Analysis frequency	For each of the **four** line items: $f(x_i) = \dfrac{1}{6} * (x_i - 1) * \dfrac{1}{4}$

Table 7.8: Continued

PMS design score (COMP)		

A.12	Reporting frequency	For each of the **six** performance measure categories the respondent scores:

$$f(x_i) = \frac{1}{6} * \frac{1}{8} \text{ if reported irregularly,}$$

$$\frac{2}{8} \text{ if reported less than annually,}$$

$$\frac{3}{8} \text{ if reported annually,}$$

$$\frac{4}{8} \text{ if reported semi-annually,}$$

$$\frac{5}{8} \text{ if reported quarterly,}$$

$$\frac{6}{8} \text{ if reported monthly,}$$

$$\frac{7}{8} \text{ if reported weekly,}$$

$$\frac{8}{8} \text{ if reported daily}$$

A.14	Informal communication frequency	$$f(x_i) = \frac{1}{6} * (x_i - 1)$$
A.17	Modification intensity	$$f(x_i) = \frac{\ln(x_i)}{\ln(\text{max. no. of modified measures})}$$

Performance measurement actors (ACT)		

A.18	Involved actors	For each of the **eight** line items:

$$f(x_i) = \frac{1}{3} * x_i * \frac{1}{8}$$

Notes: x_i = respondent's manifestation; $f(x)$ = score transformation function; ln = natural logarithm; max = maximum; no. = number; a = reverse coded score

7.2.1.2 *Performance measurement effectiveness*

The success and failure of PMS has been subject to several empirical analyses in the performance measurement literature (e.g. *Ittner et al.* (2003); *Said et al.* (2003)). An essential measure of PMS success is its effectiveness. Section B in questionnaire B and section C in questionnaire A focus on the perceived performance measurement effectiveness. Performance measurement effectiveness is operationalized in two scores by four elements (table 7.9). Both questionnaires incorporate all four elements of performance measurement effectiveness in order to evaluate possible perception differences between the two respondent groups. The **goal attainment score (GOA)** encompasses the objective achievement of the SSO and the goal attainment of the PMS objectives. The **satisfaction score (SAT)** contains the perceived overall satisfaction by the SSO managers and the PMS acceptance by the SSO employees. Both scores represent a tool which allows for the measurement of PMS effectiveness in SSOs. The scores are necessary since the effectiveness of PMS in SSOs cannot be measured by objectively observable data (e.g. in annual reports).

Element B.1 addresses the question to what extent PMS support SSOs in achieving their objectives. In line with the essential SSO objectives elaborated in section 2.1.3, this element contains six items. The proxy **SSO objective achievement** has been used in a similar vein by *Sterzenbach* (2010). In contrast to his operationalization, this study employs six instead of four major SSO objectives. Moreover, *Sterzenbach* has subdivided the SSO objectives into twelve subordinate goals in order to thoroughly determine the SSOs' objective achievement (*Sterzenbach* (2010), p. 430). However, this operationalization refrains from such a level of detail since his findings indicate that respondents are not able to differentiate between, for example twelve varying financial objectives. Notably, this study uses seven-point instead of five-point rating scales. Similar to *Sterzenbach's* operationalization, element B.1 applies rank-ratings to weigh the items according to their relative importance for the SSO. Although rankings should be used with caution due to the limited time of the respondents, they enhance the score's robustness.

Table 7.9 presents the formation of the GOA and the SAT score.

Table 7.9: The performance measurement effectiveness score

	Performance measurement effectiveness	
Item	**Element**	**Calculation scheme for score-transformation**
		Goal attainment score (GOA)
B.1	SSO objective achievement	For each of the **six** SSO objectives the respondent scores:

$$f(x_i) = \frac{1}{6} * (x_i - 1) * \frac{1}{6} * \frac{6}{6} \text{ if ranked as first,}$$

$$\frac{5}{6} \text{ if ranked as second,}$$

$$\frac{4}{6} \text{ if ranked as third,}$$

$$\frac{3}{6} \text{ if ranked as fourth,}$$

$$\frac{2}{6} \text{ if ranked as fifth,}$$

$$\frac{1}{6} \text{ if ranked as sixth,}$$

B.2 — PMS goal attainment — For each of the **six** performance measurement objectives the respondent scores:

$$f(x_i) = \frac{1}{6} * (x_i - 1) * \frac{1}{6} * \frac{6}{6} \text{ if ranked as first,}$$

$$\frac{5}{6} \text{ if ranked as second,}$$

$$\frac{4}{6} \text{ if ranked as third,}$$

$$\frac{3}{6} \text{ if ranked as fourth,}$$

$$\frac{2}{6} \text{ if ranked as fifth,}$$

$$\frac{1}{6} \text{ if ranked as sixth,}$$

(*continued on next page*)

Table 7.9: Continued

Satisfaction score (SAT)		
B.3	Overall satisfaction	$f(x_i) = \frac{1}{6} * (x_i - 1)$
B.4	PMS acceptance	$f(x_i) = \frac{1}{6} * (x_i - 1)$

Notes: x_i = respondent's manifestation; $f(x)$ = score transformation function

The second element comprises the respondents' perceived **PMS goal attainment** and also consists of the six most essential objectives. The operationalized objectives that are commonly pursued with PMS are based on the contribution of *Gleich* ((2001), pp. 418–420). Similar to item B.1, B.2 also uses rank-ratings to evaluate the importance of the objectives for the SSOs' PMS. A higher ranking of the PMS objective by the respondent paired with a high degree of perceived goal attainment consequently results in a high GOA score, while a high degree of perceived goal attainment paired with a low relevance of the objective results in a lower score.

A further measure of PMS effectiveness is the **perceived overall satisfaction** with the PMS of the SSO managers and management accountants. This element is operationalized as a single item using a seven-point rating scale, where a value of one indicates a high dissatisfaction and a value of seven indicates a high satisfaction. This item has already been used in a similar manner by *Raake* ((2008), p. 156).

The fourth element **PMS acceptance** completes the SAT score and focuses on the perceived acceptance of the PMS by the SSO employees. This single item and its subsequent score transformation is operationalized in line with item B.3. Several empirical findings associate an effective PMS with a successful involvement of all relevant stakeholders (e.g. *Gleich* (2001); *Kaplan/Norton* (1996)). However, not only the actors directly involved in the performance measurement process are of significance, but also the perceptions of other SSO employees have to be reflected since they may be indirectly affected by the PMS. Therefore, item B.4 encourages the respondents to change their perspective. A PMS which is only accepted by the SSO managers and management accountants struggles to be effective in the long run.

A potential drawback of the operationalized questionnaire items is the dependence on **self-assessments** of the SSO managers and SSO management accountants, because independent and directly observable proxies (e.g. capital market data) are not applicable. Therefore, the obtained questionnaire data are incapable of isolating the effects of the SSO's PMS from other effects that drive the MNC's success.

The GOA and the SAT score are used to descriptively supplement the case study results and to investigate in the explanatory analysis whether PMS design is associated with PMS effectiveness.

7.2.2 Operationalization of the explanatory factors

In addition to the questions on PMS effectiveness, questionnaire A contains questions on possible **contingency factors** that might impact PMS design. As outlined in the basic hypotheses development in section 4.2.1, the potential determinants are subdivided into three groups: external, MNC-related and SSO-related context factors. The operationalization of these influencing factors serves to test the refined hypotheses.

7.2.2.1 Environmental factors

This study operationalizes **perceived environmental uncertainty** (PEU) by evaluating five dimensions of uncertainty: *behavior of customers, behavior of suppliers, behavior of competitors, political and legal environment, and economic environment*. The predictability of these five items is assessed on a seven-point rating scale ranging from *not at all* to *completely*. The five items are averaged and subsequently aggregated to a PEU score. In accordance with the argumentation in the previous section, this item also uses rank-ratings to weigh the relative importance of PEU factors for the MNCs. In order to calculate the PEU score, the items are reverse coded since a higher value indicates a lower PEU.

Closely related to the PEU is the environmental hostility which serves as a second contingency factor for PMS design. *Chenhall* emphasizes the influence of environmental hostility on the design of MCS. Therefore, the survey for SSO managers employs three items to assess the competitive environment of the MNCs. The **competition intensity** is operationalized as *price, product,* and *resource competition intensity*. In line with the procedure for PEU, this item also averages and aggregates the three items to a competition intensity score for each respondent. A higher value on the seven-point rating scale implies a higher competition intensity.

7.2.2.2 MNC factors

Product diversity is operationalized by three items which estimate the heterogeneity of the *development, manufacturing, sales and distribution processes* for the products and services of the respective MNC. A high value on the seven-point rating scale demonstrates a high product diversity. The explanatory notes supplementing this question point out that the term *product* also includes services, in case a MNC mainly offers services.

The **organizational complexity of the MNC** represents another contingency factor and is measured by three indicators following the conceptualization of *Blau* and *McKinley* as well as of *Damanapur* (*Blau/McKinley* (1979), pp. 208–210; *Damanpour* (1996), p. 701). First, the number of hierarchical levels serves as a measure of hierarchical complexity. Second, the organizational structure of the group management board is another indicator of structural complexity. Each indicator is transformed to a score between zero and one, depending on the complexity level. Third, this study uses the respondent's task complexity as a third indicator for the MNC's organizational complexity (*Campbell* (1988), pp. 40–43). Question A.3 captures four different dimensions of task complexity. On a seven-point rating scale, the respondent indicates the extent to which the respective dimensions describe his work environment in the respective MNC. A higher value on the scale is equivalent to a higher task complexity. The three components of the structural complexity score are subsequently aggregated and averaged.

In line with the argumentation of indicator A.8 the **heterogeneity of the IT infrastructure** of the MNC is taken into account as a potential determinant and is operationalized by using five items. On a seven-point rating scale, the respondent assesses the heterogeneity of the MNC's IT infrastructure, whereby the first three items are reverse-coded and thus a low value indicates high heterogeneity. This indicator is also informed by the findings of the case study analyses. Furthermore, item A.8 investigates the number of implemented ERP systems in the MNC as the importance of the ERP landscape for the SSO's PMS has been highlighted in several interviews. A large number of implemented ERP systems may increase the PMS design complexity of the SSO, since the data has to be collected from several ERP systems and performance measures may have to be calculated differently to ensure a cross-system comparability.

The MNC's **top management support** is included as a further context factor and operationalized by three items which assess top management support in cases of conflicts and in the daily business. A high value on the seven-point rating scale implies high support for the PMS of the SSO by the MNC's top management.

As outlined in the hypothesis refinement, this study investigates the potential influence of the **collaboration intensity** between the **group controlling** and the SSO. Collaboration intensity is measured by using a seven-point rating scale. In accordance with previous indicators, the item is transformed into a score between zero and one.

7.2.2.3 SSO factors

The **geographical dispersion of SSCs** is operationalized by using an ordinal scale. The four items *onshore, nearshore, offshore and farshore* are used and transformed into a score between zero and one. A high score implies that the SSCs of the SSOs are geographically far apart from each other, which makes a holistic performance measurement across several SSCs more complex.

The degree of the SSO's independence is described by making reference to its **legal and economic independence**. This potential determinant has already been empirically tested by *Sterzenbach*, who investigated the influence of SSO design characteristics on MCS (*Sterzenbach* (2010), pp. 377–378). This indicator is operationalized as a dummy variable (0 = total dependence, 1 = legal and/or economic independence).

Indicator B.4 examines the applied **center concepts in SSOs**. Since the descriptive results of *Sterzenbach* and the interviews with the SSO management accountants suggest that SSOs mainly use cost and profit centers to control their operational business, these two are used for the explicative analysis and operationalized as dummy variables (*Sterzenbach* (2010), p. 353).

Similar to the MNC's organizational complexity, the **structural complexity of the SSO** is considered as another contingency factor. The SSO's structural complexity is operationalized through the questions B.5 and B.6 by using the two indicators functional and geographical complexity. Both indicators are operationalized as dummy variables. First, the respondents indicate if more than one functional area has been transferred to the SSO. Monofunctional SSOs receive a zero score. Multifunctional SSOs that render services for at least two different corporate functions in one SSC receive a score of 1.0. Second, geographical complexity is defined as the SSO's mono- or multigeographical service provision. SSOs that offer their services for several countries yield a score of 1.0, whereas SSOs that render services to a single country receive a zero score.

A potential influencing factor on PMS design addresses the question whether the SSO's customers are obliged to contract SSO services. This indicator has also been used in prior research by *Sterzenbach* to analyze the influence of SSO design characteristics on MCS (*Sterzenbach* (2010), pp. 390–391). The **obligation to contract** is operationalized as a dummy variable.

SLA design describes another contingency variable, since compliance with SLAs is often monitored by relying on performance measures. Therefore, the design of SLAs between customers and SSOs is measured by a total of ten items, which shed light on the governed aspects in SLAs. The more aspects SLAs regulate, the higher the SLA design score (one governed item refers to a score of 0.1; ten governed items refer to a score of 1.0).

The **average time spent** for exemplary **management accounting tasks** in SSOs is addressed in questionnaire A in order to test hypothesis H_{1c7}. Thus, the time spent by SSO management accountants for performance measurement activities may affect PMS design. The more attention SSO controlling departments pay to the two items *KPI analyses* and *reporting*, the higher the PMS design score.

Standardization takes a prominent role in SSOs and may impact PMS design. Based on the conceptualization of standardization in section 2.1.3 and on the empirical findings of *Tempel* and *Walgenbach*, *Wolfsgruber* and *Schulz* in the context of cost accounting, this study distinguishes between **formal and factual standardization** (*Tempel/Walgenbach* (2007), p. 18; *Wolfsgruber* (2011), pp. 86–88; *Schulz* (2018), pp. 27–41). The degree of the SSO's formal standardization is operationalized with a total of five items in B.11, while the degree of the SSO's factual standardization is determined in questionnaire item B.12. The degree of factual and formal standardization is measured using seven-point rating scales, whereby the items of each of the two indicators are averaged and transformed into a score between zero and one. A high score implies a high degree of standardization.

The variety of **SSO customer requirements** completes the set of SSO-specific contingency factors. Indicator B.13 operationalizes a total of nine specific customer requirements and surveys their importance for SSO customers by using a seven-point rating scale. A drawback of this operationalization is that SSO managers assess the customer expectations, because SSO customers were not surveyed in this study. In accordance with previously outlined potential determinants, the nine operationalized SSO customer requirements are also transformed into a score between zero and one. The higher the score, the more differentiated are the requirements of the SSO customers.

7.2.3 Operationalization of the control variables

Control variables are of significance for the explicative analyses because their influence on the dependent variable (e.g. performance measurement effectiveness) can be determined and controlled. For example, performance measurement effectiveness may not only be driven by PMS design but also by other influencing factors. In order to isolate the effect of PMS design on its effectiveness, common drivers are considered as control variables in the regressions. Previous literature finds that size is an important contextual variable of MCS (e.g. *Chenhall* (2003); *Gleich* (2001); *Kagelmann* (2001); *Khandwalla* (1972); *Merchant* (1981); *Sterzenbach* (2010)). *Khandwalla* states that large firms use more sophisticated controls compared to small firms. (*Khandwalla* (1972), pp. 275–285). *Merchant* analyzes that large, diverse firms use more sophisticated budgets (*Merchant* (1981), pp. 813–829). Moreover, *Bruns* and *Waterhouse* find that managers of large firms perceive their administrative controls more sophisticated than managers of smaller firms (*Bruns* and *Waterhouse* (1975), pp.177–203). The case study results corroborate the findings on size as a contingency factor of MCS. For instance, the cross-case analysis illustrates that the larger firms CommCo, ChemCo and HealthCo have more SSO management accountants at their disposal compared to the smaller firms, such as EngineerCo and MedTechCo. Hence, this study uses five control variables that relate to size.

Firm size is a frequently used control variable in MCS research (*Chenhall* (2003), pp. 148–150). The size of a MNC has an influence on the PMS design, as larger MNCs have, for example, more subsidiaries and thus more SSO customers. As opposed to their smaller counterparts, larger MNCs are able to invest more resources into the PMS of their SSO. Moreover, larger MNCs usually have more SSO employees than smaller ones, which implies a higher coordination and communication effort. The MNCs' size is operationalized by using four items, namely the annual sales, the number of employees, the number of subsidiaries, and the number of countries in which the MNC operates. The regression models use annual sales as a primary proxy for firm size. To control for the validity of annual sales as a firm size proxy, all regression models are also calculated with the remaining size proxies. All variables refer to the FY 2015. The annual sales and number of employees have been collected from the databases *Compustat* and *Amadeus*. Missing values have been taken from the annual reports of the respective firms. The annual sales and the number of employees are calculated as the natural logarithm to reflect the non-linearity of large values.

Moreover, the **size of the MNCs' group controlling department** is operationalized by retrieving the number of employees, since the same arguments apply as for the other size controls. Furthermore, the **MNCs' organizational structure** is operationalized by using a dummy variable (*organization by business segments/geographic region or by a matrix organization*). A matrix organization implies more coordination and communication effort for SSOs, since the managerial and functional power to direct is spread across a number of players so that SSO customers in a matrix organization have to deal with several counterparts with the same decision-making authority. This also results in a higher PMS design score as, for instance, the SLA reporting has to be adapted to different user groups.

SSO size is included as another control variable (*Sterzenbach* (2010), pp. 374–375). It is measured by the two items number of SSO employees and number of SSCs. The maturity of the SSO serves as a third control variable. It is included in the regression analyses because SSOs, which have been established two years ago, are likely to have less complexity in their PMS compared to SSOs existing for more than twenty years. **SSO maturity** is measured by surveying the SSO's year of foundation and subsequently deducting the year of foundation from 2016. This variable is also used as the natural logarithm.

7.3 Methods of data analysis

This section presents the methods of data analysis used to gauge the empirical results of the quantitative study. Section 7.3 is subdivided in two main parts. Section 7.3.1 introduces the descriptive statistics, which are applied to describe the survey results of PMS design in SSOs. Moreover, section 7.3.1 provides information about the applied methods for the bivariate correlation analyses. Section 7.3.2 summarizes the multiple regression models used for the explicative analyses. Furthermore, section 7.3.2 presents an overview of the major assumptions on which the regression models are based. This section concludes with the specification of the essential measures to assess the fit of the regression model.

7.3.1 Descriptive statistics and mean comparisons

Descriptive statistics aim to yield information about the distribution and manifestation of variables by identifying the most important characteristics in the data of the target population (*Döring/Bortz* (2016), p. 631). The following descriptive statistics on the SSO's performance measurement characteristics use two measures to describe the central tendency of a frequency distribution for metric and dichotomized nominal variables. The tables for the empirical results contain the arithmetic mean and the median which is less sensitive with regard to outliers (*Auer* (2016), p. 49; *Cleff* (2015), pp. 37–49; *Eid et al.* (2017), pp. 154–158; *Riesenhuber* (2009), pp. 9–10). In addition to the arithmetic mean and the median, the tables also indicate the minimum and maximum values as well as the first quartile Q1 (25%) and the third quartile Q3 (75%) in order to better assess the composition of the data (*Eid et al.* (2017), pp. 159–161). Moreover, the tables provide information about the dispersion of the data set by including the standard deviation. The standard deviation specifies the extent to which the measured values spread around the arithmetic mean (*Auer* (2016), pp. 31–32; *Eid et al.* (2017), pp. 161–164).

This study conducts **parametric tests** to verify whether two group-means differ significantly from each other (*Auer* (2016), pp. 247–252). In contrast to parametric tests, non-parametric tests do not require a known distribution of the examined characteristic (*Eid et al.* (2017), p. 281). Furthermore, the choice of test depends on whether the underlying samples are paired or unpaired. A paired sample refers to measured values that originate from the same person (e.g. the SSO manager completes the same questionnaire at two different points in time), that come from different persons who naturally belong together (e.g. twins) or that come from different persons who have been assigned to each other (*Eid et al.* (2017), pp. 367–368). Since this study applies a dyadic research design, in which the SSO managers and management accountants are paired, the latter pre-requisite for a paired sample exists. Moreover, two additional assumptions have to be met to perform a parametric t-test. First, omnibus tests assume **normally distributed data** (*Eid et al.* (2017), pp. 371–372). In line with the literature of test theory, this study's sample sizes satisfy the prerequisite of the central limit theorem (n > 30) (*Auer/Rottmann* (2015), p. 284). Since none of the variables to be tested has a sample size of less than thirty, this study does not use further tests to verify the normal distribution of the data. Second, parametric tests require **variance homogeneity** of the data (*Eid et al.* (2017), pp. 408–409). In case of variance heterogeneity, this study performs a Welch-test instead of a t-test due to its robustness against heteroscedasticity (*Eid et al.* (2017), pp. 336–338).

The subsequent empirical results present **bivariate correlation analyses** to investigate the isolated statistical relationship between each (independent) determinant variable and the (dependent) PMS design variable. For this purpose, bivariate correlation analyses present the correlation coefficients according to *Bravais-Pearson* and the rank correlations according to *Spearman* (*Cleff* (2015), pp. 98–109). Whereas *Pearson's* correlation coefficients determine linear associations of metrically scaled variables (*Auer/Rottmann* (2015), p. 95), the *Spearman* rank correlation coefficients are suitable to detect a monotonic relationship between ordinally scaled variables (*Pospeschill* (2006), pp. 354–355). As opposed to *Pearson's* correlation coefficients, *Spearman's* rank correlation coefficients allow for a lower scale of measurement (*Cleff* (2015), p. 102). Both correlation coefficients vary between minus one and plus one so that coefficients between minus one and zero indicate a negative association between two variables and coefficients between zero and plus one express a positive association (*Auer* (2016), p. 36). Moreover, the magnitude of the correlation coefficient reflects the strength of the association between both variables. In accordance with the classification of *Eid et al.*, this study defines the magnitude of the correlation coefficient between 0.00 and 0.20 as weak, between 0.21 and 0.40 as moderate and between 0.41 and 1.00 as strong (*Eid et al.* (2017), p. 540).

All of the aforementioned tests and correlation analyses indicate significant differences between the group means (respectively significant associations between two variables) by using the denomination of the asterisks *, ** and ***. The asterisks describe the **significance levels** $p < 0.1$ (marginally significant), $p < 0.05$ (significant), and $p < 0.01$ (highly significant) (*Auer* (2016), pp. 130–139).

7.3.2 Multiple regression analysis

The empirical analysis uses multiple regression models to investigate potential statistical relationships between the identified determinants and PMS design as well as to analyze potential associations between PMS design and its effectiveness. The explicative analysis in the following section uses **ordinary-least-square regression models** (OLS) to test the hypotheses refined in chapter six (*Auer* (2016), p. 198; *Backhaus et al.* (2016), p. 574; *Dreger et al.* (2014), p. 24; *Winker* (2017), p. 137). As opposed to the isolated view of bivariate correlation analyses, OLS regression models allow to test whether several independent variables simultaneously affect a dependent variable (*Cleff* (2015), p. 143). However, the modeling of a regression analysis involves four major assumptions.

First, the **residuals** have to be **identically distributed**, otherwise dependencies between residuals and independent variables suggest heteroscedasticity (*Backhaus et al.* (2016), p. 103). In order to prevent biased results due to possible variance heterogeneity, this study uses heteroscedastic-consistent standard errors (*White* estimators) in all regression models (*White* (1980), pp. 817–838). Second, the residuals themselves should **not** be **auto-correlated**, since otherwise the influence of the regression coefficients on the dependent variable is over-estimated (*Winker* (2017), pp. 176–177). However, autocorrelation particularly emerges in time series analyses and thus is less relevant to this study (*Winker* (2017), p. 176). Nevertheless, the used *White* estimators are robust against a violation of the autocorrelation condition (*Dreger et al.* (2014), p. 94). Third, the explanatory variables should be independent of each other (*Cleff* (2015), pp. 160–163). Correlations between the determinants cause **multicollinearity** so that in case of perfect multicollinearity between two determinants, one of the two would not add any explanatory value (*Dreger et al.* (2014), p. 66). Strong multicollinearity may lead to an ambiguous interpretability of the regression model (*Winker* (2017), p. 169). This study examines the existence of multicollinearity by calculating variance inflation factors (VIFs) for all regression models (*Auer* (2016), p. 208; *Backhaus et al.* (2016), p. 107). A VIF below the threshold of ten suggests that multicollinearity does not affect the interpretability of the regression model (*Chatterjee/Hadi* (2015), pp. 248–251). Fourth, the underlying data of the regression models have to be **asymptotically normally distributed** in order to yield unbiased results (*Backhaus et al.* (2016), p. 110). Hence, the assumptions of the central limit theorem are considered to be met if thirty or more observations are available, which is the case in all regression models (*Auer/Rottmann* (2015), p. 284).

Furthermore, a potential misspecification of the regression models originates from the correlation of one or more independent variables with the error term of the regression induced by **endogeneity** (*Winker* (2017), p. 183). The three main sources of endogeneity are correlated omitted variables, reversed causality, and measurement errors (*Kajüter/Nienhaus* (2016), p. 476). Particularly in survey research these are evoked by the non-response bias and the common method bias (*Antonakis et al.* (2010), p. 109; *Podsakoff et al.* (2003), pp. 879–881). While the non-response bias is already addressed during the sample description, the common method bias is avoided by the dyadic research design (*Kajüter/ Nienhaus* (2016), p. 517). Nevertheless, endogeneity still remains an issue and will be discussed in the limitations of this study.

All regression models use two-tailed t-tests for undirected and one-tailed t-tests for directed hypotheses (*Auer* (2016), p. 247; *Backhaus et al.* (2016), p. 91). Since all variables in OLS regression models have to be scaled metrically, this study dichotomizes ordinally scaled variables so that they are incorporated into the regression models as dummy variables (*Dreger et al.* (2014), p. 26; *Winker* (2017), pp. 198–202). All regression tables indicate the adjusted R^2 and the F-statistic to indicate the **fit of the regression model**. The F-test verifies whether the coefficient of determination significantly differs from zero (*Auer* (2016), p. 253; *Backhaus et al.* (2016), p. 86). A F-value differing significantly from zero signals that the modeled regression has sufficient explanatory power (*Auer/Rottmann* (2015), pp. 470–471). More-over, all regression tables indicate the adjusted R^2 as a further measure for the goodness of the fit (*Winker* (2017), p. 155). R^2 indicates how much variation of the dependent variable can be explained by the independent variables (*Auer/Rottmann* (2015), pp. 431–432). Since the measure R^2 grows with an increasing number of independent variables even if the added independent variables do not add explanatory power, this study uses the adjusted R^2, which controls for this effect (*Winker* (2017), p. 155).

7.4 Empirical results

The presentation of the empirical results is subdivided into four main parts, which correspond to the three research questions. Section 7.4.1 presents the descriptive findings of this study and thus provides insights into the current state of **PMS design in SSOs** of MNCs in Germany, Austria and Switzerland. Sections 7.4.1.1 to 7.4.1.3 provide descriptive evidence on performance measures, the performance measurement process and the performance measurement actors. In addition, section 7.4.1.4 descriptively analyzes the PMS design score. Section 7.4.2.1 provides descriptive evidence on **PMS determinants**. Subsequently, section 7.4.2.2 and 7.4.2.3 address the second research question by explaining which determinants influence the PMS design in SSOs. Section 7.4.3 concludes the empirical findings by investigating the associations between PMS design in SSOs and its **effectiveness**, which addresses the third research question. Section 7.4.4 discusses the empirical findings.

7.4.1 PMS design in SSOs

As described in section 2.2, this study defines PMS design in three substantial dimensions. The dimension of performance measures is based on the PMS contents and describes the quantity, composition and the focus of performance measures in the PMS of SSOs. The descriptive evidence on the performance measurement process provides insights how performance measurement takes place in SSOs. This dimension is particularly concerned with the four subprocesses performance measure selection, data collection, evaluation and modification. Furthermore, this section presents the findings on performance measurement actors.

7.4.1.1 Performance measures

The **number of performance measures** used in SSOs varies significantly in corporate practice as suggested by the standard deviation of 90.9 (table 7.10). The comparison of minimum and maximum values shows that the largest and the smallest PMS differ by a total of 520 performance measures. However, the maximum value, the standard deviation and the mean of 47.8 performance measures are driven by two outliers (521 and 435 performance measures). The median is a more robust measure against outliers and indicates that a PMS of this sample's SSOs encompasses twenty-two performance measures.

With regard to the **performance measurement categories**, the descriptive analysis finds that performance measures with reference to process quality and productivity are most commonly used in SSOs. The leading position of process-related measures, indicated by the highest mean and median among all catego-ries, is not reflected in the displayed ranking of these categories according to their importance for the SSO. According to the ranking, performance measures with reference to revenues, costs, profit and loss are most important for the SSO managers, whereas performance measures with reference to process quality and productivity only rank second. Although performance measures with reference to revenues, costs, profit and loss are ranked as the most important measure category, the SSO's PMS only contain on average 9.6 measures in this cate-gory. By contrast, the number of SSOs using cost-profit-related measures (51) highlights their prevalence. The findings describe that performance measures in other categories are less common and also less important for SSO managers. For example, performance measures with reference to organizational development are ranked as the least significant (26). The findings on the prevalence of finan-cial and process-related performance measures corroborate with the results of the cross-case analysis. A reason for the rather low prevalence of performance measures with reference to employee satisfaction and organizational develop-ment could be that the development of performance measures in these cate-gories seems to be substantially more difficult as suggested by ChemCo's SSO manager.

Table 7.10: Performance measures in SSOs per category

	Number of performance measures in SSOs								
n = 53	Mean	Std. dev.	Q25	Median	Q75	Min	Max	N	Rank
Total	47.8	90.9	11	22	47	1	521	53	
... thereof performance measures with reference to...									
... revenues, costs, profit & loss	9.6	10.6	3	5	12	1	60	51	1
... customer satisfaction	5.2	4.7	2	4	6	1	20	42	3
... process quality & productivity	30.5	79.0	3	5	24	1	407	43	2
... process automation	5.3	5.9	1	3	6	1	20	38	4
... employee satisfaction	5.4	6.8	2	4	5	1	34	34	5
... organizational development	2.9	1.9	1	2	5	1	5	26	6

The proportion of **financial and non-financial performance measures** is near-balance, although the non-financial measures (53%) overweigh the financial measures in SSOs. This finding seems consistent with the prevalence of process-oriented performance measures in table 7.10. Moreover, the cross-case analysis supports the survey findings as five of the seven case companies maintain a PMS which either has an almost balanced number of financial and non-financial performance measures or a PMS which contains slightly more non-financial performance measures. Even though related literature emphasizes the importance of non-financial measures for a company's success (*Ittner/ Larcker* (2003), p. 2), prior studies find that financial measures dominate in corporate practice (*Bhimani* (1994), p. 36; *Fowler* (1996), p. 54; *Grüning* (2002), p. 150). The proportion of non-financial performance measures unveiled in figure 7.5 may follow a general trend towards the use of non-financial measures. The proportion of **absolute measures and ratios** reveals a similar picture compared to the proportion of financial and non-financial measures with a slight overweight in favor of absolute measures.

Only 40% of all SSOs link the variable remuneration of the SSO employees to their PMS. The sub-sample (21) to the right-hand side of figure 7.5 shows that only one out of three **performance measures is relevant for the variable remuneration** of SSO employees. The case company findings confirm the rather low coupling of SSO performance measures and variable remuneration as it is

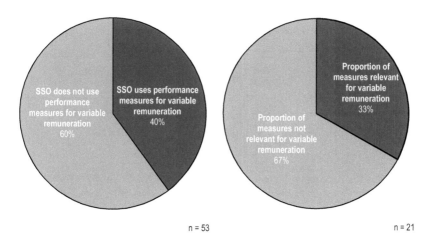

Figure 7.5: Use and proportion of measures linked to variable remuneration

only applied for senior hierarchical levels in CommCo' SSO. The PAT points out that linking performance measures to variable remuneration may reduce moral hazard. The less pronounced coupling of performance measures to the variable remuneration of SSO employees at lower management tiers may induce opportunistic behavior of the SSO employees, such as shirking. In addition, the correlation analyses of *Grüning* associate measures linked to remuneration with a higher validity, reliability and objectivity compared to measures that are not linked to the remuneration system (*Grüning* (2002), pp. 289–290).

7.4.1.2 Performance measurement process

This section presents the descriptive analysis of the performance measurement process according to the main process steps performance measure selection, performance measure data collection, performance measure evaluation and performance measure revision (figure 7.6).

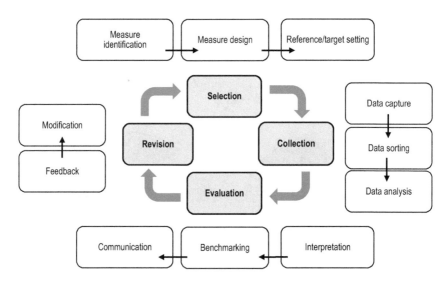

Figure 7.6: The performance measurement process (own illustration based on *Bourne et al.* (2000), p. 757, *Kaplan and Norton* (2000), pp. 71–72, and *Neely et al.* (2000), p. 1132–1134)

Performance measure selection

A median of four and the highest average (3.8) among all alternatives suggest that SSOs predominantly use brainstorming sessions for the **selection of new performance measures** (table 7.11). The CommCo case indicates that management escalations and issues in current operations lead to brainstorming sessions that trigger the development of new performance measures. Suggestions for new performance measures by other departments (3.5), the use of PMS from other SSOs as a role model (3.5), the trial and error method and specialized literature (3.3) also play a role to select new performance measures. By contrast, the majority of the SSOs (59%) does not use consultancy firms to develop new performance measures. Notably, several SSOs condition the performance measure development on the data availability in their IT system by using predefined measures (3.0). The EngineerCo and the MedTechCo case suggest that cost-benefit considerations drive the use of predefined measures which are available in IT-systems. The distribution of responses on the scale imply that only a few SSOs extensively use one particular method for the performance measure development. The results of the cross-case analysis confirm the variety of methods used to select new performance measures.

Table 7.11: Performance measure development

To what extent do the following statements describe the development process of new performance measures for your SSO?									
n = 53			Distribution (scale: 1 = not at all…7 = completely)						
New performance measures are developed by using…	Mean	Std. dev.	1	2	3	4	5	6	7
…brainstorming sessions	3.8	2.1	19%	17%	9%	<u>10%</u>	19%	17%	9%
…suggestions of other departments	3.5	1.9	19%	19%	<u>13%</u>	13%	13%	21%	2%
…literature & conventions	3.3	2.0	26%	21%	<u>11%</u>	6%	19%	11%	6%
…the PMS of more mature SSOs as a role model	3.5	1.9	21%	17%	<u>17%</u>	6%	24%	11%	4%
…consulting firms	2.0	1.5	<u>59%</u>	13%	9%	11%	4%	2%	2%
…predefined measures in new information systems	3.0	1.6	24%	19%	<u>9%</u>	23%	23%	2%	0%
…the trial and error method	3.3	1.9	20%	26%	<u>8%</u>	11%	19%	10%	6%

median underlined

In essence, the mean values indicate that SSOs apply three different strategies to define **performance measure targets** (table 7.12): targets are based on previous year's figures (4.9), SSO management expectations (5.2) and the experience of the process managers (4.9). By contrast, capital market requirements (2.0) play a subordinate role for the target formation. The AgriCo case describes the relevance of the SSO's management expectations for the target setting process since the SSO management determines the SSO strategy, which is subsequently operationalized in performance measure targets. However, PAT suggests a potential drawback if SSOs set performance measure targets based on SSO management expectations, because SSO managers and process owners (agents) may have an incentive to put their own interests over those of the SSO management (principal).

Table 7.12: Performance measure target definition

To what extent do the following statements describe the strategy by which the targets for performance measures are defined in your SSO?									
n = 53			Distribution (scale: 1 = not at all...7 = completely)						
Targets for performance measures are based on...	Mean	Std. dev.	1	2	3	4	5	6	7
... previous year's figures.	4.9	1.7	8%	4%	6%	11%	<u>30%</u>	24%	17%
... an external benchmarking.	3.3	1.8	23%	17%	9%	<u>24%</u>	15%	6%	6%
... an internal benchmarking.	3.8	1.9	21%	11%	8%	<u>13%</u>	24%	19%	4%
... capital market requirements.	2.0	1.5	<u>57%</u>	17%	7%	9%	4%	6%	0%
... SSO management expectations.	5.2	1.3	0%	4%	10%	11%	<u>26%</u>	38%	11%
... the practical experience of the process owners.	4.9	1.6	5%	6%	6%	17%	<u>23%</u>	30%	13%

median underlined

The EngineerCo case demonstrates that process managers tend to set lower performance measure targets in order to safely meet the SSO's management expectations instead of setting ambitious but achievable performance measure targets. Thus, performance measure targets based on SSO management expectations may imply a dilemma since the target setting usually requires the experience of the SSC and the process managers. A potential remedy for moral hazard are performance measure targets based on an internal (3.8) or external (3.3) benchmarking, which is also commonly applied in SSOs. The cross-case findings substantiate that benchmarking is used by SSOs to define performance measure targets.

Performance measure data collection

SSOs primarily use ERP systems (89%) and spreadsheets (85%) to collect the required data for their performance measures (figure 7.7). Frequently, data from the ERP systems are subtracted at first and subsequently edited in spreadsheets. Almost half of the surveyed SSO management accountants state that they use software solutions with the possibility to analyze big data. The MedTechCo and the HealthCo case provide explanations for the growing relevance of big data analyzing information systems. The use of big data information systems for the **performance measure data collection** overcomes the limited capacities of spreadsheets and enables SSO management accountants to visualize data streams. Among the 11% of other information systems listed, SSOs mainly use ticketing systems from which the data are collected for the performance measures.

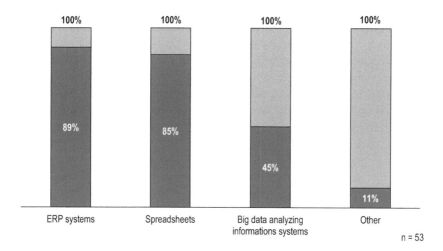

Figure 7.7: MIS used for performance measure data collection

The survey results underpin the notion of the case study findings that data collection for performance measures incorporates a considerable workload for SSO employees. The median suggests that SSOs employ two FTEs to collect, aggregate, validate and edit data (table 7.13).

Table 7.13: FTE allocation to performance measure data collection activities

How many FTEs perform the following process steps for the performance measure data collection?								
n = 53	Mean	Std. dev.	Q25	Median	Q75	Min	Max	n
Total	4.1	5.0	0.5	2	6	0.1	19	50
Data collection from back-end systems	0.8	1.0	0.1	0.4	1	0	5	42
Data aggregation	0.6	0.8	0	0.2	1	0	3	34
Corrections/bug fixes	0.5	0.7	0	0.2	1	0	3	36
Merging different data sources into the target system	0.8	1.0	0.1	0.3	1	0	3	40
Plausibility checks	0.6	0.9	0.1	0.2	1	0	4	38
Data editing	0.8	1.1	0.1	0.3	1	0	5	45

The mean (4.1 FTEs) is even higher since a considerable number of SSOs employs more than 10 FTEs to collect performance measure data (maximum value: 19 FTEs). Looking at the data collection activities performed in SSOs, the data collection from back-end systems has to be considered as most resource-intensive (mean: 0.8). Since this activity implies the mere compiling of data from different systems, automation potential seems inferable. The same applies to the mean of 0.8 FTE, which reflects the merging of different data sources into the target system. Performance measure data aggregation (0.6), bug fixes (0.5) and plausibility checks (0.6) of performance measure data require slightly less resources. While most SSOs need to collect data from back-end systems and subsequently edit retrieved data, only 34 (resp. 36) SSOs need to aggregate (resp. correct) collected data for further processing. The CommCo case shows that SSO controlling departments make efforts to outsource the data collection procedures for their performance measures to the IT department in order to reduce their own workload.

The **automation degree for the data collection of performance measures** in SSOs unveils mixed evidence (table 7.14). Collecting data for performance measures with reference to revenues, costs, profit and loss as well as for measures with reference to process automation have the highest automation degree (5.0). The surveyed SSO management accountants indicate that performance measure data collcection for measures with reference to process automation (4.5), process quality and productivity (3.9) and employee satisfaction (3.8) is partially automated. By contrast, the data collection of performance measures with reference to organizational development and customer satisfaction are least automated. The PharCo case points out that data for performance measures with reference to customer satisfaction are not always accessible from digital databases and thus difficult to automate.

Table 7.14: Automation of data collection by performance measure category

To what extent do you automatically collect the required data for the performance measures in the following categories?									
n = 53	Distribution (scale: 1 = entirely manually…7 = fully automatically)								
	Mean	Std. dev.	1	2	3	4	5	6	7
Performance measures with reference to…									
… revenues, costs, profit & loss	5.0	1.7	6%	8%	4%	8%	<u>30%</u>	24%	20%
… customer satisfaction	3.6	1.9	19%	15%	15%	<u>12%</u>	27%	5%	7%
… process quality & productivity	3.9	1.6	7%	11%	23%	<u>27%</u>	14%	11%	7%
… process automation	4.5	1.7	8%	8%	6%	24%	<u>24%</u>	16%	14%
… employee satisfaction	3.8	1.7	12%	12%	18%	<u>25%</u>	18%	9%	6%
… organizational development	3.4	1.6	16%	16%	12%	<u>32%</u>	16%	4%	4%

median underlined

Evaluation

The quantitative study finds that SSO management accountants predominately use two analysis types to **evaluate performance measures** (table 7.15). Variance analyses and time-series comparisons have the highest means (5.2) and are therefore often performed in SSOs to evaluate performance measures. In addition, the EngineerCo case illustrates that SSO management accountants do not analyze performance measures on their own, but with the assistance of the process managers. By contrast, the survey findings indicate that SSOs use an internal (3.2) or external (2.5) benchmarking less frequently compared to variance analyses and time-series comparisons. Notably, the survey results differ from the case study findings since the majority of the case companies regularly performs an internal or external benchmarking to analyze performance measures. For example, the HealthCo and the MedTechCo case use an external *Hackett* benchmarking to analyze their administrative costs per processed invoice. Since an external benchmarking entails considerable costs, many SSOs abstain from it.

Table 7.15: Types of performance measure analyses

How often do you use the following types of performance measure analyses?									
n = 53	Distribution (scale: 1 = very rarely...7 = very often)								
	Mean	Std. dev.	1	2	3	4	5	6	7
Variance analyses	5.2	1.6	4%	4%	6%	19%	<u>22%</u>	17%	28%
Time-series comparisons	5.2	1.5	0%	6%	8%	17%	<u>26%</u>	19%	24%
Internal benchmarking	3.2	1.8	25%	21%	<u>11%</u>	17%	13%	11%	2%
External benchmarking	2.5	1.4	30%	<u>32%</u>	13%	13%	10%	2%	0%

median underlined

The cross-case analysis reveals mixed results regarding the benefits of an internal benchmarking of performance measures. Whereas EngineerCo' SSO managers are satisfied with the gained insights based on an internal benchmarking between their SSCs, HealthCo's SSO managers voice concerns about the limited comparability of their SSCs.

Figure 7.8 sheds light on how performance measure analyses are communicated in SSOs. SSO management accountants most frequently use figures and tables (75%) or charts and diagrams (72%) to **publish and communicate performance measures analyses**. 53% of the SSO management accountants add comments and explanatory notes next to the charts and diagrams in order to explain them in greater detail. Applications for mobile devices are less frequently used in SSOs (9%). In a similar vein, ERP-based information systems that enable the report users to make extensive changes are scarcely used (13%). The effort involved in the provision of such reports appears to be an obstacle. 45% of the SSOs already use dashboards, in which the SSO manager receives a visualization of the most important performance measures. The survey results support the cross-case analysis findings that *Excel* and *PowerPoint* are still most commonly used to publish performance measure reports. The PharCo case supplements the survey results with the SSO managers' ambition to provide performance measure dashboards with real-time data.

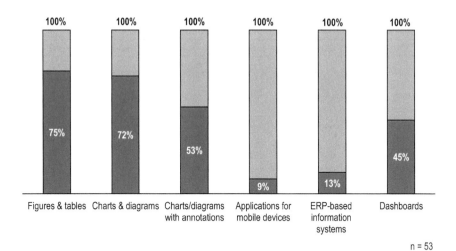

Figure 7.8: PMS reporting tools used to communicate performance measure analyses

The survey findings on the performance measure **reporting frequency** unveil that SSO management accountants report their performance measures most frequently on a monthly basis (table 7.16). This finding is valid to performance measures with reference to revenues, costs, profit and loss, process quality and productivity and process automation. By contrast, performance measures with reference to employee satisfaction are predominantly reported annually. Performance measures with reference to customer satisfaction and organizational development are reported on a quarterly basis. The slower reporting frequency may be attributable to a manual data collection, for example by using surveys to assess the SSO employee satisfaction. However, the fact that performance measures with reference to employees, customers, and organizational development are reported at larger intervals suggests that SSO managers mainly require measures with reference to financials and processes to control their organization. The vast majority of the SSOs reports its performance measures on a regular basis. The cross-case analysis indicates that the performance measure reporting frequency depends on contingency factors, such as the length of the customer relationship and the hierarchical level of the performance measure reporting recipient.

Table 7.16: Reporting frequency by performance measure category

Which category of performance measures do you report in which frequency?								
				Frequency				
Performance measures with reference to...	Daily	Weekly	Mon-thly	Quart-erly	Semi-annually	Annu-ally	Less than annually	Irregu-larly
... revenues, costs, profit & loss	6%	4%	<u>68%</u>	18%	2%	0%	0%	2%
... customer Satisfaction	0%	0%	39%	<u>15%</u>	12%	22%	7%	5%
... process quality & productivity	2%	14%	<u>61%</u>	9%	7%	2%	0%	5%
... process automation	3%	8%	<u>65%</u>	16%	5%	0%	0%	3%
... employee satisfaction	0%	0%	21%	15%	9%	<u>46%</u>	6%	3%
... organizational development	0%	0%	44%	<u>24%</u>	8%	16%	0%	8%

n = 53   median underlined

The frequency of informal communication among SSO employees about performance measures is an indicator to what extent the PMS is embedded in the organization. The median (4.0) and the mean (3.8) unveil that performance measures are fairly frequently subject to informal discussions among SSO employees (table 7.17). This finding corroborates with the mixed results of the cross-case analysis.

Table 7.17: Informal conversation frequency on performance measures

How often do you have an informal conversation with other SSO employees on performance measures of your PMS?									
n = 53		Distribution (scale: 1 = very rarely...7 = very often)							
	Mean	Std. dev.	1	2	3	4	5	6	7
Conversation frequency	3.8	1.2	4%	9%	24%	<u>36%</u>	19%	8%	0%

median underlined

After an initial enthusiasm, the SSO employees of EngineerCo have quickly lost interest in the discussion about SSO performance measures. By contrast, the SSO employees of MedTechCo discuss KPI developments quite often.

Revision

30% of the SSOs in this sample revise their PMS less frequently than annually (figure 7.9). By contrast, 23% of the SSOs change their PMS annually. Only 24% of the SSO management accountants state that they **revise the SSO's PMS** more frequently than annually. Moreover, 30% of the SSO management accountants modify the SSO's PMS on an irregular basis. The survey findings diverge from the results of the cross-case analysis where five out of seven SSOs revised their PMS within the last twelve months. The diverging findings indicate the presence of conflicting goals with respect to the performance measure modification frequency. On the one hand, performance measures should be linked to the SSO's strategy. The HealthCo and the ChemCo case demonstrate that changing environmental conditions have an impact on the SSO's PMS. For example, altering legal requirements continuously transform their SSOs' PMS. On the other hand, the MedTechCo case suggests that the continuity of the PMS is important to grasp a deeper understanding of trends over a longer period of time. Moreover, report recipients disapprove ongoing performance measure modifications because they will then struggle to interpret those KPIs.

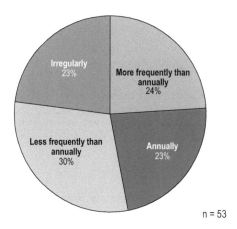

Figure 7.9: Performance measure modification frequency

SSOs make PMS modifications in varying intensities, which becomes evident due to the minimum (0) and maximum (160) values (table 7.18). While 40% of all SSOs have not made any adjustments to their PMS over the past twelve months, several SSOs made substantial changes in their set of performance measures. On average, SSOs eliminate 4.3 and add 9.2 performance measures. Hence, the PMS of a SSO averagely grows by five performance measures per year. Thus, SSOs add performance measures to their PMS more easily than eliminating them. The results of the quantitative study diverge from the results of the qualitative study. The cross-case analysis describes that case companies either change their PMS moderately or intend to eliminate performance measures with a 'big bang' rather than adding new ones. By considering the modification intensity in relation to the age of the SSO, the descriptive analysis yields a more nuanced perspective on this process step. The PMS of SSOs founded less than eight years ago are growing on average with only 1.9 performance measures per year. By contrast, SSOs that are founded more than eight years ago are growing with ten performance measures per year. This finding is also surprising and contradicts the case study results. The interviews with the SSO management accountants suggest that less mature SSOs are still in the implementation phase of their PMS and thus tend to add more performance measures compared to more mature SSOs which only slightly revise their PMS. An explanation for this finding could be that less mature SSOs initially focus on process bundling, standardization and automation and take care of PMS modifications not before the SSO is in a steady state.

Table 7.18: Eliminated and added performance measures

Eliminated and added performance measures over the past twelve months								
n = 53	Mean	Std. dev.	Q25	Median	Q75	Min	Max	n
Eliminated measures	4.3	10.9	0	0	2	0	60	23
Added measures	9.2	23.4	0	2	10	0	160	35
Difference	+ 4.9		0	+ 2	+ 8	0	+ 100	+ 12

Having detailed the descriptive survey results of the performance measurement process, the following section addresses the descriptive findings on the performance measurement actors.

7.4.1.3 Performance measurement actors

Table 7.19 stresses that PMS design in SSOs rests with different groups of actors. In essence, four groups of actors have a major influence on the SSO's PMS: the

SSO executive board, the SSC heads, the process managers and the SSO controlling. The **SSC heads** take the leading role in defining performance measure objectives (77%) followed by the SSO executive board (55%). The process owners (49%) and the SSO controlling (45%) are also fairly involved in the performance measure target setting process. By contrast, SSO employees (9%) and other groups of actors who cannot be assigned to the SSO (e.g. the group controlling) play only a subordinate role for the performance measure target setting. This finding is consistent with the case studies and extant literature since the decision-makers are responsible to set the objectives for their organization.

With regard to the PMS reporting, the survey results illustrate that this sample's SSOs involve various stakeholders in their communication of performance measure reports. 91% of the SSOs report KPIs to their **SSO management board** and also 85% of the SSC heads receive a KPI reporting. Thus, it can be stated that SSOs keep their management informed about the performance development of their organization. In addition, 77% of the process owners and still 58% of the SSO employees receive performance measure reports suggesting that SSOs fairly acquaint their employees about current performance developments. The results describe that only 53% of the SSO controlling departments receive KPI reports. A reason for the rather low percentage could be that SSO management accountants are rather sending KPI reports than receiving them. Furthermore, SSO-external performance measurement actors, such as the group management board (51%) and the group controlling (42%) receive KPI reports of the SSO in several MNCs. Contrarily, performance measure reports are rarely communicated to external service providers (23%).

Similar to the performance measure target selection, the SSC heads (70%) and the SSO executive board (55%) are the most frequently involved groups of performance measurement actors in the PMS revision process. Although the **SSO controlling department** takes part in the performance measure modification process in several SSOs (32%), it is striking that neither the SSO nor the group controlling takes a leading role. This finding contradicts the results of the cross-case analysis, since in the case studies primarily the SSO management accountants coordinated the modification of the SSO's PMS. However, the case studies and the survey reveal that many SSOs do not have a controlling department so that the coordination of the PMS modification has to be transferred to other performance measurement actors. The rather low involvement of the **process managers** (36%) in the PMS revision process is also surprising, because the case analyses of HealthCo and EngineerCo unveil that process managers guide the SSO controlling department if performance measures do not measure what they are supposed to measure and therefore have to be changed. In line with the cross-case analysis, the descriptive analysis indicates that SSO employees and SSO-external actors do not play a significant role for the PMS modification.

Table 7.19: Involvement of actors in the performance measurement process

Which of the following actors are involved in the three performance measurement process steps specified below?			
n = 53	...defines performance measure targets.	...receives performance measure reports.	...decides to add & eliminate performance measures.
The SSO executive board...	55%	**91%**	55%
The SSC head...	**77%**	85%	**70%**
The process owner...	49%	77%	36%
The SSO controlling...	45%	53%	32%
The SSO employee...	9%	58%	6%
The group management board...	13%	51%	17%
The group controlling...	23%	42%	21%
The outsourcing service provider...	4%	23%	4%

Having presented the descriptive findings of the PMS design components (measures, processes and actors), the following section summarizes PMS design in SSOs on an aggregated level based on the PMS design score.

7.4.1.4 Score aggregation and summary

The PMS design score (COMP) incorporates twelve elements that are subdivided into the **three subscores** performance measures (MEAS), performance measurement process (PROC), and performance measurement actors (ACT).

The **subscore MEAS** consists of the three elements number of performance measures, number of covered performance measure categories and the proportion of performance measures linked to variable remuneration (figure 7.10). The score of each MEAS element is added and then divided by three. The number of performance measures contributes with a value of 0.50 to the MEAS score. However, the average score of 0.50 does not adequately reflect the survey findings since it is driven by SSOs with a particularly high number of performance measures and by SSOs with only few KPIs. The analysis of the MEAS score desscribes that the SSOs' PMS cover a wide range of performance measure categories (0.74). Although performance measure categories, such as performance measures with reference to SSO employee and customer satisfaction are less intensively used in SSOs compared to financial and process quality performance measures, the survey findings describe that the majority of the PMS in SSOs contain the full range of performance measurement categories. The wide coverage of performance measure categories could be a peculiarity of PMS in SSOs. For example, PMS on group level rarely include KPIs with reference to process quality and automation since process quality performance measures are rather required for operational control. By contrast, PMS for production plants barely incorporate performance measures for customer satisfaction or organizational development. The low proportion of performance measures linked to variable remuneration (0.13) diminishes the MEAS score (0.46). In light of the PAT, the descriptive findings suggest that the low coupling of performance measures and variable remuneration may induce moral hazard, such as shirking.

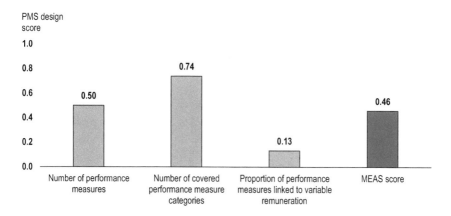

Figure 7.10: Composition of the MEAS score

The **subscore PROC** contains eight elements which represent the essential steps of the performance measurement process (figure 7.11).

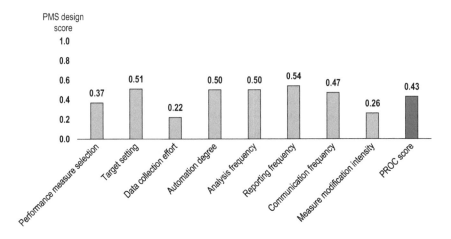

Figure 7.11: Composition of the PROC score

The score for the performance measure selection (0.37) is slightly below the aggregated PROC score (0.43). The survey results illustrate that only few SSOs make extensive use of one particular method to select new performance measures, albeit brainstorming sessions are most commonly used. By contrast, the score analysis shows that the target setting process is more pronounced compared to other steps in the performance measurement process (0.51). SSOs frequently base their performance measure targets on previous year's figures, management expectations and the experience of process managers. Moreover, SSOs sometimes apply an internal and external benchmarking to set KPI targets. The strong integration of process managers in the performance measure target setting process seems to be a characteristic of PMS in SSOs. According to the PAT, performance measure targets based on management expectations and the experience of process managers imply moral hazard.

Although some SSOs undertake a considerable effort to collect data for performance measures, the overall picture looks different. The rather low score for the data collection effort indicates that this process step of the surveyed SSOs is less pronounced (0.22) compared to the performance measure selection and evaluation activities. The data collection from back-end systems, the merging of different data sources into the target system and data editing require the most time and labor to collect performance measure data. The rather low score for the data collection effort seems consistent to the rather high automation degree score for the data collection of performance measures (0.50). The score is driven by a high automation degree for the data collection of performance measures with reference to revenues, costs, profit and loss as well as for performance measures with reference to process automation.

The scores for the three process steps performance measure analysis (0.50), reporting (0.54) and communication frequency (0.47) refer to the subprocess performance measure evaluation and are all above the average value of the PROC score. This finding suggests that the performance measure evaluation is the most pronounced subprocess of the four subprocesses performance measure selection, data collection, evaluation and revision. The descriptive analysis finds that SSO management accountants analyze performance measures quite frequently. Particularly, variance analyses and time-series comparisons are often used by SSOs to evaluate their current level of performance. The management accountants of the surveyed SSO predominately report performance measures on a monthly basis, although several SSOs also implemented a daily reporting for process quality KPIs. By contrast, performance measures with reference to customer and employee satisfaction are reported in larger time intervals. Furthermore, the score for the informal conversation frequency reveals that SSO employees often have informal conversations about SSO performance measures. The frequent interaction among SSO employees with regard to performance measures can be interpreted as an indicator for the embeddedness of the PMS in the organization.

The comparatively low score for the performance measure modification intensity indicates that this process step in the performance measurement process is pursued by the SSOs with a rather low intensity. 40% of SSO management accountants state that the SSO's PMS has not been revised within the last 12 months. In essence, the breakdown of the PROC score shows that the two subprocesses performance measure and target selection as well as performance measure evaluation are more pronounced compared to the two subprocesses performance measure data collection and performance measure revision.

The **subscore ACT** encompasses eight different groups of actors and describes their involvement in the performance measurement process (figure 7.12). The ACT score confirms the findings of the descriptive analysis by illustrating that mainly four groups of actors are involved in the performance measurement process: the SSO management board, the SSC managers, the process managers and the SSO management accountants. Particularly, SSC managers participate in all relevant performance measurement process steps and thus have a major influence on the SSO's PMS (0.77). The survey results stress that the SSO management board predominately receives performance measures reports but is also quite often involved in the performance measures selection and revision process (0.67). SSO process managers frequently play an important role for the performance measure target setting and are often responsible for the definition of performance measures (0.54). Another peculiarity of PMS in SSOs seems to be the low involvement of SSO management accountants in the performance measurement process (0.43). Nevertheless, SSO management accountants are an important group of performance measurement actors as they coordinate the PMS modification in many SSOs of this sample. By contrast, the SSO employees (0.25), the group management board (0.27) and the group controlling department (0.28) are of minor importance for PMS design in SSOs. Finally, outsourcing partners are rarely involved in the performance measurement process of SSOs.

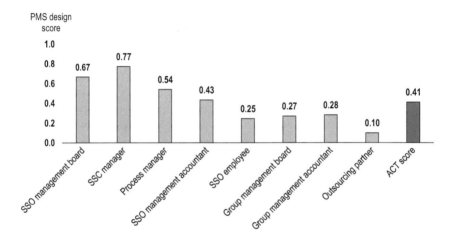

Figure 7.12: Composition of the ACT score

The three subscores MEAS (0.46), PROC (0.43) and ACT (0.41) are aggregated to the **PMS design score** (0.41). The results indicate an average degree of PMS design complexity in SSOs (table 7.20). With regard to the performance measure score, it is noteworthy that the link between the remuneration system and the PMS is less pronounced and thus barely contributes to the PMS design score. By contrast, SSOs cover on average a considerable number of performance measurement categories with their PMS, yielding a comparatively high score. The performance measurement process score unveils a relatively pronounced performance measure analysis and communication effort by the SSOs. However, the performance measure data collection and modification process of the PMS seems less pronounced compared to the performance measure selection and analysis process. The ACT score uncovers an ambiguous picture. The descriptive findings stress that most SSOs involve four groups of actors: the SSO management board, the SSC managers, the process managers and the SSO controlling department. However, PMS design in SSOs is mainly driven by SSC managers and not by SSO management accountants as suggested by the case study findings and extant literature.

Table 7.20: Summary of the PMS design score

	PMS design score	
Item	**Subscore/element**	**Mean**
A.1.1	Number of performance measures	0.50
A.1.2	Number of performance measure categories	0.74
A.6	Number of measures linked to the remuneration system	0.13
MEAS score	**Performance measures**	**0.46**
A.4	Performance measure selection	0.37
A.7	Target setting	0.51
A.10	Data collection	0.22
A.11	Automation degree	0.50
A.13	Analysis frequency	0.50
A.12	Reporting frequency	0.64
A.14	Informal communication frequency	0.47
A.17	Performance measure modification intensity	0.26
PROC score	**Performance measurement process**	**0.43**
A.18	Involved actors	0.41
ACT score	**Performance measurement actors**	**0.41**
COMP score	**PMS design score**	**0.43**

The PMS design score displayed in table 7.20 is based on a formative construct that incorporates several manifest variables. In order to control the extent to which the operationalized PMS design score matches the PMS design perceived by the respondents, the questionnaire entails five items that reflect the perceived performance measurement process (table 7.21). The items are reverse-coded so that a high value on the rating scale indicates a low **CONTROL score**. The comparison with the PROC score reveals that the perceived (0.42) and measured (0.43) performance measurement process barely differ, which is interpreted as an indicator for the robustness of the construct. However, the small deviation between the PROC and the CONTROL score could also be caused by the error of central tendency.

Table 7.21: PMS design control score

To what extent do you agree with the following statements?									
n = 53	**Distribution (scale: 1 = not at all…7 = completely)**								
I find it easy,…	**Mean**	**Std. dev.**	**1**	**2**	**3**	**4**	**5**	**6**	**7**
… to decide for which SSO areas we should develop performance measures.	5.0	1.5	4%	4%	6%	15%	<u>30%</u>	26%	15%
… to define new performance measures.	4.2	1.3	4%	8%	15%	<u>28%</u>	30%	13%	2%
… to figure out which data needs to be collected to calculate performance measures.	4.6	1.5	4%	2%	20%	15%	<u>21%</u>	34%	4%
… to integrate new performance measures into the existing PMS.	4.1	1.7	8%	13%	15%	<u>15%</u>	24%	21%	4%
… to eliminate performance measures no longer required.	4.3	1.9	8%	13%	19%	9%	<u>17%</u>	17%	17%
CONTROL score		0.42							

median underlined

7.4.2 Determinants of PMS design in SSOs

The following section is subdivided into three parts. First, the descriptive analysis presents potential determinants that may impact PMS design in SSOs. As outlined in the operationalization of the explanatory factors, the determinants of PMS design in SSOs are subdivided into the three groups external, MNC-related and SSO-related contingency factors. Particularly, the analysis of the SSO-related contingency factors is of importance since this study emphasizes the particular setting of a SSO in which performance measurement takes place. The results are compared whenever possible with the findings of other studies from prior SSO literature and the case study findings. The second part details the bivariate correlation analyses in order to reveal associations between the variables under investigation. These provide first indications of the determinants' influence on PMS design in SSOs. The third part uses multiple regressions to analyze the associations between determinants and PMS design so that (in contrast to the bivariate correlation analyses) the interaction of determinants is taken into account. The regression analyses also investigate possible effects on the subscores in more detail.

7.4.2.1 Descriptive analysis

7.4.2.1.1 External context

Perceived environmental uncertainty and competition intensity

SSO managers perceive the economic **environment** of their MNCs as rather unpredictable (mean 3.5), whereas they assess the behavior of customers as rather predictable (mean 4.4) (table 7.22). The interviews with MedTechCo and EngineerCo support the perceived importance of the SSO customers' behavior as a determinant of the SSO's performance measures. The general economic environment, such as the development of exchange rates or economic trends in emerging markets also affects the SSO's PMS as suggested by the cross-case analysis. By contrast, the survey findings illustrate that the behavior of suppliers (4.2), competitors (4.0) and the political and legal environment (4.1) is neither predictable nor unpredictable for SSO managers. The results describe that SSO managers rank the behavior of customers as most important for the MNC (1), while they attribute the least importance to the behavior of suppliers (5).

Table 7.22: Perceived environmental uncertainty

How predictable are the following factors in your company's environment?										
n = 71			Distribution (scale: 1 = not at all…7 = completely)							
	Mean	Std. dev.	1	2	3	4	5	6	7	Rank
Behavior of customers	4.4	1.1	0%	6%	17%	<u>28%</u>	35%	14%	0%	1
Behavior of suppliers	4.2	0.9	0%	6%	11%	<u>42%</u>	35%	6%	0%	5
Behavior of competitors	4.0	1.2	3%	7%	24%	<u>35%</u>	22%	6%	3%	2
Political and legal environment	4.1	1.3	3%	8%	21%	<u>31%</u>	21%	13%	3%	4
Economic environment	3.5	1.1	0%	20%	<u>32%</u>	31%	13%	4%	0%	3

median underlined

The survey results indicate that the MNCs of the SSOs are in an intense **competitive environment** (table 7.23). Primarily, SSO managers perceive the MNC's price competition as very intense (5.9). Moreover, the product competition on global markets also seems to be characterized by a high intensity (5.2). However, the SSO managers state that the competition for resources, such as personnel and funds is less intense compared to price and product competition (4.1). The case studies suggest that a competitive environment also affects the SSO's KPIs and the performance measurement process since a difficult competitive environment increases the reliance on quantifiable, reliable information provided by the PMS.

Table 7.23: Perceived competition intensity

	How do you assess the competitive environment in your industry with regard to the following competition categories?								
n = 71	Distribution (scale: 1 = not at all intense...7 = very intense)								
	Mean	**Std. dev.**	**1**	**2**	**3**	**4**	**5**	**6**	**7**
Price competition	5.9	1.0	0%	0%	3%	4%	24%	<u>42%</u>	27%
Product competition	5.2	1.4	1%	0%	11%	16%	<u>24%</u>	30%	18%
Resource competition	4.1	1.4	1%	10%	27%	<u>24%</u>	20%	14%	4%

median underlined

7.4.2.1.2 MNC context

Product differentiation and organizational structure

This sample's MNCs indicate that their products and services neither completely differ from each other nor do they resemble each other (table 7.24). The differentiation applies to the development (4.3) as well as to the manufacturing (4.3) and the sales processes (4.3) of the MNC's products and services. The underlined median (5) and the mean value of the three processes do not indicate considerable differences regarding the degree of differentiation. A high degree of **product differentiation** also implies a high degree of complexity for the SSO's service provision because the MNC's subsidiaries (the SSO customers) confront the SSO with varying preconditions and requirements. The complexity resulting from the MNC's differing development, manufacturing and sales processes is also reflected in the PMS as described in the EngineerCo case study. However, the rather small deviations between the items could also be caused by the error of central tendency.

Table 7.24: Differentiation of products and services

To what extent do the products/services of your company differ on average in their...								
n = 71	Distribution (scale: 1 = not at all...7 = completely)							
	Mean	Std. dev.	1	2	3	4	5	6	7
...development processes?	4.3	1.7	5%	13%	13%	17%	<u>31%</u>	7%	14%
...manufacturing processes?	4.3	1.9	7%	16%	13%	14%	<u>24%</u>	8%	18%
...sales and distribution processes?	4.3	1.7	4%	13%	15%	17%	<u>27%</u>	11%	13%

median underlined

The **MNC's organizational structure** may affect the SSO's PMS in four different ways. First, the MNC's organizational structure is a complexity driver for the SSO's PMS. Figure 7.13 shows that a matrix organization (42%) and an organization by business segments (44%) are the two predominant organizational forms in this study's sample. This finding corroborates with the results of the cross-case analysis. The interviews emphasize that a matrix organization entails more counterparts for SSO managers compared to other organizational forms. The cross-case analysis illustrates that matrix organizations induce a multitude of relationships between the SSO and the business units in the performance measurement process, which increases the coordination effort for SSO management accountants. The cross-jurisdictions resulting from matrix organizations arise in a lesser extent in an organization by segments or geographic regions (14%).

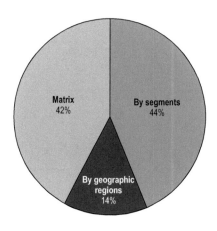

n = 71

Figure 7.13: MNCs' organizational structure

Second, the **hierarchical structure** adds to the MNC's organizational complexity. Table 7.36 indicates a median value of five existing hierarchical levels in this sample's MNCs. The specified minimum (1) and maximum values (12) suggest that there is a wide range of hierarchical levels among the MNCs. The mean of 4.7 is slightly lower compared to the median. More hierarchical levels in a MNC imply more differentiated reporting requirements in the performance measurement process and more reporting addressees. The case study findings suggest that KPI reports vary according to the level of hierarchy in their information content.

Table 7.25: Hierarchical structure of MNCs

How many hierarchical levels exist between a SSO employee and the group management board?							
n = 71	Mean	Std. dev.	Q25	Median	Q75	Min	Max
Total	4.7	2.0	3	5	6	1	12

The **composition of the management board** is a third element for the MNC's organizational complexity. Figure 7.14 emphasizes that 59% of this sample's MNC board members have more than one corporate function under their responsibility, whereas a joint responsibility of all board members is seldom (6%). 35% of the surveyed SSO managers state that their board members have one corporate function under their responsibility. As outlined in chapter two, SSOs are primarily focused on end-to-end processes and less on functional silos. Since end-to-end processes in the SSOs usually involve several operational functions (e.g. the purchase-to-pay process includes the operational functions purchasing, accounting and finance), its PMS may be subject to a potential influence by the management board structure. For example, if the central purchasing department is assigned to a board member other than the finance department, the potential for conflicts and the required coordination effort increases as soon as the PMS design aims at selecting performance measures for the entire end-to-end process. This is also the case for multifunctional SSOs (e.g., the HR and the finance function are under the responsibility of two different board members). Thus, PMS design in SSOs may depend on the composition of the management board.

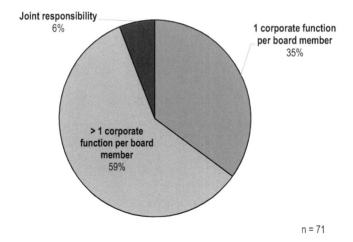

Figure 7.14: MNCs' management board structure

Fourth, the **perceived task complexity** represents another component of the MNCs' organizational complexity. A total of four proxies capture the item task complexity which shed light on the different facets of a SSO managers' area of responsibility (table 7.26). In general, SSO managers perceive their tasks as complex. An average of 5.6 illustrates that the frequent interaction with SSO employees contributes to the task complexity of SSO managers. Particularly, they perceive the constant exchange with other functional areas as a challenging requirement for their daily work (6.0). Moreover, the different kinds of knowledge (such as technical know-how, legal knowledge and language skills) that SSO managers need for their day-to-day work add to the SSO managers' task complexity (5.6). Frequent job profile changes for SSO managers also play a role for their perceived task complexity (4.5). Since the survey results report a strong involvement of SSO managers in the performance measurement process, their perceived task complexity may impact PMS design in SSOs.

Table 7.26: SSO managers' task complexity

	Perceived task complexity							
n = 71	Distribution (scale: 1 = not at all...7 = completely)							
	Mean	Std. dev.	1	2	3	4	5	6	7
Frequent interaction with SSO employees	5.6	1.3	1%	0%	6%	8%	21%	<u>37%</u>	27%
Frequent job profile changes	4.5	1.5	3%	11%	13%	14%	<u>35%</u>	18%	6%
Different kinds of knowledge are required	5.6	1.1	0%	1%	3%	10%	25%	<u>37%</u>	24%
Involvement of different functional areas	6.0	1.1	0%	0%	4%	9%	11%	<u>39%</u>	37%

median underlined

IT infrastructure and top management support

A further potential contingency factor on the SSO's PMS is the IT landscape of the surveyed MNCs. The cross-case analysis emphasizes the importance of **ERP systems** for the MNCs' IT system architecture, since ERPs are used for almost all business and support processes. A median of five implemented ERP systems among this sample's MNCs suggests a rather heterogeneous system landscape (table 7.27). The mean value of 15 ERPs and the standard deviation of 36.4 imply large differences among the MNCs. The maximum value of 250 ERPs in a single MNC indicates that harmonization efforts of the system landscape advances in large MNCs at varying speeds. However, the maximum value represents an outlier of a large German industrial engineering and steel production conglomerate. The interviews with the SSO managers during the case studies reveal that the harmonization of the ERP systems remains an important objective for SSO managers since a harmonized ERP landscape enables process standardization and automation. The case study findings report that ERP systems play an important role for the performance measure data collection process. More ERP systems are equivalent to more system interfaces which results in an increased performance measure data consolidation effort.

Table 7.27: Number of implemented ERP-Systems

n = 71	How many ERPs does your company have in use?						
	Mean	Std. dev.	Q25	Median	Q75	Min	Max
Total	15.2	36.4	2	5	10	1	250

Moreover, MNCs use other IT systems, which also play a role for the **homogeneity of the IT-infrastructure**. Table 7.28 shows four proxies for IT-infrastructure heterogeneity. A mean value of 4.4 indicates that the MNC's IT-systems are rather integrated into the existing ERP systems in order to avoid interfaces. For the same reason the MNC's IT systems are rather cross-functionally interconnected (4.5) so that, for example, the sales and the finance departments store their performance measure data on the same IT platform. The results indicate that MNCs tend to buy new software centrally for all subsidiaries (4.8). By contrast, the HealthCo case finds that a decentralized purchase of software results in a more difficult performance measure data collection. Moreover, this sample's MNCs customize their IT-systems locally only to a very limited extent (3.3) in order to avoid IT system heterogeneity, which is associated with higher running and maintenance costs.

Table 7.28: IT-infrastructure homogeneity

IT-infrastructure homogeneity									
n = 71	Distribution (scale: 1 = not at all…7 = completely)								
	Mean	Std. dev.	1	2	3	4	5	6	7
IT-systems are fully integrated into ERP system(s)	4.4	1.5	3%	10%	16%	18%	<u>25%</u>	24%	4%
IT-systems are cross-functionally interconnected	4.5	1.5	4%	6%	18%	18%	<u>27%</u>	18%	9%
New software is procured centrally	4.8	1.8	4%	14%	11%	4%	<u>19%</u>	34%	14%
Subsidiaries are authorized to customize IT-systems	3.3	1.8	18%	27%	<u>14%</u>	11%	13%	13%	4%

median underlined

This finding mirrors the results of the cross-case analysis. The proxy is reverse-coded so that a lower mean value suggests a lower IT-infrastructure homogeneity. Apart from the ERP system landscape, the survey results of the SSO managers indicate that they consider their IT infrastructure as rather homogeneous, although indirect questions certainly have to be interpreted a little more carefully.

To achieve their PMS objectives, SSO managers often depend on the **support of the MNC's top management**, for example through a project sponsor in the executive board who provides the SSO' PMS with the necessary resources. A prerequisite for support is that the MNC's top management devotes its attention to the SSO. A mean value of 4.5 provides some evidence that SSO managers perceive their MNC's top management as rather attentive to SSO matters (table 7.29). Furthermore, the survey results suggest a somewhat indifferent top management support for SSO managers in case of conflicting goals with subsidiaries (4.2). The cross-case analysis illustrates that subsidiaries have to transfer support processes to the SSO, which results in a power shift from the local to the SSO management. This power shift is often accompanied by conflicts that require top management involvement. Another indicator for the support of the SSO's PMS is the top management's constant interest in KPI reports from the SSO controlling department. The survey results suggest a decent interest of the MNC's top management in the SSO's KPI reports (4.5). The CommCo case study supports the survey results, whereas the findings of the EngineerCo and the AgriCo case studies indicate missing top management support for the SSO's PMS. In essence, the survey results supplemented with the case study findings indicate that the MNC's top management behavior may impact the design of the SSO's PMS.

Table 7.29: Perceived top management support

Perceived top management support									
n = 71		**Distribution (scale: 1 = not at all…7 = completely)**							
	Mean	**Std. dev.**	**1**	**2**	**3**	**4**	**5**	**6**	**7**
Top management is attentive to SSO matters	4.5	1.7	3%	14%	11%	14%	<u>23%</u>	27%	8%
Top management support in case of conflicting goals with subsidiaries	4.2	1.6	3%	18%	13%	<u>24%</u>	15%	23%	4%
Top management is interested in KPI reports from the SSO	4.5	1.8	8%	8%	10%	14%	<u>23%</u>	27%	10%

median underlined

Group controlling

Since the SSO controlling may adopt standardized procedures from the group controlling to gain the MNC's legitimacy, the group controlling department size, the PMS on group controlling level and the cooperation intensity between the group controlling and the SSO are possible determinants for PMS design in SSOs. A median value of 30 group management accountants implies that this sample's MNCs have rather large group controlling departments (table 7.30). The strongly deviating mean value (100.6) and the high standard deviation of 178.4 here again point to large differences between the MNCs' with respect to their **group controlling size**. Moreover, the survey results find that 70% of the MNCs in this sample have a **PMS on group level**. A PMS on group level may induce an alignment between the SSO's and the group's PMS as suggested by coercive isomorphism.

Table 7.30: Group controlling department size

How many employees are working for the group controlling of your company?							
n = 71	**Mean**	**Std. dev.**	**Q25**	**Median**	**Q75**	**Min**	**Max**
Total	100.6	178.4	10	30	65	2	800

However, table 7.31 does not suggest a very close collaboration between the SSO and the group controlling. A mean value of 3.9 indicates a rather moderate **collaboration intensity** between the two controlling departments. The interviews in the case studies confirm the impression of rather weak interconnections between the performance measurement activities in the SSO and the group controlling departments. By contrast, the experts of EngineerCo and CommCo emphasize a rather intense collaboration between both departments.

Table 7.31: Collaboration intensity between SSO and group controlling

How do you characterize the collaboration intensity between the group controlling and the SSO?									
n = 71 Distribution (scale: 1 = no collaboration at all...7 = very close collaboration)									
	Mean	Std. dev.	1	2	3	4	5	6	7
Collaboration intensity	3.9	1.5	4%	23%	10%	<u>24%</u>	23%	15%	1%

median underlined

7.4.2.1.3 SSO context

SSO size

Table 7.32 indicates that this study's sample encompasses large and mature SSOs. A mean value of 832.4 SSO employees (a median of 250 SSO employees) supports this statement about the **SSOs' size.** However, the mean is affected by an outlier with 8,000 SSO employees so that the median value seems to be more reliable. Prior research finds lower mean values with regard to the number of SSO employees. While the majority of the SSOs in the sample of *Kagelmann's* study employed around 50 employees (*Kagelmann* (2001), p. 18), the SSOs in *Sterzenbach's* sample operate with more than 100 employees (*Sterzenbach* (2010), p. 342). Moreover, this study's results suggest a mean value of 4.3 SSCs (a median of 3 SSCs) per SSO. However, the maximum value of 30 SSCs provides again an indication for an outlier. This finding seems consistent with the German samples of *Kagelmann* ((2001), p. 98) and *Sterzenbach* ((2010), p. 341). Furthermore, this study's survey findings report an average SSO maturity of 9.0 years (a median of 7 years). The maximum value reflects that SSOs should not be considered as a new-fashioned phenomenon in the German-speaking world, since the oldest SSO of this study's sample has already been founded in 1990. Notably, the studies of *Sterzenbach* and *Kagelmann* are based on differnt sample sizes so that the results are hardly comparable.

Table 7.32: SSO characteristics

SSO characteristics							
n = 71	**Mean**	**Std. dev.**	**Q25**	**Median**	**Q75**	**Min**	**Max**
Number of SSCs	4.3	4.8	1	3	5	1	30
Number of SSO employees	832.4	1.600	50	250	800	6	8.000
SSO maturity (in years)	9	5.8	3	7	13	1	27

Geographic dispersion and legal as well as economic independence

Figure 7.15 unveils the **geographic dispersion** of the SSCs. 58% of the SSOs implemented a SSC onshore in their country of origin. The case study results complement this finding with the interviews of six SSO managers stating that one of their SSCs is located onshore next to the headquarters' site. Prior research reports a lower percentage of onshore SSCs compared to this study (*Sterzenbach* (2010), p. 347). The share of nearshore SSCs is lower compared to the percentage of onshore SSCs (32%). Notably, the indicated percentage of the farshore SSCs (37%) is higher than the share of offshore SSCs (32%). It is striking that many MNCs do not refrain from operating a SSC even in remote regions. The cross-case analysis finds that labor arbitrage is a major reason for establishing farhore SSCs.

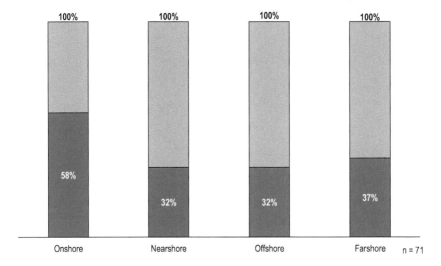

Figure 7.15: Geographic dispersion of SSCs

47% of this sample's SSOs do not have legal autonomy and are also economically dependent on the parent company or a subsidiary of the group (figure 7.16). The cross-case analysis reveals that a minimum size of SSOs seems to be a prerequisite for legal independence since legal autonomy is associated with a considerable effort. By contrast, 28% of the SSOs are **legally and economically independent**. Moreover, 11% are only legally independent so that 39% of this sample's SSOs are designed as a legally independent entity. The findings altogether mirror the results from *Sterzenbach's* analysis (*Sterzenbach* (2010), p. 352). However, compared to the results of *Kagelmann* (58% legally independent) this study unveils a smaller proportion of legally independent SSOs (*Kagelmann* (2001), p. 99). As opposed to this sample, 75% of the MNCs in *Kagelmann's* study are headquartered in the US (*Kagelmann* (2001), p. 17). Moreover, 40% of the SSCs in his study are located in Ireland, where the formation of a legally independent company is less costly, which is a plausible explanation for the higher share of legally independent SSOs. The survey results describe that only 14% of the SSOs are economically independent from their parent company, although the MedTechCo case study associates a higher cost transparency and accountability with economic independence.

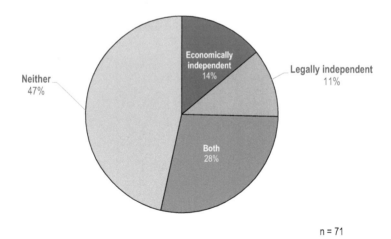

Figure 7.16: Legal and economic independence of SSOs

Center concepts and SSO configuration

Figure 7.17 highlights that economic accountability in SSOs is operationalized with **cost centers**. 97% of this sample's SSOs use cost centers to control their organization. Prior research reports significantly lower shares (*Kagelmann* (2001), p. 104; *Sterzenbach* (2010), p. 353). The proportion of SSOs that encompass a profit responsibility by using profit centers is considerable lower (21%). The descriptive analysis of *Sterzenbach* finds a slightly higher share of SSOs that use profit centers (*Sterzenbach* (2010), p. 353). Other center concepts, such as revenue centers are scarcely prevalent (1%). The cross-case analysis illustrates that the SSO managers in the qualitative sample prefer cost centers since they are not supposed to make profits with their SSO.

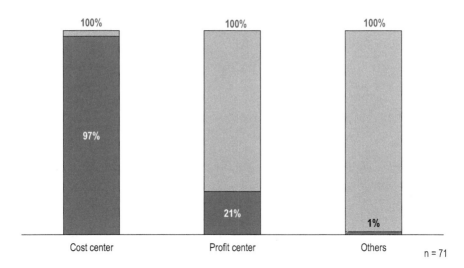

Figure 7.17: Center concepts in SSOs

Concerning the **functional configuration of SSOs,** the descriptive findings of the questionnaires indicate that multifunctional SSOs prevail (figure 7.18). 54% of this sample's SSOs bundle corporate functions, such as finance, HR and IT in the same SSC. 18% of the surveyed SSO managers state that their SSO incorporates several functions which are assigned to different SSCs. By contrast, 28% of the SSO managers report that their SSO encompasses only one corporate function. The cross-case analysis reveals that SSO managers prefer multifunctional SSOs at one location in order to yield more economies of scope. However, the HealthCo case suggests that performance measurement is more challenging in multifunctional SSOs as the controlling department has to include a greater heterogeneity of support processes in the PMS compared to monofunctional SSOs.

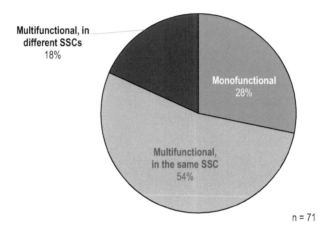

Figure 7.18: Functional configuration of SSOs

Figure 7.19 emphasizes that the majority of this sample's SSOs provide their services for different divisions and for several countries (69%). SSOs, which provide their services for several divisions but only for one country, are notably less represented (24%). SSOs, which are monogeographic and monodivisional, are less prevalent (13%), just as SSOs which provide their services for a single division but in several countries (8%). The cross-case analysis mirrors the prevalence of **multidivisional and multigeographical SSOs**. In addition to the configuration of the SSO's current service provision, the MedTechCo and the AgriCo case highlight that monodivisional and monogeographical SSOs are sometimes a precursor to multigeographical SSOs.

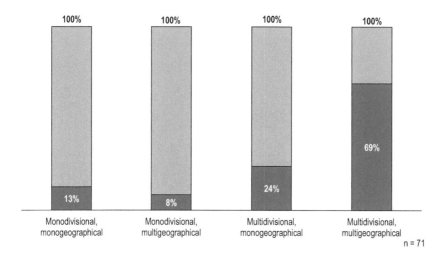

Figure 7.19: Configuration of the service provision in SSOs

Obligation to contract and use of SLAs

51% of the surveyed SSO managers indicate that internal SSO customers are subject to an **obligation to contract** (figure 7.20). Moreover, 35% of the SSOs in this sample state that their SSO customers are at least partially obliged to render the SSO's service. In total, this results in 86% of the SSOs which force their subsidiaries completely or at least partially to contract with the SSO. Prior research by *Kagelmann* and *Sterzenbach* suggest lower shares of SSO customers that are obliged to render services (*Kagelmann* (2001), p. 121; *Sterzenbach* (2010), p. 354). The survey findings corroborate with the results of the cross-case analysis. The case studies reveal that MNCs tend to force internal customers to contract with the SSO in order to secure a minimum transaction volume for the SSO and to avoid contentious negotiations between the SSO and its customers.

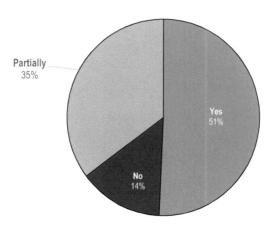

n = 71

Figure 7.20: Obligation to contract for internal SSO customers

80% of this sample's SSOs use **SLAs** to shape their relationships with internal customers (figure 7.21). The widespread use of SLAs mirrors the case study results. By contrast, the descriptive findings of *Kagelmann* and *Sterzenbach* (95%) suggest a broader application of SLAs (*Kagelmann* (2001), p. 118; *Sterzenbach* (2010), p. 355). Furthermore, the HealthCo case points out that SLA design has implications for the SSO's PMS design because SLAs often contain performance measures to monitor service quality. This equally applies to the monitoring of SLAs between the SSO and its outsourcing service providers. Figure 7.22 illustrates that 76% of the SSOs in this sample employ outsourcing service providers for at least one of their support processes. 55% of the surveyed SSO managers confirm that they use SLAs to define their contractual relationship with those outsourcing providers. By contrast, 24% of this sample's SSOs do not outsource at all so that the remaining 21% of the SSOs do not use SLAs although they maintain a contractual relationship with at least one outsourcing service provider. The HealthCo case highlights that the SSO management accountants use the PMS to monitor its outsourcing service providers. In addition, the SSO managers use the KPI reporting to signal to the SSO customers that the SSO is bound to the agreed service levels by providing a (voluntary) performance measure reporting. However, the cross-case analysis suggests that monitoring the outsourcing service provider and signaling compliance to the internal SSO customers is associated with a considerable effort in the SSO controlling department.

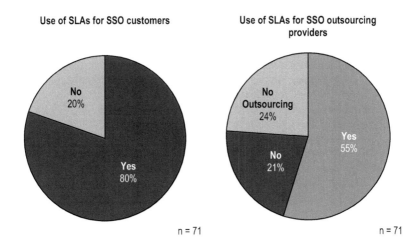

Figure 7.21: Use of SLAs

The SSOs of this sample value four components of SLAs (figure 7.22). 96% of the SSOs define a service scope in their SLAs. In addition, the involved contractual parties (86%), the distribution of roles and responsibilities (84%) and the agreed delivery dates for the service provision (82%) are commonly used SLA design components. Surprisingly, only 56% of the SLAs comprise pricing models. Possibly, the SSOs' pricing models are negotiated otherwise or change frequently so that an ongoing adjustment in the SLAs seems too cumbersome. Actions for continuous improvement (23%) and customer satisfaction measures (14%) play only a subordinate role in SLAs. The low percentage of the continuous improvement component corresponds to the descriptive evidence of *Sterzenbach*, who also indicates a low prevalence of improvement measures in SLAs in his sample (*Sterzenbach* (2010), p. 355). By contrast, this analysis finds that 56% of the SSOs include process quality measures in their SLA design which supports the assumption that SLA design has an impact on PMS design. Contingencies (51%) and payment terms (47%) also prevail quite often as a component of SLA design.

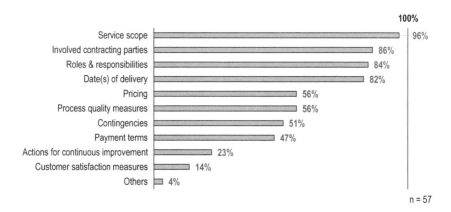

Figure 7.22: SLA design

SSO controlling and SSO customers

46% of the SSOs in this sample have their own **SSO controlling department** (figure 7.23). 11% of the SSOs with an own controlling department implemented a controlling department in each of their SSCs. On the one hand, this is an unexpected evidence since *Sterzenbach* already identified a broader spread of SSO controlling departments (68%) in 2010 (*Sterzenbach* (2010), p. 359). Notably, the SSOs of this sample are both larger and more mature compared to *Sterzenbach's* sample. Hence, it seems assumable that the control of larger organizational units strengthens the need for an own controlling department. On the other hand, the fact that 46% of this sample's SSO do not have a SSO controlling department is consistent with the results already presented in the sample description, illustrating that many SSOs do not use a PMS. Furthermore, the cross-case analysis reveals that the reason for the mediocre prevalence of controlling departments in SSOs is their persistent resource scarcity. The ChemCo case study describes the cautious viewpoint of the responsible SSO manager with regard to investments in a SSO controlling department.

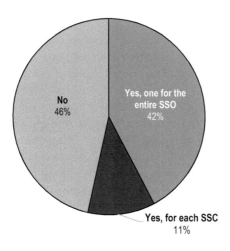

Figure 7.23: SSO controlling departments in SSOs

Table 7.33 underpins the notion of a careful investment policy in controlling capacities by demonstrating a median value of five management accountants who are employed in a SSO controlling department. However, the maximum value (100) and the standard deviation (21.6) of this sample suggest that the SSOs have a different emphasis on the SSO controlling activities. On average, 13.5 SSO management accountants work in a SSO controlling department.

Table 7.33: SSO controlling size

SSO controlling size						
n = 39	Mean	Std. dev.	Q25	Median	Q75	Min	Max
Number of SSO controlling employees	13.5	21.6	2	5	15	1	100

With regard to the **controlling tasks in SSOs**, SSO management accountants fulfil four major tasks, which can be described as genuine controlling tasks (figure 7.24). Cost accounting (22%), followed closely by budgeting and planning (18%) and reporting (18%), account for the highest share of working time. The controlling task KPI calculations and analyses is an essential component of the performance measurement process and also describes an important task for SSO management accountants (17%). Preparing investment appraisals and feasibility studies (6%) as well as the organization and coordination of projects (8%) are less frequently performed controlling tasks of SSO management accountants. Remarkably, risk management plays only a subordinate role in their day-to-day work (2%), although SSO managers and management accountants characterize a preventive risk management as an important SSO objective. In a similar vein, the cross-case analysis emphasizes budgeting, planning, KPI analyses and reporting as the most time-consuming controlling tasks for SSO management accountants. As opposed to the survey results, cost and profit accounting is less represented in the qualitative sample. Moreover, the case studies reveal that four interviewed SSO management accountants are obliged to fulfil tasks from other SSO areas so that less working time remains for genuine controlling tasks. This may lead to an insufficient task fulfilment of the SSO management accountants with regard to the performance measurement process.

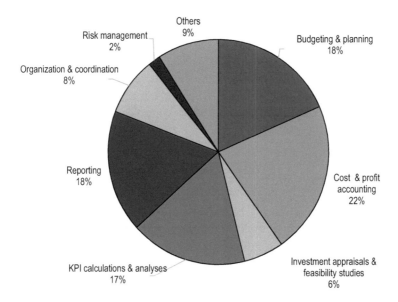

Figure 7.24: SSO controlling tasks for SSO management accountants

The survey findings unveil that SSO managers are particularly sensitive to four basic **requirements of SSO customers** (table 7.34). According to the mean values, a timely service provision is the most important SSO customer requirement (6.0). In addition to a timely service provision, SSO customers value a quick responsiveness to their requests by the SSOs (5.9). Moreover, a constant level of service quality plays an important role for SSO customers (5.7). The professional experience and competence of SSO employees is also of particular relevance for SSO customers according to the managers (5.7). Furthermore, the continuity of the counterparts within the SSO is an important requirement of the SSO customers (5.4). Remarkably, SSO managers rate the offered level of service fees as less significant compared to other customer requirements (5.3). The SSO customers also put emphasis on the flexible consideration of specific customer requirements (5.2) and whether the SSO employees are familiar with the particularities of the SSO customer's business areas (5.2). Suggestions for process improvements by the SSO are the least significant requirement for SSO customers (4.4). A limitation of these findings is that instead of the SSO customers the SSO managers evaluated the SSO customer requirements. However, the comparison with the study on service quality in HR SSOs conducted by *Röder*, who surveyed a total of 763 SSO customers, suggests converging results. For example, *Röder's* SSO customers assess the responsiveness to customer requirements and the professional expertise of SSO employees also as the most important customer requirements (*Röder* (2012), p. 168). Notably, the SSO customers in his sample evaluate the timeliness of the service provision as less significant compared to this sample's SSO managers (*Röder* (2012), p. 169). However, the CommCo case study illustrates that the SSOs in the qualitative sample measure only to a limited extent whether they meet their customers' requirements.

Table 7.34: SSO customer requirements

How important are the following criteria for the customers of your SSO?									
n = 71	Distribution (scale: 1 = not important...7 = very important)								
	Mean	Std. dev.	1	2	3	4	5	6	7
Service fees	5.3	1.8	6%	4%	13%	1%	18%	<u>25%</u>	32%
Timely service provision	6.0	1.1	1%	1%	0%	3%	17%	<u>42%</u>	35%
Consistent service level	5.7	1.2	1%	0%	4%	8%	21%	<u>37%</u>	28%
Professional expertise of the SSO employees	5.7	1.0	0%	0%	3%	7%	25%	<u>42%</u>	23%
Flexible consideration of specific customer requirements	5.2	1.3	0%	1%	10%	21%	<u>18%</u>	34%	15%
Self-initiated suggestions for improvements by the SSO	4.4.	1.3	0%	7%	15%	<u>35%</u>	18%	20%	4%
SSO employees are familiar with particularities of the customer business areas	5.2	1.1	0%	0%	6%	25%	<u>28%</u>	30%	11%
Quick response to customer requests	5.9	1.0	0%	0%	4%	4%	20%	<u>39%</u>	32%
Continuity of the SSO counterparts	5.4	1.3	1%	1%	7%	7%	25%	<u>42%</u>	15%

median underlined

Process standardization

As outlined in the operationalization of the quantitative study, **process standardization** can be subdivided into formal and factual standardization. The survey findings on the current state of formal process standardization in SSOs measure the degree of process standardization that is observable by the existence of established guidelines, a comprehensive process documentation and templates. In essence, the survey findings describe that SSO managers perceive their processes as rather standardized. This finding mirrors the results of the cross-case analysis. A mean of 5.4 for a constant documentation of the SSO's standard processes and a mean of 5.3 for the existence of established guidelines underpin the notion of a rather high degree of formal process standardization. However, a mean of

3.8 with regard to the question about necessary deviations from the standard process in the interest of the MNC and a mean of 3.3 for necessary deviations in the interest of the SSO, suggest that SSOs still take local particularities into account. The EngineerCo and the CommCo case studies confirm that some SSO guidelines and templates are not applicable to all SSO customers so that a deviation from the standard procedures is necessary.

Table 7.35: Formal process standardization in SSOs

Formal process standardization in SSOs									
n = 71		Distribution (scale: 1 = not at all…7 = completely)							
	Mean	Std. dev.	1	2	3	4	5	6	7
Established guidelines	5.3	1.5	0%	7%	7%	10%	20%	<u>35%</u>	21%
Documentation of processes	5.4	1.5	1%	3%	9%	13%	21%	<u>28%</u>	25%
Deviations from the standard process only in exceptional cases	4.4	1.6	3%	11%	20%	<u>20%</u>	15%	21%	10%
In the interest of the SSO, employees have to deviate from the standard processes	3.3	1.6	7%	35%	<u>13%</u>	20%	14%	10%	1%
In the interest of the company, employees have to deviate from the standard processes.	3.8	1.5	6%	23%	14%	<u>20%</u>	25%	11%	1%

median underlined

The hypothesis development in chapter four emphasizes that guidelines and routines can be adopted differently due to a varying context so that under the surface of formal standardization a decoupling of the genuine meaning takes place, which can be defined as factual standardization. Overall, the survey sample suggests mixed results with regard to the degree of factual process standardization in SSOs. Notably, table 7.36 reveals lower means for the factual compared to the formal standardization. Particularly, local requirements (4.7) and local information systems (3.7) cause constant deviations from the standard process. By contrast, deviations from the SSO's standard processes due to a higher resource consumption (2.6) and due to overcomplicated standard procedures (2.7) are rather seldom. The HealthCo case study confirms the result that deviations from the standard process are caused by local requirements.

Moreover, the cross-case analysis illustrates that deviations between the formal and factual degree of process standardization impinge on other SSO objectives, such as process automation.

Table 7.36: Factual process standardization in SSOs

Factual process standardization in SSOs									
n = 71	**Distribution (scale: 1 = not at all…7 = completely)**								
Deviations, because…	**Mean**	**Std. dev.**	**1**	**2**	**3**	**4**	**5**	**6**	**7**
…standard process does not comply with local requirements.	4.7	2.0	16%	21%	5%	21%	<u>11%</u>	16%	10%
…standard process does not comply with local information systems.	3.7	1.8	21%	16%	5%	<u>26%</u>	16%	16%	0%
…standard process is too complicated.	2.7	1.5	26%	<u>37%</u>	16%	5%	11%	5%	0%
…standard process causes a higher resource consumption.	2.6	1.4	42%	<u>26%</u>	11%	5%	11%	5%	0%

median underlined

Power and know-how promotors

The descriptive evidence on performance measurement actors unveiled that PMS design in SSOs involves various actors. As outlined in the hypotheses development, the promotor model suggests that the development of the SSO's PMS depends on performance measurement actors who are willing and able to promote performance measurement in their organization. **Power promotors** support the development of the SSO's PMS design by providing financial and human resources. The mean values of the descriptive analysis support the results of the cross-case analysis stating that the SSO executive board (5.1) and the SSC heads (5.2) contribute to the PMS design by acting as power promotors (table 7.37). In addition, the median (6) indicates a strong agreement among the respondents on the question of who provides resources for their PMS. By contrast, the group management board plays a subordinate role for promoting PMS design in SSOs (2.8).

Table 7.37: PMS power promotors in SSOs

To what extent do the following actors support the development of your SSO's PMS by providing financial resources and/or personnel capacity?									
n = 53	Distribution (scale: 1 = not at all…7 = completely)								
	Mean	Std. dev.	1	2	3	4	5	6	7
The SSO executive board	5.1	1.7	2%	8%	11%	11%	17%	<u>25%</u>	26%
The SSC head	5.2	1.7	2%	4%	19%	6%	17%	<u>24%</u>	28%
The group management board	2.8	1.6	30%	15%	<u>21%</u>	19%	7%	6%	2%

median underlined

A heterogeneous SSO environment imposes a variety of process-specific challenges for performance measurement activities in SSOs and requires a high degree of expertise of the responsible performance measurement actors. **Know-how promotors** contribute to the SSO's PMS design with their expertise. The mean values in table 7.38 describe that the process owners with their expertise contribute the most to the development of the SSOs' PMS design (5.6). The case study results illustrate that process owners take a leading role for the selection of new performance measures. In addition, the cross-case analysis finds that process managers contribute with their expertise to set realistic performance measure targets and support SSO management accountants and SSC managers during the performance measure evaluation. Apart from the process managers, the SSC heads add their knowledge to the further improvement of the PMS (5.1). Notably, the survey results indicate that also the SSO executive board promotes the SSO's by sharing the performance measurement expertise (4.6). The cross-case analysis reveals that the SSO executive board is particularly involved in the target setting and performance measure modification process. Surprisingly, SSO management accountants contribute to the PMS design with their expertise only to a limited extent (4.2). The outlined descriptive evidence regarding the SSO controlling may serve as an explanation since 46% of this sample's SSOs do not have a controlling department. The SSO employees (3.5), the group controlling department (2.4) and the outsourcing service providers (1.8) are less relevant as know-how promotors for PMS design in SSOs.

Table 7.38: PMS know-how promotors in SSOs

To what extent do the following actors contribute to PMS improvements with their expertise?									
n = 53			Distribution (scale: 1 = not at all…7 = completely)						
	Mean	Std. dev.	1	2	3	4	5	6	7
The SSO executive board	4.6	1.9	9%	8%	9%	13%	<u>23%</u>	23%	15%
The SSC head	5.1	1.5	2%	6%	9%	13%	<u>23%</u>	30%	17%
The process owner	5.6	1.4	4%	0%	4%	9%	21%	<u>36%</u>	26%
The SSO controlling	4.2	2.0	15%	10%	9%	<u>17%</u>	21%	15%	13%
The SSO employee	3.5	1.6	17%	15%	9%	<u>28%</u>	21%	8%	2%
The group controlling	2.4	1.6	38%	<u>28%</u>	15%	6%	6%	5%	2%
The outsourcing service provider	1.8	1.4	<u>64%</u>	15%	6%	6%	7%	2%	0%

median underlined

Process and relationship promotors

The described performance measurement process requires a considerable coordination effort. As illustrated in the hypotheses development, **process promotors** help to overcome administrative barriers with their organizational knowledge. Table 7.39 points out that process owners and SSC heads can be considered as process promotors. A mean of 4.9 for the process owners and a mean of 4.4 for the SSC managers is a somewhat unexpected finding since the coordination of the performance measurement process is a genuine task for SSO management accountants. The findings of the CommCo and the HealthCo case studies substantiate the assumption that the SSO controlling department slips into the role of the process promotor. However, the survey findings imply a rather weak coordination effort by the SSO controlling department (3.8). Again, an explanation for this finding may be the fact that about half of this sample's SSOs does not have a controlling department. The SSO employees (3.0) and the group controlling (2.0) play a subordinate role in the coordination of the performance measurement process. In essence, it remains a controversial issue which organizational unit of the SSO is best suited to coordinate performance measurement activities.

Table 7.39: PMS process promotors in SSOs

	To what extent do the following actors coordinate performance measurement activities within your SSO?								
n = 53	Distribution (scale: 1 = not at all…7 = completely)								
	Mean	**Std. dev.**	**1**	**2**	**3**	**4**	**5**	**6**	**7**
The SSC head	4.4	2.1	15%	11%	10%	11%	11%	23%	19%
The process owner	4.9	1.7	4%	11%	4%	13%	27%	26%	15%
The SSO controlling	3.8	2.1	23%	15%	4%	15%	21%	9%	13%
The SSO employee	3.0	1.6	24%	19%	15%	23%	13%	4%	2%
The group controlling	2.0	1.6	60%	15%	8%	7%	6%	0%	4%

median underlined

A successful PMS design in SSOs depends very much on the cooperation of the performance measurement actors with other departments and stakeholders outside the SSO. **Relationship promotors** help to overcome dependency barriers caused by an asymmetric balance of power. Table 7.40 indicates that the role of the relationship promotor is not assigned to a particular performance measurement actor, but assumed by four groups of actors. Indeed, the SSC heads (4.2) show the highest mean value. However, the average values of the SSO executive board (3.8) and the process owners (3.9) are only slightly lower. Hence, this finding suggests that different actors maintain relationships with co-workers outside the SSO and cooperate with them during the performance measurement process. The cross-case analysis provides several examples of a cross-departmental collaboration regarding performance measurement matters. Again, SSO employees are less relevant as relationship promotors which is suggested by the rather low mean value of 2.6.

Table 7.40: PMS relationship promotors in SSOs

	To what extent do the following actors cooperate with departments outside the SSO in relation to your PMS?								
n = 53	Distribution (scale: 1 = not at all…7 = completely)								
	Mean	**Std. dev.**	**1**	**2**	**3**	**4**	**5**	**6**	**7**
The SSO executive board	3.8	2.1	25%	6%	13%	13%	19%	13%	11%
The SSC head	4.2	2.1	15%	9%	17%	11%	10%	19%	19%
The process owner	3.9	2.0	17%	15%	6%	17%	25%	9%	11%
The SSO controlling	3.5	2.1	26%	13%	8%	15%	19%	10%	9%
The SSO employee	2.6	1.5	30%	25%	15%	17%	9%	4%	0%

median underlined

7.4.2.1.4 Summary

The descriptive analysis on determinants of PMS design in SSOs presents a number of contextual factors in which PMS design takes place. This sample's MNCs are subject to a considerable **competition intensity** which may increase the SSO's formal controls, such as the PMS. Moreover, SSO managers perceive the **IT-infrastructure** of their MNCs as rather harmonized which may facilitate the performance measure data collection process. The descriptive findings indicate a strong support for the SSO's PMS from the **MNC's top management** so that the performance measurement activities may be promoted by higher hierarchical levels.

This sample's SSOs locate their **SSCs geographically dispersed**. Apart from nearshore SSCs, a considerable proportion of this sample's SSOs have a SSC in a remote region which may add to the complexity of PMS design. Furthermore, the SSO managers state that the majority of the SSOs render their services to a **multidivisional and multigeographical** customer base. Thus, the SSO customer base is spread across several countries and the SSO has to render services for subsidiaries with different business models, products and services. The heterogeneous SSO customer base may be also reflected in the SSO's PMS. The majority of this sample's SSOs obliges its SSO customers to contact with the SSO in order to secure a minimum transaction volume. The **obligation to contract** may impinge on KPI reporting activities since the SSO has a lower incentive to voluntarily signal that the SSO is bound to the agreed service levels by means of process and service quality performance measures. 80% of this sample's SSOs use **SLAs** to manage their SSO customer relationships. SLAs may foster PMS design since the descriptive evidence on SLA design emphasizes that SSOs often encompass performance measures in their SLAs. In addition, SLAs are commonly used to shape the relationship between SSOs and outsourcing service providers. The survey findings illustrate that 76% of the SSOs in this sample employ outsourcing providers which need to be monitored by means of the SSO's PMS. However, almost half of the SSOs in this sample do not have a **SSO controlling department** which is consistent to the finding that many SSOs do not use a PMS. A missing SSO controlling department may adversely affect the PMS design since performance measurement activities have to be done by other SSO departments and performance measurement actors who perform PMS design tasks in addition to their actual job. The survey findings illustrate that SSOs are commonly controlled with **cost centers**. Furthermore, the survey findings suggest that SSO managers perceive their processes as rather standardized although the formal degree of **process standardization** seems to be more pronounced compared to the degree of factual standardization. Standardized support processes may facilitate performance measurement activities since less plausibility checks are required and performance measure data is easier to collect.

The descriptive analysis provides some evidence that the SSO executive board and the SSC heads are perceived as significant **power promotors** of PMS design by investing financial and human resources into the development of the SSO's PMS. In addition, process owners contribute with their expertise to the SSO's PMS design as **know-how promotors**. The descriptive analysis finds that process owners and SSC heads slip into the role of **process promotors** as they coordinate the performance measurement process.

In essence, the descriptive analysis provides some evidence on potential determinants of PMS design. The following correlation analysis extends the descriptive findings and aims to substantiate the presumed relationships between PMS design in SSOs and the described contingency factors.

7.4.2.2 Correlation analysis

This section uses bivariate correlation analyses to investigate the relationship between PMS design in SSOs and the determinants described in the previous sections. The correlation analysis measures the strength and the direction between the PMS design and the respective contingency factors so that the analysis provides an indication whether a pairwise association between the determinant and PMS design in SSOs exists. Thus, the correlation analysis assesses the applicability of the following regression models. The following table provide the pairwise *Pearson* and the *Spearman* correlation coefficients between the independent (context and control variables) and the dependent variables (COMP, GOA, and SAT). Notably, the sample size amounts to 50 observations. The reduced sample size is attributable to the dyadic research design of the quantitative study. Since the SSO managers answered the questions concerning the SSO determinants and the SSO management accountants answered the questions with regard to the PMS design in SSOs, the sample for the correlation analysis only includes MNCs of which two completed questionnaires are available. Thus, MNCs of which only one survey for the SSO determinants or for the PMS design is available, cannot be considered in the sample of the correlation analysis. This explains the difference to the sample size of the descriptive findings.

Table 7.41: Pearson and Spearman correlation matrix

		Pearson and Spearman correlation matrix										
	(1)	(2)	(3)	(4)	(5)	(6)	(7)	(8)	(9)	(10)	(11)	(12)
(1) Perceived environmental uncertainty	1.00	0.03	-0.18	-0.09	-0.13	-0.05	-0.08	0.16	0.11	-0.12	-0.01	0.03
(2) Competition intensity	0.05	1.00	0.07	0.22	-0.01	0.24*	-0.18	0.01	0.18	-0.18	0.21	-0.32**
(3) Product diversity	-0.17	0.12	1.00	-0.04	0.15	-0.06	-0.20	-0.10	0.09	0.21	-0.07	-0.07
(4) MNC organizational complexity	-0.11	0.22	-0.00	1.00	-0.03	-0.04	0.08	-0.01	-0.35**	-0.13	-0.08	0.04
(5) MNC IT infrastructure heterogeneity	-0.08	0.03	0.16	-0.04	1.00	-0.24*	0.06	-0.00	-0.01	0.02	0.19	-0.37***
(6) MNC top management support	-0.05	0.24*	-0.08	-0.01	-0.23	1.00	0.26*	-0.23	0.16	0.05	0.26*	0.12
(7) Group controlling collaboration intensity	-0.05	-0.18	-0.22	0.12	0.05	0.31**	1.00	-0.15	-0.18	-0.00	-0.06	0.06
(8) Geographical dispersion of SSCs	0.13	-0.10	-0.07	-0.11	0.07	-0.29**	-0.12	1.00	-0.01	-0.02	0.10	-0.09
(9) SSO legal and economic independence	0.09	0.16	0.10	-0.35**	0.05	0.18	-0.18	0.01	1.00	0.19	0.13	-0.16

Table 7.41: Continued

					Pearson and Spearman correlation matrix							
	(1)	(2)	(3)	(4)	(5)	(6)	(7)	(8)	(9)	(10)	(11)	(12)
(10) SSO center concept	-0.10	-0.16	0.23	-0.14	-0.02	-0.01	-0.01	-0.00	0.18	**1.00**	0.06	0.08
(11) SSO structural complexity	-0.06	0.21	0.01	-0.09	0.15	0.31**	-0.03	0.12	0.15	0.09	**1.00**	-0.37***
(12) Obligation to contract	0.05	-0.21	-0.07	0.01	-0.35**	0.10	0.06	-0.08	-0.16	0.10	-0.36***	**1.00**
(13) SLA complexity	0.12	0.29**	-0.02	0.10	0.02	0.16	0.02	0.17	0.23	-0.02	0.26*	-0.12
(14) Time spent on PMS tasks	-0.15	0.17	0.14	0.05	0.15	0.05	-0.03	-0.01	0.16	-0.11	0.15	-0.34**
(15) SSO customer requirements	0.07	0.31**	0.03	0.32**	0.13	0.05	0.10	0.08	0.16	-0.10	0.10	-0.22
(16) Degree of process standardization	0.07	-0.11	0.22	0.07	0.01	-0.18	-0.28*	0.08	0.01	0.03	-0.15	0.11
(17) Power promotors	-0.10	0.24*	0.06	-0.08	-0.02	0.18	-0.04	-0.08	0.04	-0.08	0.25*	-0.04
(18) Know-how promotors	-0.18	0.15	0.10	0.13	-0.04	0.22	0.20	0.04	-0.05	0.03	0.24*	-0.13
(19) Process promotors	-0.16	0.14	0.04	0.06	0.02	0.16	0.23	0.06	-0.06	-0.15	0.05	-0.19
(20) Relationship promotors	-0.14	0.11	0.07	0.13	-0.13	0.16	0.09	-0.12	-0.04	-0.01	0.11	-0.05

(continued on next page)

Table 7.41: Continued

		Pearson and Spearman correlation matrix										
	(1)	(2)	(3)	(4)	(5)	(6)	(7)	(8)	(9)	(10)	(11)	(12)
(21) MNC size	0.03	0.36**	0.24*	0.23	0.14	-0.11	-0.35**	0.23	0.16	-0.35**	0.01	-0.33**
(22) MNC organizational structure	0.17	0.13	0.02	-0.06	-0.08	0.10	-0.26*	0.16	-0.15	-0.12	-0.01	0.03
(23) MNC group controlling size	0.18	0.29**	0.12	0.21	0.05	-0.09	-0.15	0.34**	-0.11	-0.22	0.05	-0.18
(24) SSO size	-0.06	0.15	0.08	-0.04	0.25*	-0.18	-0.27*	0.36***	0.27*	-0.18	0.35**	-0.26*
(25) SSO maturity	-0.02	-0.10	-0.01	-0.05	-0.05	-0.31**	0.06	0.38***	-0.25*	-0.11	-0.07	-0.09
(26) COMP	-0.11	0.20	0.10	-0.03	0.15	0.26*	-0.15	0.10	0.16	-0.08	0.37***	-0.25*
(27) GOA	0.29**	0.11	-0.24	0.11	-0.27*	0.16	-0.05	0.06	-0.04	-0.21	0.06	-0.07
(28) SAT	0.12	0.12	-0.09	0.24*	-0.08	0.07	-0.02	0.07	0.01	-0.09	0.24*	0.03

Notes: table displays the Spearman correlation coefficients above and the Pearson correlations below the diagonal of 1.00.

Table 7.41: Continued

							Pearson and Spearman correlation matrix									
	(13)	(14)	(15)	(16)	(17)	(18)	(19)	(20)	(21)	(22)	(23)	(24)	(25)	(26)	(27)	(28)
(1) Perceived environmental uncertainty	0.18	-0.12	0.07	0.10	-0.10	-0.21	-0.16	-0.11	0.05	0.20	0.29**	0.00	-0.06	-0.08	0.30**	0.13
(2) Competition intensity	0.29**	0.24*	0.25*	-0.16	0.16	0.08	0.10	0.10	0.41***	0.12	0.28**	0.23	-0.02	0.22	0.03	-0.02
(3) Product diversity	-0.04	0.21	0.03	0.19	0.06	0.10	0.08	0.03	0.22	0.06	0.13	0.09	0.03	0.02	-0.28**	-0.12
(4) MNC organizational complexity	0.16	-0.03	0.30**	0.04	-0.09	0.19	0.12	0.18	0.29**	-0.07	0.25*	0.04	-0.02	0.07	0.11	0.31**
(5) MNC IT infrastructure heterogeneity	-0.03	0.20	0.09	-0.05	0.00	-0.01	0.03	-0.15	0.10	-0.08	-0.08	0.20	-0.09	0.14	-0.34**	-0.09
(6) MNC top management support	0.15	0.09	0.08	-0.13	0.14	0.16	0.15	0.21	-0.16	0.10	-0.08	-0.19	-0.36**	0.27*	0.13	0.05
(7) Group controlling collaboration intensity	0.01	0.01	0.13	-0.30**	-0.09	0.20	0.22	0.10	-0.36**	-0.28*	-0.19	-0.28*	0.01	-0.17	-0.01	-0.00
(8) Geographical dispersion of SSCs	0.31**	-0.02	0.04	0.10	-0.12	0.07	0.08	-0.13	0.29*	0.22	0.39***	0.41***	0.37***	0.14	0.13	0.13

(continued on next page)

Table 7.41: Continued

							Pearson and Spearman correlation matrix									
	(13)	(14)	(15)	(16)	(17)	(18)	(19)	(20)	(21)	(22)	(23)	(24)	(25)	(26)	(27)	(28)
(9) SSO legal and economic independence	0.20	0.22	0.12	0.04	0.07	-0.06	-0.07	-0.07	0.17	-0.15	-0.12	0.27*	-0.23	0.20	-0.09	-0.07
(10) SSO center concept	-0.12	-0.09	-0.12	0.03	-0.06	0.07	-0.12	-0.01	-0.33***	-0.13	0.25*	-0.16	-0.04	-0.07	-0.16	-0.13
(11) SSO structural complexity	0.23	0.10	0.06	-0.18	0.26*	0.16	0.07	0.09	0.03	-0.03	0.01	0.32**	-0.17	0.44***	0.09	0.22
(12) Obligation to contract	-0.18	-0.38***	-0.22	0.11	-0.01	-0.10	-0.23	-0.03	-0.32**	0.03	-0.12	-0.26*	-0.10	-0.25*	0.11	0.08
(13) SLA complexity	**1.00**	0.20	0.34**	0.13	0.01	0.35**	0.39***	0.18	0.32**	0.20	0.34**	0.43***	-0.02	0.43***	0.17	0.28**
(14) Time spent on PMS tasks	0.19	**1.00**	0.10	-0.16	-0.20	-0.07	0.36***	-0.06	0.34**	-0.06	-0.04	0.35**	0.08	0.25*	-0.16	-0.12
(15) SSO customer requirements	0.36**	0.14	**1.00**	0.09	0.07	0.28*	0.32**	0.13	0.19	-0.21	0.26*	0.06	-0.05	0.14	0.08	0.42***
(16) Degree of process standardization	0.10	-0.07	0.11	**1.00**	0.06	0.04	0.12	0.05	0.23	0.17	0.49***	0.13	-0.03	-0.10	0.20	0.07
(17) Power promoters	0.09	-0.17	0.06	0.07	**1.00**	0.60***	0.24*	0.44***	-0.09	0.17	0.04	-0.02	-0.19	0.42***	0.20	0.26*
(18) Know-how promoters	0.42***	-0.04	0.27*	0.07	0.62***	**1.00**	0.69***	0.55***	-0.10	0.13	0.07	0.09	0.04	0.45***	0.03	0.32**

Table 7.41: Continued

	(13)	(14)	(15)	(16)	(17)	(18)	(19)	(20)	(21)	(22)	(23)	(24)	(25)	(26)	(27)	(28)
										Pearson and Spearman correlation matrix						
(19) Process promotors	0.34**	0.31**	0.33**	0.16	0.28*	0.68***	**1.00**	0.39***	0.14	0.12	0.19	0.22	0.07	0.34**	-0.05	0.17
(20) Relationship promotors	0.27*	0.03	0.11	0.05	0.46***	0.57***	0.39***	**1.00**	-0.04	0.14	0.13	-0.01	-0.16	0.33**	-0.10	0.23
(21) MNC size	0.27*	0.32**	0.28*	0.23	-0.04	-0.06	0.16	0.01	**1.00**	0.09	0.54***	0.68***	0.22	0.31**	0.12	0.00
(22) MNC organizational structure	0.16	-0.03	0.12	-0.19	0.19	0.14	0.11	0.15	0.10	**1.00**	0.30**	0.20	-0.13	0.04	-0.14	0.01
(23) MNC group controlling size	0.24*	-0.00	0.49***	0.27*	0.08	0.08	0.21	0.08	0.56***	0.35**	**1.00**	0.44***	0.12	0.06	0.27*	0.29**
(24) SSO size	0.39***	0.37***	0.14	0.12	0.00	0.12	0.19	0.02	0.61***	0.21	0.45***	**1.00**	0.34***	0.42***	-0.05	0.10
(25) SSO maturity	-0.02	0.08	-0.03	-0.02	-0.18	0.08	0.07	-0.17	0.21	-0.09	0.17	0.37***	**1.00**	-0.06	0.11	-0.17
(26) COMP	0.44***	0.28**	0.00	0.15	0.44***	0.55***	0.43***	0.37***	0.34**	0.07	0.02	0.41***	0.04	**1.00**	0.27*	0.22
(27) GOA	0.20	-0.13	0.15	0.12	0.16	0.04	-0.02	-0.09	0.25*	-0.07	0.28**	0.02	0.06	0.28**	**1.00**	0.31**
(28) SAT	0.47***	-0.04	0.14	0.43***	0.27*	0.34**	0.19	0.29	0.20	0.02	0.25*	0.19	-0.13	0.32**	0.44***	**1.00**

Notes: table displays the Spearman correlation coefficients above and the Pearson correlations below the diagonal of 1.00.

The table shows the *Spearman* correlation coefficients above and the *Pearson* correlations below the diagonal. As opposed to the *Pearson* correlations, the non-parametric *Spearman* rank-order correlation test does not assume normally distributed data, continuous variables and a linear relationship between the two variables. Since the operationalization of variables sporadically entails variables that are measured on an ordinal scale, *Spearman's* correlations supplement the *Pearson's* correlations. Both methods illustrate that the correlation coefficients of the two tests barely differ. Hence, the following section uses the more robust *Spearman* correlations to analyze the most important bivariate associations.

Overall, the correlation table suggests that the majority of the correlation coefficients show the expected direction suggesting that the operationalized proxies seem well-specified. However, the correlation matrix indicates several weak and moderate coefficients so that the correlations between the independent and dependent variables should be interpreted carefully. As outlined in section 7.3, the strength of a correlation between 0.00 and 0.20 is interpreted as weak, whereas a correlation strength between 0.21 and 0.40 is considered as moderate and between 0.41 and 1.00 as strong. The correlation matrix reveals a total of nine significant correlations between context factors and the dependent variable PMS design.

First, top management support is positively associated with PMS design at a 10% level using a two-tailed test ($r = 0.27$, $p < 0.1$). Without considering other variables, this finding suggests that **top management support** enhances PMS design in SSOs. However, a bivariate correlation cannot rule out that the direction is reversed, such that PMS design positively influences top management support or a third unknown variable exists. Second, in line with the hypothesis, the **SSO's structural complexity** is positively associated with COMP ($r = 0.44$, $p < 0.01$). This allows for the interpretation that the SSO's organizational design choices, such as establishing mono- or multifunctional SSCs as well as a mono- or multigeographical service provision affects PMS design. This finding seems consistent with conceptual literature and is supported by the case study results.

Third, an existing **obligation to contract** for SSO customers is negatively correlated with COMP ($r = -0.25$, $p < 0.1$). This rather weak association supports prior research indicating that SSOs, which rely on contract obligation for the MNC's subsidiaries, do not have to cope with a market-like competitive situation and thus are less dependent on a rather exhaustive PMS design. Fourth, **SLA design** is positively associated with COMP ($r = 0.43$, $p < 0.01$). This correlation is consistent with the detailed descriptive findings on SLA design. Since sophistically designed SLAs often entail process quality and customer satisfaction measures, it seems reasonable that SLA design positively influences the SSO's PMS design complexity. Fifth, the **time spent on PMS tasks** of the SSO controlling department correlates positively with the PMS design ($r = 0.25$, $p < 0.1$). This finding allows for the interpretation that SSO controlling departments, which appoint a comparably high number of FTEs to the KPI analysis and reporting, operate with a well-developed PMS.

Sixth, **power promotors** are strongly correlated with PMS design in SSOs ($r = 0.42$, $p < 0.01$). This finding coincidences with the underlying promotor model and the case study results. This result supports the notion that the existence of power promotors fosters the development of PMS in SSOs. Seventh, the existence of **know-how promotors** is positively associated with PMS design in SSOs ($r = 0.45$, $p < 0.01$). In line with the cross-case analysis, this finding substantiates the assumption that PMS design in SSOs requires performance measurement actors with a high degree of expertise. The eighth finding of the correlation analysis reports a moderate correlation between **process promotors** and PMS design ($r = 0.34$, $p < 0.05$). This result indicates that the existence of process promotors that coordinate the performance measurement process is positively associated with PMS design in SSOs. Ninth, the bivariate analysis finds that the existence of **relationship promotors** moderately correlates with PMS design in SSOs ($r = 0.33$, $p < 0.05$). This finding is in accordance with the illustrated promotor model even though the cross-case analysis does not reveal an unambiguous result regarding the performance measurement actors that embody relationship promotors.

With regard to the control variables, the correlation matrix points out that the MNC's and the SSO's size are positively associated with COMP. This finding supports prior MCS research that underpins the impact of size on MCS in contingency-based studies. Notably, the significant correlation between the MNC's size and COMP applies to all operationalized **MNC size** proxies ($r = 0.31$, $p < 0.05$). The **SSO's size** is operationalized by the number of SSO employees and reveals a slightly stronger correlation to COMP compared to MNC's size ($r = 0.42$, $p < 0.01$).

Moreover, the bivariate correlation analysis unveils a significant positive correlation between PMS design and the **goal attainment** perceived by the SSO managers ($r = 0.27$, $p < 0.1$). This result supports the expected positive association between COMP and performance measurement effectiveness. In essence, the correlation matrix illustrates that the associations between independent and dependent variables are consistent with the majority of the outlined hypotheses.

7.4.2.3 Regression analysis

The following regressions analyze whether the associations revealed in the bivariate correlations persist if other independent variables are simultaneously taken into account. Thereby, this section refers to the second research question and analyzes the extent to which the context factors are associated with PMS design in SSOs. This section intends to test the hypotheses refined in chapter six.

In line with the hypotheses, the tables indicate the predicted sign of the independent variables next to the coefficients. The PMS design score (COMP) is at the top of the table and represents the dependent variable, while the independent variables follow in a descending order. Control variables without a predicted sign are at the bottom of the table. All regressions are based on the OLS method. The asterisks behind the correlation coefficients indicate the statistical significance of the correlations at a 10%, 5% or 1% level. Whenever a directed hypothesis has been stated (recognizable by the expected sign), the reported significance level is based on **one-tailed tests**. Whenever an undirected hypothesis has been stated, the reported significance level is based on two-tailed tests. Similar to the bivariate correlation analysis, the sample size for the following regression models is also restricted to 50 observations due to the requirement of two completed questionnaires.

The regression analysis on determinants of PMS design in SSOs is based on the two models (A) and (B) (table 7.42). Both models entail 20 contingency and 5 control variables. As opposed to model (A), model (B) incorporates **industry and country fixed effects** to control for unobserved heterogeneity across firms.

Table 7.42: Regression analysis on determinants of PMS design

	Regression analysis on determinants of PMS design					
			Model (A)		Model (B)	
H	Variables	E.S.	Coefficient	t-value	Coefficient	t-value
H1a_1	Perceived environmental uncertainty	(+)	0.230	(1.57)	0.105	(0.72)
H1a_2	Competition intensity	(+)	-0.050	(-0.44)	-0.005	(-0.04)
H1b_1	Product diversity	(+)	-0.004	(-0.10)	0.030	(0.63)
H1b_2	MNC organizational complexity	(+)	0.010	(0.58)	0.019	(0.10)
H1b_3	MNC IT system heterogeneity	(+)	0.087	(1.26)	0.099	(1.51)
H1b_4	MNC top management support	(+)	0.238	(2.86) ***	0.303	(3.60) ***
H1b_5	Group controlling collaboration intensity	(+)	0.157	(2.91) ***	0.168	(2.99) ***
H1c_1	Geographical dispersion of SSCs	(+)	0.097	(1.50)	0.194	(2.37) **
H1c_2	SSO legal and economic independence	(+/-)	-0.062	(-1.46)	-0.079	(-1.82) *
H1c_3	SSO center concept	(-)	0.011	(0.38)	0.011	(0.35)
H1c_4	SSO structural complexity	(+)	-0.103	(-0.71)	-0.169	(-1.05)
H1c_5	Obligation to contract	(-)	-0.039	(-0.93)	-0.041	(-1.21)
H1c_6	SLA design	(+)	0.085	(1.39)	0.103	(1.47)
H1c_7	Time spent on PMS tasks	(+)	0.079	(1.58)	0.083	(1.73) *
H1c_8	SSO customer requirements	(+)	-0.147	(-0.78)	-0.015	(-0.07)
H1c_9	Degree of process standardization	(-)	0.016	(0.14)	-0.003	(-0.03)
H1d_1	Power promotors	(+)	0.165	(1.71) *	0.190	(2.09) **
H1d_2	Know-how promotors	(+)	0.174	(0.83)	0.181	(0.88)
H1d_3	Process promotors	(+)	0.007	(0.06)	-0.016	(-0.12)
H1d_4	Relationship promotors	(+)	0.067	(1.29)	0.031	(0.55)
Contr.	MNC size		0.014	(0.09)	0.011	(0.07)
Contr.	MNC group controlling size		-0.179	(-1.95)	-0.170	(-1.86)
Contr.	MNC organizational structure		-0.068	(-1.99)	-0.062	(-1.86)
Contr.	SSO size		0.262	(1.64)	0.284	(1.89) *

(continued on next page)

Table 7.42:   Continued

		Regression analysis on determinants of PMS design			
		Model (A)		Model (B)	
H	Variables	E.S. Coefficient	t-value	Coefficient	t-value
Contr.	SSO maturity	-0.016	(-0.29)	-0.036	(-0.69)
	Constant	-0.087	(-0.53)	-0.099	(-0.58)
	Country fixed effects	No		Yes	
	Industry fixed effects	No		Yes	
	N	50		50	
	adj. R2	75.18%		81.85%	
	F-stat	9.08		8.56	
	Prob > F	0.000		0.000	
	VIFmax	8.36		9.07	

While industry fixed effects capture systematic differences across firms within industries, country fixed effects control for unobserved differences in the country-specific environments of Germany, Austria, and Switzerland.

The F-value of 9.08 suggests a **good fit of the regression** model (A). The F-value of model (B) is only slightly lower so that a good fit can be assumed for both models. Model (A) demonstrates an adjusted R^2 of 75.18%, signaling a high explanatory power. Model (B) indicates that industry and country fixed effects contribute to the explanatory power of the regression model which results in an adjusted R^2 of 81.85%. The maximum VIFs of model (A) (8.36) and (B) (9.07) are below the threshold of ten, which implies that multicollinearity does not pose a problem. The regression model uses robust White estimators so that it meets the assumptions of heteroscedasticity and autocorrelation.

The regression models include perceived environmental uncertainty and competition intensity as external context factors. Both determinants do not show a significant association with the dependent variable COMP in neither of the two regressions so that the hypotheses H1a_1 and H1a_2 are rejected.

The MNC-specific contingency factors product diversity and the MNC's organizational complexity also yield no significant coefficients and thus do not provide evidence for H1b_1 and H1b_2. While the regression models do not indicate a significant association between IT system heterogeneity and COMP (H1b_3), there is a positive association between the **MNC's top management support** for the SSO and the PMS design in model (A)(coef. 0.238, $p < 0.01$) and (B) (coef. 0.303, $p < 0.01$). This finding corroborates with the results of the bivariate correlation analysis and the findings of the qualitative study. The predicted positive association is highly significant in both models at the 1% level and supports H1b_4. Hence, based on the theoretical foundation and the cross-case results, this finding suggests that the MNC's top management support encourages performance measurement actors to enhance the SSO's PMS design and to actively engage in the performance measurement process. Moreover, both regression models reveal a highly significant association of the **collaboration intensity between the MNC's group controlling and the SSO** and its PMS design. The predicted positive association is highly significant at the 1% level for model (A) (coef. 0.157, p < 0.01) and model (B) (coef. 0.168, p < 0.01) providing evidence for H1b_5. The result of the regression analysis coincides with the findings of the CommCo and the EngineerCo case studies indicating that an intense collaboration between the SSO and the group controlling is advantageous for the SSO's PMS design.

With regard to the SSO-specific context factors, model (A) neither unveils a significant association between the geographical dispersion of SSCs and PMS design in SSOs nor between its legal and economic independence and PMS design. However, both coefficients point in the right direction. By contrast, model (B) controls for the systematic differences across firms within an industry and country and reports that the **geographic dispersion of SSCs** is positively associated with its PMS design. This finding is significant at a 5% level (coef. 0.194, p < 0.05) so that model (B) supports H1c_1. The regression analysis substantiates the results of the ChemCo case study and fosters the assumption that geographical distance between SSCs creates information asymmetries which performance measurement actors intend to reduce through an elaborated PMS design. In addition, model (B) indicates that the **legal and economic independence of SSOs** is negatively associated with their PMS design. This association is significant at a 10% level and supports H1c_2 (coef. -0.079, p < 0.10). Thus, model (B) confirms the results of the CommCo and ChemCo case studies by stating that a clear delineation of (profit) responsibility facilitates the performance measurement process since less coordination effort is required. Notably, H1c_2 is an undirected hypothesis so that only for the negative direction a significant association could be found.

The results of both regression models do not provide support for a significant association between the dominating center concept in SSOs and COMP (H1c_3). Moreover, the analysis implies that the SSO's mono- or multigeographical (respectively mono- or multidivisional) service provision does not determine PMS design in SSOs (H1c_4). There is no significant association between an existing obligation to contract for SSO customers and PMS design in SSOs (H1c_5). Both regression models do not find a significant association between the design of the SLAs and the dependent variable even though the p-value is close to the ten per cent level (H1c_6). Furthermore, model (A) does not yield a significant association between the time spent of SSO management accountants for performance measurement tasks and COMP (H1c_7). By contrast, model (B) reveals the predicted significant positive association between the **time spent of SSO management accountants for performance measurement tasks** and PMS design in SSOs which is significant at a 10% level (coef. 0.083, p < 0.10). This finding confirms the results of the cross-case analysis and provides supporting evidence for H1c_7. The result suggests that a strong emphasis on performance measurement tasks of the involved actors promotes PMS design in SSOs. The regression tables do not indicate that the prevailing degree of process standardization in SSOs is associated with the PMS design in SSOs (H1c_8). Moreover, both models do not provide evidence for a significant association between the requirements of SSO customers and COMP (H1c_9).

By contrast, both models reveal a significant positive association between the existence of **power promotors** and PMS design in SSOs. Model (A) (coef. 0.165, p < 0.10) and model (B) (coef. 0.190, p < 0.05) corroborate with the results of the cross-case analysis and the promotor model on which hypothesis H1d_1 is based on. The results for H1d_1 suggest that the existence of power promotors fosters a pronounced PMS design in SSOs. The descriptive analysis of the survey findings and the case studies indicate that the SSO management and SSC managers are perceived as power promotors in SSOs. Thus, the regression analysis provides further support for the assumption that the presence of SSO managers, who act as sponsors for the SSO's PMS, has a positive impact on its design. However, the basic regression model does not yield significant associations between PMS design and know-how promotors (H1d_2) or process promotors (H1d_3). Finally, there is also no significant association between relationship promotors and PMS design in SSOs (H1d_4).

Apart from the context factors outlined in the hypotheses, the control variables included in the regression model (A) do not indicate significant associations with the dependent variable COMP. However, model (B) reveals a significant positive association between the **SSO size** (number of SSO employees) and its PMS design (coef. 0.284, p < 0.10). This result does not seem surprising due to the cross-case findings and prior contingency-based research (e.g. *Chenhall* (2003); *Richter/Brühl* (2016)).

In addition to the two models that examine the COMP score as a dependent variable, this section also exploits the three descriptively analyzed subscores (measures, process, actors). The subscore analysis serves to verify the robustness of the found associations in the two analyzed regression models and also to yield further associations between contingency factors and PMS design in SSOs.

Table 7.43 presents the regression models for the **three subscores** describing the dimensions performance measures (MEAS), performance measurement process (PROC), and performance measurement actors (ACT), which are denominated as the models (1), (2) and (3) in the following presentation of the results. The F-values differ significantly from zero, indicating a good fit of all three models. The p-values suggests that all subscore regression models are highly significant. The maximum VIF (9.08) is below the threshold of ten, suggesting that multicollinearity is not an issue. The regression models (2) and (3) show an adjusted R^2 of 89.70% (70.40%), implying a high explanatory power. Model (1) indicates a slightly lower adjusted R^2 of 69.74%. All models incorporate country and industry fixed effects. Again, the regression models use robust White estimators so that all models meet the assumptions of heteroscedasticity and autocorrelation.

The analysis of the three subscores reveals nine essential findings. First, the analysis of the subscore ACT in regression model (3) reveals a significant positive association between the **environmental uncertainty** perceived by the SSO managers and PMS design (coef. 0.476, $p < 0.10$). Hence, this finding provides supportive evidence for H1a_1, although the main score COMP does not show a significant association. This finding suggest that a high degree of environmental uncertainty perceived by SSO managers is associated with a high number of involved performance measurement actors.

Second, the results of the three subscore regression models provide support for the insights gained in the main regression models, emphasizing that the **support of the MNC's top management** are also significantly associated with PMS design (H1b_4). The support of MNC's top management is significantly associated with the performance measures in model (1) (coef. 0.438, $p < 0.01$), with the performance measurement process in model (2) (coef. 0.121, $p < 0.01$) and the performance measurement actors in model (3) (coef. 0.351, $p < 0.05$). Thus, the subscore analysis implies that all of the three conceptualized elements of

PMS design in SSO seem to be more pronounced when the MNC's top management provides support for the further development of the PMS.

Table 7.43: Regression analysis on determinants of PMS design – subscore analysis

			Regression analysis on determinants of PMS design – subscore analysis					
			Model 1 – MEAS			Model 2 – PROC		Model 3 – ACT	
H	Variables	E.S.	Coef.	t-value	Coef.	t-value	Coef.	t-value
H1a_1	Perceived environ-mental uncertainty	(+)	-0.086	(-0.27)	-0.074	(-0.66)	0.476	(2.01)*
H1a_2	Competition intensity	(+)	-0.339	(-1.41)	0.048	(0.71)	0.275	(1.04)
H1b_1	Product diversity	(+)	-0.002	(-0.02)	0.052	(1.33)	0.040	(0.47)
H1b_2	MNC orga-nizational complexity	(+)	0.524	(1.37)	-0.278	(-2.82)	-0.189	(-0.50)
H1b_3	MNC IT system heterogeneity	(+)	0.160	(1.11)	-0.066	(-1.87)	0.203	(1.56)
H1b_4	MNC top management support	(+)	0.438	(3.45)***	0.121	(3.05)***	0.351	(2.23)**
H1b_5	Group con-trolling col-laboration intensity	(+)	0.349	(3.34)***	0.098	(2.62)**	0.056	(0.54)
H1c_1	Geographical dispersion of SSCs	(+)	0.199	(1.62)	0.099	(3.28)***	0.283	(1.52)
H1c_2	SSO legal and economic independence	(+/-)	-0.080	(-1.00)	-0.038	(-1.65)	-0.118	(-1.43)
H1c_3	SSO center concept	(-)	-0.022	(-0.35)	-0.025	(-1.49)	0.078	(1.33)
H1c_4	SSO struc-tural complexity	(+)	-0.176	(-1.01)	-0.035	(-0.75)	-0.294	(-1.15)
H1c_5	Obligation to contract	(-)	-0.079	(-1.30)	0.012	(0.61)	-0.055	(-0.81)
H1c_6	SLA design	(+)	0.206	(1.82)*	0.045	(1.12)	0.059	(0.44)
H1c_7	Time spent on PMS tasks	(+)	0.051	(0.49)	0.078	(3.15)***	0.120	(1.31)
H1c_8	SSO customer requirements	(-)	-0.044	(-0.11)	-0.004	(-0.03)	0.003	(0.00)

Table 7.43: Continued

Regression analysis on determinants of PMS design – subscore analysis								
			Model 1 – MEAS		Model 2 – PROC		Model 3 – ACT	
H	Variables	E.S.	Coef.	t-value	Coef.	t-value	Coef.	t-value
H1c_9	Degree of process standardization	(+)	0.189	(0.83)	-0.086	(-1.06)	-0.112	(-0.50)
H1d_1	Power promotors	(+)	0.280	(1.59)	-0.092	(-1.30)	0.383	(2.02)*
H1d_2	Know-how promotors	(+)	-0.028	(-0.07)	0.313	(2.50)**	0.257	(0.71)
H1d_3	Process promotors	(+)	0.095	(0.36)	-0.028	(-0.39)	-0.115	(-0.50)
H1d_4	Relationship promotors	(+)	-0.053	(-0.46)	0.074	(2.20)**	0.071	(0.68)
Contr.	MNC size		-0.449	(-1.54)	0.144	(1.45)	0.337	(0.83)
Contr.	MNC group controlling size		-0.168	(-0.98)	0.037	(0.65)	-0.380	(-1.64)
Contr.	MNC organizational structure		-0.123	(-2.19)	-0.060	(-3.02)	-0.003	(-0.04)
Contr.	SSO size		0.464	(1.53)	0.106	(1.21)	0.283	(1.13)
Contr.	SSO maturity		0.031	(0.27)	-0.065	(-2.18)	-0.074	(-0.69)
	Constant		-0.133	(-0.36)	0.307	(2.31)	-0.470	(-1.12)
	Country fixed effects		YES		YES		YES	
	Industry fixed effects		YES		YES		YES	
	N		50		50		50	
	adj. R2		69.74%		89.70%		70.40%	
	F-stat		4.66		18.86		8.66	
	Prob > F		0.000		0.000		0.000	
	VIFmax		9.07		9.07		9.07	

Third, the regression models (1) and (2) confirm the results of the COMP score models (A) and (B) indicating that the **collaboration intensity between the MNC's group controlling department and the SSO** is positively associated with PMS design in SSOs (H1b_5). While the regression models (1) of the subscore MEAS (coef. 0.349, p < 0.01) and (2) of the subscore PROC (coef. 0.098, p < 0.05) reveal significant coeffecients, the regression analysis of the subscore ACT (model (3)) does not reveal a significant association between the two variables. This finding insinuates that an intense collaboration between the SSO and the group controlling amplifies the content of the PMS, such as the number of performance measures, and the performance measurement process, such as the intensity of the performance measure evaluation and the KPI reporting.

Fourth, the analysis of the subscore regression model (2) specifies that the significant positive association between the **geographic dispersion of SSCs** and PMS design revealed in model (B) of the COMP regression analysis is mainly driven by the subscore PROC (coef. 0.099, p < 0.01). By contrast, the regression models (1) and (3) do not find significant associations. This finding partially supports H1c_1 and indicates that the geographical distance between the SSCs is associated with the amplification of the performance measurement process. For example, a KPI reporting in multiple languages and an increased effort for the performance measure data collection process across several SSC locations in varying time zones requires a more advanced PMS design. Fifth, there is a significant positive association between SLA and PMS design in the regression model (1) for the subscore MEAS (coef. 0.206, p < 0.10). This result suggests that an elaborated **SLA design** is associated with a growing number of performance measures and performance measure categories, which provides some evidence for H1c_6. This finding is consistent with the results of the cross-case analysis since several SSO managers point out that service levels are regularly evaluated through performance measures, which are included in SLAs between the SSO and its customers. However, the regression models (2) and (3) for the subscores PROC and ACT do not display significant associations with SLA design.

Sixth, the regression analysis of model (2) for the subscore PROC points out that the found positive association between the **time spent of SSO management accountants for performance measurement tasks** and PMS design in SSOs found earlier is driven by the PROC score (coef. 0.078, p < 0.01). This finding suggests that a strong emphasis on performance measurement tasks of the involved actors is associated with an enhanced performance measurement process in SSOs. Hence, regression model (2) provides further supporting evidence for H1c_7. By contrast, no significant associations between the two variables can be found in model (1) and (3), although the coefficients point in the predicted direction.

Seventh, the regression analysis of the subscore ACT in model (3) confirm the significant positive association between **power promotors** and PMS design (coef. 0.383, p < 0.10). The supportive evidence for H1d_1 insinuates that the existence of power promotors is associated with a high number of involved performance measurement actors. This finding corroborates with the case study results as the SSO management accountants of MedTechCo and HealthCo illustrate that their SSO managers have to act as role models that engage in the performance measurement process if they intend to inspire potential performance measurement actors. By contrast, models (1) and (2) do not provide evidence for a significant association between the existence of power promotors and PMS design in SSOs.

Eighth, model (2) unveils a significant positive association between the existence of **know-how promotors** and the PROC score (coef. 0.313, $p < 0.05$). In accordance with the cross-case analysis, this association substantiates the assumption that the performance measurement process requires actors with a high degree of expertise, such as experts for the KPI analyses, benchmarking and reporting. Therefore, this finding partially supports H1d_2 and underpins the results of the qualitative study. Regression model (1) and (3) do not yield significant associations between know-how promotors and the subscores MEAS and ACT.

Ninth, model (2) indicates a significant positive association between the existence of **relationship promotors** and the PROC score (coef. 0.074, $p < 0.05$). This finding also substantiates the relevance of the promotor model. The result suggests that the existence of performance measurement actors who are willing and able to establish substantial relationships to other organizational units (e.g. SSC managers) is associated with an amplified performance measurement process. However, neither model (1) nor model (3) confirms the found association. Moreover, the cross-case analysis yields diverging results so that this finding has to be interpreted with caution.

In essence, the regression analyses of the three subscores supplements the outlined results of the COMP score regressions by contributing to a more detailed answer to the second research question. Having presented the results of the regression analyses on the determinants of PMS design in SSOs, the following section provides descriptive evidence on the effectiveness of PMS in SSOs.

7.4.3 Performance measurement effectiveness

7.4.3.1 Descriptive analysis

As described in the construct measurement, this study measures performance measurement effectiveness in two dimensions. **Goal attainment (GOA)** incorporates the objective achievement of the SSO and the goal attainment of the PMS objectives perceived by the SSO managers. **Satisfaction (SAT)** consists of the perceived overall satisfaction of the SSO managers and the perceived PMS acceptance. In addition, the descriptive analysis supplements the results of the questionnaire for the SSO managers with the answers of the SSO management accountants in order to compare both data sets.

Goal attainment

Overall, SSO managers indicate that their PMS supports them to achieve the SSO's objectives. In particular, SSO managers state that the PMS assisted them to **attain the goal** of cost reduction (4.8) and to ensure compliance with internal policies over the past three years (4.5) (table 7.44). Moreover, the PMS moderately supports SSO managers in increasing the SSO's customer satisfaction (4.4), standardizing and automating support processes (4.3) and increasing the motivation of SSO employees (4.3). However, the PMS of the SSOs seems to offer little support for the SSO managers when it comes to post-merger integrations (3.2).

With regard to the prevalence of SSO objectives, cost reduction (n = 65) and process standardization (n = 63) are most often mentioned by the SSO managers followed by compliance (n = 53) and customer satisfaction (n = 46). Notably, only a minority of the SSO managers defines increasing the satisfaction of SSO employees (n = 18) and facilitating post-merger integrations (n = 19) as SSO objectives.

Table 7.44: PMS support for SSO objectives perceived by managers

SSO managers: Please rank the SSO objectives according to their importance for the SSO. To what extent has the PMS supported you to reach the specified SSO objectives over the past 3 years?										
n = 71			Distribution (scale: 1 = not at all…7 = completely)							
	Mean	Std. dev.	1	2	3	4	5	6	7	Rank	n
Reduce costs	4.8	1.7	7%	3%	11%	11%	<u>34%</u>	14%	20%	1	65
Increase customer satisfaction	4.4	1.6	9%	4%	11%	24%	<u>24%</u>	22%	6%	2	46
Ensure compliance with internal policies	4.5	1.7	9%	6%	6%	19%	<u>32%</u>	19%	9%	4	53
Standardize & automate processes	4.3	1.8	15%	5%	3%	18%	<u>31%</u>	23%	5%	3	63
Increase employee satisfaction	4.3	1.8	11%	11%	6%	17%	<u>33%</u>	11%	11%	6	18
Facilitate post-merger integrations	3.2	1.7	21%	11%	<u>27%</u>	26%	5%	5%	5%	5	19

median underlined

Furthermore, the SSO managers rank cost reduction (1) and increasing the SSO's customer satisfaction (2) as particularly important. Despite SSO managers giving the second highest priority among all SSO objectives to an increasing customer satisfaction, their current PMS design supports them only to a limited extent (4.4). The high importance of customer satisfaction for SSO managers contradicts its consideration in the SSOs' PMS. The descriptive analysis on PMS design in SSOs revealed that, on average, only five performance measures are used to measure customer satisfaction, which is the second-lowest value of all performance measure categories.[42] Standardizing and automating support processes (3) as well as ensuring compliance with internal policies (4) rank behind cost reduction and customer satisfaction. In accordance with the low prevalence of the two SSO objectives among **SSO managers**, post-merger integrations and increasing the SSO employee satisfaction are ranked last.

Table 7.45 indicates similar results for the dataset of **SSO management accountants**. On average, SSO management accountants are slightly more satisfied with the support of the PMS to achieve the SSOs' objectives than SSO managers, but the p-values imply no significant differences in the mean comparisons for the six SSO objectives. Similar to the SSO managers, SSO management accountants value the support of the SSO's PMS for the objectives cost reduction (5.0) and compliance with internal policies (4.7) the most. By contrast, SSO management accountants perceive the PMS support for the standardization and automation of support processes as more helpful compared to the SSO managers (4.8), whereas the perceived PMS support for customer satisfaction is slightly weaker (4.3). Moreover, the perceived support of the SSO's PMS to attain the goals SSO employee satisfaction (4.5) and facilitating post-merger integrations (3.8) is also slightly stronger compared to the results of the SSO managers. Although the mean differences between the two datasets are not significant, it is plausible that the designer of the PMS is slightly more satisfied with the outcome of his work than the user.

---

42 Refer to section 7.4.1.1 (pp. 205 – 206).

Table 7.45: PMS support for SSO objectives perceived by management accountants

SSO management accountants: Please rank the SSO objectives according to their importance for the SSO. To what extent has the PMS supported you to reach the specified SSO objectives over the past 3 years?										
n = 53			Distribution (scale: 1 = not at all...7 = completely)							
	Mean	Std. dev.	1	2	3	4	5	6	7	Rank	n
Reduce costs	5.0	1.6	4%	2%	10%	15%	<u>29%</u>	19%	21%	1	48
Increase customer satisfaction[a]	4.3	1.4	5%	8%	10%	<u>28%</u>	28%	18%	3%	2	39
Ensure compliance with internal policies[b]	4.7	1.5	3%	6%	9%	21%	<u>29%</u>	23%	9%	4	34
Standardize & automate processes[c]	4.8	1.5	4%	2%	15%	17%	<u>31%</u>	19%	12%	3	48
Increase employee Satisfaction[d]	4.5	1.6	9%	0%	14%	18%	<u>27%</u>	27%	5%	5	22
Facilitate post-merger integrations[e]	3.8	1.4	0%	23%	23%	<u>23%</u>	16%	15%	0%	6	13

median underlined

Notes: Mean differences between datasets (p-values): [a] = 0.38, [b] = 0.73, [c] = 0.47, [d] = 0.24, [e] = 0.66, [f] = 0.46

Regarding the importance of the SSO objectives, the ranking of the SSO management accountants remains the same as for the SSO managers by one exception. Increasing the SSO employee satisfaction is ranked as more important (5), whereas the post-merger integration ranks last (6).

Most SSO managers use their PMS to identify room for improvement for their processes (table 7.46). Consistently, this **PMS objective** has the highest priority and is also being pursued by the SSOs with the highest intensity among all PMS objectives (5.4). Apart from the identification of potential for process optimization (1), the majority of the SSO managers stresses that the communication of results is of significant importance (2) and also pursued with a high intensity (5.0). Moreover, attaining learning effects for SSO employees (3) and understanding causal connections (4) constitute important objectives. Both PMS objectives are pursued with a moderate intensity (4.6 and 4.8). By contrast, the motivation of employees (5) and the sharing of knowledge and information

(6) is of minor importance to SSO managers. Consequently, the motivation of SSO employees is pursued less intensively according to the SSO managers (4.4). The descriptive findings reveal that the importance of the PMS objectives ranked by the SSO managers is not always consistent with the pursued intensity. For example, **SSO managers** intensively pursue the sharing of knowledge and information with their PMS (5.0), even though they do not assign a high priority to this objective. Concurrently, they pursue the achievement of learning curve effects with a lower intensity.

Table 7.46: PMS objectives and pursuance perceived by managers

SSO managers: Please rank the PMS objectives according to their importance for the SSO. How intensively do you pursue the specified PMS objectives of your SSO?											
n = 71			Distribution (scale: 1 = not at all intensive...7 = very intensive)								
	Mean	Std. dev.	1	2	3	4	5	6	7	Rank	n
Identify process improvements	5.4	1.5	1%	6%	4%	2%	34%	25%	28%	1	65
Motivate employees	4.4	1.3	5%	0%	19%	19%	38%	19%	0%	5	21
Communicate results	5.0	1.4	2%	6%	6%	14%	30%	30%	12%	2	50
Attain learning effects for SSO employees	4.6	1.3	3%	6%	6%	26%	37%	17%	5%	3	35
Understand causal relations	4.8	1.4	2%	7%	9%	11%	35%	29%	7%	4	45
Encourage the sharing of information and knowledge	5.0	1.0	0%	0%	10%	17%	41%	28%	4%	6	29

median underlined

The **SSO management accountants** confirm the assessment of the SSO managers (table 7.47). However, there are three major differences between the two datasets. First, the SSO management accountants state that the communication of results is the PMS objective which is pursued with the highest intensity (5.7) so that the identification of improvement potentials for the SSOs' support processes is ranked second, although SSO management accountants and SSO managers indicate the same level of intensity (5.0). A t-test unveils that the mean differences between both datasets with regard to the perceived intensity of communicating results are significant on a 95% level. This finding suggests that SSO management accountants perceive the intensity of communicating results significantly higher compared to the SSO managers. Moreover, the SSO management accountants perceive the intensity for the objectives knowledge and information sharing (5.3), understanding causal relations (5.1) and attain learning effects for SSO employees (5.0) slightly higher than the SSO managers. Second, SSO management accountants rate the intensity by which the SSO uses the PMS to motivate employees also higher (4.9). Third, understanding causal relations (3) by using the PMS has a higher priority for SSO management accountants than for SSO managers, whereas learning curve effects rank lower in the dataset of the SSO management accountants (4). Apart from this minor difference, both groups consent on the importance of the PMS objectives. Notably, only the mean difference with regard to the PMS objective to communicate results is statistically significant.

Table 7.47: PMS objectives and pursuance perceived by management accountants

SSO management accountants: Please rank the PMS objectives according to their importance for the SSO. How intensively do you pursue the specified PMS objectives of your SSO?										
n = 53			**Distribution (scale: 1 = not at all intensive…7 = very intensive)**							
	Mean	**Std. dev.**	**1**	**2**	**3**	**4**	**5**	**6**	**7**	**Rank**	**n**
Identify process improvements[a]	5.4	1.4	0%	2%	13%	8%	23%	<u>27%</u>	27%	1	48
Motivate employees[b]	4.9	1.1	0%	0%	14%	18%	<u>45%</u>	14%	9%	5	22
Communicate results[c]	5.7	1.2	0%	0%	9%	5%	25%	<u>30%</u>	31%	2	44
Attain learning effects for SSO employees[d]	5.0	1.4	0%	10%	4%	10%	<u>43%</u>	20%	13%	4	30
Understand causal relations[e]	5.1	1.3	0%	3%	12%	15%	<u>27%</u>	31%	12%	3	31
Encourage the sharing of information and knowledge[f]	5.3	1.2	0%	0%	7%	19%	<u>26%</u>	33%	15%	6	27

median underlined

Notes: Mean differences between datasets (p-values): [a] = 0.91, [b] = 0.33, [c] = 0.02**, [d] = 0.28, [e] = 0.50, [f] = 0.26

Satisfaction

SSO managers (4.3) and SSO management accountants (4.2) are moderately satisfied with their PMS (table 7.48). As highlighted in the tables 7.49 and 7.50, the **degree of satisfaction** stems from different sources. The perception of both respondent groups does not differ significantly. However, this finding may be subject to a tendency to the mean so that it should be interpreted with caution.

Table 7.48: PMS satisfaction

	Overall, how satisfied are you with the PMS of your SSO?								
	Distribution (scale: 1 = highly dissatisfied...7 = highly satisfied)								
	Mean	Std. dev.	1	2	3	4	5	6	7	n
SSO managers	4.3	1.2	1%	6%	18%	<u>30%</u>	24%	21%	0%	71
SSO management accountants	4.2	1.3	0%	15%	15%	<u>21%</u>	32%	17%	0%	53

Note: Mean differences between datasets (p-values): 0.62 median underlined

The perceived **acceptance of the PMS** by SSO employees displays a similar picture (table 7.49). The PMS acceptance of the SSO management accountants (4.3) is slightly higher than the acceptance of the SSO managers (4.1). Again, a tendency to the mean seems to be an issue. The p-values do not indicate a significant deviation between both datasets.

Table 7.49: PMS acceptance

	To what extent do SSO employees accept the PMS?								
	Distribution (scale: 1 = not at all...7 = completely)								
	Mean	Std. dev.	1	2	3	4	5	6	7	n
SSO managers	4.1	1.1	0%	10%	15%	<u>37%</u>	28%	10%	0%	71
SSO management accountants	4.3	1.2	0%	10%	15%	<u>28%</u>	30%	17%	0%	53

Note: Mean differences between datasets (p-values): 0.40 median underlined

Having outlined the descriptive findings on PMS effectiveness, the following section concludes with a regression analysis that examines associations between PMS design and its effectiveness.

7.4.3.2 Regression analysis

This section addresses the third research question by investigating whether PMS design is associated with performance measurement effectiveness.

Table 7.50 outlines the regression models for the **performance measurement effectiveness**, which are subdivided into model (A) for the perceived goal attainment and model (B) for the perceived satisfaction. Both models indicate F-values differing significantly from zero (model A: 7.43; model B: 5.80), suggesting a good fit of the regressions. The maximum VIF (9.37) is below the threshold of ten for both models, which implies that multicollinearity seems not to be an issue. The regression models use robust White estimators so that both models meet the assumptions of heteroscedasticity and autocorrelation. Both regression models (A) and (B) display an acceptable adjusted R^2 of 73.11% (A) and 62.96% (B), indicating that PMS design and the determinants of PMS design explain in both models to a large extent variances in the perceived performance measurement effectiveness. Notably, the regression models (A) and (B) analyze solely whether the association between the independent variable PMS design in SSOs (COMP) and the dependent variables goal attainment (GOA) and satisfaction (SAT) is significant, in order to test hypothesis H2. All other variables serve merely as control variables to improve the explanatory power of the regression models, since this study does not aim to state a hypotheses about associations between contingency factors (such as SLA design in SSOs) and performance measurement effectiveness. The explicative results on the impact of PMS determinants on PMS design in SSOs have been detailed in section 7.4.2.3. As outlined before, the number of observations is restricted to 50 due to the dyadic research design.

The dependent variable GOA (model (A)) combines two forms of goal attainment. The first indicator measures the extent to which SSOs achieve their objectives according to the SSO managers and the second indicator measures the extent to which the objectives associated with the implementation of a PMS have been achieved. Both indicators are equally weighted in the GOA score. The regression analysis of model (A) reveals a significant association between the **SSO managers' goal attainment** and PMS design (coef. 0.850, $p < 0.05$). This finding suggests that a well-marked PMS design supports SSO managers to achieve their goals. Hence, the results of the regression analysis provides supporting evidence for H2.

The dependent variable SAT (model (B)) also combines two indicators. The first indicator measures the **SSO managers' satisfaction** with regard to their PMS. The second indicator measures the extent to which the PMS finds acceptance among the SSO employees. Again, both indicators are equally weighted in

Table 7.50: Regression analysis on performance measurement effectiveness

			Model (A) – GOA		Model (B) – SAT	
H	**Variables**	**E.S.**	**Coefficient**	**t-value**	**Coefficient**	**t-value**
H2	PMS design (COMP)	(+)	0.850	(2.32) **	0.408	(0.65)
	Perceived environmental uncertainty		0.124	(0.62)	0.146	(0.28)
	Competition intensity		-0.219	(-1.47)	-0.343	(-1.09)
	Product diversity		-0.051	(-0.80)	-0.078	(-0.61)
	MNC organizational complexity		0.238	(1.17)	0.454	(0.80)
	MNC IT system heterogeneity		-0.258	(-2.89)	-0.210	(1.51)
	MNC top management support		-0.090	(-0.72)	-0.208	(-0.84)
	Group controlling collaboration intensity		-0.002	(-0.02)	0.073	(0.44)
	Geographical dispersion of SSCs		-0.153	(-1.63)	-0.097	(-0.37)
	SSO legal and economic independence		0.066	(1.11)	-0.045	(-0.32)
	SSO center concept		-0.060	(-1.35)	-0.020	(-0.23)
	SSO structural complexity		0.070	(0.57)	0.220	(0.88)
	Obligation to contract		0.005	(0.12)	0.058	(0.68)
	SLA design		0.073	(0.71)	0.196	(0.95)
	Time spent on PMS tasks		-0.074	(-0.94)	0.116	(0.90)
	SSO customer requirements		0.118	(0.47)	0.767	(1.34)
	Degree of process standardization		0.068	(0.36)	0.151	(0.44)
	Power promotors		0.098	(0.61)	0.105	(0.39)
	Know-how promotors		-0.416	(-1.42)	0.121	(0.19)
	Process promotors		0.118	(0.72)	-0.073	(-0.19)
	Relationship promotors		-0.232	(-2.41)	-0.121	(-0.68)
	MNC size		-0.101	(-0.42)	-0.145	(-0.37)
	MNC group controlling size		0.287	(1.97)	0.107	(0.52)
	MNC organizational structure		-0.050	(-0.96)	-0.024	(-0.28)
	SSO size		-0.255	(-0.97)	-0.151	(-0.36)
	SSO maturity		0.033	(0.39)	-0.134	(-0.88)
	Constant		0.347	(1.35)	-0.126	(-0.24)
	Country fixed effects		YES		YES	
	Industry fixed effects		YES		YES	
	n		50		50	
	adj. R2		73.11%		62.96%	
	F-stat		7.43		5.80	
	Prob > F		0.000		0.000	

Table heading (spanning): Regression analysis on the effectiveness of PMS design in SSOs the SAT score. The regression analysis of model (B) does not show a significant association between the SSO managers' satisfaction and PMS design, although the coefficients point in the expected direction (coef. 0.408, p > 0.10). Therefore, regression model (B) does not yield supporting evidence for H2. In essence, the results of both regression models partially support H2.

In both regressions a few control variables are significantly associated with the dependent variables GOA and SAT. However, those significant associations are not subject to this study's research questions since the research questions do not investigate the coherence between, for example, SSO size and the SSO manager's goal attainment.

In order to elaborate on the results of the two regression models on performance measurement effectiveness and to yield further evidence, this study also analyzes potential associations between the three elements of PMS design in SSOs (measures, processes and actors) and its effectiveness (table 7.51 to 7.53). The F-values differ significantly from zero, indicating a good fit of all three models. The p-values suggests that all subscore regression models are highly significant. The regression models show an adjusted R^2 of 68.87% (62.80%), implying a high explanatory power.

The extended analysis of the three **performance measurement subscores** (MEAS, PROC and ACT) yields a significantly positive association between GOA and MEAS implying that particularly the performance measures foster a higher goal attainment of the SSO managers (coef. 0.356, p < 0.05). Thus, it is conceivable that PMS contents, such as the number of performance measures and the considered performance measurement categories assist SSO managers to attain their goals. However, the analysis of the subscores PROC and ACT do not find a significantly positive association between the performance measurement process as well as the performance measurement actors in SSOs and the SSO managers' goal attainment (GOA), although the coefficients point in the predicted direction. In addition, the association between the subscore ACT and the SSO managers' goal attainment is almost significant at a 10% level. Furthermore, there is no significant association between the three subscores (MEAS, PROC, ACT) and the SSO managers' satisfaction (SAT), which is in line with table 7.50.

The small sample size of 50 observations suggests an **extended descriptive analysis** to grasp a better understanding of the found association between PMS design in SSOs and performance measurement effectiveness. The extended descriptive analysis subdivides the sample of the 50 SSOs into two groups of 25 SSOs in order to describe the results of the regression analyses on performance measurement effectiveness more precisely (table 7.54). The first group consists of 25 SSOs with a lower PMS design score (mean of group 1: 0.34). The second group of 25 SSOs has a higher PMS design score (mean of group 2: 0.51).

Table 7.51: Regression analysis on PMS effectiveness – subscore analysis MEAS

H	Variables	E.S.	GOA Coefficient	GOA t-value	SAT Coefficient	SAT t-value
				Regression analysis on the effectiveness of PMS design- subscore MEAS		
H2	Performance measures (MEAS)	(+)	0.356	(2.15) **	0.197	(0.61)
	Perceived environmental uncertainty		0.244	(1.25)	0.206	(0.37)
	Competition intensity		-0.102	(-0.53)	-0.279	(-0.91)
	Product diversity		-0.025	(-0.33)	-0.065	(-0.52)
	MNC organizational complexity		0.067	(0.28)	0.359	(0.73)
	MNC IT system heterogeneity		-0.231	(-2.37)	-0.202	(-1.12)
	MNC top management support		0.012	(0.10)	-0.172	(-0.74)
	Group controlling collaboration intensity		0.017	(0.17)	0.072	(0.44)
	Geographical dispersion of SSCs		-0.059	(-0.59)	-0.057	(-0.25)
	SSO legal and economic independence		0.027	(0.45)	-0.061	(-0.45)
	SSO center concept		-0.043	(-0.97)	-0.012	(-0.13)
	SSO structural complexity		-0.011	(-0.08)	0.186	(0.78)
	Obligation to contract		-0.001	(-0.02)	0.057	(0.65)
	SLA design		0.087	(0.79)	0.197	(0.93)
	Time spent on PMS tasks		-0.022	(-0.27)	0.140	(1.06)
	SSO customer requirements		0.121	(0.46)	0.770	(1.36)
	Degree of process standardization		-0.002	(-0.01)	0.112	(0.32)
	Power promotors		0.160	(0.97)	0.127	(0.48)
	Know-how promotors		-0.252	(-0.82)	0.201	(0.34)
	Process promotors		0.071	(0.40)	-0.098	(-0.26)
	Relationship promotors		-0.187	(-1.89)	-0.098	(-0.55)
	MNC size		0.068	(0.24)	-0.052	(-0.15)
	MNC group controlling size		0.202	(1.37)	0.070	(0.38)
	MNC organizational structure		-0.056	(-1.30)	-0.025	(-0.30)
	SSO size		-0.179	(-0.66)	-0.127	(-0.31)
	SSO maturity		-0.008	(-0.09)	-0.155	(-1.05)
	Constant		0.310	(1.10)	-0.140	(-0.26)
	Country fixed effects		YES		YES	
	Industry fixed effects		YES		YES	
	n		50		50	
	adj. R2		68.87%		62.82%	
	F-stat		3.47		6.21	
	Prob > F		0.003		0.000	

Table 7.52: Regression analysis on PMS effectiveness – subscore analysis PROC

H	Variables	E.S.	GOA Coefficient	GOA t-value	SAT Coefficient	SAT t-value
	Regression analysis on the effectiveness of PMS design- subscore PROC					
H2	PM process (PROC)	(+)	0.842	(1.08)	-0.486	(-0.47)
	Perceived environmental uncertainty		0.276	(1.55)	0.153	(0.29)
	Competition intensity		-0.264	(-1.41)	-0.322	(-1.01)
	Product diversity		-0.069	(-0.92)	-0.040	(-0.33)
	MNC organizational complexity		0.488	(1.53)	0.328	(0.51)
	MNC IT system heterogeneity		-0.118	(-1.40)	-0.202	(-1.17)
	MNC top management support		0.012	(0.46)	-0.026	(-0.12)
	Group controlling collaboration intensity		0.058	(0.71)	0.189	(1.27)
	Geographical dispersion of SSCs		-0.072	(-0.49)	0.030	(0.14)
	SSO legal and economic independence		0.031	(0.46)	-0.095	(-0.71)
	SSO center concept		-0.030	(-0.79)	0.028	(-0.31)
	SSO structural complexity		-0.044	(-0.31)	0.134	(0.55)
	Obligation to contract		-0.039	(-0.71)	0.047	(0.50)
	SLA design		0.123	(1.17)	0.260	(1.26)
	Time spent on PMS tasks		-0.069	(-0.65)	0.188	(1.14)
	SSO customer requirements		0.109	(0.35)	0.760	(1.30)
	Degree of process standardization		0.137	(0.69)	0.108	(0.31)
	Power promotors		0.337	(1.81)	0.138	(0.46)
	Know-how promotors		-0.526	(-1.38)	0.347	(0.47)
	Process promotors		0.128	(0.83)	-0.093	(-0.25)
	Relationship promotors		-0.268	(-2.16)	-0.072	(-0.36)
	MNC size		-0.213	(-0.84)	-0.070	(-0.16)
	MNC group controlling size		0.110	(0.93)	0.056	(0.28)
	MNC organizational structure		-0.051	(-0.87)	-0.079	(-0.80)
	SSO size		-0.103	(-0.37)	0.016	(0.04)
	SSO maturity		0.058	(0.53)	-0.181	(-1.17)
	Constant		0.004	(0.01)	-0.017	(-0.03)
	Country fixed effects		YES		YES	
	Industry fixed effects		YES		YES	
	n		50		50	
	adj. R2		65.63%		62.42%	
	F-stat		4.72		5.93	
	Prob > F		0.000		0.000	

Table 7.53: Regression analysis on PMS effectiveness – subscore analysis ACT

			GOA		SAT	
H	**Variables**	**E.S.**	**Coefficient**	**t-value**	**Coefficient**	**t-value**
H2	PM actors (ACT)	(+)	0.258	(1.61)	0.175	(0.60)
	Perceived environmental uncertainty		0.091	(0.43)	0.106	(0.21)
	Competition intensity		-0.294	(-1.77)	-0.394	(-1.18)
	Product diversity		-0.036	(-0.49)	-0.072	(-0.55)
	MNC organizational complexity		0.303	(1.44)	0.496	(0.84)
	MNC IT system heterogeneity		-0.226	(-2.50)	-0.205	(-1.12)
	MNC top management support		0.078	(0.70)	-0.146	(-0.76)
	Group controlling collaboration intensity		0.127	(1.40)	0.131	(0.93)
	Geographical dispersion of SSCs		-0.062	(-0.72)	-0.067	(-0.27)
	SSO legal and economic independence		0.029	(0.50)	-0.056	(-0.41)
	SSO center concept		-0.071	(-1.49)	-0.030	(-0.33)
	SSO structural complexity		0.002	(0.01)	0.202	(0.84)
	Obligation to contract		-0.015	(-0.29)	0.051	(0.59)
	SLA design		0.145	(1.52)	0.227	(1.14)
	Time spent on PMS tasks		-0.035	(-0.53)	0.129	(1.00)
	SSO customer requirements		0.105	(0.35)	0.761	(1.29)
	Degree of process standardization		0.094	(0.43)	0.169	(0.47)
	Power promotors		0.161	(0.94)	0.116	(0.41)
	Know-how promotors		-0.329	(-1.12)	0.150	(0.25)
	Process promotors		0.134	(0.79)	-0.059	(-0.16)
	Relationship promotors		-0.224	(-2.01)	-0.121	(-0.66)
	MNC size		-0.179	(-0.68)	-0.199	(-0.47)
	MNC group controlling size		0.240	(1.51)	0.104	(0.47)
	MNC organizational structure		-0.102	(-2.10)	-0.049	(-0.58)
	SSO size		-0.087	(-0.29)	-0.085	(-0.22)
	SSO maturity		0.022	(0.23)	-0.136	(-0.86)
	Constant		0.384	(1.33)	-0.085	(-0.16)
	Country fixed effects		YES		YES	
	Industry fixed effects		YES		YES	
	n		50		50	
	adj. R2		68.75%		62.67%	
	F-stat		3.85		5.82	
	Prob > F		0.002		0.000	

Table 7.54: Extended descriptive analysis on performance measurement effectiveness

	n	Mean PMS design score	P-value	Mean GOA Score	P-value	Mean SAT Score	P-value
Extended descriptive analysis on performance measurement effectiveness							
Low PMS design score	25	0.34		0.36		0.51	
High PMS design score	25	0.51	0.00 ***	0.44	0.01 **	0.59	0.11

Two results are drawn from this supplementary descriptive analysis. First, the comparison of the GOA score between the two groups underpins the findings of the regression analyses. SSOs with a higher PMS design score also have a higher GOA score. Second, the group of SSOs with the higher PMS design score also has a higher SAT score, although the difference between the two groups is at conventional levels statistically not significant.

Several SSO managers voiced doubts during the case study interviews that more performance measures are inevitably better. Some experts stated that too many involved performance measurement actors can also be ineffective. Hence, the following analysis investigates whether a higher PMS design score is always associated with a higher perceived performance measurement effectiveness (table 7.55). Therefore, this study divides the sample of 50 SSOs into four groups based on the PMS design score quartiles. The first quartile has the lowest PMS design score (0.28), the second quartile has an under average PMS design score (0.40), the third quartile has an above PMS design score (0.46), while the fourth quartile of SSOs has the highest PMS design score (0.57).

Table 7.55: Diminishing marginal utility of PMS design in SSOs

	N	Mean PMS design score	Diff.	Mean GOA Score	Diff.	Mean SAT Score	Diff.
Diminishing marginal utility of PMS design in SSOs							
Lowest PMS design score	13	0.28		0.36		0.46	
Under average PMS design score	12	0.40	+ 0.12	0.36	+/- 0	0.56	+ 0.10
Above average PMS design score	12	0.46	+ 0.06	0.45	+ 0.09	0.60	+ 0.04
Highest PMS design score	13	0.57	+ 0.11	0.43	- 0.02	0.58	- 0.02

Comparing the PMS design scores of the groups with their corresponding scores for goal attainment and managerial satisfaction offers a few interesting insights. Although the average PMS design score increases by 0.12 between the first and second quartile, the GOA score remains unchanged between the two quartiles. By contrast, the SAT score increases by 0.10. This result indicates that extending a PMS, which is only rudimentarily developed, serves rather the SSO managers' satisfaction than a higher goal attainment. A comparison of the second (PMS design score under average) and the third quartile (above average) illustrates that the GOA and the SAT score increase by 0.06 (0.04). However, a comparison between the third and the fourth quartile reveals that the GOA and the SAT score slightly decrease, although the PMS design score between both quartiles increases by 0.11. This contrary tendency suggests that managerial satisfaction and goal attainment are perceived a little lower by SSO managers with the most advanced PMS compared to SSO managers with an above average PMS design. In essence, this descriptive finding suggests a diminishing marginal utility for PMS design in SSOs.

Due to the small sample size, the descriptive results cannot be analyzed in an additional regression analysis. However, the findings of the supplementary descriptive analyses on performance measurement effectiveness may trigger future research on a **diminishing marginal utility of PMS design in SSOs**.

Having presented the empirical results, the following section outlines a comprehensive discussion of the findings.

7.4.4 Summary and discussion

This section is subdivided into five parts and discusses the empirical results from different angles. First, the qualitative and quantitative findings are integrated to emphasize converging, complementary and diverging results of both research approaches. Second, this section discusses possible reasons why some of the hypotheses are not supported by the regression analyses. Third, the findings are discussed with reference to prior research. Fourth, the results are discussed with reference to the theoretical framework on which this study is based. Fifth, this section stresses the particularities of PMS design in SSOs.

7.4.4.1 Integration of the qualitative and the quantitative findings

PMS design in SSOs

The cross-case analysis and the survey findings unveil large differences between the SSOs with regard to the number of **performance measures** in their PMS. The samples of both research approaches emphasize the prevalence of non-financial process and quality measures. The survey findings complement the results of the cross-case analysis by describing that other performance measure categories, such as customer and employee satisfaction measures, are indeed used less intensively than process-related performance measures, but are still included in the most PMS of the SSOs. The qualitative findings mirror the survey results by illustrating that SSOs rarely link performance measures to remuneration systems.

With regard to the **performance measurement process** the quantitative and the qualitative analyses describe that most SSOs use different approaches to select performance measures for their PMS, even though brainstorming sessions are most commonly applied. The survey findings and the case study results indicate that performance measure targets are based on previous year's figures and the process manager's experience. As opposed to the case studies, the quantitative study finds that management expectations are also regularly taken into account when setting performance measure targets. The survey analysis reveals that the data collection from back-end systems, the merging of different data sources into the target system and data editing require the most time to collect performance measure data. Whereas the survey findings suggest a rather high automation degree for the data collection of performance measures, the cross-case analysis yields diverging results since the majority of the case companies struggle to automate the performance measure data collection due to large data volumes and a heterogeneous IT-landscape. The case studies mirror the findings of the quantitative study stating that variance analyses and time-series comparisons are most frequently used in SSOs to analyze performance measures. In contradistinction to the interviews with the experts of the case companies the survey results find that benchmarking is barely used for the performance measure analysis. The quantitative and the qualitative study describe that SSOs report their KPIs mainly on a monthly basis. The case studies supplement the survey results stating that performance measures with reference to customer and employee satisfaction are reported in larger time intervals since the data required for those KPIs is usually collected through questionnaires. Both studies emphasize that the PMS modification is a rather disregarded part of the performance measurement process. In addition to the survey findings, the cross-case analysis shows that the combination of few but extensive PMS modifications suggests a *big bang* instead of a continuous improvement of the SSO's PMS.

Both studies show that the SSO management board, the SSC managers, the process managers and the SSO management accountants are the most prevalent **performance measurement actors**. The quantitative and the qualitative analysis stresses that the SSO management board and the SSC managers are predominately involved in the performance measure selection, the target setting and the revision process. In addition to the survey findings, the case studies indicate a strong engagement of the process managers in the target setting process. As opposed to the survey results, the case studies find that process managers commonly analyze performance measures. Both studies indicate that SSO management accountants are usually responsible to collect performance measure data and to analyze KPIs. Moreover, the cross-case analysis mirrors the survey findings by stating that a substantial proportion of the SSOs in both samples do not employ SSO management accountants.

Determinants of PMS design in SSOs

The quantitative and qualitative analysis of the **external contingency factors** describes that SSO managers perceive their environment as neither predictable nor unpredictable. However, the regression analysis of the PMS design subscore ACT unveils that a rather unpredictable environment perceived by SSO managers is associated with a high number of involved actors in the performance measurement process. This finding suggests that SSO managers intend to encounter the perceived uncertainty by involving more performance measurement actors.

With respect to the **MNC-specific context factors**, both studies reveal a rather high degree of product differentiation and competition intensity for both sample's MNCs. Moreover, the studies find that matrix organizations prevail as the MNCs' organizational setup. The cross-case findings supplement the survey results by indicating that MNCs with matrix organizations are exposed to various interfaces which increases the MNCs' organizational complexity. As opposed to the case study results, the survey study suggests a rather harmonized IT-infrastructure. The cross-case analysis describes that SSOs struggle with multiple ERP-systems and additional interfaces which negatively impacts PMS design. However, this finding is not supported by the regression analysis. By contrast, the qualitative study corroborates with the descriptive survey results with regard to the significance of the MNC's top management support for the SSO's PMS design. In addition, the regression analyses find a significant positive association between the MNC's top management support and the PMS design suggesting that top management support promotes a more pronounced PMS design in SSOs. This finding is valid for the three PMS design subscores (measures, processes, actors). The association between top management support and PMS design is strengthened by the results of the bivariate correlation analysis.

The case studies find little evidence for a close cooperation between the SSO and the group controlling. By contrast, the regression analysis unveils that a close cooperation between the SSO and the group controlling department is positively associated with PMS design indicating that an intense collaboration between both organizations enhances particularly the PMS content, such as the number and diversity of performance measures as well as the performance measurement process.

Regarding the **SSO-specific context factors** the survey findings support the results of the cross-case analysis stating that the majority of both samples' SSOs establish their SSCs geographically dispersed. Both studies find that many SSOs have nearshore SSCs. Moreover, a considerable proportion of SSOs in both samples establishes SSCs in remote regions. The case study analysis complements the quantitative findings by indicating that smaller SSOs locate one of their SSCs next to the headquarters' site. In addition, both studies illustrate that the SSCs provide their services for multiple operational functions and to several regions. The regression analysis yields a significant positive association between the geographic dispersion of SSCs and PMS design which supports the assumption that SSOs especially enhance the performance measurement process to cope with information asymmetries that emerge due to the geographical distance. Both studies describe that about half of the SSOs operate as a legally and economically independent entity. Moreover, the regression analysis finds a negative association between the legal and economic independence of SSOs and its PMS design suggesting that legal and economic independence simplifies the design of the PMS since less coordination effort with other organizational units is required.

Furthermore, the quantitative and the qualitative analysis unveils that the majority of the managers use cost centers for controlling their SSOs. In a similar vein, both studies find that the majority of the MNCs obliges their internal customers to contract with the SSO. The cross-case analysis extends this finding by illustrating that SSO managers use the contract obligation to secure a minimum transaction volume. The qualitative findings mirror the survey results with regard to the prevalence of SLAs as an important tool to define the relationship between the SSO and its customers. The SSO managers of both samples state that SSO customers are particularly demanding with regard to a timely service provision and the service quality. In addition, the regression analysis of the PMS design subscores yields a positive association between SLAs and PMS design in SSOs. This finding indicates that an elaborated SLA design in SSOs fosters the content of the PMS since service levels are monitored with performance measures of the SSO's PMS.

In accordance with the findings that a significant proportion of the SSOs has neither employed management accountants nor implemented a PMS, both samples describe that almost half of the SSOs do not have a SSO controlling department. The case study results add to this finding by describing that SSO managers refrain from the establishment of a SSO controlling department because they fear the costs associated with the setup. The quantitative and the qualitative study illustrate that SSO management accountants primarily perform genuine controlling tasks, such as cost accounting, budgeting, reporting and KPI analyses. The regression analysis unveils a significant positive association between the time a SSO management accountant spends on PMS tasks and PMS design in SSOs which reinforces the assumption that a strong focus on KPI analyses and reporting of the involved performance measurement actors enhances PMS design in SSOs. Furthermore, both studies suggest that SSO managers perceive the support processes performed by their SSOs as rather standardized although the quantitative analysis unveils a higher degree of formal standardization compared to the degree of factual standardization.

The survey study underpins the results of the cross-case analysis with regard to the promotor model. Both studies indicate that the SSO executive board and the SSC managers are perceived as power promotors who support performance measurement in SSOs by means of financial and personnel resources. Moreover, the cross-case analysis complements this result by illustrating that the absence of power promotors leads to dissatisfaction with regard to the PMS design in SSOs. The regression analysis finds a positive association between power promotors and PMS design in SSOs which suggests that SSO managers who act as sponsors of the PMS encourage other actors to become more involved in the performance measurement process. Moreover, the descriptive evidence of both studies illustrates that process managers contribute with their process-specific expertise to the SSO's PMS by acting as know-how promotors. The regression analysis of the PMS design subscores reveals a positive association between the existence of know-how promotors and the performance measurement process which indicates that process managers contribute to an amplified PMS design with their knowledge during the KPI target setting and analysis process.

The quantitative and the qualitative analysis describe that SSC managers and process owners foster PMS design by coordinating performance measurement activities by slipping into the role of process promotors. Both studies yield ambiguous results with regard to potential relationship promotors so that a specific performance measurement actor cannot be assigned. Under the precondition that a performance measurement actor can be considered as a relationship promotor, the regression analysis of the PMS design subscores yields a positive association between the existence of relationship promotors and PMS design in SSOs. This finding substantiates the hypothesis that performance measurement actors who are willing to establish meaningful relationships to other organizational units promote the performance measurement process. The collaboration between different organizational units (e.g. the accounts receivable department and the customer service) in the performance measurement process enables a better understanding of causal relationships between performance measures (for instance, a quick handling of complaints in the customer service department lowers the number of dunning letters sent by mistake).

Performance measurement effectiveness

With regard to the **PMS effectiveness**, the descriptive evidence of the survey and the case studies indicate that SSO managers perceive the SSO's PMS as rather effective since it assists them to attain the SSO objectives. In particular, both studies emphasize that the PMS provides support to achieve the SSO's objectives of cost reduction and compliance. Moreover, most SSO managers in both studies state that they intend to enable process improvements, gain transparency and communicate results by implementing a PMS. However, several SSO managers of the case companies voiced doubts on whether the PMS ensures process transparency and thus allows to detect causal relations. This may be a reason why SSO managers of both samples are only moderately satisfied with their PMS. Another reason for a moderate PMS satisfaction may be found in the discrepancy between the significance of a PMS objective according to the SSO managers and the intensity with which the objective is pursued. Furthermore, the regression analysis substantiates the descriptive evidence of both studies by revealing that PMS design is positively associated with the goal attainment perceived by the SSO managers. This finding suggests that an amplified PMS supports SSO managers to achieve their objectives. However, an extended descriptive analysis of the regression results suggests a diminishing marginal utility of PMS design in SSOs.

7.4.4.2 Review of the results

Hypotheses not supported by the empirical findings

The research design and the course of the study offer five possible explanations why ten **hypotheses are not supported** by the results. First, the small sample size could have a negative effect on the results of the multivariate regression analyses. A total of 74 SSO managers and management accountants completed a survey. However, the dyadic research design requires two surveys for each MNC: one for the independent variables (SSO managers) and one for the dependent variables (SSO management accountants). Due to the dyadic research design only 50 pairs of surveys are usable for the regression analyses. Although a dyadic research design offers advantages concerning the common method bias, it impinges on the survey sample size.

Second, the validity of the constructs under research may be limited. Proxies simplify the underlying construct so that the construct does not always exactly measure what it is supposed to measure. The more abstract a construct, the more difficult is a precise construct measurement. This concern might especially affect the hypotheses on the organizational complexity of the MNC and on the structural complexity of the SSO since both are not supported by this study's results.

Third, the fact that predominately hypotheses with reference to external and MNC-specific contingency factors find little supportive evidence suggests that SSO managers struggle to give meaningful survey answers concerning external and MNC-specific contextual factors. It seems to be easier for SSO managers to answer questions on SSO-specific contingency factors than answering questions on the MNC's competition intensity or product diversity. This may be due to the fact that SSO managers are more familiar with their direct surroundings. Fourth, the descriptive findings of some determinants indicate that a tendency to the mean could be an issue. The error of central tendency implies that the survey responses have only small variances, which may also impair the results of the regression analyses. Fifth, some of the case companies' experts seize several contingency factors as powerful determinants of PMS design, such as the IT system heterogeneity or the degree of process standardization, which is not confirmed to the same extent by the SSO managers who are part of the survey study.

Table 7.56 summarizes the results of the hypotheses tests. For eleven hypotheses the regression analyses finds supportive evidence, whereas ten hypotheses are not supported.

Table 7.56: Summary of the hypotheses testing

Summary of the hypotheses testing				
			Effectiveness	
Hypothesis	Variable	Result	Goal attainment	Satisfaction
H_{1a_1}	Perceived environmental uncertainty	**partially supported** (0.59)		
H_{1a_2}	Competition intensity	not supported (0.76)		
H_{1b_1}	Product diversity	not supported		

(continued on next page)

Table 7.56: Continued

| | Summary of the hypotheses testing | | | |
| | | | Effectiveness | |
Hypothesis	Variable	Result	Goal attainment	Satisfaction
H_{1b_2}	MNC organizational complexity	not supported		
H_{1b_3}	MNC IT system heterogeneity	not supported		
H_{1b_4}	MNC top management support	**supported**		
H_{1b_5}	Group controlling collaboration intensity	**supported**		
H_{1c_1}	Geographical dispersion of SSCs	**partially supported**		
H_{1c_2}	SSO legal and economic independence	**supported**		
H_{1c_3}	SSO center concept	not supported		
H_{1c_4}	SSO structural complexity	not supported		
H_{1c_5}	Obligation to contract	not supported		
H_{1c_6}	SLA design	**partially supported**		
H_{1c_7}	Time spent on PMS tasks	**supported**		
H_{1c_8}	SSO customer requirements	not supported		
H_{1c_9}	Degree of process standardization	not supported		
H_{1d_1}	Power promotors	**supported**		
H_{1d_2}	Know-how promotors	**partially supported**		
H_{1d_3}	Process promotors	not supported		
H_{1d_4}	Relationship promotors	**partially supported**		
$H_{2\_1/2}$	Effectiveness	**partially supported**	**supported**	not supported

Reference to prior research

Prior research that is most closely related to this study are *Kagelmann* (2001), *Sterzenbach* (2010) and *Gleich* (2001). The studies by *Kagelmann* (2001) and *Sterzenbach* (2010) use a comparable research design with regard to the SSO-specific determinants. The study of *Gleich* (2001) shows similarities with regard to the descriptive investigation of PMS design. As outlined in the state of research, however, an empirical study that combines the two essential elements *PMS design* and *SSOs* does not exist. Moreover, the descriptive evidence of the three studies is not comparable with this study's descriptive results since the mentioned studies are based on different samples. The study of *Sterzenbach* (2010) focuses on determinants of the SSO controlling in a broader sense so that PMS design plays only a subordinate role in his empirical analysis. The explicative analysis of *Gleich* (2001) applies a different operationalization of PMS design so that his findings seem to be also comparable only to a limited extent. Unfortunately, there is no prior research related to PMS design in SSOs that applies a MMRD so that this study's integrated results are difficult to compare with the aforementioned studies.

Hence, even though *Sterzenbach's* contribution does not find a significant association between SSO controlling and the SSO's legal and economic independence, his finding does not necessarily contradict this study's finding regarding the legal and economic independence of SSOs. By contrast, the found positive association between perceived environmental uncertainty and PMS design is in line with prior research. Several authors indicate that a higher degree of perceived environmental uncertainty is associated with more elaborated MCS (*Chapman* (1998); *Chenhall/Morris* (1986); *Gordon/Narayanan* (1984)). Moreover, prior research emphasizes the prevalence of non-financial measures in corporate practice (*Bhimani* (1994), p. 36; *Fowler* (1996), p. 54; *Grüning* (2002), p. 150). Therefore, the descriptive evidence that non-financial measures dominate the SSO's PMS also is in line with prior research on PMS design.

Reference to the theoretical framework

The discussion of the results with reference to the theoretical framework provides some support for the underlying theoretical assumptions.

The empirical findings of the regression analyses stressed the importance of contextual factors that determine PMS design in SSOs and its effectiveness. Since the results of the regression analyses support the majority of the outlined hypotheses, the findings seem to be consistent with the underlying **contingency framework**. This allows for the conclusion that an effective PMS design in SSOs depends on its environment. Due to the contingency framework's lack of analytical specificity, this study's theoretical framework rests on the three theoretical pillars NIS, agency theory and the promotor model.

NIS offers reasonable explanations that SSO managers (institutional actors) use the SSO's PMS (i.e. a MCS) to reduce environmental uncertainty. In accordance with NIS, the regression analyses reveal that environmental uncertainty perceived by SSO managers is associated with a more sophisticated PMS design in terms of involved performance measurement actors. Furthermore, the regression analyses indicate that a close cooperation between the SSO and the group controlling department is positively associated with the SSO's PMS design. Imitating the PMS of the MNC's group controlling reduces the risk for the SSO management to be called into question by the MNC's management. Thus, this finding is in line with NIS, since isomorphism is a reasonable strategy as it is economic for the SSO to mimic the MNC's PMS. Moreover, the basic assumption of institutional isomorphism implies that SSO managers intend to cope with the expectations of the MNC's top management. The more the SSO's PMS meets the expectations of the MNC's top management, the more likely it is that the MNC management will support the SSO's PMS. The regression analyses supports the notion of institutional isomorphism suggesting a significant positive association between the MNC's top management support for the SSO's PMS design.

Due to manifold information asymmetries among the SSO actors, **agency theory** constitutes the second theoretical pillar on which the empirical study is based. PMS design is a potential means of mitigation for problems that emerge in principal-agent relationships in SSOs. The descriptive findings reveal that geographical distance between the SSCs creates a higher information asymmetry between the SSO management (principals) and the SSC heads (agents) compared to a pure onshore SSO so that a more elaborated PMS design promises to be a remedy for moral hazard. SSC heads use the PMS reporting to signal towards the SSO management that the SSC acts in line with the SSO's interest. By contrast, the SSO management uses the PMS to monitor whether the SSC's actions are consistent with the SSO's objectives. The regression analysis yields a significant positive association between the geographic dispersion of SSCs and PMS design. This finding reinforces the presumption that PMS design in SSOs reduces information asymmetries which occur due to the geographical distance. Furthermore, the positive association between SLA design and PMS design addresses the relationship between SSO customers (principals) and SSO managers (agents). A sophisticated PMS design that encompasses process quality and customer satisfaction measures signals that the SSO acts on behalf of its customers.

In light of the PAT, the descriptive findings suggest that the low coupling of performance measures and variable remuneration may induce moral hazard, such as shirking. Even though principal agent theory may allege reasons for a variable remuneration on a larger scale, the findings indicate that SSOs seem to reserve such compensation schemes only for senior hierarchical levels.

The third theoretical pillar constitutes the **promotor model** which serves as a basis to analyze the associations between PMS promotors and PMS design in SSOs. The promotor model allows for the assumption that SSO managers act as power promotors as their hierarchical position enables them to allocate financial and personnel resources to the PMS design in SSOs. In accordance with the promotor model, the regression analyses find a positive association between power promotors and PMS design in SSOs. Moreover, the regression models of the PMS design subscores reveal a positive association between the existence of know-how promotors and the performance measurement process. The descriptive evidence reveals that process owners commonly have a pronounced understanding of the SSO's processes so that they are able to define and analyze performance measures. The findings of the regression analyses indicate that process managers contribute as know-how promotors to an amplified PMS design. Furthermore, the regression analyses of the PMS design subscores yield a positive association between the existence of relationship promotors and PMS design in SSOs. This finding is consistent with the underlying promotor model. By contrast, this study could not find explicative evidence for a positive association between process promotors and PMS design in SSOs. This could be explained by the circumstance that SSO management accountants who typically act as process promoters do not exist in many SSOs of this study's sample.

Characteristics of PMS design in SSOs

The presented results provide some indications for a discussion on potential **characteristics of PMS design in SSOs.**

The prevailing number of process-related performance measures in SSOs stands out with regard to the descriptive findings. A vast number of process-related KPIs underpins the importance for SSOs to improve process and service quality as well as to automate and standardize the MNCs' support processes. The strong focus on process KPIs may set the PMS design in SSOs apart from other PMS, for example the PMS on group level. However, a strong emphasis on a single performance measure category may lead to an underrepresentation of other SSO objectives in the PMS, such as enhancing the SSOs' risk management. The high number of operational performance measures may also be attributable to the geographical dispersion of SSCs which subsequently leads to a dispersion of the performance measurement actors. As unveiled by the regression analyses, geographical distance between performance measurement actors adds complexity to the performance measurement process which increases the need for process-specific performance measures.

Apart from the geographical dispersion of SSCs, SSOs provide services to a demanding customer base of different regions and business segments. The wide coverage of performance measure categories could be another peculiarity of PMS design in SSOs. For example, PMS on group level rarely include KPIs with reference to process quality and automation since process quality performance measures are rather required for operational control. By contrast, PMS for production plants barely incorporate performance measures for customer satisfaction or organizational development. In addition, the descriptive analysis finds that PMS modification is a rather neglected part in the performance measurement process of SSOs. Although SSOs seldom modify their PMS they tend to make extensive modifications instead of continuously improving it. Since the literature rather assumes a continuous PMS improvement, *big bang* PMS modifications seem to be another characteristic of the performance measurement process in SSOs.

Moreover, the strong integration of process managers in the performance measurement process seems to be a characteristic of PMS in SSOs. The regression models revealed that process managers act as know-how promotors in all parts of the performance measurement process (target setting, data collection, analysis and modification). This characteristic is closely related to the low involvement of SSO management accountants with regard to PMS design in SSOs. The descriptive findings demonstrate that many SSOs engage in performance measurement activities without employing SSO management accountants in their organization. In line with this finding, many SSOs have not established a SSO controlling department. In general, the results reveal a rather low institutionalization of performance measurement in SSOs which constitutes another particularity of PMS design.

Finally, the feedback of the non-respondents indicates a considerable number of SSOs which neither pursue performance measurement activities nor have a PMS. This finding implies that such organizations may prefer other MCS for behavioral control and decision-making or do not use MCS at all. The low institutionalization of PMS design in SSOs is remarkable since SSOs are not a completely new phenomenon in corporate practice and are constantly growing in terms of the number of SSOs and their importance for MNCs.

8 Conclusions

This study analyzes PMS design in SSOs of MNCs. Drawing on the empirical results, this chapter summarizes the main findings and elaborates on their implications. Moreover, this chapter illustrates this study's contribution to existing research. It discusses limitations of this study and considers avenues for future research.

8.1 Main findings and implications

In recent years, SSOs are of growing relevance in research and corporate practice. On the one hand, MNCs combine a number of benefits by implementing SSOs, such as cost reductions, process quality improvements and an improved risk management. On the other hand, MNCs voice concerns about potential negative impacts on the MNC's effectiveness due to a lowered service quality and a lack of acceptance among employees. A major reason for the ongoing controversy of the SSOs' outcome is closely related to the shortcoming of measuring their performance. Hence, the SSOs' relevance in corporate practice contradicts the uncertainty about its effectiveness to drive the MNC's success.

To date, literature on MCS in SSOs is substantially characterized by anecdotal evidence. There is little evidence on current performance measurement practices in SSOs. Hence, PMS design in SSOs marks a blind spot in prior MCS research. Moreover, evidence on determinants of PMS design in SSOs and its effectiveness remains scarce. Therefore, this study pursued the following three research objectives to reduce the research gap:

- an explorative descriptive analysis of the current PMS design in SSOs;
- an explicative analysis of potential determinants on PMS design in SSOs;
- an explicative analysis of associations between PMS design and its effectiveness.

The three outlined research objectives necessitated two different research approaches. This study employed a MMRD that combined case study and survey research in a sequential exploratory research design. The applied research design enabled a more exhaustive analysis of performance measurement practices in SSOs compared to an isolated analysis of the three research objectives. The integration of qualitative and quantitative findings allowed for a triangulation of the empirical findings.

The empirical analyses required a **conceptual foundation** which was detailed in chapter two. The second chapter illustrated the most important characteristics of SSOs and discussed the major objectives of this new organizational form. Moreover, the second chapter also described the three essential components of PMS design (measures, processes, actors). Chapter three reviewed the most **relevant empirical literature** related to PMS design and SSOs. In line with the research design, the literature review was structured according to qualitative and quantitative studies. The review uncovered the existing research gap and refined the research design. The fourth chapter developed a **sound theoretical foundation** and presented contingency theory, NIS, agency theory and the promotor model as a solid basis for the developed hypotheses. Chapter five presented this study's research design. It introduced case study and survey research and detailed the applied **MMRD**. The sixth chapter provided the first part of the **case study analyses** on firm level. The second part derived implications from a detailed cross-case analysis. Furthermore, chapter six refined the basic hypotheses. Chapter seven provided **descriptive evidence** on PMS design in SSOs and descriptively analyzed its contingency factors. Moreover, the seventh chapter investigated in an explicative analysis whether potential **determinants** are associated with PMS design. Finally, chapter seven analyzed whether PMS design is associated with its **effectiveness**.

Main findings

The analysis of the three research questions revealed the following major findings:

RQ 1   How are PMS in SSOs designed?

The empirical analysis of the first research question unveiled four major findings which are related to the underlying conceptual framework of PMS design in SSOs (measures, processes, actors).

First, the case study analyses and the descriptive survey results suggested large differences among SSOs with regard to the **performance measures**. The number of performance measures incorporated in the PMS varied significantly across the SSOs. The findings indicated that process related, non-financial performance measures dominate the SSOs' PMS. Moreover, PMS of SSOs commonly entail a wide range of performance measure categories so that most PMS not only contain process-related and financial KPIs, but also KPIs with reference to customer satisfaction, risk management and organizational development.

Second, the descriptive evidence on the **performance measurement process** revealed that the modification of the SSO's PMS is a rather disregarded part of the performance measurement process. As a consequence, the number of KPIs in a SSO's PMS grows over time. Moreover, the findings suggest that SSOs tend to modify their PMS seldom but in an extensive manner instead of pursuing a continuous PMS improvement.

Third, the descriptive analysis unveiled that the SSO management board, SSC managers, process managers and SSO management accountants are the most prevalent **performance measurement actors** in SSOs. However, the analysis found that a considerable number of SSOs do not employ management accountants.

Fourth, the feedback of the non-respondents described that a significant proportion of the SSOs do not have a PMS in place. Moreover, this study found that almost half of the SSOs do not have a SSO controlling department, which suggests a low institutionalization of performance measurement practices in SSOs.

RQ 2   What determines the design of PMS in SSOs?

This study employed multiple regression analyses which revealed that **ten determinants** are associated with PMS design in SSOs.

The analysis of **external and MNC-specific determinants** unveiled that a rather unpredictable environment perceived by SSO managers is associated with a high number of involved actors in the performance measurement process. Thus, SSO managers tend to encounter uncertainty by involving more performance measurement actors. Moreover, this study found a significant positive association between the MNC's top management support and PMS design suggesting that perceived top management support promotes an elaborated PMS design. Furthermore, the regression analysis revealed that a close cooperation between the SSO and the group controlling department is a determinant of PMS design. An intense collaboration between both organizations expands particularly the number and diversity of performance measures.

The analysis of the **SSO-specific determinants** found that geographic distance between SSCs is a contingency factor for PMS design. This finding supports the assumption that SSOs enhance their PMS to cope with information asymmetries that arise from geographical distance. Moreover, the legal and economic independence of SSOs determines PMS design. Furthermore, the results revealed that the use of SLAs is positively associated with PMS design in SSOs. This finding implies that the use of SLAs in SSOs fosters PMS design since service levels are commonly monitored with performance measures of the SSO's PMS. In addition, the empirical analysis unveiled a significant association between the time a SSO management accountant spends on PMS tasks and PMS design in SSOs which reinforces the assumption that a strong focus on KPI analyses and reporting of the involved performance measurement actors enhances PMS design in SSOs.

In accordance with the **promotor** model, this study found that power promotors determine PMS design in SSOs which suggests that SSO managers who act as sponsors of the PMS foster PMS design. In addition, the analyses revealed that know-how promotors are another contingency factor for PMS design indicating that process managers who act as know-how promotors contribute to an amplified PMS design with their process-specific knowledge. Finally, the results substantiated the hypothesis that relationship promotors are a contextual factor that is positively associated with PMS design.

RQ 3   What determines the PMS effectiveness in SSOs?

The descriptive analysis unveiled that SSO managers consider a PMS as effective if their PMS enables them to initiate process improvements, gain transparency and communicate results. Moreover, this study found descriptive evidence that the SSOs' PMS provide support for SSO managers to achieve the objectives of cost reduction and compliance. In addition, the regression analysis on performance measurement effectiveness revealed that PMS design determines the SSO managers' goal attainment. Hence, an advanced PMS contributes to a more effective goal attainment of the SSO managers. However, this study also found some evidence for a diminishing marginal utility for PMS design in SSOs, which raises doubts whether a more advanced PMS design (e.g. more performance measures) is always more effective.

Implications

This study's results yields five implications for SSO managers as the users of the SSOs' PMS and for SSO management accountants as the designers of the SSOs' PMS. The first three implications are addressed to SSO managers and the latter two are directed to SSO management accountants.

First, this study highlighted that **SSO managers** benefit from an advanced PMS design. Therefore, it is striking that about one third of the surveyed SSOs did not implement a PMS although it is associated with a higher managerial goal attainment. Moreover, about half of the surveyed SSOs do not have a controlling department and do not employ SSO management accountants despite the growing relevance of SSOs for its MNCs. Hence, this study's results might encourage SSO managers to institutionalize PMS in their organizations. Since the coordination of the SSO's performance measurement seems a genuine task of SSO management accountants, SSO managers may foster the institutionalization of performance measurement activities in a SSO controlling department. A separate organizational controlling unit within the SSO promises a distinct area of responsibility and contributes to a professionalization of performance measurement tasks in SSOs.

Second, the findings unveiled that PMS in SSOs grow over time. SSO managers should not hesitate to eliminate measures that have become superfluous. This study's results provided some evidence for a diminishing marginal utility of PMS design, which also applies to the number of performance measures in a PMS. If the number of performance measures becomes too large, it is barely feasible for SSO managers to draw meaningful conclusions from it and to derive actions. A steadily growing number of performance measures involves the danger that performance measure data are collated for their own sake. Hence, SSO managers may pay attention if previously created measures are still required and if the number of performance measures is still at a manageable level.

Third, the analysis found that promotors have a positive impact on PMS design. The descriptive and explicative evidence emphasized the importance of power and know-how promotors for PMS design in SSOs. The case study results coincided with the findings of the quantitative study. Moreover, the within-case analysis provided two examples which illustrate the problems that arise in the performance measurement process if PMS promotors cannot be found within the SSO. The within-case analyses described that without power and know-how promotors, SSOs run the risk that performance measurement activities are discontinued. Therefore, SSO managers should act as power promotors for their PMS by providing financial and personnel resources for its development. In addition, it is essential for the PMS design that SSO managers identify potential know-how promotors in their organization and encourage other performance measurement actors to become a promotor of the SSO's PMS.

Fourth, this study revealed that PMS modifications are a rather ignored part of the performance measurement process in SSOs. **SSO management accountants** rarely adjust the PMS. The descriptive evidence exposed that *if* SSO management accountants modify the SSO's PMS, they have to make substantial changes. The findings with regard to the PMS modification frequency and extent imply conflicting goals for SSO management accountants. In correspondence with this study's contingency framework, SSO management accountants need to adapt their performance measures if SSOs change strategies due to an altering environment. However, they also need to convey steadiness to PMS reporting recipients in order to enable an enhanced understanding of trends over time. Hence, SSO management accountants should direct their attention to a continuous but less extensive PMS modification.

Fifth, this study illustrated the prevalence of non-financial, process-specific performance measures as a particularity of PMS in SSOs. The strong focus on process KPIs is certainly beneficial to achieve the SSO objectives process standardization, process automation and process quality. Yet, the analysis emphasized that SSO managers pursue further objectives in their SSOs. Particularly, compliance with applicable laws, accounting standards and internal guidelines is of significance for SSO managers. However, the descriptive evidence on PMS design in SSOs suggested an underrepresentation of performance measures which are not related to process improvements. In particular, PMS contain only few performance measures with reference to risk management and organizational development. Therefore, SSO management accountants may ensure that their PMS adequately covers the area of risk management. In essence, SSO management accountants should pay attention that the SSO's PMS is in the right balance of performance measures.

Contribution

The contribution of the empirical findings to the existing research is threefold.

First, this study's results go beyond prior research by offering a **comprehensive descriptive overview** of PMS design in SSOs and its determinants. The effort associated with primary data collection pays off with a detailed understanding of the performance measure composition, an in-depth analysis of the performance measurement process and a sound description of the essential performance measurement actors in SSOs. The focus on PMS design adds to the nascent research stream that analyzes MCS in SSOs. The detailed descriptive analysis revealed some particularities of PMS design in SSOs, such as the emphasis on process-related performance measures and the strong integration of process managers in the performance measurement process.

This study's results broaden prior research by revealing **SSO-specific determinants** that are associated with PMS design. The results of the determinant analysis have implications for researchers and practitioners. For researchers, the results of this study are useful because some of the SSO-specific determinants associated with PMS design have not yet been tested for other MCS. For SSO managers and management accountants, the determinant analysis revealed some of the aforementioned implications for PMS design in SSOs.

Moreover, this study contributes to the existing body of performance measurement literature by investigating the **promotors** of the performance measurement process in SSOs. To date, this study is the first to explore the influence of promotors on PMS design and their role in the performance measurement process. Therefore, this study provides first insights that especially power and know-how promotors play an important role for PMS design in SSOs. In addition, this study provides explicative evidence that performance measurement effectiveness is affected by its design. The additional descriptive analyses on performance measurement effectiveness ensure a more differentiated interpretation of the findings so that this study provides some initial evidence for a diminishing marginal utility of PMS design in SSO.

Second, this study is the first in SSO research that uses a MMRD which allows for the triangulation of qualitative and quantitative findings. The combination of qualitative and quantitative results in one **research design** yields a more complete picture of PMS design in SSOs. The within-case analysis provides valuable insights into the specific context of a MNC in which performance measurement takes place and adds to existing contingency-based MCS research. Moreover, the within-case analysis illustrates the different perspectives of the performance measurement actors on PMS design in their SSOs. Therefore, the within-case analysis yields some good examples of best practices, but also unveils some pitfalls which should be avoided by practitioners. The cross-case analysis systematically outlines commonalities and differences in the PMS design between the case companies. The integration of the cross-case results and the quantitative findings is beneficial to the explanatory power of this study's results. Furthermore, the triangulation of the quantitative and qualitative results might be useful for researchers because diverging results are a trigger for further research. In addition, the applied dyadic survey research design allows for the separation of the designer and the user of the SSO's PMS and may thus provide more reliable results compared to other research designs since it avoids common method bias.

Third, this study offers a **sound conceptualization of PMS design** by dividing PMS design into the three components measures, processes and actors. Based on this conceptualization, this study uses a PMS design score to analyze PMS design in SSOs. Since the PMS design score is applicable to other settings, this study may contribute to the measurability and comparability of PMS design. Finally, the explicative results provide some evidence for the underlying theoretical framework. Thereby, this study's findings contribute to the existing body of research on PAT, NIS and the promotor model.

8.2 Limitations and outlook

Limitations

The research design entails seven major limitations. Five limitations are associated with the survey results, whereas the latter two refer to the applied MMRD.

First, the **generalizability** of the results may be constrained. This study investigates SSOs of MNCs from Germany, Austria, and Switzerland. Therefore, it seems questionable whether this study's results generalize to other settings. Performance measurement may be perceived very differently in another cultural context. For example, countries with a tendency towards uncertainty avoidance may associate informal discussions on performance measures with emotional stress and thus avoid this element of the performance measurement process.

Second, the rather small **sample size** is an issue in this study and may impair the reliability of the findings. In general, primary data collection in management accounting research often involves small sample sizes. Although a total of 74 MNCs participated in this study, only 50 MNCs completed both questionnaires. Albeit the number of observations is consistent to the central limit theorem, a small sample size implies that hypotheses are rejected more frequently compared to studies with a large sample size, in which even small effect sizes may be statistically significant. By contrast, all MNCs in Germany, Austria and Switzerland with more than € 100 million annual sales were asked to participate in this research project so that probably only a few MNCs operating with a SSO were not covered by this study. Hence, the basic population seems rather small.

Third, another limitation of this study consists in **endogeneity**. The applied dyadic research design may mitigate endogeneity through common method bias. However, the explicative studies only yield statistical associations so that causal claims cannot be inferred based on the results. Moreover, reversed causality could be an issue in the explicative analyses. As a consequence, PMS design may determine top management support and not, as expected, vice versa.

Fourth, this study uses proxies to operationalize the conceptualized constructs into survey items. Therefore, proxies have to simplify the underlying construct so that a discrepancy between the gauged proxy and the real life phenomenon may emerge. As a consequence, the **validity of the measurement constructs** may be restricted. Moreover, this study remains silent whether all important variables are captured. Furthermore, the formation of a PMS design score always remains a subjective endeavor.

Fifth, the survey results may suffer from **response biases**. Even though the non- and late response bias tests do not reveal differences in the respondents' response style, there may be other biases, such as extreme response styles or central tendency biases. Although this study identified experts as survey respondents for both questionnaires, this research design is not able to control whether the identified respondent completed the survey.

Sixth, case study research also entails some drawbacks which might constrain the explanatory power of the case study results. The sample **selection rationale** for the case companies might be an issue. Although this study details its case study sample selection criteria transparently, the case selection is neither mutually exclusive nor collectively exhaustive. Furthermore, this study uses expert interviews to collect the data for the case study analysis. However, face-to-face interviews and the applied structuring-thematic coding are exposed to subjectivity as the researcher in qualitative research approaches takes an active part in the research process.

Seventh, the integration of qualitative and quantitative results might lead to a **flawed interpretation of the findings**. Although a MMRD allows to triangulate the empirical findings of both approaches, the interpretation of the results that combine the expert testimonials with the survey results may be biased. Since expert statements largely refer to personal opinions, this approach cannot rule out alternative interpretations for the quantitative descriptive evidence. By contrast, this study pursues an embedded sampling strategy, implying that qualitative findings emanate from MNCs which also participated in the quantitative study.

Outlook

The limitations reveal four potential **avenues for future research**.

First, future studies may use a similar research design in a **different setting** to address the possibly impaired generalizability of this study. Given the SSCs' geographical dispersion, future SSO research on performance measurement may focus on other intercultural settings. Cultural factors, such as language and local particularities may affect PMS outcome. Moreover, other cultural settings may have other performance measurement traditions, which could impact PMS design. Empirical studies on differing cost accounting traditions suggest a potential influence of culture on PMS design (*Schulz* (2018); *Schröder* (2015)).

Second, future research on the SSO's performance measurement may draw on **longitudinal studies** in order to unveil long-term effects of the SSO's performance measurement initiatives. Furthermore, this study's research design could not derive causal inferences. Therefore, future studies may employ experimental research designs in which researchers are able to control for most conditions. As this study concentrates on performance measurement effectiveness by analyzing the SSO managers' goal attainment and their satisfaction, experimental research designs may use other proxies for effectiveness instead (e.g. observable capital market measures).

Third, this study's descriptive findings on a **diminishing marginal utility of PMS design** in SSOs suggest that SSO managers may challenge whether the benefits of an advanced PMS design justifies the invested effort. Thus, future studies may draw on explicative analyses to further investigate whether PMS effectiveness is affected by a diminishing marginal utility.

Fourth, future studies may address other MCS since prior research indicates that SSOs use an entire set of MCS to control their organization. Furthermore, future research may analyze **MCS as a package** as suggested by *Malmi* and *Brown* (*Malmi/Brown* (2008), p. 291). This study focused on already implemented PMS in SSOs. Therefore, future qualitative research may investigate how PMS are implemented in SSOs.

Appendix A

Performance Measurement in Shared Service Organizations

Interview Guideline

Company / City: _____

Interviewee / Function: _____

Date / Time: _____

Definition of Terms

Performance Measurement: A Performance Measurement System quantifies the efficiency and/or effectiveness of actions based on performance measures.

Shared Service Organization: A Shared Service Organization (SSO) consolidates and performs support processes for more than one organizational unit and operates like a business under market conditions to enhance the efficiency and effectiveness of its corporation. A SSO may consist of more than one Shared Service Center (SSC) at different locations.

I Context of the Performance Measurement System

A Company Context

1. How would you describe the fundamentals of your group organization?
2. How do you assess the IT landscape of your finance, accounting and controlling organization?

B Shared Service Center Organization

3. How would you describe the fundamentals of your SSO?
4. Which processes have been integrated in your SSO and which processes are you planning to integrate in the next three years?
5. To what extent does your SSO use outsourcing partners for the execution of sub-processes?
6. Please explain briefly the design of your SSC controlling.
7. How would you describe the collaboration between the group and SSC controlling?

II Objectives

1. Which objectives does your SSO pursue and how would you prioritize them?
2. What role does process standardization play for the objectives of your SSO?

Figure A-1 (1/2): Interview guideline

III Design of the Performance Measurement System

1. How would you describe the fundamentals of your Performance Measurement System (PMS)?
2. How many performance measures do you use to control your SSO?
3. How do you collect the performance measures?
4. How important are non-financial performance measures for your SSO??
5. What are the main criteria for selecting performance measures?
6. How do you collect and prepare the data for the calculation of your SSO's performance measures?
7. How do you analyze performance measures?
8. To what extent does your SSO use benchmarking to analyze performance measures?
9. How and to whom are performance measures and their development communicated?
10. To what extent and in which frequency do you modify your PMS?
11. To what extent is the PMS of your SSO linked to other PMS in the group?
12. Which particularities has the PMS of your SSO compared to other PMS in your group?

IV Impact on success

1. What characterizes a good PMS in your opinion?
2. How satisfied are you currently with your PMS?
3. Where do you see room for improvement for your PMS?
4. How do you assess the acceptance of your SSO's PMS among the SSO employees?

Figure A-1 (2/2): Interview guideline

Appendix B

WESTFÄLISCHE
WILHELMS-UNIVERSITÄT
MÜNSTER

IUR
Lehrstuhl für Internationale
Unternehmensrechnung
Prof. Dr. Peter Kajüter

Performance Measurement in Shared Service Organizations

Motivation

This questionnaire is part of an international research project conducted by the Chair of International Accounting at the University of Münster (Germany). The objective of this research project is to analyze the design of performance measurement in shared service organizations in multinational corporations. Therefore, contextual factors as well as information about the design of the performance measurement and its effects are surveyed.

Contents:

A	Information about your company
B	Information about your Shared Service Organization (SSO)
C	Effects on the Performance Measurement System (PMS)
D	Personal Information

Please note:

This questionnaire is **strictly confidential**. All data will be aggregated and used for statistical purposes only. Results are published exclusively in aggregated form such that conclusions on individual persons or companies cannot be drawn. Personal information is solely collected to ensure the quality of the survey.

This questionnaire is designed for companies of different sizes. It is therefore possible that certain questions do not apply to your company or appear to be unnecessary to you. For this research project, however, **complete** and **truthful** answers are of utmost importance. If you have little or no information to answer certain questions, we would like to ask you for your **subjective assessment**. Please tick the correct answer(s) or enter your details in the appropriate boxes.

For questions and suggestions please do not hesitate to contact:

Friedrich Kalden

E-Mail: friedrich.kalden@wiwi.uni-muenster.de

Telephone: +49 (0)251/ 83 22815

Figure B-1 (1/7): Survey SSO manager

Definition of terms

Performance Measurement System (PMS): A Performance Measurement System quantifies the efficiency and/or effectiveness of actions based on performance measures.

Shared Service Organization (SSO): A Shared Service Organization consolidates and performs support processes for more than one organizational unit and operates like a business under market conditions to enhance the efficiency and effectiveness of its corporation. A SSO may consist of more than one Shared Service Center (SSC) at different locations.

Section A - Information about you company

A.1	To what extent do the products/services of your company differ on average in their...	1 = not at all, ... completely = 7						
		1	2	3	4	5	6	7
	... development processes?	□	□	□	□	□	□	□
	... manufacturing processes?	□	□	□	□	□	□	□
	... sales and distribution processes?	□	□	□	□	□	□	□

A.2	Please provide the following information for the previous fiscal year of your group: (If you are not aware of the exact numbers, approximate numbers are sufficient.)
	Number of fully consolidated subsidiaries: _____ (subsidiaries)
	Number of countries in which your group operates: _____ (countries)

A.3	To what extent do the following statements describe your area of responsibility?	1 = not at all, ... completely = 7						
		1	2	3	4	5	6	7
	In order to fulfil my projects/tasks successfully, I have to exchange ideas with many employees.	□	□	□	□	□	□	□
	My job profile changes frequently.	□	□	□	□	□	□	□
	My area of responsibility requires different kinds of knowledge (e.g. technical knowledge, legal knowledge, language skills).	□	□	□	□	□	□	□
	In order to fulfil my projects/tasks successfully, I have to involve different functional areas (e.g. procurement, IT, logistics).	□	□	□	□	□	□	□

A.4	Which organizational structure is closest to your company? (Please only tick one):
	□ Organization by business segments □ Organization by geographic regions □ Matrix organization

A.5	How many hierarchical levels exist between a SSO employee (without personnel responsibility) and the group management board? (If the SSCs of your SSO have different hierarchical levels, please answer the question from the perspective of the most mature SSC. If you are not aware of the exact numbers, approximate numbers are sufficient.)
	_____ (Number of hierarchical levels)

A.6	How predictable are the following factors in your company's environment?

Please rank in the last column the environmental factors according to their importance for your company (1 = highest importance).	1 = not at all predictable, ... very predictable = 7							Rank
	1	2	3	4	5	6	7	
Behavior of customers (e.g. customer requirements, demand)	□	□	□	□	□	□	□	
Behavior of suppliers (e.g. pricing, resource availability)	□	□	□	□	□	□	□	
Behavior of competitors (e.g. pricing, market penetration)	□	□	□	□	□	□	□	
Political and legal environment (e.g. laws, regulations)	□	□	□	□	□	□	□	
Economic environment (e.g. exchange rates, economic trends)	□	□	□	□	□	□	□	

Figure B-1 (2/7): Survey SSO manager

A.7	How do you assess the competitive environment in your industry with regard to the following competition categories?	1 = not at all intensive,... very intensive = 7						
		1	2	3	4	5	6	7
	Price competition	☐	☐	☐	☐	☐	☐	☐
	Product competition	☐	☐	☐	☐	☐	☐	☐
	Resource competition	☐	☐	☐	☐	☐	☐	☐

A.8	How many enterprise resource planning (ERP) systems does your company have in use? (If you are not aware of the exact numbers, approximate numbers are sufficient.)
	✎_____ (Number of ERP Systems in use)

A.9	To what extent do the following statements describe the IT infrastructure of your company?	1 = not at all,............. completely = 7						
		1	2	3	4	5	6	7
	The existing information systems are fully integrated into the ERP system(s) (e.g. workflow systems, ticketing systems, reporting systems).	☐	☐	☐	☐	☐	☐	☐
	The existing information systems are cross-functionally interconnected (e.g. management accounting/controlling information systems are connected to purchasing information systems).	☐	☐	☐	☐	☐	☐	☐
	New software is procured centrally for all subsidiaries.	☐	☐	☐	☐	☐	☐	☐
	Subsidiaries are authorized to make local adaptations of the information systems (customizing).	☐	☐	☐	☐	☐	☐	☐

A.10	Which organizational structure is the closest to your group management board? (Please only tick one):
	☐ Each member of the group management board is responsible for a maximum of one corporate function (e.g. finance or HR).
	☐ At least one member of the group management board is responsible for more than one corporate function (e.g. finance and HR).
	☐ The group management board is jointly responsible for the corporate functions.

A.11	To what extent do you agree with the following statements?	1 = not at all,............. completely = 7						
		1	2	3	4	5	6	7
	The SSO is given particular attention by the group management board.	☐	☐	☐	☐	☐	☐	☐
	The SSO receives support from the group management board in case of conflicting goals with subsidiaries (e.g. during the transfer of previously locally performed support processes to the SSO).	☐	☐	☐	☐	☐	☐	☐
	The group management board expects a status report by the SSO management on a regular basis.	☐	☐	☐	☐	☐	☐	☐

A.12	How many employees are working for the group controlling of your company? (If you are not aware of the exact numbers, approximate numbers are sufficient.) ✎_____ (Number of employees)

A.13	Does a Performance Measurement System (PMS) for the company exist at the level of group controlling?
	☐ Yes ☐ No

A.14	How do you characterize the collaboration intensity between the group controlling and the SSO?

		1	2	3	4	5	6	7	
	1 = no collaboration at all	☐	☐	☐	☐	☐	☐	☐	7 = very close collaboration

Section B – Information about your Shared Service Organization

B.1	Please provide the following information about the SSO of your group: (If you are not aware of the exact numbers, approximate numbers are sufficient.)
	Number of Shared Service Centers (SSCs) that belong to the SSO: ✎_____ (SSC)
	Number of employees that work for the SSO: ✎_____ (Employees)
	Year of foundation for the SSO: ✎_____ (Year of foundation)

Figure B-1 (3/7): Survey SSO manager

B.2	Where are the SSCs of your SSO geographically located? (Multiple answers possible)
	☐ Onshore, in the country of the corporate HQ (e.g. corporate HQ in Germany, at least 1 SSC in Germany).
	☐ Nearshore, in a neighboring country of the corporate HQ (e.g. corporate HQ in Germany, at least 1 SSC in a neighboring country).
	☐ Offshore, on the same continent as the corporate HQ (e.g. corporate HQ in Germany, at least 1 SSC in Europe).
	☐ Farshore, on another continent as the corporate HQ (e.g. corporate HQ in Germany, at least 1 SSC outside Europe).
B.3	Is the SSO of your group legally and/or economically independent? (Please only tick one):
	☐ Economically independent (profit responsibility of the SSO). ☐ Both.
	☐ Legally independent (SSO as a separate legal entity). ☐ Neither
B.4	Which center concepts are used in your company's SSO? (Multiple answers possible):
	☐ Cost Center ☐ Profit Center ☐ Other (e.g. Investment Center, Revenue Center): ✎
B.5	Which organizational form applies to your company's SSO? (Please only tick one):
	☐ Monofunctional (e.g. the SSO only performs finance or HR processes).
	☐ Multifunctional, spatially united (the SSO performs processes for at least 2 different functions in 1 SSC).
	☐ Multifunctional, spatially divided (the SSO performs processes for at least 2 different functions, each function in its own SSC).
B.6	How do the SSCs provide their services? (Multiple answers possible):
	☐ Monodivisional, monogeographical (a SSC renders services to 1 business segment in 1 country).
	☐ Monodivisional, multigeographical (a SSC renders services to a business segment in more than 1 country).
	☐ Multidivisional, monogeographical (a SSC renders services to more than 1 business segment in 1 country).
	☐ Multidivisional, multigeographical (a SSC renders services to more than 1 business segment in more than 1 country).
B.7	Are internal customers (e.g. subsidiaries) obliged to accept the services rendered by the SSO?
	☐ Yes ☐ No ☐ Partially
B.8	Does the SSO use Service Level Agreements (SLAs) to shape their customer relationships?
	☐ Yes ☐ No ➔ If not, please proceed with B.9.

Which of the following aspects are governed by SLAs? (Multiple answers possible) — **Yes**

	Yes
Service scope	☐
Date(s) of delivery	☐
Involved contracting parties	☐
Process quality performance measures (e.g. allowed error rates)	☐
Roles and responsibilities	☐
Customer satisfaction performance measures (e.g. allowed complaint rates)	☐
Pricing	☐
Contingencies	☐
Actions to be taken for performance improvements	☐
Payment terms	☐
Other aspects: ✎	

B.9	Does the SSO use Service Level Agreements (SLAs) to shape their business relationships with outsourcing service providers?
	☐ Yes ☐ No ☐ The SSO does not cooperate with outsourcing service providers
B.10	Does your SSO have its own controlling department?
	☐ Yes, a controlling department for the entire SSO ☐ Yes, a controlling department in each SSC ☐ No ➔ If not, please proceed with B.11.

How many employees are working for the controlling department in your SSO? (If you are not aware of the exact numbers, approximate numbers are sufficient.)

✎ _____ (Number of employees who are working in the SSO controlling department)

What is the average time spent by a management accountant in your SSO with the following tasks?

	Percentage of time spent per task
Budgeting/planning tasks (e.g. capacity planning, personnel deployment)	%
Cost and profit accounting (e.g. variance analyses)	%
Investment appraisals/feasibility studies	%
KPI calculations/analyses	%

Page 4

Figure B-1 (4/7): Survey SSO manager

Reporting/communication tasks	%
Organization and coordination tasks (e.g. coordination with other departments)	%
Risk management	%
Other tasks:	%
	∑ 100%

B.11 To what extent do the following statements describe the (sub-)process execution in your SSO?

1 = not at all, ... completely = 7

	1	2	3	4	5	6	7
The SSO established instructions/guidelines on how particular process steps are to be executed.	□	□	□	□	□	□	□
Standard processes are comprehensively documented (e.g. as a standard operating procedure).	□	□	□	□	□	□	□
The SSO creates individual solutions for its customers that deviate from the standard process in exceptional cases only.	□	□	□	□	□	□	□
In the interest of the SSO, management accountants sometimes have to deviate from the standard processes.	□	□	□	□	□	□	□
In the interest of the company, management accountants sometimes have to deviate from the standard processes.	□	□	□	□	□	□	□

B.12 To what extent do the following statements apply to your SSO?

1 = not at all, ... completely = 7

Deviations from the standard process are necessary, because ...

	1	2	3	4	5	6	7
... the standard process does not comply with local requirements (e.g. local GAAP, tax regulations, market requirements).	□	□	□	□	□	□	□
... local information systems do not comply with the standard process (e.g. local software, ERP systems, workflow systems).	□	□	□	□	□	□	□
... the standard process is too complicated.	□	□	□	□	□	□	□
... the standard process would cause a significantly higher resource consumption compared to an individual solution.	□	□	□	□	□	□	□
... of other reasons (if yes, please specify): _____	□	□	□	□	□	□	□

B.13 How important are the following criteria for the customers of your SSO?

1 = not important, ..., very important = 7

	1	2	3	4	5	6	7
Service fees	□	□	□	□	□	□	□
Timely service provision	□	□	□	□	□	□	□
Consistent service level	□	□	□	□	□	□	□
Professional expertise of the SSO employees	□	□	□	□	□	□	□
Flexible consideration of specific customer needs	□	□	□	□	□	□	□
Self-initiated suggestions for improvements by the SSO	□	□	□	□	□	□	□
SSO employees are familiar with particularities of the customer business areas	□	□	□	□	□	□	□
Quick response to customer requests	□	□	□	□	□	□	□
Continuity of the SSO counterparts	□	□	□	□	□	□	□
Other criteria (please specify) _____	□	□	□	□	□	□	□

Figure B-1 (5/7): Survey SSO manager

Section C – Effects of the Performance Measurement System

C.1 To what extent has the PMS of the SSO supported you to reach the following objectives over the past 3 years?

Please rank in the last column the SSO objectives according to their importance for the SSO (1 = highest importance). If your SSO does not pursue an objective, please do not rank it.

	No objective of the SSO	1 = not at all,................., completely = 7							Rank
		1	2	3	4	5	6	7	
Reduce costs	☐	☐	☐	☐	☐	☐	☐	☐	
Increase customer satisfaction	☐	☐	☐	☐	☐	☐	☐	☐	
Ensure compliance with internal policies	☐	☐	☐	☐	☐	☐	☐	☐	
Automate support processes	☐	☐	☐	☐	☐	☐	☐	☐	
Increase employee satisfaction	☐	☐	☐	☐	☐	☐	☐	☐	
Facilitate post-merger integrations	☐	☐	☐	☐	☐	☐	☐	☐	
Additional objectives (please name): _____	☐	☐	☐	☐	☐	☐	☐	☐	

C.2 How intensively do you pursue the following PMS objectives of your SSO?

Please rank in the last column the SSO objectives according to their importance for the SSO (1 = highest importance). If your SSO does not pursue an objective, please do not rank it.

	No objective of the SSO	1 = not at all intensive,..., very intensive = 7							Rank
		1	2	3	4	5	6	7	
Identify process improvements	☐	☐	☐	☐	☐	☐	☐	☐	
Motivate employees	☐	☐	☐	☐	☐	☐	☐	☐	
Communicate results	☐	☐	☐	☐	☐	☐	☐	☐	
Achieve learning effects from successes and failures for SSO employees	☐	☐	☐	☐	☐	☐	☐	☐	
Understand causal relations	☐	☐	☐	☐	☐	☐	☐	☐	
Encourage the sharing of information and knowledge	☐	☐	☐	☐	☐	☐	☐	☐	
Additional objectives (please name): _____	☐	☐	☐	☐	☐	☐	☐	☐	

C.3 Overall, how satisfied are you with the Performance Measurement System of your SSO?

1 = highly unsatisfied	1	2	3	4	5	6	7	7 = highly satisfied
	☐	☐	☐	☐	☐	☐	☐	

C.4 To what extent do SSO employees accept the Performance Measurement System?

1 = not at all	1	2	3	4	5	6	7	7 = completely
	☐	☐	☐	☐	☐	☐	☐	

Figure B-1 (6/7): Survey SSO manager

Section D – Personal information

D.1	Please provide the following information:		
	Since when have you been working for your company?	✎ _____	(Year)
	Since when have you been working for the SSO of your company?	✎ _____	(Year)
	What is your nationality?	✎ _____	(Nationality)
	What is your job title? ✎ _____		(e.g. Managing Director SSO)
	Do you have personnel responsibility?	☐ Yes	☐ No

Thank you for your support!

We would like to thank you for the time that you have invested in this questionnaire. Your answers are very important for the success of this research project and will be treated strictly confidential. After completing the analyses, we are pleased to provide you with a personal result report.

☐   Please tick this box if you are interested in the results of our study.

Your name: _____

Company: _____

Address: _____

    _____

E-Mail-Address: _____

Telephone number: _____

Any comments on the research project:

For questions and suggestions please do not hesitate to contact:

Friedrich Kalden

E-Mail: friedrich.kalden@wiwi.uni-muenster.de

Telephone: +49 (0)251/ 83 22815

Figure B-1 (7/7): Survey SSO manager

Appendix C

WESTFÄLISCHE
WILHELMS-UNIVERSITÄT
MÜNSTER

IUR
Lehrstuhl für Internationale
Unternehmensrechnung
Prof. Dr. Peter Kajüter

Performance Measurement in Shared Service Organizations

Motivation

This questionnaire is part of an international research project conducted by the Chair of International Accounting at the University of Münster (Germany). The objective of this research project is to analyze the design of performance measurement in shared service organizations in multinational corporations. Therefore, contextual factors as well as information about the design of the performance measurement and its effects are surveyed.

Contents:

A   Design of Performance Measurement Systems

B   Effects of Performance Measurement Systems

C   Personal Information

Please note:

This questionnaire is **strictly confidential.** All data will be aggregated and used for statistical purposes only. Results are published exclusively in aggregated form. Conclusions on individual persons or companies cannot be drawn. Personal information is solely collected to ensure the quality of the survey.

This questionnaire is designed for companies of different sizes. It is therefore possible that certain questions do not apply to your company or appear to be unnecessary to you. For this research project, however, **complete** and **truthful** answers are of utmost importance. If you have little or no information to answer certain questions, we would like to ask you for your **subjective assessment.** Please tick the correct answer(s) or enter your details in the appropriate boxes.

For questions and suggestions please do not hesitate to contact:

Friedrich Kalden

E-Mail: friedrich.kalden@wiwi.uni-muenster.de

Telephone: +49 (0)251/ 83 22815

Figure C-1 (1/9): Survey SSO management accountant

Definition of terms

Performance Measurement System (PMS): A Performance Measurement System quantifies the efficiency and/or effectiveness of actions based on performance measures.

Shared Service Organization (SSO): A Shared Service Organization consolidates and performs support processes for more than one organizational unit and operates like a business under market conditions to enhance the efficiency and effectiveness of its corporation. A SSO may consist of more than one Shared Service Center (SSC) at different locations.

Section A – Design of Performance Measurement Systems

Section A.1 – Contents of the Performance Measurement System

A.1   Please specify the number of performance measures in the Performance Measurement System (PMS) of your Shared Service Organization (SSO) in the following performance measurement categories and rank the performance measurement categories according to their importance for the SSO (1 = highest importance, 2 = second highest importance, etc.).

	Number	Rank
Performance measures w.r.t. revenues, costs and profit/loss (e.g. revenue/year, IT-costs/FTE)		
Performance measures w.r.t. customer satisfaction (e.g. complaint rates, response time)		
Performance measures w.r.t. quality and productivity (e.g. error rates, cycle times)		
Performance measures w.r.t. process automation (e.g. touchless rates)		
Performance measures w.r.t. employee satisfaction (e.g. churn rates)		
Performance measures w.r.t. organizational development (e.g. training days/FTE)		
Others :		

A.2   Please indicate the percentages of financial and nonfinancial performance measures in the PMS of your SSO: Financial performance measures contain all performance measures that are expressed pecuniary (e.g. revenue/customer). Non-financial performance measures contain, therefore, all performance measures which are not expressed directly monetarily (e.g. invoices/FTE). If you are not aware of the exact percentages, approximate percentages are sufficient.

     _____% of financial performance measures.
+   _____% of non-financial performance measures.
=   100 %

A.3   Please specify the percentages of performance measures in the PMS of your SSO, which are calculated as absolute figures and of such measures, which are calculated as ratios.

     _____% of performance measures calculated in absolute figures (e.g. 1.2 Mn. processed invoices).
+   _____% of performance measures calculated as a ratio (e.g. 10,000 processes invoices/FTE).
=   100 %

Figure C-1 (2/9): Survey SSO management accountant

Section A.2 – Performance Measurement Process

A.4 To what extent do the following statements describe the development process of new performance measures for the PMS of your SSO?

	1 = not at all,............., completely = 7						
	1	2	3	4	5	6	7
We arrange brainstorming sessions with SSO employees to generate new measures.	☐	☐	☐	☐	☐	☐	☐
Functional areas outside the SSO suggest new performance measures to us (e.g. SSO customers or group controlling).	☐	☐	☐	☐	☐	☐	☐
We consult specialized literature and/or visit conventions to develop new ideas for performance measures.	☐	☐	☐	☐	☐	☐	☐
We are oriented towards the performance measures used by Multinational Corporations (MNCs) with a more mature SSO.	☐	☐	☐	☐	☐	☐	☐
We employ consulting services to enhance our set of performance measures.	☐	☐	☐	☐	☐	☐	☐
We adapt performance measures that are given by default in recently implemented information systems (e.g. data mining software).	☐	☐	☐	☐	☐	☐	☐
We refine existing performance measures using the trial and error method.	☐	☐	☐	☐	☐	☐	☐

A.5 Does the SSO use the PMS for a variable remuneration of SSO employees?

☐ Yes ☐ No ➔ If not, please proceed with A.7.

Please indicate the percentage of performance measures that are linked to the remuneration system: (If you are not aware of the exact percentages, approximate percentages are sufficient.)

_____% of performance measures linked to the remuneration system.

A.6 To what extent do the following statements describe the strategy by which performance measure targets are set in your SSO?

Performance measure targets are based on ...	1 = not at all,............., completely = 7						
	1	2	3	4	5	6	7
... previous year's figures.	☐	☐	☐	☐	☐	☐	☐
... an external benchmarking.	☐	☐	☐	☐	☐	☐	☐
... an internal benchmarking.	☐	☐	☐	☐	☐	☐	☐
... capital market requirements.	☐	☐	☐	☐	☐	☐	☐
... management expectations.	☐	☐	☐	☐	☐	☐	☐
... the practical experience of process owners.	☐	☐	☐	☐	☐	☐	☐
... other strategies (please specify): _____	☐	☐	☐	☐	☐	☐	☐

A.7 To what extent do you agree with the following statements?
I find it easy,...

	1 = not at all,............., completely = 7						
	1	2	3	4	5	6	7
... to decide for which SSO areas we should generate performance measures.	☐	☐	☐	☐	☐	☐	☐
... to define new performance measures.	☐	☐	☐	☐	☐	☐	☐
... to figure out which data needs to be collected to calculate the performance measures.	☐	☐	☐	☐	☐	☐	☐
... to integrate new performance measures into the existing PMS.	☐	☐	☐	☐	☐	☐	☐
... to eliminate performance measures no longer required.	☐	☐	☐	☐	☐	☐	☐

Figure C-1 (3/9): Survey SSO management accountant

A.8 Which information systems do you use to collect data for the performance measures of your PMS? (Multiple answers possible):
- ☐ Enterprise Resource Planning (ERP) Systems
- ☐ Spreadsheets (e.g. Excel) respectively software solutions based on spreadsheets (e.g. macros, add-ons)
- ☐ Software solutions based on the ERP(s) with the possibility to analyze big data (e.g. Celonis)
- ☐ Other information systems (please specify) _____

A.9 How many SSO FTEs (Example 1 FTE = 2 half time employees) are employed to perform the following process steps for the performance measure data collection?

	Number of FTE
Data collection from back-end systems	
Data aggregation	
Corrections/bug fixes	
Merging different data sources into the target system	
Plausibility checks	
Data editing (e.g. visualization, formatting)	

A.10 To what extent do you collect the required data for the performance measures of your PMS automatically in the following performance measurement categories?

1 = entirely manually,... fully automatically = 7

	1	2	3	4	5	6	7
performance measures w.r.t. revenues, costs and profit/loss	☐	☐	☐	☐	☐	☐	☐
performance measures w.r.t. customer satisfaction	☐	☐	☐	☐	☐	☐	☐
performance measures w.r.t. quality and productivity	☐	☐	☐	☐	☐	☐	☐
performance measures w.r.t. process automation	☐	☐	☐	☐	☐	☐	☐
performance measures w.r.t. employee satisfaction	☐	☐	☐	☐	☐	☐	☐
performance measures w.r.t. organizational development	☐	☐	☐	☐	☐	☐	☐
Others:	☐	☐	☐	☐	☐	☐	☐

A.11 Which performance measurement category of your PMS is reported in which frequency? If you are reporting performance measures of a certain category in different frequencies (e.g. per week and per month), please select the frequency for which you are reporting the majority of performance measures.

Performance measures w.r.t...	Daily	Weekly	Monthly	Quarterly	Half-yearly	Yearly	Less frequently than yearly	Sporadically
...revenues, costs and profit/loss	☐	☐	☐	☐	☐	☐	☐	☐
...customer satisfaction	☐	☐	☐	☐	☐	☐	☐	☐
...quality and productivity	☐	☐	☐	☐	☐	☐	☐	☐
...process automation	☐	☐	☐	☐	☐	☐	☐	☐
...employee satisfaction	☐	☐	☐	☐	☐	☐	☐	☐
...organizational development	☐	☐	☐	☐	☐	☐	☐	☐
...other performance measure categories	☐	☐	☐	☐	☐	☐	☐	☐

Figure C-1 (4/9): Survey SSO management accountant

A.12 How often do you use the following types of performance measure analyses?	1 = very rarely,............., very often = 7						
	1	2	3	4	5	6	7
Variance analyses (e.g. target-actual comparison)	☐	☐	☐	☐	☐	☐	☐
Time-series comparisons (e.g. actual vs. previous year)	☐	☐	☐	☐	☐	☐	☐
Internal benchmarking (e.g. SSC 1 vs. SSC 2)	☐	☐	☐	☐	☐	☐	☐
External benchmarking (e.g. actual vs. Hackett-benchmark)	☐	☐	☐	☐	☐	☐	☐

A.13 How often do you have an informal conversation with other SSO employees on performance measures of your PMS?

	1	2	3	4	5	6	7	
1 = very rarely	☐	☐	☐	☐	☐	☐	☐	7 = very often

A.14 How are performance measures reported by the SSO? (Multiple answers possible):

In the form of...

☐ ... figures and tables in a spreadsheet (e.g. in Excel)
☐ ... charts and diagrams (e.g. in PowerPoint)
☐ ... charts and diagrams with extensive annotations (e.g. in PowerPoint)
☐ ... applications for mobile devices (e.g. mobile phones, tablets)
☐ ... information systems with the possibility of making substantial adjustments (e.g. IBM Cognos/TM1)
☐ ... elaborately designed applications with the ability to make small adjustments (e.g. dashboards)
☐ ... other forms (please specify): _____

A.15 In which frequency do you change the performance measure definitions/calculation schemes of your PMS?

(Please only tick one):

☐ more frequently than annually   ☐ annually   ☐ less frequently than annually   ☐ irregularly

A.16 How many performance measures have been eliminated from the PMS over the past 12 months and how many have been added?

✎ _____ (eliminated performance measures)   ✎ _____ (added performance measures)

Section A.3 – Performance Measurement Actors

A.17 Which of the following actors are involved in the three performance measurement process steps specified below? (Multiple answers possible):

	...decided to add/eliminate performance measures.	...defines performance measure objectives.	...receives performance measure reports.
The SSO executive board (e.g. the Managing Director of the SSO)...	☐	☐	☐
The SSC heads (e.g. the Head of SSC A)...	☐	☐	☐
The process owners (e.g. the GPO order-to-cash)...	☐	☐	☐
The SSO controlling...	☐	☐	☐
The SSO employees...	☐	☐	☐
The group management board...	☐	☐	☐
The group controlling...	☐	☐	☐

Figure C-1 (5/9): Survey SSO management accountant

The business partners (e.g. an outsourcing service provider)	□	□	□
Other actors: _____	□	□	□

A.18   To what extent do the following actors support the development of your SSO's PMS? (e.g. by providing financial resources and/or personnel capacity)

1 = not at all, ... completely = 7

	1	2	3	4	5	6	7
The SSO executive board (e.g. the Managing Director of the SSO)	□	□	□	□	□	□	□
The SSC head (e.g. the Head of SSC A)	□	□	□	□	□	□	□
The group management board	□	□	□	□	□	□	□

A.19   To what extent do the following actors contribute to PMS improvements with their expertise?

1 = not at all, ... completely = 7

	1	2	3	4	5	6	7
The SSO executive board (e.g. the Managing Director of the SSO)	□	□	□	□	□	□	□
The SSC heads (e.g. the Head of SSC A)	□	□	□	□	□	□	□
The process owners (e.g. the GPO order-to-cash)	□	□	□	□	□	□	□
The SSO controlling	□	□	□	□	□	□	□
The SSO employees	□	□	□	□	□	□	□
The group controlling	□	□	□	□	□	□	□
The business partners (e.g. an outsourcing service provider)	□	□	□	□	□	□	□

A.20   To what extent do the following actors coordinate performance measurement activities within your SSO?

1 = not at all, ... completely = 7

	1	2	3	4	5	6	7
The SSC heads (e.g. the Head of SSC A)	□	□	□	□	□	□	□
The process owners (e.g. the GPO order-to-cash)	□	□	□	□	□	□	□
The SSO controlling	□	□	□	□	□	□	□
The SSO employees	□	□	□	□	□	□	□
The group controlling	□	□	□	□	□	□	□

A.21   To what extent do the following actors cooperate with departments outside the SSO with regard to your PMS?

1 = not at all, ... completely = 7

	1	2	3	4	5	6	7
The SSO executive board (e.g. the Managing Director of the SSO	□	□	□	□	□	□	□
The SSC heads (e.g. the Head of SSC A)	□	□	□	□	□	□	□
The process owners (e.g. the GPO order-to-cash)	□	□	□	□	□	□	□
The SSO controlling	□	□	□	□	□	□	□
The SSO employees	□	□	□	□	□	□	□

Figure C-1 (6/9): Survey SSO management accountant

A.22   To what extent do you agree with the following statements?

	1 = not at all................. completely = 7						
	1	2	3	4	5	6	7
The PMS of our SSO is closely aligned to a model established in theory (such as the Balanced Scorecard).	☐	☐	☐	☐	☐	☐	☐
The PMS of our SSO is consciously not based on established models.	☐	☐	☐	☐	☐	☐	☐
The PMS of our SSO contains performance measures which are probably not available in any other corporation.	☐	☐	☐	☐	☐	☐	☐
The PMS of our SSO serves more as a long-term strategy than for short-term improvement activities.	☐	☐	☐	☐	☐	☐	☐
Technical feasibility plays a greater role for the performance measure selection than the requirements of the process managers.	☐	☐	☐	☐	☐	☐	☐
Performance measure definitions and calculation schemes are comprehensively documented in our SSO.	☐	☐	☐	☐	☐	☐	☐
The automation of the performance measure data collection and performance measure analysis has top priority for the PMS of our SSO	☐	☐	☐	☐	☐	☐	☐
Our SSO organizes meetings with the management on a regular basis to discuss the performance measure development.	☐	☐	☐	☐	☐	☐	☐
The extent to which the resources invested in the PMS pay off is difficult to assess.	☐	☐	☐	☐	☐	☐	☐

Section B – Effects of the Performance Measurement System

B.1   To what extent has the PMS supported you to accomplish the following objectives over the past 3 years?

Please rank the PMS objectives in the last column according to their importance for the SSO (1 = highest importance). If your SSO does not pursue an objective, please do not rank it.

	Not an objective of the SSO	1 = not at all,................ completely = 7							Rank
		1	2	3	4	5	6	7	
Reduce costs	☐	☐	☐	☐	☐	☐	☐	☐	
Increase customer satisfaction	☐	☐	☐	☐	☐	☐	☐	☐	
Ensure compliance with internal policies	☐	☐	☐	☐	☐	☐	☐	☐	
Automate support process	☐	☐	☐	☐	☐	☐	☐	☐	
Increase employee satisfaction	☐	☐	☐	☐	☐	☐	☐	☐	
Facilitate post-merger integration	☐	☐	☐	☐	☐	☐	☐	☐	
Other objectives: _____	☐	☐	☐	☐	☐	☐	☐	☐	

B.2   How intensively do you pursue the following PMS objectives of your SSO?

Please rank in the last column the PMS objectives according to their importance for the SSO (1 = highest importance). If your SSO does not pursue an objective, please do not rank it.

	Not an objective of the SSO	1 = not at all intensive,...., very intensive = 7							Rank
		1	2	3	4	5	6	7	
Identify process improvements	☐	☐	☐	☐	☐	☐	☐	☐	
Motivate employees	☐	☐	☐	☐	☐	☐	☐	☐	
Communicate results	☐	☐	☐	☐	☐	☐	☐	☐	
Achieve learning effects for SSO employees	☐	☐	☐	☐	☐	☐	☐	☐	
Understand causal relations	☐	☐	☐	☐	☐	☐	☐	☐	
Encourage the sharing of information and knowledge	☐	☐	☐	☐	☐	☐	☐	☐	
Other objectives: _____	☐	☐	☐	☐	☐	☐	☐	☐	

Figure C-1 (7/9): Survey SSO management accountant

B.3   Overall, how satisfied are you with the Performance Measurement System of your SSO?

	1	2	3	4	5	6	7	
1 = highly dissatisfied	□	□	□	□	□	□	□	7 = highly satisfied

B.4   To what extent do SSO employees accept the Performance Measurement System?

	1	2	3	4	5	6	7	
1 = not at all	□	□	□	□	□	□	□	7 = completely

Section C – Personal information

C.1   Please provide the following personal information:

Since when have you been working for your company?   _____ (year)
Since when have you been working for the SSO of your company?   _____ (year)
What is your nationality?   _____ (nationality)
What is your job title?   _____   (e.g. SSC Management Accountant)
Do you have personal responsibility?   □ Yes   □ No

Figure C-1 (8/9): Survey SSO management accountant

Thank you for your support!

We would like to thank you for the time that you have invested in this questionnaire. Your answers are very important for the success of this research project and will be treated strictly confidential. After completing the analyses, we are pleased to provide you with a personal result report.

☐ Please tick this box if you are interested in the results of our study.

Your name: _____

Company: _____

Address: _____

_____

E-Mail-Address: _____

Telephone number: _____

Any comments on the research project:

For questions and suggestions please do not hesitate to contact:
Friedrich Kalden
E-Mail: friedrich.kalden@wiwi.uni-muenster.de
Telephone: +49 (0)251/ 83 22815

Figure C-1 (9/9): Survey SSO management accountant

Bibliography

Abdallah, W. M./Alnamri, M. (2015): Non-financial performance measures and the BSC of multinational companies with multi-cultural environment: An empirical investigation., in: Cross Cultural Management 22 (4), pp. 594–607.

Abernethy, M. A./Chua, W. F. (1996): A field study of control system "redesign": the impact of institutional processes on strategic choice, in: Contemporary Accounting Research, 13 (2), pp. 569–606.

Aguirre, D./Couto, V./Disher, C./Neilson, G. (1998): Shared services: management fad or real value, New York 1998.

Aharoni, Y. (1971): Definition of a Multinational Corporation, in: Quarterly Review of Economics and Business, 11 (3), pp. 27–37.

Akerlof, G. A. (1970): The market for "lemons": Quality uncertainty and the market mechanism, in: The Quarterly Journal of Economics, 84 (3), pp. 488–500.

Aksin, O./Masini, A. (2008): Effective strategies for internal outsourcing and offshoring of business services: An empirical investigation, in: Journal of Operations Management, 26 (2), pp. 239–256.

Albert, H. (2000): Kritischer Rationalismus: vier Kapitel zur Kritik illusionären Denkens, Tübingen 2000.

Allen, P./Maguire, S./McKelvey, B. (2011): The sage handbook of complexity and management, Thousand Oaks 2011.

Allen, T. J. (1967): Communications in the research and development laboratory, in: Technology Review, 70 (1), pp. 31–37.

Allen, T. J. (1970): Communication networks in R & D laboratories, in: R&D Management, 1 (1), pp. 14–21.

Allweyer, T. (2005): Geschäftsprozessmanagement: Strategie, Entwurf, Implementierung, Controlling, Herdecke 2005.

Al-Omiri, M./Drury, C. (2007): A survey of factors influencing the choice of product costing systems in UK organizations, in: Management Accounting Research, 18 (4), pp. 399–424.

Alparslan, A. (2006): Strukturalistische Prinzipal-Agenten-Theorie: Eine Reformierung der Hidden-Action-Modelle aus der Perspektive des Strukturalismus, Dissertation Universität Duisburg-Essen, Wiesbaden 2006.

Alvesson, M./Kärreman, D. (2004): Interfaces of control. Technocratic and socio-ideological control in a global management consultancy firm, in: Accounting, Organizations and Society, 29 (3), pp. 423–444.

Amaratunga, D./Baldry, D. (2002): Moving from performance measurement to performance management, in: Facilities, 20 (5/6), pp. 217–223.

Anthony, R. N. (1965): Planning and control systems: a framework for analysis, Harvard 1965.

Anthony, R. N./Govindarajan, V./Hartmann, F. G. H./Kraus, K./Nilsson, G. (2007): Management Control Systems, 12th. ed., New York 2007.

Antonakis, J./Bendahan, S./Jacquart, P./Lalive, R. (2010): On making causal claims: A review and recommendations, in: The Leadership Quarterly, 21 (6), pp. 1086–1120.

Armstrong, J. S./Overton, T. S. (1977): Estimating nonresponse bias in mail surveys, in: Journal of Marketing Research, 14 (3), pp. 396–402.

Arrow, K. J. (1984): The Economics of Agency, Stanford 1984.

Atkinson, A. (1998): Strategic performance measurement and incentive compensation, in: European Management Journal, 16 (5), pp. 552–561.

Atkinson, A. A./Waterhouse, J. H./Wells, R. B. (1997): A stakeholder approach to strategic performance measurement, in: Sloan Management Review, 38 (3), pp. 25–37.

Auer, B. R./Rottmann, H. (2015): Statistik und Ökonometrie für Wirtschaftswissenschaftler, 3rd. ed., Wiesbaden 2015.

Auer, L. v. (2016): Ökonometrie, 7th. ed., Berlin 2016.

Azorín, J. M./Cameron, R. (2010): The application of mixed methods in organisational research: A literature review, in: Electronic Journal of Business Research Methods, 8 (2), pp. 95–105.

Azzone, G./Masella, C./Bertelè, U. (1991): Design of performance measures for time-based companies, in: International Journal of Operations & Production Management, 11 (3), pp. 77–85.

Backhaus, K./Erichson, B./Plinke, W./Weiber, R. (2018): Multivariate Analysemethoden, 15th. ed., Berlin 2016.

Balkcom, J. E./Ittner, C. D./Larcker, D. F. (1997): Strategic performance measurement: Lessons learned and future directions, in: Journal of Strategic Performance Measurement, 1 (2), pp. 22–32.

Balling, J./Gössi, M. (2001a): Mit Shared Services Supportprozesse optimieren, Wie Geschäftseinheiten durch Shared-Service-Center entlastet werden können, in: Management, 70 (9), pp. 21–25.

Balling, J./Gössi, M. (2001b): Shared Services Konzept im Trend, in: Schweizer Treuhänder, 75 (9), pp. 819–824.

Bandilla, W. (2002): Web surveys – an appropriate mode of data collection for the social sciences, in: Online Social Sciences, 1 (1), pp. 1–6.

Bangemann, T. O. (2005): Shared services in finance and accounting, Aldershot 2005.

Bartel, R. (1990): Charakteristik, Methodik und wissenschaftsmethodische Probleme der Wirtschaftswissenschaften, in: Wirtschaftswissenschaftliches Studium 19 (2), pp. 54–59.

Bartlett, C. A./Ghoshal, S. (2002): Managing across borders: The transnational solution, Boston 2002.

Baumann, P. (2008): Erkenntnistheorie, 3rd. ed., Stuttgart 2015.

Becker, F. G. (1995): Anreizsysteme als Führungsinstrumente, in: Handwörterbuch der Führung, 2 (1), pp. 34–45.

Becker, W./Bluhm, K./Kunz, C./Mayer, B. (2008): Gestaltung von Shared Service Centern in internationalen Konzernen, in: Bamberger Betriebswirtschaftliche Beiträge, 158 (1), pp. 1–55.

Becker, W./Rech, S. (2013): Wertschöpfungsorientiertes Dienstleistungscontrolling, in: Controlling 25 (10), pp. 515–521.

Berger, T. G. (2007): Service-Level-Agreements, Darmstadt 2007.

Bergeron, B. (2002): Essentials of shared services, Hoboken 2002.

Bergman, M. M. (2011): The good, the bad, and the ugly in mixed methods research and design, in: Journal of Mixed Methods Research, 5 (4), pp. 271–275.

Bertalanffy, L. v. (1972): The history and status of general systems theory, in: Academy of Management Journal, 15 (4), pp. 407–426.

Bhimani, A. (1994): Monitoring performance measures in UK manufacturing companies, in: Management Accounting: Magazine for Chartered Management Accountants, 72 (1), pp. 34–37.

Birnberg, J. G./Shields, M. D./Young, S. M. (1990): The case for multiple methods in empirical management accounting research (with an illustration from budget setting), in: Journal of Management Accounting Research, 2 (1), pp. 33–66.

Bititci, U./Garengo, P./Dörfler, V./Nudurupati, S. (2012): Performance measurement: Challenges for tomorrow, in: International Journal of Management Reviews, 14 (3), pp. 305–327.

Bititci, U. S./Carrie, A. S./McDevitt, L. (1997): Integrated performance measurement systems: a development guide, in: International Journal of Operations & Production Management, 17 (5), pp. 522–534.

Bititci, U. S./Nudurupati, S. S./Turner, T. J./Creighton, S. (2002): Web enabled performance measurement systems: Management implications, in: International Journal of Operations & Production Management, 22 (11), pp. 1273–1287.

Bititci, U. S./Turner, U./Begemann, C. (2000): Dynamics of performance measurement systems, in: International Journal of Operations & Production Management, 20 (6), pp. 692–704.

Blau, J. R./McKinley, W. (1979): Ideas, complexity, and innovation, in: Administrative Science Quarterly, 24 (2), pp. 200–219.

Bogner, A./Littig, B./Menz, W. (2014): Interviews mit Experten: eine praxisorientierte Einführung, Berlin 2014.

Bohnert, F. S. (2010): Kennzahlen im Controlling von Dienstleistungen, in: Controlling-Berater, 1 (9), pp. 49–62.

Bonner, S. E./Sprinkle, G. B. (2002): The effects of monetary incentives on effort and task performance: theories, evidence, and a framework for research, in: Accounting, Organizations and Society, 27 (4), pp. 303–345.

Borchardt, A./Göthlich, S. E. (2009): Erkenntnisgewinnung durch Fallstudien, in: Albers, S./Klapper, D./Konradt, U./Walter, A./Wolf, J. (eds.): Methodik der empirischen Forschung, Wiesbaden 2009, pp. 33–48.

Boulding, K. E. (1956): General systems theory—the skeleton of science, in: Management Science, 2 (3), pp. 197–208.

Bourne, M./Franco, M./Wilkes, J. (2003): Corporate performance management, in: Measuring Business Excellence, 7 (3), pp. 15–21.

Bourne, M./Kennerley, M./Franco-Santos, M. (2005): Managing through measures: a study of impact on performance, in: Journal of Manufacturing Technology Management, 16 (4), pp. 373–395.

Bourne, M./Melnyk, S./Faull, N./Franco-Santos, M./Kennerley, M./Micheli, P./Martinez, V./Mason, S./Marr, B./Gray, D. (2007): Towards a definition of a business performance measurement system, in: International Journal of Operations & Production Management, 27 (8), pp. 784–801.

Bourne, M./Mills, J./Wilcox, M./Neely, A./Platts, K. (2000): Designing, implementing and updating performance measurement systems, in: International Journal of Operations & Production Management, 20 (7), pp. 754–771.

Bourne, M./Neely, A./Platts, K./Mills, J. (2002): The success and failure of performance measurement initiatives, in: International Journal of Operations & Production Management, 22 (11), pp. 1288–1310.

Brandau, M./Endenich, C./Trapp, R./Hoffjan, A. (2013): Institutional drivers of conformity–Evidence for management accounting from Brazil and Germany, in: International Business Review, 22 (2), pp. 466–479.

Breid, V. (1995): Aussagefähigkeit agencytheoretischer Ansätze im Hinblick auf die Verhaltenssteuerung von Entscheidungsträgern, in: Zeitschrift für betriebswirtschaftliche Forschung, 47 (9), pp. 821–854.

Brislin, R. W. (1970): Back-translation for cross-cultural research, in: Journal of Cross-cultural Psychology, 1 (3), pp. 185–216.

Brose, P. (1984): Konzeption, Varianten und Perspektiven der Kontingenztheorie, in: Journal für Betriebswirtschaft, 5 (5), pp. 230–243.

Brühl, R. (2017): Wie Wissenschaft Wissen schafft – Wissenschaftstheorie für Sozial- und Wirtschaftswissenschaften, 2nd. ed., Stuttgart 2017.

Bruhn, M. (2003): Internal service barometers: Conceptualization and empirical results of a pilot study in Switzerland, in: European Journal of Marketing, 37 (9), pp. 1187–1204.

Bruhn, M./Stauss, B. (2005): Dienstleistungscontrolling, Berlin 2005.

Bruns, W. J./Waterhouse, J. H. (1975): Budgetary control and organization structure, in: Journal of Accounting Research, 13 (2), pp. 177–203.

Busi, M./Bititci, U. S. (2006): Collaborative performance management: present gaps and future research, in: International Journal of Productivity and Performance Management, 55 (1), pp. 7–25.

Camp, R. (1994): Benchmarking, München 1994.

Campbell, D. J. (1988): Task complexity: A review and analysis, in: Academy of Management Review, 13 (1), pp. 40–52.

Campbell, D. T. (1957a): Factors relevant to the validity of experiments in social settings, in: Psychological Bulletin, 54 (4), p. 297–297.

Campbell, D. T./Fiske, D. W. (1959): Convergent and discriminant validation by the multitrait-multimethod matrix, in: Psychological Bulletin, 56 (2), p. 81–81.

Campbell, N. R. (1957b): Foundations of Science: The Philosophy of Theory and Experiment, New York 1957.

Campenhausen, C./Rudolf, A. (2001): Shared Services-profitabel für vernetzte Unternehmen, in: Harvard Business Manager, 23 (1), pp. 82–94.

Cappallo, S. (2006): Funktionen und Ziele wissenschaftlichen Fortschritts aus strukturationstheoretischer Perspektive, in: Zelewski, S. (ed.): Fortschritt in den Wirtschaftswissenschaften, Wiesbaden 2006, pp. 19–48.

Caracelli, V. J./Greene, J. C. (1993): Data analysis strategies for mixed-method evaluation designs, in: Educational Evaluation and Policy Analysis, 15 (2), pp. 195–207.

Carter, A. P. (**1998**): Measuring the Performance of a Knowledge-Based Economy, in: Neef, D./Siesfeld, A./Cefola, J. (eds.): The Economic Impact of Knowledge, Woburn 1998, pp. 203–213.

Chakrabarti, A. K. (**1974**): The role of champion in product innovation, in: California Management Review, 17 (2), pp. 58–62.

Chandler, A. D. (**1990**): Strategy and structure: Chapters in the history of the industrial enterprise, Cambridge 1990.

Chang, C. J./Kuo, T./Wu, A. (**2013**): Strategy Alignment and Performance Evaluation for Shared Service Centers: A Longitudinal Study on the Role of Balanced Scorecard, Working Paper, San Diego State University.

Chapman, C. S. (**1997**): Reflections on a contingent view of accounting, in: Accounting, Organizations and Society, 22 (2), pp. 189–205.

Chapman, C. S. (**1998**): Accountants in organisational networks, in: Accounting, Organizations and Society, 23 (8), pp. 737–766.

Charmaz, K./Belgrave, L. L. (**2010**): Grounded theory as an emergent method, in: Hesse-Biber, S. N./Leavy, P. (eds.): Handbook of emergent methods, New York 2010, pp. 155–172.

Chatterjee, S./Hadi, A. S. (**2012**): Regression analysis by example, 5th. ed., Hoboken 2012.

Chen, M.-C./Yang, T./Li, H.-C. (**2007**): Evaluating the supply chain performance of IT-based inter-enterprise collaboration, in: Information & Management, 44 (6), pp. 524–534.

Chenhall, R. H. (**2003**): Management control systems design within its organizational context: findings from contingency-based research and directions for the future, in: Accounting, Organizations and Society, 28 (2–3), pp. 127–168.

Chenhall, R. H./Morris, D. (**1986**): The impact of structure, environment, and interdependence on the perceived usefulness of management accounting systems, in: Accounting Review, 61 (1), pp. 16–35.

Child, J. (**1972**): Organizational structure, environment and performance: The role of strategic choice, in: Sociology, 6 (1), pp. 1–22.

Chmielewicz, K. (**1994**): Forschungskonzeptionen der Wirtschaftswissenschaft, 3rd. ed., Stuttgart 1994.

Chow, C. W./van der Steede, W. (**2006**): The Use and Usefulness, in: Management Accounting Quarterly, 7 (3), pp. 1–8.

Cleff, T. (**2015**): Deskriptive Statistik und Explorative Datenanalyse. Eine computergestützte Einführung mit Excel, SPSS und STATA, 3rd. ed., Wiesbaden 2015.

Coase, R. H. (1937): The nature of the firm, in: Economica, 4 (16), pp. 386–405.

Coenenberg, A. G./Fischer, T. M./Günther, T. (2016): Kostenrechnung und Kostenanalyse, 9th, ed., Stuttgart 2016.

Cokins, G. (2004): Performance management: finding the missing pieces, Hoboken 2004.

Collins, K. M. T./Onwuegbuzie, A. J./Jiao, Q. G. (2007): A mixed methods investigation of mixed methods sampling designs in social and health science research, in: Journal of Mixed Methods Research, 1 (3), pp. 267–294.

Collins, K. M. T./Onwuegbuzie, A. J./Sutton, I. L. (2006): A model incorporating the rationale and purpose for conducting mixed methods research in special education and beyond, in: Learning Disabilities: A Contemporary Journal, 4 (1), pp. 67–100.

Collis, J./Hussey, R. (2013): Business research: A practical guide for undergraduate and postgraduate students, 4th. ed., London 2013.

Cooke, F. L. (2006): Modeling an HR shared services center: Experience of an MNC in the United Kingdom, in: Human Resource Management, 45 (2), pp. 211–227.

Corbin, J./Strauss, A./Strauss, A. L. (2015): Basics of qualitative research, 4th. ed., Thousand Oaks 2015.

Covaleski, M./Evans, J. H./Luft, J./Shields, M. D. (2007): Budgeting research: three theoretical perspectives and criteria for selective integration, in: Chapman, C. S. (ed.): Handbook of management accounting research, Amsterdam 2007, pp. 587–624.

Creswell, J. W. (2013): Research design: Qualitative, quantitative, and mixed methods approaches, Thousand Oaks 2013.

Creswell, J. W./Hanson, W. E./Clark Plano, Vicki L./Morales, A. (2007): Qualitative research designs: Selection and implementation, in: The Counseling Psychologist, 35 (2), pp. 236–264.

Cyert, R. M./March, J. G. (1963): A behavioral theory of the firm, 2nd. ed., Englewood Cliffs 1963.

Damanpour, F. (1996): Organizational complexity and innovation: developing and testing multiple contingency models, in: Management Science, 42 (5), pp. 693–716.

Davis, S./Albright, T. (2004): An investigation of the effect of balanced scorecard implementation on financial performance, in: Management Accounting Research, 15 (2), pp. 135–153.

Davis, T. (2005): Integrating shared services with the strategy and operations of MNEs, in: Journal of General Management, 31 (2), pp. 1–17.

Deimel, K./Quante, S. (2003): Prozessoptimierung durch Shared Service Center, in: Controlling, 15 (6), pp. 301–307.

Dellinger, A. B./Leech, N. L. (2007): Toward a unified validation framework in mixed methods research, in: Journal of Mixed Methods Research, 1 (4), pp. 309–332.

Denscombe, M. (2008): Communities of practice: A research paradigm for the mixed methods approach, in: Journal of Mixed Methods Research, 2 (3), pp. 270–283.

Denscombe, M. (2014): The good research guide, 5th. ed., Berkshire 2014.

Denzin, N. K. (1978): Sociological methods: A sourcebook, Berkshire 1978.

DeVellis, R. F. (2016): Scale development: Theory and applications, Thousand Oaks 2016.

Diamantopoulos, A./Riefler, P. (2008): Formative Indikatoren: Einige Anmerkungen zu ihrer Art, Validität und Multikollinearität, in: Zeitschrift für Betriebswirtschaft, 78 (11), pp. 1183–1196.

Dillman, D. A. (1991): The design and administration of mail surveys, in: Annual Review of Sociology, 17 (1), pp. 225–249.

Dillman, D. A./Bowker, D. K. (2001): The web questionnaire challenge to survey methodologists, in: Online Social Sciences, 1 (1), pp. 53–71.

DiMaggio, P./Powell, W. W. (1983): The iron cage revisited: Collective rationality and institutional isomorphism in organizational fields, in: American Sociological Review, 48 (2), pp. 147–160.

DiMaggio, P. J./Powell, W. W. (1991): Introduction, in: Powell, W. (ed.): The new institutionalism in organizational analysis, Chicago 1991, pp. 1–41.

Dittrich, J./Braun, M. (2004): Business process outsourcing, Stuttgart 2004.

Dixon, J. R. (1990): The new performance challenge: Measuring operations for world-class competition, Burr Ridge 1990.

Dollery, B./Akimov, A. (2007): Critical review of the empirical evidence on shared services in local government, Working Paper, University of New England.

Donaldson, L. (1999): The normal science of structural contingency theory, in: Clegg, S. (ed.): Studying organization, London 1999, pp. 51–70.

Döring, N./Bortz, J. (2016): Forschungsmethoden und Evaluation, 5th. ed., Berlin 2016.

Dossi, A./Patelli, L. (2010): You learn from what you measure: financial and non-financial performance measures in multinational companies, in: Long Range Planning, 43 (4), pp. 498–526.

Doumeingts, G./Clave, F./Ducq, Y. (1995): ECOGRAI – a method to design and to implement performance measurement systems for industrial organizations, in: Rolstadas, A. (ed.): Benchmarking – Theory and Practice, London 1995, pp. 350–368.

Dreger, C./Kosfeld, R./Eckey, H.-F. (2014): Ökonometrie, 5th. ed., Wiesbaden 2014.

Dressler, S. (2007): Shared services, business process outsourcing und offshoring – Die moderne Ausgestaltung des Back Office – Wege zu Kostensenkung und mehr Effizienz im Unternehmen, Wiesbaden 2007.

Drury, C./Tayles, M. (2005): Explicating the design of overhead absorption procedures in UK organizations, in: The British Accounting Review, 37 (1), pp. 47–84.

Easterby-Smith, M./Thorpe, R./Jackson, P. (2012): Management research, London 2012.

Eccles, R. G. (1990): The performance measurement manifesto, in: Harvard Business Review, 69 (1), pp. 131–137.

Eichenberg, T./Bursy, R. (2016): Management von internationalen HR Shared Service Centern: Implementierungsempfehlungen und Best Practice, Berlin 2016.

Eicker, S./Kress, S./Lelke, F. (2005): Kennzahlengestützte Geschäftssteuerung im Dienstleistungssektor – Ergebnisse einer empirischen Untersuchung, in: Zeitschrift für Controlling & Management, 49 (6), pp. 408–414.

Eid, M./Gollwitzer, M./Schmitt, M. (2017): Statistik und Forschungsmethoden, 5th. ed., Weinheim 2017.

Eisenhardt, K. M. (1989a): Agency theory: An assessment and review, in: Academy of Management Review, 14 (1), pp. 57–74.

Eisenhardt, K. M. (1989b): Building theories from case study research, in: Academy of Management Review, 14 (4), pp. 532–550.

Eisenhardt, K. M./Graebner, M. E. (2007): Theory building from cases: Opportunities and challenges, in: Academy of Management Journal, 50 (1), pp. 25–32.

Engstermann, F. (2015): Reengineering von Finanz-, Controlling- und Accountingprozessen, in: Zeitschrift für internationale und kapitalmarktorientierte Rechnungslegung, 15 (9), pp. 443–452.

Erdmann, M.-K. (2003): Supply chain performance measurement, in: Schlüchtermann, J. (ed.): Produktionswirtschaft und Industriebetriebslehre, 3rd. ed. 2003, pp. 1–388.

Erlei, M./Leschke, M./Sauerland, D. (2016): Institutionenökonomik, 3rd. ed., Stuttgart 2016.

Erzberger, C./Kelle, U. (2010): Making inferences in mixed methods: the rules of integration, in: Tashakkori, A. (ed.): Sage handbook of mixed methods in social & behavioral research, 2nd., ed., Los Angeles 2010, pp. 457–488.

Evans, H./Ashworth, G./Gooch, J./Davies, R. (1996): Who needs performance management?, in: Managment Accounting, 74 (11), pp. 20–25.

Ewert, R./Wagenhofer, A. (2014): Interne Unternehmensrechnung, 8th. ed., Berlin 2014.

Ezzamel, M. (1990): The impact of environmental uncertainty, managerial autonomy and size on budget characteristics, in: Management Accounting Research, 1 (3), pp. 181–197.

Fama, E. F./Jensen, M. C. (1983): Separation of ownership and control, in: The Journal of Law and Economics, 26 (2), pp. 301–325.

Farndale, E./Paauwe, J./Hoeksema, L. (2009): In-sourcing HR: shared service centres in the Netherlands, in: The International Journal of Human Resource Management, 20 (3), pp. 544–561.

Farrell, D. (2004): Beyond offshoring: assess your company's global potential, in: Harvard Business Review, 82 (12), pp. 82–90, 148.

Fayol, H. (1970): Administration, Paris 1970.

Ferreira, A./Otley, D. (2009): The design and use of performance management systems: An extended framework for analysis, in: Management Accounting Research, 20 (4), pp. 263–282.

Ferreira, L. D./Merchant, K. A. (1992): Field research in management accounting and control: a review and evaluation, in: Accounting, Auditing & Accountability Journal, 5 (4), pp. 3–34.

Fielding, N. G. (2012): Triangulation and mixed methods designs: Data integration with new research technologies, in: Journal of Mixed Methods Research, 6 (2), pp. 124–136.

Fischer, L. D. (2006): Internationalität der Unternehmung: aktueller Forschungsstand, Analyse und Konzeptualisierung, Dissertation Universität Bamberg, Bamberg 2006.

Fischer, T. M./Hirsch, S./Dornbusch, D./Ollmann, S./Schründer, C. P./Vollmer, M. (2017): Performance Management in der SSO, in: Fischer, T. M./

Vollmer, M. (eds.): Erfolgreiche Führung von Shared Services, Berlin 2017, pp. 117–148.

Fischer, T. M./Möller, K./Schultze, W. (2015): Controlling – Grundlagen, Instrumente und Entwicklungsperspektiven, 2nd. ed., Stuttgart 2015.

Fischer, T. M./Sterzenbach, S. (2006): ZP-Stichwort: Shared Service Centers, in: Zeitschrift für Planung & Unternehmenssteuerung, 17 (1), pp. 123–128.

Fischer, T. M./Sterzenbach, S. (2007): Shared Service Center-Controlling – Ergebnisse einer empirischen Studie in deutschen Unternehmen, in: Controlling, 19 (8), pp. 463–472.

Fisher, J. (1992): Use of non-financial performance measures, in: Journal of Cost Management, 6 (1), pp. 31–38.

Fisher, J. (1995): Contingency-based research on management control systems: categorization by level of complexity, in: Journal of Accounting Literature, 14 (1), p. 24–24.

Fisher, J. G. (1998): Contingency theory, management control systems and firm outcomes: past results and future directions, in: Behavioral Research in Accounting, 10 (1), p. 47–47.

Flamholtz, E. G./Das, T. K./Tsui, A. S. (1985): Toward an integrative framework of organizational control, in: Accounting, Organizations and Society, 10 (1), pp. 35–50.

Flick, U. (2014a): An introduction to qualitative research, Thousand Oaks 2014.

Flick, U. (2014b): Qualitative Sozialforschung: Eine Einführung, 6th. ed., Hamburg 2014.

Flick, U. (2014c): Triangulation, in: Bohnsack, R./Flick, U./Lueders, C./Reichertz, J. (eds.): Qualitative Sozialforschung, 6th edn. 2014, pp. 1–125.

Flyvbjerg, B. (2006): Five misunderstandings about case-study research, in: Qualitative Inquiry, 12 (2), pp. 219–245.

Folan, P./Browne, J. (2005): A review of performance measurement: Towards performance management, in: Computers in Industry, 56 (7), pp. 663–680.

Folkerts, L./Hauschildt, J. (2002): Personelle Dynamik in Innovationsprozessen, in: Die Betriebswirtschaft, 62 (1), pp. 7–23.

Forst, L. I. (1999): Outstanding service is an inside job, in: The Journal for Quality and Participation, 22 (2), p. 58–58.

Forza, C./Salvador, F. (2000): Assessing some distinctive dimensions of performance feedback information in high performing plants, in: International Journal of Operations & Production Management, 20 (3), pp. 359–385.

Fowler, C. (1996): TQM in NZ: What impact?, in: Australian Accountant, 66 (1), pp. 53–54.

Fowler, F. J. (2013): Survey research methods, Thousand Oaks 2013.

Franco, M./Bourne, M. (2003): Factors that play a role in "managing through measures", in: Management Decision, 41 (8), pp. 698–710.

Frank, U. (2003): Einige Gründe für eine Wiederbelebung der Wissenschaftstheorie, in: Die Betriebswirtschaft, 63 (3), pp. 278–292.

Frank, U. (2007): Wissenschaftstheorie, in: Köhler, R./Küpper, H.-U./Pfingsten, A. (eds.) Handwörterbuch der Betriebswirtschaft, 6th. ed., Stuttgart 2007, pp. 2010–2017.

Frey, S./Pirker, F./Eynde, K. V. (2008): Change-Management in nationalen und internationalen Shared-Service-Center-Projekten, in: Keuper, F./Oecking, C. (eds.): Corporate Shared Services: Bereitstellung von Dienstleistungen im Konzern, Wiesbaden 2008, pp. 279–309.

Fritze, A.-K. (2013): Shared Service Center, in: Controlling: 25 (3), pp. 159–162.

Fritze, A.-K./Küpper, V./Möller, K./Reimann, A. (2013): Shared Services für Controlling-Prozesse – Umsetzungsstandards und Gestaltungsfaktoren, in: Controlling, 25 (11), pp. 634–640.

Fuchs, J. (2010): Performance-Management: Die dynamische Interaktion zwischen Performance Measurement, Management Control & Organisationsentwicklung, München 2010.

Fülbier, R. U. (2004): Wissenschaftstheorie und Betriebswirtschaftslehre, in: WiSt – Wirtschaftswissenschaftliches Studium, 33 (5), pp. 266–271.

Furck, K. (2005): Shared Services am Beispiel der Deutschen Lufthansa AG, in: Zeitschrift für Controlling & Management, 49 (1), pp. 64–71.

Garengo, P./Bititci, U. (2007): Towards a contingency approach to performance measurement: an empirical study in Scottish SMEs, in: International Journal of Operations & Production Management, 27 (8), pp. 802–825.

Gates, S. (1999): Aligning strategic performance measures and results, New York 1999.

Gemünden, H. G. (1985): Promotors: key persons for the development and marketing of innovative industrial products, in: Backhaus, K./Wilson, D. (eds.): Industrial Marketing: A German-American Perspective, Berlin et al. 1985, pp. 134–166.

Gemünden, H. G./Salomo, S./Hölzle, K. (2007): Role models for radical innovations in times of open innovation, in: Creativity and Innovation Management, 16 (4), pp. 408–421.

Gemünden, H. G./Salomo, S./Hölzle, K./Walter, A./Schmidthals, J. (2006): Technologieorientierte Innovationskooperationen bei hochinnovativen Produktentwicklungen, in: Wertschöpfungsnetzwerke, 1 (1), pp. 165–187.

Gericke, C. G. (2002): Evolutionäres E-Business Performance Measurement: ein Ansatz zur Messung der Electronic Business Performance, Dissertation Universität Zürich, Zürich 2002.

Ghoshal, S./Bartlett, C. A. (1990): The multinational corporation as an interorganizational network, in: Academy of Management Review, 15 (4), pp. 603–626.

Gladen, W. (2002): Performance measurement als Methode der Unternehmenssteuerung, in: HMD-Praxis der Wirtschaftsinformatik (227), pp. 5–16.

Gladen, W. (2014): Performance Measurement: Controlling mit Kennzahlen, 6th. ed., Berlin 2014.

Glaser, B./Strauss, A. (1967): Grounded theory: The discovery of grounded theory, in: Sociology The Journal of the British Sociological Association, 12 (1), pp. 27–49.

Gläser, J./Laudel, G. (2019): Experteninterviews und qualitative Inhaltsanalyse, 5th. ed., Berlin 2019.

Gleich, R. (1997): Performance Measurement, in: Die Betriebswirtschaft, 57 (1), pp. 114–118.

Gleich, R. (2001): Das System des Performance Management – Theoretisches Grundkonzept, Entwicklungs- und Anwendungsstand, München 2001.

Gleich, R. (2002): Performance Measurement: Grundlagen, Konzept und empirische Erkenntnis, in: Controlling, 14 (8), pp. 447–454.

Gleich, R. (2011): Performance Measurement – Konzepte, Fallstudien und Grundschema für die Praxis, 2nd. ed., München 2011.

Gleich, R./Petschnig, M./Schmidt, T. (2010): Controlling von Dienstleistungen. Besonderheiten bei Anforderungen und Lösungsansätzen, in: Der Controlling-Berater, 2 (9), pp. 25–46.

Globerson, S. (1985): Issues in developing a performance criteria system for an organization, in: International Journal of Production Research, 23 (4), pp. 639–646.

Göbel, E. (2002): Neue Institutionenökonomik: Konzeption und betriebswirtschaftliche Anwendungen, Stuttgart 2002.

Goh, M./Prakash, S./Yeo, R. (2007): Resource-based approach to IT shared services in a manufacturing firm, in: Industrial Management & Data Systems, 107 (2), pp. 251–270.

Gonzalez, R./Gasco, J./Llopis, J. (2006): Information systems offshore outsourcing: A descriptive analysis, in: Industrial Management & Data Systems, 106 (9), pp. 1233–1248.

Goode, M./Malik, A. (2011): Beyond budgeting: the way forward, in: Pakistan Journal of Social Sciences, 31 (2), pp. 207–214.

Goold, M. (1991): Strategic control in the decentralized firm, in: MIT Sloan Management Review, 32 (2), p. 69–69.

Gordon, L. A./Narayanan, V. K. (1984): Management accounting systems, perceived environmental uncertainty and organization structure: an empirical investigation, in: Accounting, Organizations and Society, 9 (1), pp. 33–47.

Grady, M. W. (1991): Performance measurement: implementing strategy, in: Strategic Finance, 72 (12), p. 49–49.

Granlund, M./Lukka, K. (1998): It's a small world of management accounting practices, in: Journal of Management Accounting Research, 10 (1), p. 153–153.

Granlund, M./Malmi, T. (2002): Moderate impact of ERPS on management accounting: a lag or permanent outcome?, in: Management Accounting Research, 13 (3), pp. 299–321.

Grant, G./McKnight, S./Uruthirapathy, A./Brown, A. (2007): Designing governance for shared services organizations in the public service, in: Government Information Quarterly, 24 (3), pp. 522–538.

Green, S. G./Welsh, M. A. (1988): Cybernetics and dependence: Reframing the control concept, in: Academy of Management Review, 13 (2), pp. 287–301.

Greene, J. C. (2006): Toward a methodology of mixed methods social inquiry, in: Research in the Schools, 13 (1), pp. 93–98.

Greene, J. C./Caracelli, V. J./Graham, W. F. (1989): Toward a conceptual framework for mixed-method evaluation designs, in: Educational Evaluation and Policy Analysis, 11 (3), pp. 255–274.

Grochla, E. (1978): Einführung in die Organisationstheorie, Stuttgart 1978.

Grossman, R. J. (2010): Saving Shared Services HR managers who strive to operate this popular business model find that one size rarely fits all, in: HR Magazine, 55 (9), p. 26–26.

Grüning, M. (2002): Performance Measurement Systeme: Messung und Steuerung von Unternehmensleistung, Berlin 2002.

Guerrieri, P./Meliciani, V. (2005): Technology and international competitiveness: the interdependence between manufacturing and producer services, in: Structural Change and Economic Dynamics, 16 (4), pp. 489–502.

Gul, F. A. (**1991**): The effects of management accounting systems and environmental uncertainty on small business managers' performance, in: Accounting and Business Research, 22 (85), pp. 57–61.

Gundavelli, V./Mohanty, L. (**2004**): A Whole New World: Shared Services for Receivables Management, in: Business Credit, 106 (8), pp. 52–55.

Günther, T./Grüning, M. (**2002**): Performance Measurement-Systeme im praktischen Einsatz, in: Controlling: 14 (1), pp. 5–13.

Hair, J. F./Black, W. C./Babin, B. J. (**2019**): Multivariate data analysis: A global perspective, 8th. ed., New York 2019.

Hall, M. (**2008**): The effect of comprehensive performance measurement systems on role clarity, psychological empowerment and managerial performance, in: Accounting, Organizations and Society, 33 (2), pp. 141–163.

Hall, R. (**2012**): Mixed methods: In search of a paradigm, London 2012.

Hart, O./Holmstrom, B. (**1989**): The theory of contracts, in: Bewley, T. F. (ed.): Advances in Economic Theory: Fifth World Congress, Cambridge 1989, pp. 71–157.

Hartmann-Wendels, T. (**1989**): Principal-Agent-Theorie und asymmetrische Informationsverteilung, in: Zeitschrift für Betriebswirtschaft, 59 (7), pp. 714–734.

Hasse, R./Krücken, G. (**2015**): Neo-Institutionalismus, 2nd. ed., Bielefeld 2015.

Hauschildt, J. (**2001**): Promotoren-Erfolgsfaktoren für das Management von Innovationen, in: Zeitschrift Führung und Organisation, 70 (6), pp. 332–337.

Hauschildt, J./Chakrabarti, A. K. (**2013**): Arbeitsteilung im Innovationsmanagement, in: Hauschildt, J./Gemünden, H. G. (eds.): Promotoren: Champions der Innovation, 3rd. ed., Berlin 2013, pp. 67–87.

Hauschildt, J./Kirchmann, E. (**1997**): Arbeitsteilung im Innovationsmanagement: Zur Existenz und Effizienz von Prozesspromotoren, in: Zeitschrift Führung und Organisation, 66 (1), pp. 68–74.

Hauschildt, J./Kirchmann, E. (**2001**): Teamwork for innovation – the 'troika' of promotors, in: R&D Management, 31 (1), pp. 41–49.

Hauschildt, J./Kirchmann, E. (**2013**): Arbeitsteilung im Innovationsmanagement: Zur Existenz und Effizienz von Prozesspromotoren, in: Hauschildt, J./ Gemünden, H. G. (eds.): Promotoren: Champions der Innovation, 3rd. ed., Berlin 2013, pp. 89–110.

Hauschildt, J./Schewe, G. (**2000**): Gatekeeper and process promotor: key persons in agile and innovative organizations, in: International Journal of Agile Management Systems, 2 (2), pp. 96–103.

Held, M./Nutzinger, H. G. (2003): Perspektiven einer Allgemeinen Institutionenökonomik, Marburg 2003.

Hellinger, C. (1999): Kernkompetenzbasiertes Outsourcing in Kreditgenossenschaften: eine transaktionskostenökonomische Analyse unter besonderer Berücksichtigung von Netzwerkstrukturen, Dissertation Univeristät Regensburg, Regensburg 1999.

Herbert, I. P./Seal, W. B. (2012): Shared services as a new organisational form: Some implications for management accounting, in: The British Accounting Review, 44 (2), pp. 83–97.

Heskett, J. L./Schlesinger, L./Jones, T. (1994): Putting the service-profit chain to work, in: Harvard Business Review, 72 (2), pp. 164–174.

Hilgers, D. (2008): Performance management, Dissertation Universität Hamburg, Wiesbaden 2008.

Himme, A. (2009): Gütekriterien der Messung: Reliabilität, Validität und Generalisierbarkeit, in: Albers, S./Klapper, D./Konradt, U./Walter, A./Wolf, J. (eds.): Methodik der empirischen Forschung, Wiesbaden 2009, pp. 485–500.

Hirsch, S. (2016): Performance Management in Shared Services, in: Friedrich, R./Reimsbach, D. (eds.): Entwicklungen und Perspektiven des Finanz- und Rechnungswesens, Köln 2016, p. 127–127.

Hoffmann, O. (2000): Performance Management: Systeme und Implementierungsansätze, 3rd. ed., Bern 2000.

Hofmann, C. (2001): Balancing financial and non-financial performance measures, Hanover 2001.

Hollich, F./Otter, T./Scheuermann, H. D. (2008): Shared Services: Foundation, Practice and Outlook, München 2008.

Holtbrügge, D./Welge, M. (2015): Internationales Management: Theorien, Funktionen, Fallstudien, 6th. ed., Stuttgart 2015.

Horngren, C. T./Srikant, D./Madhav, R. (2009): Cost accounting: A managerial emphasis, 14th. ed., London 2009.

Horsch, A. (2005): Agency und Versicherungsintermediation, in: WiSt-Wirtschaftswissenschaftliches Studium, 33 (9), pp. 531–536.

Horváth, P./Gleich, R./Seiter, M. (2019): Controlling, 14th. ed., München 2019.

Horváth, P./Mayer, R. (1995): Konzeption und Entwicklungen der Prozeßkostenrechnung, in: Männel, W. (ed.): Prozesskostenrechnung: Bedeutung, Methoden, Branchenerfahrungen, Softwarelösungen, Berlin 1995, pp. 59–86.

Horváth, P./Seiter, M. (2009): Performance measurement, in: Die Betriebs wirtschaft, 69 (3), p. 393–393.

Howell, J. M./Higgins, C. A. (1990): Champions of technological innovation, in: Administrative Science Quarterly, 35 (2), pp. 317–341.

Hungenberg, H. (1995): Zentralisation und Dezentralisation: strategische Entscheidungsverteilung in Konzernen, Wiesbaden 1995.

Hutzschenreuter, T./Dresel, S./Ressler, W. (2007): Offshoring von Zentralbereichen, Berlin 2007.

Ibold, F./Mauch, H. (2008): Shared-Services zwischen Zentralisierung und Dezentralisierung, in: Keuper, F./Oecking, C. (eds.): Corporate Shared Services: Bereitstellung von Dienstleistungen im Konzern, Wiesbaden 2008, pp. 377–385.

Ihantola, E.-M./Kihn, L.-A. (2011): Threats to validity and reliability in mixed methods accounting research, in: Qualitative Research in Accounting & Management, 8 (1), pp. 39–58.

Imoisili, O. A. (1986): Task complexity, budget style of evaluating performance and managerial stress: an empirical investigation, New York 1986.

Ittner, C. D./Larcker, D. F. (1998): Innovations in performance measurement: Trends and research implications, in: Journal of Management Accounting Research, 10 (1), p. 205–205.

Ittner, C. D./Larcker, D. F. (2001): Assessing empirical research in managerial accounting: a value-based management perspective, in: Journal of Accounting and Economics, 32 (1), pp. 349–410.

Ittner, C. D./Larcker, D. F. (2003): Coming up short on non-financial performance measurement, in: Harvard Business Review, 81 (11), pp. 88–95.

Ittner, C. D./Larcker, D. F./Randall, T. (2003): Performance implications of strategic performance measurement in financial services firms, in: Accounting, Organizations and Society, 28 (7), pp. 715–741.

Jahns, C./Hartmann, E./Bals, L. (2006): Offshoring: Dimensions and diffusion of a new business concept, in: Journal of Purchasing and Supply Management, 12 (4), pp. 218–231.

Janssen, M./Joha, A. (2004): Issues in relationship management for obtaining the benefits of a shared service center, in: Proceedings of the 6th International Conference on Electronic Commerce, pp. 219–228.

Janssen, M./Joha, A. (2006): Motives for establishing shared service centers in public administrations, in: International Journal of Information Management, 26 (2), pp. 102–115.

Janssen, M./Joha, A. (2008): Emerging shared service organizations and the service-oriented enterprise: Critical management issues, in: Strategic Outsourcing: An International Journal, 1 (1), pp. 35–49.

Janssen, M./Schulz, V./Brenner, W. (2010): Characteristics of shared service centers, in: Transforming Government: People, Process and Policy, 4 (3), pp. 210–219.

Jarvis, C. B./MacKenzie, S. B./Podsakoff, P. M. (2003): A critical review of construct indicators and measurement model misspecification in marketing and consumer research, in: Journal of Consumer Research, 30 (2), pp. 199–218.

Jenner, T. (2001): Zur Verwendung des Kontingenzansatzes in der betriebswirtschaftlichen Forschung, in: Das Wirtschaftsstudium, 30 (1), pp. 79–84.

Jensen, M. C./Meckling, W. H. (1976): Theory of the firm: Managerial behavior, agency costs and ownership structure, in: Journal of Financial Economics, 3 (4), pp. 305–360.

Johnson, H. T./Kaplan, R. S. (1991): Relevance lost: the rise and fall of management accounting, Boston 1991.

Johnson, N. (2009): Simply complexity: A clear guide to complexity theory, Oxford 2009.

Johnson, R. B./Onwuegbuzie, A. J. (2004): Mixed methods research: A research paradigm whose time has come, in: Educational Researcher, 33 (7), pp. 14–26.

Johnson, R. B./Onwuegbuzie, A. J./Turner, L. A. (2007): Toward a definition of mixed methods research, in: Journal of Mixed Methods Research, 1 (2), pp. 112–133.

Jorissen, A./Laveren, E./Devinck, S. (1997): Planning and control: Necessary tools for success in SMEs? – Empirical results of survey and case research on SMEs in Belgium, Antwerp 1997.

Jun, M./Cai, S. (2010): Examining the relationships between internal service quality and its dimensions, and internal customer satisfaction, in: Total Quality Management, 21 (2), pp. 205–223.

Kagelmann, U. (2001): Shared Services als alternative Organisationsform – Am Beispiel der Finanzfunktion im multinationalen Konzern, Dissertation Universität Rostock, Wiesbaden 2001.

Kajüter, P./Brühl, R./Finken, T./Steuernagel, M./Troßbach, S./Vollmer, M. (2017): Konstitutive Entscheidungen zur Vorbereitung der SSC-Implementierung, in: Fischer, T. M./Vollmer, M. (eds.): Erfolgreiche Führung von Shared Services, ZfbF-Sonderheft, Berlin 2017, pp. 25–59.

Kajüter, P./Nienhaus, M. (2016): Kausalität in der empirischen Rechnungslegungsforschung (Teil 2), in: WiSt-Wirtschaftswissenschaftliches Studium, 45 (10), pp. 516–521.

Kamal, M. M. (2012): Shared services: lessons from private sector for public sector domain, in: Journal of Enterprise Information Management, 25 (5), pp. 431–440.

Kang, G.-D./Jame, J./Alexandris, K. (2002): Measurement of internal service quality: application of the SERVQUAL battery to internal service quality, in: Managing Service Quality: An International Journal, 12 (5), pp. 278–291.

Kaplan, R. B./Murdock, L./Ostroff, F. (1991): Core process redesign, in: The McKinsey Quarterly (2), pp. 27–44.

Kaplan, R. S./Norton, D. P. (1992): The Balanced Scorecard – Measures That Drive Performance, in: Harvard Business Review, 70 (1), pp. 71–79.

Kaplan, R. S./Norton, D. P. (1996): The balanced scorecard, Boston 1996.

Kaplan, R. S./Norton, D. P. (2000): Putting the balanced scorecard to work, in: Harvard Business Review, 66 (1), pp. 1–61.

Kaspar, R. H./Ossadnik, W. (2014): Was hilft im KPI-Dschungel?, in: Controlling & Management Review, 58 (7), pp. 26–35.

Kast, F. E./Rosenzweig, J. E. (1972): General systems theory: Applications for organization and management, in: Academy of Management Journal, 15 (4), pp. 447–465.

Keegan, D. P./Eiler, R. G./Jones, C. R. (1989): Are your performance measures obsolete?, in: Strategic Finance, 70 (12), p. 45–45.

Kellermanns, F./Islam, M. (2004): US and German Activity-Based Costing: a critical comparison and system acceptability propositions, in: Benchmarking: An International Journal, 11 (1), pp. 31–51.

Kennerley, M./Neely, A. (2002): A framework of the factors affecting the evolution of performance measurement systems, in: International Journal of Operations & Production Management, 22 (11), pp. 1222–1245.

Kennerley, M./Neely, A. (2007): Performance measurement frameworks: a review, in: Neely, A. D. (ed.): Business performance measurement: theory and practice, 2nd. ed., Cambridge 2007, pp. 145–155.

Kerssens-van Drongelen, I./Fisscher, O. (2003): Ethical dilemmas in performance measurement, in: Journal of Business Ethics, 45 (1–2), pp. 51–63.

Keuper, F./Glahn, C. v. (2006): Shared-Controlling-Services–Eine Standortbestimmung unter Berücksichtigung der IT, in: Zeitschrift für Controlling & Management, 50 (2), pp. 84–93.

Keuper, F./Glahn, C. v. (2005): Der Shared-Service-Ansatz zur Bereitstellung von IT-Leistungen auf dem konzerninternen Markt, in: Wirtschaftswissenschaftliches Studium, 34 (4), pp. 190–194.

Keuper, F./Oecking, C. (2008): Corporate Shared Services, Wiesbaden 2008.

Keuper, F./Röder, S. (2009): Shared-Services-Automation – Ergebnisse einer empirisch gestützten Befragung, Hamburg 2009.

Khandwalla, P. N. (1972): The effect of different types of competition on the use of management controls, in: Journal of Accounting Research, 10 (2), pp. 275–285.

Kieser, A. (1974): Organisationsstruktur, in: Schmalenbachs Zeitschrift für betriebswirtschaftliche Forschung, 25 (9), pp. 569–590.

Kieser, A./Ebers, M. (2019): Organisationstheorien, 8th. ed., Stuttgart 2019.

Kieser, A./Kubicek, H. (2015): Organisation, 3rd. ed., Berlin 2015.

Kleining, G. (1995): Lehrbuch entdeckende Sozialforschung: Von der Hermeneutik zur qualitativen Heuristik, Weinheim 1995.

Klingebiel, N. (2001): Performance Measurement & Balanced Scorecard, München 2001.

Klingebiel, N. (2005): Shared Service Center, in: Das Wirtschaftsstudium, 34 (6), pp. 777–782.

Klingebiel, N. (2006): Offshoring. Varianten und Wirkungseffekte von Dienstleistungsverlagerungen, in: Wirtschaftswissenschaftliches Studium, 35 (9), p. 499–499.

Klingebiel, N. (2013): Integriertes Performance Measurement, Berlin 2013.

Klingebiel, N./Andreas, J. M. (2006): Outsourcing im Rechnungswesen, in: Zeitschrift für Controlling & Management, 50 (1), pp. 981–986.

Klöter, R. (1997): Opponenten im organisationalen Beschaffungsprozess, Dissertation Universität Bochum, Wiesbaden 1997.

Kornmeier, M. (2007): Wissenschaftstheorie und wissenschaftliches Arbeiten: eine Einführung für Wirtschaftswissenschaftler, Berlin 2007.

Kosiol, E. (1964): Betriebswirtschaftslehre und Unternehmensforschung, in: Zeitschrift für Betriebswirtschaft, 34 (12), pp. 743–762.

Krause, O. (2007): Performance Management: Eine Stakeholder-Nutzenorientierte und Geschäftsprozess-basierte Methode, Dissertation Universität Berlin, Berlin 2007.

Kretschmer, K. (2009): Performance Evaluation of Foreign Subsidiaries, Dissertation ESCP Berlin, Wiesbaden 2009.

Kromrey, H. (2013): Empirische Sozialforschung: Modelle und Methoden der standardisierten Datenerhebung und Datenauswertung, Berlin 2013.

Krug, T. (2008): Historische Entwicklung von Shared Accounting Services bei Siemens, in: Keuper, F. (ed.): Die moderne Finanzfunktion, Wiesbaden 2008, pp. 17–36.

Krüger, W. (1994): Organisation der Unternehmung, Stuttgart 1994.

Krüger, W./Danner, M. (2004): Bündelung von Controllingfunktionen in Shared Service Centern, in: Zeitschrift für Controlling & Management, 48 (2), pp. 110–118.

Kuckartz, U. (2019): Einführung in die computergestützte Analyse qualitativer Daten, 4rd. ed., Wiesbaden 2019.

Kuckartz, U. (2014): Mixed Methods: Methodologie, Forschungsdesigns und Analyseverfahren, Berlin 2014.

Kuckartz, U. (2018): Qualitative Inhaltsanalyse. Methoden, Praxis, Computerunterstützung, 4rd. ed., Weinheim 2018.

Küng, P./Wettstein, T. (2003): Ganzheitliches Performance-Measurement mittels Informationstechnologie, Bern 2003.

Küpper, H.-U./Friedl, G./Hofmann, C./Hofmann, Y./Pedell, B. (2013): Controlling: Konzeption, Aufgaben, Instrumente, 6th. ed., Stuttgart 2013.

Kutschker, M./Schmid, S. (2012): Internationales Management, 7th. ed., Oldenburg 2012.

Lamnek, S. (2016): Qualitative Sozialforschung, 6th. ed., Weinheim 2016.

Langfield-Smith, K. (1997): Management control systems and strategy: a critical review, in: Accounting, Organizations and Society, 22 (2), pp. 207–232.

Lautenbach, C. (2019): Kennzahlen für die Unternehmenskommunikation: Definition, Erfassung, Reporting, in: Zerfaß, A./Piwinger, M. (eds.): Handbuch Unternehmenskommunikation, 3rd. ed., Wiesbaden 2019, pp. 887–902.

Lebas, M. (1994): Managerial accounting in France. Overview of past tradition and current practice, in: European Accounting Review, 3 (3), pp. 471–488.

Lebas, M./Euske, K. (2007): A conceptual and operational delineation of performance, in: Neely, A. D. (ed.): Business performance measurement: theory and practice, 2nd. ed., Cambridge 2007, pp. 65–79.

Lebas, M. J. (1995): Performance measurement and performance management, in: International Journal of Production Economics, 41 (1–3), pp. 23–35.

Leeuw, E. de/Hox, J. J./Dillman, D. A. (2009a): Mixed-mode surveys: When and why, in: Leeuw, E. de/Hox, J./Dillman, D. A. (eds.): International handbook of survey methodology, New York 2009, pp. 299–316.

Leeuw, E. de/Hox, J. J./Dillman, D. A. (2009b): The cornerstones of survey research, in: Leeuw, E. de/Hox, J./Dillman, D. A. (eds.): International handbook of survey methodology, New York 2009, pp. 1–17.

Leysen, J./van Nuffel, L. (2006): An Integrated Approach to Risk and Performance Management, in: Perspectives on Performance, 5 (1), pp. 20–24.

Libby, T./Waterhouse, J. H. (1996): Predicting change in management accounting systems, in: Journal of Management Accounting Research, 8 (1), p. 137–137.

Lilienthal, D. (1960): The multinational corporation, New York 1960.

Lingle, J. H./Schiemann, W. A. (1996): From balanced scorecard to strategic gauges: is measurement worth it?, in: Management Review, 85 (3), pp. 56–61.

Lingnau, V. (1995): Kritischer Rationalismus und Betriebswirtschaftslehre, in: Wirtschaftswissenschaftliches Studium, 24 (3), pp. 124–129.

Lohman, C./Fortuin, L./Wouters, M. (2004): Designing a performance measurement system: A case study, in: European Journal of Operational Research, 156 (2), pp. 267–286.

Lohrmann, M./Rau, T./Riedel, A. (2015): Shared Services und Business Process Outsourcing, Weinheim 2015.

Lucey, T. (2004): Management Information Systems, 9th. ed., London 2004.

Lüdders, L. (2016): Fragebogen-und Leitfadenkonstruktion: Ein Handbuch für Studium und Berufspraxis, Bremen 2016.

Lueg, K.-E./Georgi, C./Duck, K./Multerer, C. (2017): Prozessstandardisierung, in: Fischer, T. M./Vollmer, M. (eds.): Erfolgreiche Führung von Shared Services, Berlin 2017, pp. 63–78.

Luhmann, N. (1983): Das sind Preise: Ein soziologisch-systemtheoretischer Klärungsversuch, in: Soziale Welt, 34 (2), pp. 153–170.

Lukka, K. (1990): Ontology and accounting: the concept of profit, in: Critical Perspectives on Accounting, 1 (3), pp. 239–261.

Lynch, R. L./Cross, K. F. (1995): Measure up!: Yardsticks for continuous improvement, Oxford 1995.

MacKenzie, S. B./Podsakoff, P. M./Jarvis, C. B. (2005): The problem of measurement model misspecification in behavioral and organizational research and some recommended solutions, in: Journal of Applied Psychology, 90 (4), p. 710–730.

Malmi, T./Brown, D. A. (2008): Management control systems as a package— Opportunities, challenges and research directions, in: Management Accounting Research, 19 (4), pp. 287–300.

Manfreda, K. L./Vehovar, V. (2009): Internet surveys, in: Leeuw, E. de/Hox, J./Dillman, D. A. (eds.): International handbook of survey methodology, New York 2009, pp. 264–284.

Marr, B. (2005): Corporate Performance Measurement – State of the Art, in: Controlling, 17 (11), pp. 645–652.

Marschan-Piekkari, R./Welch, C. (2004): Handbook of qualitative research methods for international business, Cheltenham 2004.

Maskell, B. H. (1991): Performance measurement for world class manufacturing: A Model for American Companies, New York 1991.

Matheis, T. (2012): Modellgestütztes Rahmenkonzept zum Performance measurement von kollaborativen Geschäftsprozessen, Dissertation Universität Saarbrücken, Berlin 2012.

Mathews, J. A./Zander, I. (2007): The international entrepreneurial dynamics of accelerated internationalisation, in: Journal of International Business Studies, 38 (3), pp. 387–403.

Mayer, H. O. (2013): Interview und schriftliche Befragung: Grundlagen und Methoden empirischer Sozialforschung, 6th. ed., Oldenburg 2013.

Mayer, T./Ottaviano, G. I. P. (2008): The happy few: The Internationalisation of European Firms, in: Intereconomics, 43 (3), pp. 135–148.

Mayntz, R./Scharpf, F. W. (1995): Der Ansatz des akteurzentrierten Institutionalismus, in: Mayntz, R. (ed.): Gesellschaftliche Selbstregelung und politische Steuerung, Frankfurt 1995, pp. 39–72.

Mayring, P. (2015): Qualitative Inhaltsanalyse: Grundlagen und Techniken, 12th. ed., Weinheim 2015.

Mayring, P. (2016): Einführung in die qualitative Sozialforschung, 6th. ed., Weinheim 2016.

McAfee, A./Brynjolfsson, E./Davenport, T. H./Patil, D. J./Barton, D. (2012): Big data, in: Harvard Business Review, 90 (10), pp. 61–67.

McWilliams, B. (1996): The measure of success, in: Across the Board, 33 (2), pp. 16–20.

Meijerink, J./Bondarouk, T. (2013): Exploring the central characteristics of HR shared services: Evidence from a critical case study in the Netherlands, in: The International Journal of Human Resource Management, 24 (3), pp. 487–513.

Meinhövel, H. (2004): Grundlagen der Principal-Agent-Theorie, in: WiSt-Wirtschaftswissenschaftliches Studium, 33 (8), pp. 470–475.

Merchant, K./Stede, W. (2007): Management control systems: performance measurement, evaluation and incentives, London 2007.

Merchant, K. A. (1990): The effects of financial controls on data manipulation and management myopia, in: Accounting, Organizations and Society, 15 (4), pp. 297–313.

Merchant, K. A./Otley, D. T. (2007): A review of the literature on control and accountability, in: Chapman, C. S. (ed.): Handbook of management accounting research, Amsterdam 2007, pp. 785–802.

Mertins, K./Anderes, D. (2009): Benchmarking, 2nd. ed., Düsseldorf 2009.

Mertens, D. M. (2015): Research and evaluation in education and psychology: Integrating diversity with quantitative, qualitative, and mixed methods, 4th. ed., Thousand Oaks 2015.

Meuser, M./Nagel, U. (2010): ExpertInneninterview, in: Becker, R. (ed.): Handbuch Frauen- und Geschlechterforschung, 3rd. ed., Wiesbaden 2010, pp. 376–379.

Meuser, M./Nagel, U. (2009): Das Experteninterview – konzeptionelle Grundlagen und methodische Anlage, in: Pickel, S. (ed.): Methoden der vergleichenden Politik- und Sozialwissenschaft, Wiesbaden 2009, pp. 465–479.

Meyer, C. (2011): Betriebswirtschaftliche Kennzahlen und Kennzahlen-Systeme, 6th. ed., Sternenfels 2011.

Meyer, J. W./Rowan, B. (1977): Institutionalized organizations: Formal structure as myth and ceremony, in: American Journal of Sociology, 83 (2), pp. 340–363.

Miller, C. (1999): A look at European shared service centers, in: Internal Auditor, 56 (6), p. 44–44.

Mintzberg, H. (1982): Structures et dynamique des organisations, Paris 1982.

Misangyi, V. F. (2016): Institutional complexity and the meaning of loose coupling: Connecting institutional sayings and (not) doings, in: Strategic Organization, 14 (4), pp. 407–440.

Moll, L. (2012): Strategische Erfolgsfaktoren von Shared Services im Personalbereich: Eine praxisorientierte Analyse zur wertorientierten Unternehmensführung, Dissertation Technische Universität Dortmund, Genf 2012.

Möller, K./Reimann, A. (2013): Shared Services für Controlling-Prozesse, St. Gallen 2013.

Morgan, D. L. (2007): Paradigms lost and pragmatism regained: Methodological implications of combining qualitative and quantitative methods, in: Journal of Mixed Methods Research, 1 (1), pp. 48–76.

Münstermann, B./Eckhardt, A./Weitzel, T. (2010): The performance impact of business process standardization: An empirical evaluation of the recruitment process, in: Business Process Management Journal, 16 (1), pp. 29–56.

Nagar, V./Rajan, M. V. (2001): The revenue implications of financial and operational measures of product quality, in: The Accounting Review, 76 (4), pp. 495–513.

Neely, A./Adams, C. (2000): Perspectives on performance: the performance prism, in: Focus Magazine for the Performance Management Professional, 4 (1), pp. 1–8.

Neely, A./Gregory, M./Platts, K. (**1995**): Performance measurement system design: a literature review and research agenda, in: International Journal of Operations & Production Management, 15 (4), pp. 80–116.

Neely, A./Gregory, M./Platts, K. (**2005**): Performance measurement system design: A literature review and research agenda, in: International Journal of Operations & Production Management, 25 (12), pp. 1228–1263.

Neely, A./Mills, J./Platts, K./Gregory, M./Richards, H. (**1996**): Performance measurement system design: Should process based approaches be adopted?, in: International Journal of Production Economics, 46 (1), pp. 423–431.

Neely, A./Mills, J./Platts, K./Richards, H./Gregory, M./Bourne, M./ Kennerley, M. (**2000**): Performance measurement system design: developing and testing a process-based approach, in: International Journal of Operations & Production Management, 20 (10), pp. 1119–1145.

Neimark, M./Tinker, T. (**1986**): The social construction of management control systems, in: Accounting, Organizations and Society, 11 (4), pp. 369–395.

Neu, D. (**1992**): The social construction of positive choices, in: Accounting, Organizations and Society, 17 (3–4), pp. 223–237.

North, D. C. (**1994**): Economic performance through time, in: The American Economic Review, 84 (3), pp. 359–368.

Olfert, K./Rahn, H.-J. (**2017**): Einführung in die Betriebswirtschaftslehre, 12th. ed., Kiel 2017.

Olfert, K./Rahn, H.-J. (**2019**): Organisation, 18th. ed., Herne 2019.

Onwuegbuzie, A. J./Johnson, R. B. (**2006**): The validity issue in mixed research, in: Research in the Schools, 13 (1), pp. 48–63.

Onwuegbuzie, A. J./Leech, N. L. (**2007**): Validity and qualitative research: An oxymoron?, in: Quality & Quantity, 41 (2), pp. 233–249.

O'Reilly, C. A. (**1980**): Individuals and information overload in organizations: is more necessarily better?, in: Academy of Management Journal, 23 (4), pp. 684–696.

Osterloh, M./Frost, J. (**2006**): Prozessmanagement als Kernkompetenz, 5th. ed., Wiesbaden 2006.

Otley, D. (**1999**): Performance management: a framework for management control systems research, in: Management Accounting Research, 10 (4), pp. 363–382.

Otley, D. T. (**1978**): Budget use and managerial performance, in: Journal of Accounting Research, 16 (1), pp. 122–149.

Otley, D. T. (**1980**): The contingency theory of management accounting: achievement and prognosis, in: Accounting, Organizations and Society, 5 (4), pp. 413–428.

Otley, D. T. (**1992**): The contingency theory of management accounting: achievement and prognosis: Readings in Accounting for Management Control 1992, pp. 83–106.

Otley, D. T./Berry, A. J. (**1980**): Control, organisation and accounting, in: Accounting, Organizations and Society, 5 (2), pp. 231–244.

Otley, D. T./Emmanuel, C./Merchant, K. (**1990**): Accounting for management control, 2nd. ed., London 1990.

Ouchi, W. G. (**1979**): A conceptual framework for the design of organizational control mechanisms, in: Management Science, 25 (9), pp. 63–82.

Paagman, A./Tate, M./Furtmueller, E./Bloom, J. de (**2015**): An integrative literature review and empirical validation of motives for introducing shared services in government organizations, in: International Journal of Information Management, 35 (1), pp. 110–123.

Pasteels, I. (**2015**): How to weigh survey data with a dyadic multi-actor design?, Antwerp 2015.

Peemöller, V. (**2002**): Zielsystem, in: Küpper, H. U./Wagenhofer, A. (eds.): Handwörterbuch der Unternehmensrechnung und des Controllings, 4th. ed., Stuttgart 2002, pp. 2168–2178.

Pérez, N. M. (**2009**): Service Center Organisation, Dissertation Universität Hohenheim, Wiesbaden 2009.

Perlitz, M. (**1999**): Performance Measurement, in: Gabler's Magazin, 13 (2), pp. 6–10.

Pfaff, D./Zweifel, P. (**1998**): Die Principal-Agent-Theorie, in: Wirtschaftswissenschaftliches Studium, 4 (98), pp. 184–190.

Pfänder, A. (**2009**): Auswirkungen der Zentralisierung von Organisationen auf deren Effizienz–Mechanismen, Dissertation Universität Augsburg, Augsburg 2009.

Picot, A. (**1991**): Ökonomische Theorien der Organisation, in: Ordelheide, D. (ed.): Betriebswirtschaftslehre und ökonomische Theorie, Stuttgart 1991, pp. 143–172.

Picot, A./Dietl, H./Franck, E. (**2015**): Organisation – Theorie und Praxis aus ökonomischer Sicht, 7th. ed., Stuttgart 2015.

Picot, A./Fiedler, M. (**2002**): Institutionen und Wandel, in: Die Betriebswirtschaft, 62 (3), pp. 242–259.

Podsakoff, P. M./MacKenzie, S. B./Lee, J.-Y./Podsakoff, N. P. (**2003**): Common method biases in behavioral research: a critical review of the literature and recommended remedies, in: Journal of Applied Psychology, 88 (5), p. 879–879.

Poplat, T. (**2013**): Foreign investments in BRIC countries: Empirical evidence from multinational corporations, Dissertation Universität Münster, Frankfurt 2013.

Popper, K./ Keuth, H. (**2013**): Logik der Forschung, 4th. ed., Tübingen 2013.

Popper, K. R./Keuth, H. (**2009**): Vermutungen und Widerlegungen: das Wachstum der wissenschaftlichen Erkenntnis, 2nd. ed., Tübingen 2009.

Porst, R. (**2014**): Fragebogen – Ein Arbeitsbuch, 4th. ed., Wiesbaden 2014.

Porter, M. E. (**1989**): From competitive advantage to corporate strategy, in: Asch, D. (ed.): Readings in strategic management, Barsingstoke 1989, pp. 234–255.

Pospeschill, M. (**2006**): Statistische Methoden, München 2006.

Pragnall, N./Bagan, J./Driesen, R./Greving, C. (**2015**): Global Shared Services survey, Atlanta 2015.

Pütz, T. (**2007**): Die Prüfung von Performance-Measurement-Systemen, Dissertation Universität Ulm, Düsseldorf 2007.

Quattrone, P. (**2000**): Constructivism and accounting research: towards a transdisciplinary perspective, in: Accounting, Auditing & Accountability Journal, 13 (2), pp. 130–155.

Quinn, B./Cooke, R./Kris, A. (**2000**): Shared services: mining for corporate gold, London 2000.

Raake, A. (**2008**): Strategisches performance measurement: Anwendungsstand und Gestaltungsmöglichkeiten am Beispiel des öffentlichen Personennahverkehrs, Dissertation EBS Universität für Wirtschaft und Recht, Berlin 2008.

Raffée, H. (**1974**): Grundprobleme der Betriebswirtschaftslehre, Göttingen 1974.

Raffée, H./Abel, B. (**1979**): Aufgaben und aktuelle Tendenzen der Wissenschaftstheorie in den Wirtschaftswissenschaften, in: Raffée, H. (ed.): Wissenschaftstheoretische Grundfragen der Wirtschaftswissenschaften, München 1979, pp. 1–10.

Ramphal, R. R. (**2011**): The performance of South African shared services, in: South African Journal of Industrial Engineering, 22 (1), pp. 45–54.

Rathjen, P. (**2008**): Transformation durch Shared Services: Im Spannungsfeld zwischen zentraler und dezentraler Unternehmenssteuerung, in: Keuper, F./ Neumann, F. (eds.): Finance Transformation, Wiesbaden 2008, pp. 25–44.

Rau, T./Buck, S./Butschal, C. (**2012**): Effizienzsteigerung durch Prozess-Controlling im Shared Service Center, in: Zeitschrift für Controlling & Management, 56 (3), pp. 63–68.

Raudla, R./Tammel, K. (2015): Creating shared service centres for public sector accounting, in: Accounting, Auditing & Accountability Journal, 28 (2), pp. 158–179.

Rea, L. M./Parker, R. A. (2005): Designing and constructing survey research, 3rd. ed., San Francisco 2005.

Redman, T./Snape, E./Wass, J./Hamilton, P. (2007): Evaluating the human resource shared services model: evidence from the NHS, in: The International Journal of Human Resource Management, 18 (8), pp. 1486–1506.

Reichmann, T./Kißler, M./Baumöl, U. (2017): Controlling mit Kennzahlen, 9th. ed., München 2017.

Reilly, P. (2000): HR Shared Services and the Realignment of HR, London 2000.

Reilly, P. A./Williams, T. (2003): How to get best value from HR: The shared services option, Aldershot 2003.

Richter, P. C./Brühl, R. (2016): Shared service center research: A review of the past, present, and future, in: European Management Journal, 36 (1), pp. 1–13.

Richter, R./Furubotn, E. G. (2010): Neue Institutionenökonomik – Eine Einführung und kritische Würdigung, 4th. ed., Tübingen 2010.

Riesenhuber, F. (2009): Großzahlige empirische Forschung, Wiesbaden 2009.

Risse, R./Loitz, R. (2013): Shared Service Center für die Steuerfunktion – Ziele, Hürden und Erfolgsfaktoren, in: Der Betrieb (39), pp. 2161–2168.

Röder, S. (2012): Dienstleistungsqualität von Personal-Shared-Service-Organisationen aus Kundensicht, Dissertation Steinbeis-Hochschule Berlin, Berlin 2012.

Rödler, E./Rödler, R./Müller, S. (2013): Balanced Scorecard und MIS, Bonn 2013.

Rost, K./Hölzle, K./Gemünden, H. G. (2007): Promotors or champions? Pros and cons of role specialisation for economic process, in: Schmalenbach Business Review, 59 (1), pp. 340–363.

Rothwell, A. T./Herbert, I. P./Seal, W. (2011): Shared service centers and professional employability, in: Journal of Vocational Behavior, 79 (1), pp. 241–252.

Rotter, J. B. (1990): Internal versus external control of reinforcement: A case history of a variable, in: American Psychologist, 45 (4), p. 489–489.

Said, A. A./HassabElnaby, H. R./Wier, B. (2003): An empirical investigation of the performance consequences of non-financial measures, in: Journal of Management Accounting Research, 15 (1), pp. 193–223.

Sandt, J. (2004): Management mit Kennzahlen und Kennzahlensystemen, Dissertation WHU Vallendar, Wiesbaden 2004.

Sandt, J. (2005): Performance Measurement, in: Zeitschrift für Controlling und Management, 49 (6), pp. 429–447.

Scapens, R. W. (1990): Researching management accounting practice: the role of case study methods, in: The British Accounting Review, 22 (3), pp. 259–281.

Schein, E. H. (1990): Organizational culture, in: American Psychologist, 45 (2), pp. 109–119.

Schimank, C. (2004): Shared Service Center, in: Controlling, 16 (3), pp. 171–172.

Schimank, C./Strobl, G. (2002): Controlling in Shared Service Centern, in: Gleich, R./Becker, R./Horváth, P. (eds.): Controllingfortschritte, München 2002, pp. 281–301.

Schmid, M./Maurer, A. (2003): Ökonomischer und soziologischer Institutionalismus: interdisziplinäre Beiträge und Perspektiven der Institutionentheorie und-analyse, Marburg 2003.

Schmidt, J. (2013): Eigentum und strategisches Management: eine systemtheoretische Perspektive für die mittelständische Familienunternehmung, Berlin 2013.

Schneider, D. (2019): Betriebswirtschaftslehre: Grundlagen, 2nd. ed., München 2019.

Schnell, R./Hill, P. B./Esser, E. (2018): Methoden der empirischen Sozialforschung, 11th. ed., Oldenburg 2018.

Scholl, A. (2018): Die Befragung, 4th. ed., Konstanz 2018.

Schon, D. A. (1963): Champions for radical new inventions, in: Harvard Business Review, 41 (2), pp. 77–86.

Schoonhoven, C. B. (1981): Problems with contingency theory: testing assumptions hidden within the language of contingency "theory", in: Administrative Science Quarterly, 26 (3), pp. 349–377.

Schoute, M. (2011): The relationship between product diversity, usage of advanced manufacturing technologies and activity-based costing adoption, in: The British Accounting Review, 43 (2), pp. 120–134.

Schreyer, M. (2007): Entwicklung und Implementierung von Performance Measurement Systemen, Dissertation Universität Bayreuth, Wiesbaden 2007.

Schreyögg, G. (1978): Umwelt, Technologie und Organisationsstruktur – Dissertation Universität Erlangen-Nürnberg, Bern 1978.

Schröder, M. (2014): Cost accounting in anglophone subsidiaries, Dissertation Universität Münster, Frankfurt 2014.

Schulman, D. S./Harmer, M. J./Dunleavy, J. R./Lusk, J. S. (1999): Shared services: Adding value to the business units, New York 1999.

Schulz, A. (**2018**): Cost accounting in German multinational companies, Dissertation Universität Münster, Frankfurt 2018.

Schuurmans, L./Stoller, C. (**1998**): Der Shared Service Center Trend, in: Management Zeitschrift Industrielle Organisation, 67 (6), pp. 37–41.

Schwarz, G./Schiele, J. (**2004**): Es muss nicht gleich Outsourcing sein, in: Personalwirtschaft, 7 (2004), pp. 40–43.

Schwickert, A./Fischer, K. (**1996**): Der Geschäftsprozess als formaler Prozess: Definition, Eigenschaften, Arten, in: Die Betriebswirtschaft, 47 (1), pp. 88–99.

Scott, W. (**2014**): Institutions and Organizations – Ideas, Interests, and Identities, 4th. ed., Los Angeles 2014.

Seiter, M. (**2011**): Entwicklung eines Performance Measurement-Systems für Anbieter wissensintensiver Dienstleistungen, Baden-Baden 2011.

Selden, S. C./Wooters, R. (**2011**): Structures in Public Human Resource Management Shared Services in State Governments, in: Review of Public Personnel Administration, 31 (4), pp. 349–368.

Selznick, P. (**1953**): TVA and the grass roots: A study of politics and organization, Berkeley 1953.

Selznick, P. (**2011**): Leadership in administration: A sociological interpretation, 11th. ed., Berkeley 2011.

Senge, K./Hellmann, K.-U. (**2006**): Einführung in den Neo-Institutionalismus, Berlin 2006.

Shah, B. (**1998**): Shared Services – is it for you?, in: Industrial Management Magazine, 40 (5), pp. 10–15.

Shapiro, S. P. (**2005**): Agency theory, in: Annual Review of Sociology, 31 (1), pp. 263–284.

Sharman, P. (**1995**): How to implement performance measurement in your organization, in: CMA-The Management Accounting Magazine, 69 (4), pp. 33–37.

Simon, H. A. (**1962**): The architecture of complexity, in: Proceedings of the American Philosophical Society, 106 (6), pp. 467–482.

Simons, R. (**1991**): Strategic orientation and top management attention to control systems, in: Strategic Management Journal, 12 (1), pp. 49–62.

Simons, R. (**2013**): Levers of control: How managers use innovative control systems to drive strategic renewal, Harvard 2013.

Sinkovics, R. R./Penz, E./Ghauri, P. N. (**2008**): Enhancing the trustworthiness of qualitative research in international business, in: Management International Review, 48 (6), pp. 689–714.

Smith, M. L. (2006): Multiple methodology in education research, in: Green, J. L. (ed.): Handbook of complementary methods in education research, Washington 2006, pp. 457–475.

Soeffner, H.-G. (2014): Interpretative Sozialwissenschaft, in: Mey, G./Mruck, K. (eds.): Qualitative Forschung, Wiesbaden 2014, pp. 35–53.

Sorge, A. (1991): Strategic fit and the societal effect: interpreting cross-national comparisons of technology, organization and human resources, in: Organization Studies, 12 (2), pp. 161–190.

Spence, M. (1973): Job market signaling, in: The Quarterly Journal of Economics, 87 (3), pp. 355–374.

Spremann, K. (1990): Asymmetrische Information, in: Zeitschrift für Betriebswirtschaft, 60 (5/6), pp. 561–586.

Stake, R. E. (2011): Case Studies, in: Denzin, N. K./Lincoln, Y. S. (eds.): The Sage handbook of qualitative research, 4th. ed., Los Angeles 2011, pp. 435–455.

Stede, W./Young, S. M./Chen, C. X. (2005): Assessing the quality of evidence in empirical management accounting research: The case of survey studies, in: Accounting, Organizations and Society, 30 (7), pp. 655–684.

Steen, M. (2006): Human agency in management accounting change: a cognitive approach to institutional theory, Groningen 2006.

Stein, P. (2014): Forschungsdesigns für die quantitative Sozialforschung, in: Baur, N. (ed.): Handbuch Methoden der empirischen Sozialforschung, Wiesbaden 2014, pp. 135–151.

Steinke, I. (1999): Kriterien qualitativer Forschung, Weinheim 1999.

Stephenson, D./Becker, R./Lange, P./Rau, T./Riedel, A. (2013): Controlling Shared Services (CSS)–Managing capabilities for the digital age, in: Keuper, F. (ed.): Finance bundling and finance transformation, Wiesbaden 2013, pp. 339–362.

Sterzenbach, S. (2010): Shared service Center-Controlling: theoretische Ausgestaltung und empirische Befunde in deutschen Unternehmen, Dissertation Katholische Universität Eichstätt-Ingolstadt, Frankfurt 2010.

Steuer, R./Westeppe, S. (2015): Mit Controlling Shared Services neue Wege gehen, in: Controlling & Management Review, 59 (2), p. 7–7.

Stier, W. (2013): Empirische Forschungsmethoden, 2nd. ed., Berlin 2013.

Stiglitz, J. E. (1975): The theory of "screening", education, and the distribution of income, in: The American Economic Review, 65 (3), pp. 283–300.

Stinchcombe, A. L. (1959): Bureaucratic and craft administration of production: A comparative study, in: Administrative Science Quarterly, 4 (2), pp. 168–187.

Strübing, J. (2014): Grounded Theory: Zur sozialtheoretischen und epistemologischen Fundierung eines pragmatischsten Forschungsstils, Berlin 2014.

Suska, M./Zitzen, C./Enders, W. (2011): Shared service – the 2nd Generation, Frankfurt 2011.

Suska, M./Zitzen, C./Mäns, C. (2014): Shared Services – the Edge Over, Stuttgart 2014.

Swenson, D. W. (1998): Managing costs through complexity reduction at Carrier Corporation, in: Strategic Finance, 79 (10), p. 20–20.

Tashakkori, A./Teddlie, C. (2008): Quality of inferences in mixed methods research: Calling for an integrative framework, in: Bergman, M. M. (ed.): Advances in mixed methods research: Theories and applications, Los Angeles 2008, pp. 101–119.

Taylor, F. W. (2004): Scientific management, 8th. ed., London 2004.

Teddlie, C./Tashakkori, A. (2006): A general typology of research designs featuring mixed methods, in: Research in the Schools, 13 (1), pp. 12–28.

Teddlie, C./Tashakkori, A. (2009): Foundations of mixed methods research: Integrating quantitative and qualitative approaches in the social and behavioral sciences, Los Angeles 2009.

Teddlie, C./Tashakkori, A. (2010): Major issues and controversies in the use of mixed methods in the social and behvioral sciences, in: Tashakkori, A. (ed.): Sage handbook of mixed methods in social & behavioral research, 2nd. ed., Los Angeles 2010, pp. 3–50.

Tempel, A./Walgenbach, P. (2007): Global standardization of organizational forms and management practices? What new institutionalism and the business-systems approach can learn from each other, in: Journal of Management Studies, 44 (1), pp. 1–24.

Thole, W. (2003): Wir lassen uns unsere Weltsicht nicht verwirren, in: Schweppe, C. (ed.): Qualitative Forschung in der Sozialpädagogik, Opladen 2003, pp. 43–65.

Thurmond, V. A. (2001): The point of triangulation, in: Journal of Nursing Scholarship, 33 (3), pp. 253–258.

Tolbert, P. S./Zucker, L. G. (1999): The institutionalization of institutional theory, in: Clegg, S. (ed.): Studying Organization, London 1999, pp. 169–184.

Tosi, H./Slocum, J. (1984): Contingency theory: Some suggested directions, in: Journal of Management, 10 (1), pp. 9–26.

Triplett, A./Scheumann, J. (2000): Managing shared services with ABM, in: Strategic Finance, 81 (8), pp. 40–45.

Trost, S. (2013): Koordination mit Verrechnungspreisen, Berlin 2013.

Truijens, T. G./Neumann-Giesen, A./Weber, J. (2012): Organisationsform Shared Service Center: Herausforderungen an das Controlling, Weinheim 2012.

Tuomela, T.-S. (2005): The interplay of different levers of control: A case study of introducing a new performance measurement system, in: Management Accounting Research, 16 (3), pp. 293–320.

Udy, S. (1959): "Bureaucracy" and "Rationality" in Weber's Organization Theory: An Empirical Study, in: American Sociological Review, 24 (6), pp. 791–795.

Ulbrich, F. (2008): The adoption of IT-enabled management ideas: Insights from shared services in government agencies, Stockholm 2008.

Ulrich, B. (1993): Kontingenztheorie und autopoetische Systemtheorie der Organisation: ein evaluativer Vergleich zweier organisationstheoretischer Ansätze unter besonderer Berücksichtigung der Organisations-Umwelt-Beziehung, Innsbruck 1993.

Ulrich, D. (1995): Shared services: from vogue to value, in: Human Resource Planning, 18 (3), pp. 12–23.

Ulrich, P./Hill, W. (1976): Wissenschaftstheoretische Grundlagen der Betriebs-wirtschaftslehre, in: Wirtschaftswissenschaftliches Studium, 7+8 (5), pp. 304–309.

van Denburgh, E./Cagna, D. (2000): Do more with less – Shared services centers can help other business units improve performance and lower costs, in: Electric Perspectives Magazine, 25 (1), pp. 44–55.

van Griensven, H./Moore, A. P./Hall, V. (2014): Mixed methods research–The best of both worlds?, in: Manual Therapy, 19 (5), pp. 367–371.

Voegelin, M. D./Spreiter, S. (2003): Shared-Services-Center-Konzept in Banken: Überblick über Wesen dieser Organisationsform, in: Der Schweizer Treu-händer, 77 (10), pp. 831–836.

Wagenhofer, A. (2002): Verrechnungspreise, in: Küpper, H. U./Wagenhofer, A. (eds.): Handwörterbuch der Unternehmensrechnung und des Controllings, 4th. ed., Stuttgart 2002, pp. 2074–2083.

Walgenbach, P. (2002): Neoinstitutionalistische Organisationstheorie: State of the Art und Entwicklungslinien, in: Managementforschung, 12 (2002), pp. 155–202.

Walgenbach, P./Meyer, R. (**2019**): Neoinstitutionalistische Organisationstheorie, 2nd. ed., Stuttgart 2019.

Walter, A. (**2013**): Der Beziehungspromotor: Ein personaler Gestaltungsansatz für erfolgreiches Relationship Marketing, Berlin 2013.

Walter, A./Gemünden, H. G. (**2013**): Beziehungspromotoren als Förderer interorganisationaler Austauschprozesse: Empirische Befunde, in: Hauschildt, J./ Gemünden, H. G. (eds.): Promotoren: Champions der Innovation, 3rd. ed., Berlin 2013, pp. 133–158.

Wang, S./Wang, H. (**2007**): Shared services beyond sourcing the back offices: Organizational design, in: Human Systems Management, 26 (4), pp. 281–290.

Webb, R. (**2004**): Managers' Commitment to the Goals Contained in a Strategic Performance Measurement System, in: Contemporary Accounting Research, 21 (4), pp. 925–958.

Weber, J./Linder, S. (**2008**): Neugestaltung der Budgetierung mit Better und Beyond Budgeting? Eine Bewertung der Konzepte, Weinheim 2008.

Weber, J./Neumann-Gießen, A./Jung, S. (**2006**): Steuerung interner Servicebereiche, Weinheim 2006.

Weber, J./Schäffer, U. (**2016**): Einführung in das Controlling, 15th. ed., Stuttgart 2016.

Weber, M. (**2002**): Wirtschaft und Gesellschaft: Grundriss der verstehenden Soziologie, Tübingen 2002.

Welge, M. K. (**1989**): Planung in Multinationalen Unternehmen, in: Szyperski, N. (ed.): Handwörterbuch der Planung, Stuttgart 1989, pp. 1206–1220.

Werder, A. v./Grundei, J. (**2006**): Konzeptionelle Grundlagen der Center-Organisation: Gestaltungsmöglichkeiten und Effizienzbewertung, in: Werder, A. v./Grundei, J./Stöber, H. (eds.): Organisations-Controlling, Wiesbaden 2006, pp. 11–54.

Weschke, K. (**2008**): Kulturelle Passung als Erfolgsfaktor bei HR Shared Services – Eine empirische Studie im internationalen Servicekontext, Saarbrücken 2008.

Westerhoff, T. (**2008**): Corporate Shared Services–Das Geschäftsmodell aus strategischer Unternehmenssicht, in: Keuper, F./Oecking, C. (eds.): Corporate Shared Services: Bereitstellung von Dienstleistungen im Konzern, Wiesbaden 2008, pp. 55–73.

White, H. (**1980**): A heteroskedasticity-consistent covariance matrix estimator and a direct test for heteroskedasticity, in: Journal of the Econometric Society, 48 (4), pp. 817–838.

Whittemore, R./Chase, S. K./Mandle, C. L. (2001): Validity in qualitative research, in: Qualitative Health Research, 11 (4), pp. 522–537.

Wiener, N. (1967): Cybernetics, 3rd. ed., Cambridge 1967.

Wild, J. (1993): Betriebswirtschaftliche Theorienbildung: Handwörterbuch der Betriebswirtschaft, 5th. ed. 1993, pp. 3889–3910.

Williamson, O. E. (1983): Markets and hierarchies: analysis and antitrust implications: a study in the economics of internal organization, New York 1983.

Williamson, O. E. (1990): Die ökonomischen Institutionen des Kapitalismus, Tübingen 1990.

Winker, P. (2017): Empirische Wirtschaftsforschung und Ökonometrie, 4th. ed., Heidelberg 2017.

Wisner, J. D./Fawcett, S. E. (1991): Linking firm strategy to operating decisions through performance measurement, in: Production and Inventory Management Journal, 32 (3), p. 5–5.

Wißkirchen, F. (1998): Shared Service Center als Outsourcing-Alternative bei Finanzprozessen, in: Köhler-Frost, W./Baun, H.-J. (eds.): Outsourcing, 3rd. ed., Berlin 1998, pp. 137–156.

Wißkirchen, F. (2002): Dezentrale Abläufe in einen Topf werfen, in: Personalwirtschaft, 29 (9), pp. 34–39.

Wißkirchen, F./Mertens, H. (1999): Der Shared Services Ansatz als neue Organisationsform von Geschäftsbereichsorganisationen, in: Wißkirchen, F. (ed.): Outsourcing-Projekte erfolgreich realisieren, Stuttgart 1999, pp. 79–111.

Witte, E. (1973): Das Promotoren-Modell: Organisation für Innovationsentscheidungen, Göttingen 1973.

Witte, E. (1977): Power and innovation: a two-center theory, in: International Studies of Management & Organization, 7 (1), pp. 47–70.

Witte, E. (2013): Das Gespann der Promotoren, in: Hauschildt, J./Gemünden, H. G. (eds.): Promotoren: Champions der Innovation, 3rd. ed., Berlin 2013, pp. 9–42.

Witte, E./Hauschildt, J./Grün, O. (1989): Innovative Entscheidungsprozesse: Die Ergebnisse des Projektes "Columbus", Tübingen 1989.

Witzel, A./Reiter, H. (2012): The problem-centred interview, Los Angeles 2012.

Wolf, J. (2013): Organisation, Management, Unternehmensführung, 5th. ed., Wiesbaden 2013.

Wolfsgruber, I. (2011): Kostenrechnung in international tätigen österreichischen Konzernen der Industrie, Dissertation Universität Linz, Linz 2011.

Woodward, J. (**1958**): Management and technology, London 1958.

Wrona, T. (**2005**): Die Fallstudienanalyse als wissenschaftliche Forschungs-methode, Berlin 2005.

Yin, R. K. (**2018**): Applications of case study research, 6th. ed., Thousand Oaks 2018.

Yin, R. K. (**2014**): Case study research: Design and methods, 5th. ed., Thousand Oaks 2014.

Zairi, M. (**2012**): Measuring performance for business results, Berlin 2012.

Zeckhauser, R. J./Pratt, J. W. (**1985**): Principals and agents: The structure of business, Boston 1985.

Ziegler, R. (**1973**): Typologien und Klassifikationen, in: Albrecht, G./König, R. (eds.): Soziologie, Opladen 1973, pp. 11–47.

Zimmerman, J. L. (**2001**): Conjectures regarding empirical managerial ac-counting research, in: Journal of Accounting and Economics, 32 (1), pp. 411–427.

Zitterbarth, W. (**1991**): Der Erlanger Konstruktivismus in seiner Beziehung zum Konstruktiven Realismus, in: Peschl, M. F. (ed.): Formen des Konstruktivismus in Diskussion, Wien 1991, pp. 73–87.

Zucker, L. G. (**1983**): Organizations as institutions, in: Research in the Sociology of Organizations, 2 (1), pp. 1–47.

Münsteraner Schriften zur Internationalen Unternehmensrechnung

Herausgegeben von Peter Kajüter

Band 1 Daniela Barth: Prognoseberichterstattung. Praxis, Determinanten und Kapitalmarktwirkungen bei deutschen börsennotierten Unternehmen. 2009.

Band 2 Tobias Dickmann: Controllingintegration nach M&A-Transaktionen. Eine empirische Analyse. 2010.

Band 3 Simon Esser: Produktorientiertes Kostenmanagement in der chemischen Industrie. Eine empirische Analyse. 2011.

Band 4 Christian Reisloh: Influence of National Culture on IFRS Practice. An Empirical Study in France, Germany and the United Kingdom. 2011.

Band 5 Matthias Moeschler: Cost Accounting in Germany and Japan. A Comparative Analysis. 2012.

Band 6 Martin Merschdorf: Der Management Approach in der IFRS-Rechnungslegung. Implikationen für Unternehmen und Investoren. 2012.

Band 7 Kristian Bachert: Fair Value Accounting. Implications for Users of Financial Statements. 2012.

Band 8 Daniel Blaesing: Nachhaltigkeitsberichterstattung in Deutschland und den USA. Berichtspraxis, Determinanten und Eigenkapitalkostenwirkungen. 2013.

Band 9 Christina Voets: Kulturelle Einflüsse auf die Anwendung des Impairment-Tests nach IAS 36. Eine experimentelle Untersuchung in Asien und Europa. 2013.

Band 10 Thomas Poplat: Foreign Investments in BRIC Countries. Empirical Evidence from Multinational Corporations. 2014.

Band 11 Moritz Schröder: Cost Accounting in Anglophone Subsidiaries. Empirical Evidence from Germany. 2014.

Band 12 Maximilian Saucke: Full IFRS and IFRS for SMEs Adoption by Private Firms. Empirical Evidence on Country Level. 2015.

Band 13 Martin Nienhaus: Segment Reporting under IFRS 8. Reporting Practice and Economic Consequences. 2015.

Band 14 Gregor Hagemann: Financial Reporting Quality in Emerging Economies. Empirical Evidence from Brazil and South Africa. 2017.

Band 15 Stefan Hannen: Integrated Reporting. Useful for investors? 2017.

Band 16 Alexander Schulz: Cost Accounting in German Multinational Companies. An Empirical Analysis. 2018.

Band 17 Daniela Peters: Synergy and Goodwill Controlling. Empirical Evidence on Determinants and Acquisition Performance. 2019.

Band 18 Matthias Nienaber: Preparation Processes of Nonfinancial KPIs for Management Reports. Empirical Evidence on Process Design and Determinants. 2019.

Band 19 Henrik Schirmacher: Performance Measurement Systems. Design and Adoption in German Multinational Companies. 2020.

Band 20 Friedrich Kalden: Performance Measurement in Shared Services. Empirical Evidence from European Multinational Companies. 2021.

www.peterlang.com

FRIEDRICH KALDEN

Geboren am 19. Januar 1984 in Eschwege
Staatsangehörigkeit: Deutsch

**PROMOTION AN DER
WESTFÄLISCHEN WILHELMS-UNIVERSITÄT MÜNSTER,
LEHRSTUHL FÜR BWL, INSB. INTERNATIONALE
UNTERNEHMENSRECHNUNG
PROF. DR. PETER KAJÜTER**
JULI 2020

Dissertation: Performance Measurement in Shared Services –
Empirical Evidence from European Multinational Companies

**WISSENSCHAFTLICHER MITARBEITER AM LEHRSTUHL
FÜR BWL, INSB. INTERNATIONALE UNTERNEHMENS-
RECHNUNG
PROF. DR. PETER KAJÜTER**
OKTOBER 2013 – SEPTEMBER 2017

**STUDIUM DER VOLKSWIRTSCHAFTSLEHRE AN DER
HELMUT-SCHMIDT-UNIVERSITÄT HAMBURG**
OKTOBER 2005 – DEZEMBER 2009

Abschluss: Diplom-Volkswirt

**AUSLANDSSEMESTER AN DER
UNIVERISTÉ DE BRETAGNE-SUD VANNES
IN FRANKREICH**
SEPTEMBER 2007 – FEBRUAR 2008